ARCHITECTURE IN TEXAS
1895–1945

# ARCHITECTURE IN TEXAS 1895–1945

JAY C. HENRY

 UNIVERSITY OF TEXAS PRESS, AUSTIN

Library of Congress
Cataloging-in-Publication Data

Henry, Jay C., 1939–
       Architecture in Texas : 1895–1945 /
    Jay C. Henry.—1st ed.
         p.   cm.
       Includes bibliographical references
    and index.
       ISBN 0-292-73072-1
       1. Architecture, Modern—19th
    century—Texas.  2. Architecture,
    Modern—20th century—Texas.
    3. Architecture— Texas.  I. Title.
    NA730.T5H46   1993
    720'.9764'09041—dc20          92-28931
                                       CIP

# CONTENTS

# PREFACE AND ACKNOWLEDGMENTS

When asked why he had aspired to scale Mount Everest, Sir Edmund Hillary replied: "Because it was there."

Texas also was there when Hal Box, then chairman (later dean) of architecture at The University of Texas at Arlington, invited me to join his faculty in 1972. The state was too big to be evaded or conveniently ignored. One saw a lot of it while just trying to escape; gradually I began to escape into it rather than from it. The nice thing about teaching in a university is that they pay you for pursuing your hobbies. My own cycles of discovery followed the evolving sense of what was important in scholarship on American architecture. First came the nineteenth century, particularly the Richardsonian Romanesque, which I had learned to appreciate in graduate school. Then came the Prairie School, buttressed by the *Prairie School Review* and H. Allan Brooks' monograph, always considered an essential part of American and modern architecture, and to my delight, unexpectedly discovered in Texas. After 1920, however—the terminal date of my own dissertation on Columbus, Ohio—lay a cultural desert stretching at least to the late 1930's—or so it seemed to conventional wisdom. As usual, conventional wisdom was

wrong, as scholars were beginning to realize. My introduction to regional eclecticism was the hotels of Trost and Trost in the American Southwest, which I had discovered while researching Henry Trost's Prairie School context. And so I went back and revisited things that had not seemed important the first time: the Modernistic courthouses I had overlooked in studying the Richardsonian ones, and then the Beaux-Arts Classic ones ignored in visiting the Modernistic. The desert took shape, patterns began to form, but there was no comprehensive history to serve as guide.

It seemed obvious that the history of this architecture should someday be written. Indeed, the task had begun twenty-five years ago when the first volume of the Texas Architectural Survey appeared in print under the sponsorship of the Amon G. Carter Foundation: Drury Blakeley Alexander's *Texas Homes of the Nineteenth Century* (University of Texas Press, 1966). This was followed in 1974 by the second volume: Willard B. Robinson and Todd Webb's *Texas Public Buildings of the Nineteenth Century*. Yet the twentieth century remained largely uncharted when I arrived in Texas in 1972. In the ensuing twenty years, however, a great deal of published and unpublished research has been undertaken on American architecture of the twentieth century in general and on Texas architecture in particular. Equally important, the historiography of modern architecture in America and Europe, which I have attempted to describe in the first chapter, had evolved beyond partisan apologetics to embrace all manifestations of the designed environment, *retardataire* as well as progressive. The Eclectic and Modernistic traditions that comprised the vast preponderance of constructed architecture in Texas were once again viewed as respectable fields for scholarly investigation. I felt, therefore, that the time had come to attempt a synthesis of this evolving body of research on twentieth-century architecture in Texas, and to interpret it in light of prevailing scholarship on American architecture.

This effort has been assisted by numerous benefactors, to whom thanks are due:

To two successive deans of the School of Architecture at The University of Texas at Arlington, George S. Wright and Edward M. Baum, who encouraged and supported the enterprise in various ways;

To Barbara Abbott, who patiently trained me in the use of the word processor on which the successive drafts were transcribed;

To Professor Craig Kuhner, who shared with me his professional expertise and advice as an architectural photographer, which permitted me to take acceptable photographs for publication;

To Professor Drury Blakeley Alexander, who read the manuscript and suggested useful improvements;

To Lila Stillson, who introduced me to the Architectural Drawings Collection of The University of Texas at Austin;

To the Organized Research Fund of The University of Texas at Arlington, which assisted early excursions into Texas architecture with grants to explore the Richardsonian Romanesque in Texas, the Prairie School in Texas, and the hotels of Trost and Trost in the American Southwest;

And finally, to my students, and above all to my thesis students, whose work is embedded in this monograph and reflected in the notes and bibliography, and to whom this work is dedicated:

R. Edward Brooks
Patricia Taylor Canavan
Robert Linus Canavan
Diane Hospodka Collier
Judy Schwartz Dooley
Michael Hoffmeyer
Anita Regehr Toews
Charles Watson
Cary Young

ARCHITECTURE IN TEXAS
1895–1945

# THE HISTORIOGRAPHY OF
# AMERICAN AND TEXAS ARCHITECTURE
# IN THE TWENTIETH CENTURY

The great size and wide geographical diversity of Texas, surpassed in the first respect only by Alaska and in the second perhaps only by California, suggest that a history of its architecture in the first half of the twentieth century would be of more than local or statewide interest. It might be expected to represent most, if not all, of the styles, building types, and social influences common to the deep South and the midwestern prairie; to the Great Plains and the arid Southwest; to the national ecumene and to the regional environment of the Spanish borderlands. Texas lacks only great mountains and spectacular scenery; early in this century, it lacked cities of great size and cultural influence. It had, however, perhaps more cities of intermediate size than any other state, and certainly more county seats and courthouses. If the greatest American architects did no work in Texas in this period, their influence was exerted through native or transplanted Texans who knew and imitated their work. To study Texas is to study a large cross section of America in microcosm.

Nevertheless, the period has only recently begun to attract historical attention. It has been said that each generation despises the work of its parents and rediscovers the world of its grandparents. Thirty years ago this book would not have been written. The late eclectic and modernistic traditions that are so evident in most of the architecture discussed herein were held in scholarly and professional contempt as recently as the 1960's. Architectural historians had come to grips with the nineteenth century, but tended to view it as a prelude to modern architecture, created in Europe and America in the 1890's. In that decade, the course of architectural development was thought to bifurcate into two channels, one progressive and the other reactionary. A progressive current eschewing the use of historical forms, associated with Louis Sullivan and Frank Lloyd Wright in the United States and with Hendrik Petrus Berlage, Peter Behrens, Victor Horta, Otto Wagner, Auguste Perret, et al., in Europe, developed into the mainstream of modern architecture. By the 1930's the rudiments of this progressive current were being plotted by Lewis Mumford and Henry-Russell Hitchcock in America, and by Nikolaus Pevsner and Sigfried Giedion in Europe.[1] Giedion's *Space, Time and Architecture*, first delivered as the Charles Elliot Norton Lectures at Harvard in 1938–1939 and closely following the arrival of Walter Gropius and the other Bauhaus émigrés, fused American and European modernism into a common tradition. Published in its first edition in 1941, Giedion's opus separated a mainstream of historically important constituent phenomena from a side current of transient ones. These transient phenomena, of course, included a much larger body of architects and monuments than the constituent mainstream, a fact that Giedion chose to ignore. His highly selective account of nineteenth-century precedents for modern architecture did not promote a sympathetic investigation of Victorian architecture on its own terms.

In fact, although Sullivan and Wright had a considerable following in the Progressive Era before World War I, a much larger body of architects remained committed to the habit of historical adaptation, perhaps with more refined taste and greater erudition than their Victorian predecessors—or so they believed. This late, post-Victorian Eclecticism dominated American architecture, at least in a quantitative sense, from the mid-1890's until the various strands of modernism began to appear in the 1930's. Concurrently in the 1930's, historians began to reassess the preceding century, rediscovering the world of their grandparents.

Henry-Russell Hitchcock rediscovered H. H. Richardson in 1936, fifty years after the architect's death and four years after Hitchcock and Philip Johnson had defined the International style for the Museum of Modern Art.[2] But Richardson came to be valued by Giedion and others for his protomodern qualities, as a precursor to Sullivan and Wright,

rather than for his Victorian context. In 1936, Victorian architecture was still despised as discordant and even ugly.[3] It seems significant that the generation which accepted the classically reductive spirit of International Modernism should reassess the classical revival, which had begun to succumb to Victorian aesthetics in the 1840's. In 1841 Andrew Jackson Downing denounced the Greek Revival as unsuitable for domestic architecture because it was not expressive of purpose, and ushered in a half-century of Victorian architecture in America.[4] A century later, in 1944, Talbot Hamlin, one of the leading interpreters of an elastic concept of modern design for American architects in the 1930's, published *Greek Revival Architecture in America*. It was now legitimate once again to appreciate classical simplicity and discipline, partly because contemporary modern architects saw in the Greek Revival a reflection of their own principles of design. But the Victorian interlude was still held in contempt.

This began to change in the 1950's, with the publication of two important works (both 1949 Yale dissertations) that contributed to a reassessment of Victorian architecture on its own terms. The first was Vincent Scully's *The Shingle Style and the Stick Style*, which examined American domestic architecture from Downing to Wright.[5] The second was Carroll L. V. Meeks' *The Railroad Station*, published in 1956. Narrowing his focus to the most significant building type of the nineteenth century, Meeks subjected this body of work to a rigorous art-historical methodology. Following the example of Heinrich Wölfflin,

Meeks defined nineteenth-century architecture in terms of dialectical opposition to twentieth-century modern architecture, as Wölfflin had done for Renaissance and Baroque.[6] For Meeks, the essential qualities of the nineteenth century were variety, movement, irregularity, intricacy, and roughness. He coined a term for this broad period, comparable to the Baroque style; Meeks called the style of the nineteenth century Picturesque Eclecticism. In characterizing this broad style, from 1790 until 1914, as eclectic, Meeks took what had been a pejorative term and made it methodologically descriptive. Eclecticism implies the selective use of historical models to form new combinations for contemporary use. An eclectic designer might borrow the forms and details of the Gothic or the Baroque, but would use them freely in pursuit of picturesque design values and the resolution of contemporary functional needs, and not in an attempt to revive past building types.

The 125 years of Meeks' Picturesque Eclecticism is almost as long as the Baroque period, and it is obvious that development in the arts is never static for such a long interval. In an effort to account for the evolution of style within broad periods, the French art historian Henri Focillon proposed a theory of *The Life of Forms in Art*. All broad styles, according to Focillon, evolve from youth to maturity to old age, or from an archaic to a classic, and thence to a Baroque, phase. Meeks, who had studied under Focillon at Yale in the 1940's, applied this evolutionary schema to Picturesque Eclecticism. He called the early

phase Symbolic Eclecticism, dated from 1790 to 1860, and corresponding to the classical revival and others. Meeks' second phase was dubbed Synthetic Eclecticism, dated from 1860 to 1890, and corresponded more or less to the Victorian interlude in American taste. The final, late phase, dating from 1890 to 1914 and coexisting with a noneclectic progressive strand in American architecture, he called Creative Eclecticism. This term has never satisfied other historians using Meeks' system, and Academic Eclecticism has been proposed as more appropriate, in that it draws attention to the greater reliance on accurate historical details and historically correct proportions prevalent in this phase of design.[7] This phase has been described as a revival of Revivalism,[8] reflecting the greater fidelity to historical models that characterized the period before 1860, or at least before 1840, and again after 1890. The term "revival," in fact, is often attached to component modes of Academic Eclecticism, such as the Georgian Revival or the Spanish Colonial Revival. Eclecticism and Revivalism are obviously relative terms. No Greek temples were erected in America during the Symbolic Eclectic period; the form was adapted eclectically to modern usage. After thirty years or so of Synthetic Eclecticism or Victorian taste, a greater accuracy in the use of form and detail reemerges in the Academic Eclectic period, which for purposes of this study has been extended into the 1920's and even the 1930's.

Yet, even a period of thirty or forty years is too vast to be encompassed within a single category, especially because the eclectic habit encouraged choice among competing sources or historical periods. It has been said that a generation in art is ten years, for not only do new designers enter practice, but cycles of change occur, even in the oeuvre of a single artist. Thus, with careful scrutiny it is possible to distinguish the style of the 1900's from that of the 1920's, always allowing for survivals and anticipations. In dealing with eclecticism, however, the problem is complicated by the use of alternative historical sources. It is therefore necessary to distinguish alternative modes within a single generation in design, as the Victorian Gothic and Second Empire were competing modes in the 1870's, or the English Tudor and Spanish Colonial in the 1920's. The term "mode" is perhaps best used for such contemporary eclectic alternatives, reserving the term "style" for broader categories.

If the rediscovery of Victorian (or Synthetic Eclectic) architecture dates from the 1950's, its popular appreciation is a phenomenon of the 1960's, when the orthodox traditions of modern architecture and modern city planning came under attack. Americans rediscovered their Victorian heritage, a development reflected in the Texas Architectural Survey, whose first volume, *Texas Homes of the Nineteenth Century*, was published in 1966.[9] The twentieth century before 1945 was still largely virgin territory, however, except for the Prairie School, which was seen as part of the mainstream modernism that had separated from the *retardataire* eclectic tradition.[10] Perhaps no scholar has done more to rehabili-

tate the alternative tradition in American architecture than David Gebhard.

Gebhard, who began as a Prairie School specialist in the 1950's, turned his attention next to the Moderne style of the 1920's and 1930's.[11] From the late 1930's this body of decorative art had been disdained by modern purists as "modernistic," or even as yet another eclectic style. It was separated from "authentic modern architecture" by its conservative construction and its retention of ornament, whereas International Modernism exploited progressive construction methods in a radical avant-garde manner characterized by "volume rather than mass, regularity rather than symmetry, and the elimination of ornament."[12] Although other scholars have studied this phase of the arts of design, popularizing the term Art Deco, Gebhard has concentrated on the architecture, which he prefers to call Moderne. His division of the Moderne into three component phases, the Zig-Zag, Streamlined, and PWA (Public Works Administration) Moderne, remains basic to the continuing study of this body of work, although Gebhard's terms are subject to reconsideration. I have decided to describe this body of architecture in Texas as modernistic, which serves to revive a common 1930's term and strip it of pejorative connotations, just as eclectic is no longer considered a negative term.

Gebhard went on from the Moderne to examine the Academic Eclectic tradition, concentrating on the architecture of Spanish Colonial inspiration in California, where he was joined by other researchers in this historically fertile region.[13] The basic historical distinctions made in California also seem valid for Texas, except for the Pueblo Revival, which originated in New Mexico. A romantically evocative Mission Revival, originating in California in the late 1880's, had spread to Texas early in the new century and was used sparingly until World War I as a vehicle for conveying southwestern regional character. After the war, the Mission Revival was supplanted by the much more popular Spanish Colonial Revival, which drew on historically accurate provincial Baroque sources but interpreted them with a picturesque sensibility that was prevalent in the 1920's. Although in fundamental composition and social purpose the Regional Eclectic modes and those derived from non-Hispanic sources do not differ, these two categories have been divided between Chapters 4 and 5 of this book for organizational convenience. Regional Eclecticism is a subspecies of Academic Eclecticism, and not an autonomous category, a fact borne out by the frequent recourse to a regionalized classic or regional Romanesque idiom. A few recognizable details, such as Spanish tile roofs, were frequently used to signify regional historic character. The Meso-American Revival, a minor current in the eclectic mélange of the 1920's, has also been grouped with Regional Eclecticism for editorial convenience, sanctioned by Gebhard's example.

Academic Eclecticism, as used in Chapter 4, implies architecture that is neither progressive—i.e., substantially free of historical basis— nor specifically regional in its refer-

ence to historical sources. This body of work includes the greatest part of Texas architecture between 1900 and 1930, excluding the survival of Victorian forms before 1900 and the prevalence of modernistic ones after 1930. Owing in part to the sheer number of these buildings, they have been given a primary division not by component mode or by chronological phase, but by building type, with mode and chronology as secondary principles of organization within each section. Perceptible changes can be observed in all building types about midpoint in the period, around the time of World War I, thus dividing Academic Eclecticism into two generations of design, corresponding to the earlier Mission and later Spanish Colonial phases of Regional Eclecticism.

Of all the various eclectic modes employed, by far the most common was a form of generic classicism perhaps best defined as Beaux-Arts Classic. Although it recalls somewhat the neo-classicism of the period before the Civil War—hence the sense of a revival of Revivalism—it should not be confused with this earlier style. Style should be chronologically limited to a definite time period when it was current; a later recurrence of similar forms should be given a separate definition. Beaux-Arts Classicism has the advantage of focusing attention on the increasing academicism of American architecture after 1893, the year of the Chicago Columbian Exposition. Not only did an increasing number of American architects receive formal training at the Ecole des Beaux-Arts in Paris, but American schools of architecture increasingly patterned their curricula on that of the Ecole. By World War I, perhaps a majority of practicing architects in the United States had some formal schooling in design, whereas previously the normal route to architectural practice was apprenticeship, and Beaux-Arts principles of design filtered down even to architects without formal education. At its best, the Beaux-Arts Classic stood for the flexible application of a definite vocabulary of forms and ornament to a public architecture planned to incorporate modern functions and composed to express those functions. The idea of a functional plan being legible in the exterior composition of a building is perhaps the greatest legacy of the Beaux-Arts system to modern architecture. And the Academic Eclectics thought of themselves as modern; they saw no contradiction in solving contemporary building problems within the eclectic tradition.[14]

Nevertheless, by the 1920's this eclectic tradition had begun to pall. A renewed shift to picturesque composition, difficult to resolve within the classical discipline, was one manifestation of this decline. Another was the obvious unsuitability of classical design for the dominant American building type of the modern age: the skyscraper. Among historical alternatives, the Gothic commended itself to the expression of the tall building because it was the one style to emphasize verticality in proportion. Skyscrapers were built in considerable numbers in Texas in the 1920's, not just in the major cities, but as beacons of progress and modernity in the state's larger towns. By the end of

the decade, however, classic and Gothic forms of skyscraper articulation were abandoned in favor of the modernistic idiom, which in many cases resembled merely an abstracted and stylized form of Gothic ornament. The same process is observable in smaller buildings within the eclectic repertoire. The most important examples of abstraction and stylization were provided by Bertram Grosvenor Goodhue and Paul Philippe Cret, and the influence of both men may be seen in Texas architecture from 1928 onward, although only Cret did any work personally in Texas.[15]

Cret was only one of a number of architects of national reputation to do work in Texas, including Cass Gilbert, Ralph Adams Cram, George Bossom, Kenneth Franzheim, William Lescaze, and Richard Neutra. Nevertheless, the great preponderance of the state's nonresidential architecture continued to be designed by practitioners based in Texas. Yet not just the scale of building, but also the scale of architectural practice, changed in Texas in the twentieth century. Chapter 2 opens with the work of J. Riely Gordon, the most prolific late-Victorian architect in Texas, who nevertheless left in 1902 for greater professional opportunities in New York. His place was taken by new firms of modern significance: Trost and Trost of El Paso, Sanguinet and Staats of Fort Worth and Houston, C. H. Page and Brother of Austin (later called Page Brothers), Atlee B. Ayres of San Antonio, and Lang and Witchell of Dallas, to name only the more significant organizations formed shortly after the turn of the century. These firms tended to evolve internally as they adapted to new modes of design after World War I. C. D. Hill left the employ of Sanguinet and Staats in Fort Worth to found his own practice in Dallas in 1907. Wyatt C. Hedrick bought out his partners, Sanguinet and Staats, upon their retirement in 1924, as they had evolved from Messer, Sanguinet and Messer in the 1890's. Alfred C. Finn similarly launched his practice from Sanguinet and Staats' Houston office in 1925. Robert M. Ayres joined his father, Atlee, in practice in San Antonio in the 1920's. Voelcker and Dixon joined in partnership in Wichita Falls. George L. Dahl joined the firm of Herbert M. Greene in 1924, to buy out his elder partners in 1943. All these firms adopted the modernistic idiom as a design alternative in the 1930's, just as their predecessors had given up the Richardsonian Romanesque for the Beaux-Arts Classic at the turn of the century, or occasionally for the Prairie School.

Despite all previous historiographic endeavors to rehabilitate the Academic Eclectic and modernistic traditions, however, this book is not really a revisionist history of twentieth-century architecture in Texas. A significant discussion has been included of two avant-garde tendencies, out of all proportion to their numbers of constructed buildings. The first of these is the Prairie School of the 1910's; the second is the Regional Modernism of the 1930's.

The Prairie School may be defined as a body of work deriving from the form conventions of Frank Lloyd Wright or the ornamental conventions of Louis Sullivan, or both. It was brought to Texas by both direct discipleship and indirect appreciation. In the former case, both Charles Erwin Barglebaugh and George Willis had worked for Wright at the Oak Park Studio before coming to Texas, where Barglebaugh found employment with Lang and Witchell, and Willis with Atlee B. Ayres. No such direct connection has been found to explain Prairie School conventions in the work of Trost and Trost or Sanguinet and Staats, who may have depended on publications of Wright's work in *Western Architect* and other journals. Sullivan's ornament was commercially available in plaster and terra-cotta, which explains its occurrence in the work of J. E. Flanders and in anonymous usage elsewhere. The Prairie School virtually disappeared along with other progressive manifestations of American culture in the "return to normalcy" following World War I, only to re-emerge transformed in the 1930's with Wright's rejuvenated Usonian period.

Wright's rejuvenation in the 1930's is part of the complex evolution of modern architecture in that decade. Hitchcock and Johnson's definition of the International style in 1932 was premature as an exercise in art history, and obsolete as a commentary on contemporary practice, for already by that date modern architecture was evolving toward a rapprochement with tradition: traditional forms such as pitched roofs; traditional materials such as brick, stone, and wood; and a respect for site, climate, and the particular environment. These things appear in Wright's architecture of the 1930's, as they had appeared earlier in the

Prairie School and California phases of his work. Although Wright built no architecture in Texas until after World War II, his manner is reflected in the work of Karl Kamrath of Houston and to a lesser degree in that of H. R. Meyer of Dallas. Wright had never been part of the International style, of course, but even those who had been—like Walter Gropius and Marcel Breuer, when they arrived as émigrés in America in the late 1930's— modified their styles to incorporate regional manifestations: natural materials and site-specific considerations. Chester Nagel, who studied under Gropius at Harvard in 1938, returned to Texas to transplant this modified modern style in his own house at Austin. A third tendency of 1930's modern design, distinct from the influence of Wright and the European émigrés, came from the Texas regionalists, David Williams and O'Neil Ford, who regarded the Spanish Colonial and modernistic modes with equal contempt as species of eclecticism. They sought a new point of departure in the vernacular buildings of Texas erected before the Civil War, which they viewed as uncorrupted examples of indigenous adaptation. The Texas ranch houses that they built in the 1930's may be seen as part of a general fascination with the domestic vernacular in this period. They also share with Wright, and perhaps even with Gropius and Breuer, the attempt to incorporate organic, indigenous, or vernacular qualities into an authentic modern architecture.

Domestic architecture has always been more or less a thing apart, occasionally sharing the dominant historical modes used for public architecture but more often conforming to an anonymous builder's vernacular, which eludes strict historical categorization. For that reason, it has been discussed in a self-contained chapter, although Chapters 2 and 3 do consider Shingle style and Prairie School houses along with nondomestic architecture. The chapter on domestic architecture is a drastic compression of an enormous body of material. In the fifty years covered by this study, easily 90 percent of the buildings constructed in Texas have been residential, yet only 15 percent of the monuments discussed are houses. This strange imbalance could have been avoided only by ignoring houses entirely, relegating them to a future second volume, or dismissing most of them as mere building, and not architecture. This would give a misleading impression of historical priorities in the 1990's, and therefore it was decided to be inadequate rather than misleading. Some of the houses discussed were designed by architects and reflect high styles of design, but even among such large houses for a prosperous clientele there was a tendency to draw upon the historical vernacular for sources. English Tudor and Spanish Andalusian vernacular are as common for housing in the 1920's as French Renaissance or Spanish Baroque, and before World War I such generic builders' types as the foursquare and the bungalow contend with period styles even in relatively fashionable neighborhoods. The bungalow was, in fact, the great successor to the Victorian Stick style cottage, as the symmetrical foursquare succeeded the Victorian two-story with its picturesque asymmetry. Like their Victorian predecessors, the bungalow and foursquare were often built without benefit of architect, with plans purchased by mail for execution by a carpenter-builder. Such mail-order pattern books proliferated throughout the 1920's and 1930's. It was even possible to order a complete bungalow from Sears Roebuck or other merchandisers, and have the complete kit of parts shipped by rail for local assembly. The bungalow seems to have been the true domestic vernacular in Texas for thirty years, to be killed off by the Depression and reborn after World War II as the suburban ranch house. But the bungalow was a style as well as a type, and could be extended by a variety of means to incorporate quite large houses. As a style it too changes in the 1920's to conform to the general evolution in taste toward more picturesque design, with the front chimney becoming a familiar element in the transformation.

I begin this book with 1895 rather than 1900 because the change of taste resulting from the Chicago Columbian Exposition of 1893 began to be experienced by the earlier date, although at first the new classicism was tinged in most cases with distinctly Victorian coloration. Hence, the second chapter deals with the relatively long survival of Victorian habits of design, which endure well into the first decade of the new century. The study ends with 1945 because a half-century seems like an organic unit of history, and because World War II, coming as it did on the end of the Depression, seems like a more sig-

nificant watershed than 1950, when nothing in particular happened. The book has also, for the most part, been limited to surviving monuments, except where a demolished structure illustrated essential tendencies better than any surviving example. Architecture is taken to embrace the entire built environment, including domestic and commercial work not designed by architects. Nikolaus Pevsner's distinction between a bicycle shed and Lincoln Cathedral has been rejected in favor of a more inclusive concept of design, for the domestic and commercial vernacular were built with an eye to aesthetic appeal on the part of clients and builders, however much contemporary and retrospective critics might deplore the basis for such judgments.[16] A corollary of this inclusivity, however, is that not every specimen included can be assigned a designer, or even, in certain cases, a precise date.

In selecting monuments for inclusion, I have made an effort to secure wide geographical distribution throughout the state. The buildings discussed range from Dalhart to Brownsville and from El Paso to Orange. Examples representing a common genre or type were selected with such distribution in mind, without overlooking outstanding specimens or unique types. Nevertheless, the book also had to reflect demographic changes in twentieth-century Texas, notably the growth in the size of towns and the increasing concentration of population in cities. Perhaps half the architecture discussed is found in the eight or ten cities registering a population of 100,000 or more in the 1940 federal census, and a far greater proportion was designed by firms whose head-quarters were in such cities. Metropolitan concentration is a fact of life in the twentieth century, and even quite small cities such as Big Spring or Corsicana affected urban pretensions through the construction of skyscrapers in the 1920's.

A definite shift in institutional morphology can also be observed in Texas courthouse towns in the twentieth century, along with a selective growth in population. Courthouses constructed after World War I become larger, requiring different formulas of classical design in the 1920's, and giving way to modernistic forms in the 1930's. The corner bank appears with a well-defined classical form before World War I, occasionally evolving into an office building of several floors in the 1920's. New post offices of classical mien appear in most Texas courthouse towns shortly after the turn of the century; some to be rebuilt at larger scale and in modernistic guise as projects of the Public Works Administration (PWA) in the 1930's. Carnegie libraries were also endowed in many Texas towns shortly after the turn of the century. Opera houses and lodge halls gradually give way to civic auditoriums and commercial movie theaters. New hotels appear in many Texas towns, catering not only to commercial travelers but, after World War I, also to the motoring public. Garages and service stations are constructed to serve the same clientele, fostered by the National Highway System of the 1920's. High schools appear early in the twentieth century as separate institutions, often dwarfing the courthouse in bulk, if not in grandeur and prominent location,

and by the 1920's one-story elementary schools replace the more compact forms of an earlier day. City halls develop a strangely pragmatic morphology, as public-safety functions compete with ceremonial hierarchy in the building form. Churches display the greatest stylistic diversity, as Gothic modes compete with classic and Hispanic forms. Even within a given mode, nuance and chronological evolution are perceptible. There are several forms of Ecclesiastical Gothic, for instance. Although this study does not attempt to trace the evolution of the Texas town as such, the division of Chapter 4 by building type will suggest these changes in institutional morphology, because most of the architecture conforms to Academic Eclectic modes.

The maturity of Texas culture in the twentieth century is also reflected in the founding of new colleges and universities, and the replanning of several existing campuses. Architects of national significance established the collegiate idiom for Rice and Southern Methodist universities, and for the University of Texas at Austin, while Texas architects designed new buildings at several others. The campus, in fact, becomes the principal arena for Beaux-Arts planning in the twentieth century, despite tepid efforts at urban aggrandizement in the City Beautiful period before World War I and again under sponsorship of the PWA during the Depression. Such urban projects rarely extend beyond a single building, whereas the university campuses reflect coherently planned ensembles.

The sources on which this book is

based consist of my own investigations, compiled in twenty years of teaching and traveling in Texas, and the published and unpublished research of many other investigators. The extensive body of scholarly publication in American architecture served as the referential matrix for interpreting developments in Texas, and for occasional inclusion of Texas monuments. The relatively sparse contemporaneous publication of Texas architecture in national journals was also consulted, although not slavishly respected as indicating historical significance. As for retrospective publication, the Texas Architectural Survey, published in two volumes by Drury Blakeley Alexander in 1966 and Willard B. Robinson and Todd Webb in 1974, provided a nineteenth-century foundation on which to build. Because the present study begins in 1895, it overlaps Alexander's and Robinson's work to some degree. Robinson's subsequent book, *The People's Architecture*, published in 1983 by the Texas State Historical Association, extended the work of the Architectural Survey into the present century. It covered only strictly public buildings, however, and was therefore not a comprehensive history; nor was Robinson's *Gone from Texas* of 1981, which considered only work no longer extant. Both books were valuable sources of information, however.

Only three full-scale monographs on twentieth-century Texas architects had been published when this book was written: Lloyd Engelbrecht's and June-Marie Engelbrecht's work on Henry C. Trost of El Paso, Muriel McCarthy's on David Williams of Dallas, and Howard Barnstone's on John F. Staub of Houston. All were invaluable, despite limitations. Mary Carolyn Hollyers George's monograph on O'Neil Ford has since been published but too late for inclusion. Monographic studies in the form of unpublished theses on Birdsall P. Briscoe and George L. Dahl were also consulted, as well as a considerable body of thesis research examining other aspects of Texas architecture at the universities at Arlington and Austin. Unpublished sources also included the holdings of the Architectural Drawings Collection at the University of Texas at Austin and the nomination documents for the National Register of Historic Buildings. The latter are available for public inspection at the Texas Historical Commission in Austin, although the register alone is highly questionable as an index of historical significance. The process of nomination and approval at best filters out trivial examples; it does not promote consensus on what is most significant in twentieth-century architecture in Texas. Some buildings on the register are included in this study on the basis of independent judgment, but others are omitted, and most of the included monuments are not registered at all.

Reasonable architectural guidebooks exist for Dallas, Houston, Austin, and San Antonio, sponsored by those cities' respective chapters of the American Institute of Architects. A great deal of scholarly research on the history of Texas architecture has appeared in periodical sources, three of which stand out: *Texas Architect*, published by the Texas Society of Architects; *Per-*

*spective,* published for twelve volumes by the Texas Chapter of the Society of Architectural Historians; and *CITE: The Architecture and Design Review of Houston,* published by the Rice Design Alliance. Each in its own way has catered to a broad constituency that includes professional and amateur architectural historians. Citations from these journals abound in the notes and bibliography.

The subject matter of this book can be bracketed conveniently between J. Riely Gordon's Waxahachie courthouse and O'Neil Ford's Chapel in the Woods at Texas Woman's University in Denton. The former represents the culmination of Victorian design in the Richardsonian Romanesque as rendered by its foremost interpreter in Texas. The latter represents the comparable maturity of Texas Regionalism of the 1930's, bound up with the revival of craftsmanship and a springboard to Ford's distinguished corpus of post–World War II design. Both Gordon's and Ford's work are relatively well known, although the substantive monographs under preparation on each designer had not yet been published when this book was written. Between Gordon and Ford lies a historical period of some thirty or forty years that is still only partially understood despite some twenty years of incremental research summarized above and included in the notes and bibliography. I felt that the time had come to attempt a synthesis of this information, and to interpret it in light of prevailing scholarship on American architecture. It may be argued that such a systematic interpretation is premature, and that the subject would benefit by another ten or twenty years of patient research. Although such reservations are certainly apt, a case can be made for the provisional thesis as a catalyst for future revision. The interpretation and conclusions contained herein will doubtless be challenged by others to follow. Indeed, if the book is deemed obsolete in ten years and is superseded in twenty, it will have accomplished its purpose.

# THE SURVIVAL OF PAST TRADITIONS

## THE RICHARDSONIAN ROMANESQUE

Henry Hobson Richardson, the acknowledged leader of the architectural profession in the United States, died in 1886. Since before the Civil War, American architects had worked in a variety of High Victorian modes of design originating in Europe: the Second Empire, the Victorian Gothic, the Italianate, the Queen Anne. All of these modes were eclectic, in that elements of past historical styles were employed in new combinations to solve the problems of the nineteenth century. To this succession of European fashions, Richardson added his unique interpretation of the Romanesque with the design of Trinity Church in Boston of 1872–1877 (FIG. 2.01). The Richardsonian Romanesque was the first of the Victorian eclectic modes to be invented in the United States by an American designer, and the first to have a reciprocal influence on Europe.[1] Although Richardson's sources were the Romanesque churches of medieval Europe, his combination of elements was so original that his manner was identified by contemporaries as the Richardsonian Romanesque, and recognized as authentically American. Richardson's most influential commissions had

been for institutional buildings: small-town public libraries, college buildings, town halls—institutions preeminently identified with American culture. Despite the widespread admiration for his work, Richardson's personal manner had not been imitated much before his death. Now that "his death had extinguished envy,"[2] however, the Richardsonian Romanesque very nearly became "the characteristic architectural expression of American civilization,"[3] and by 1890 was being imitated everywhere, including Texas.

The dominant institutional building type in nineteenth-century Texas was the county courthouse, and dozens of these were rebuilt in the Richardsonian Romanesque in the 1890's. The most prolific designer of Richardsonian Romanesque courthouses in Texas was J. Riely Gordon of San Antonio. After working for W. C. Dodson of Waco in the 1880's, Gordon had served an apprenticeship with the Office of the Supervising Architect of the Treasury in Washington, D.C., and returned to Texas to superintend construction of the federal courthouse and post office in San Antonio. The architectural practice thus established became the most important in Texas until Gordon moved to New York in

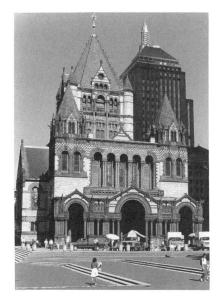

FIG. 2.01
TRINITY CHURCH,
Boston. 1872–1877.
Henry Hobson Richardon, architect.

FIG. 2.02
ELLIS COUNTY COURTHOUSE,
Waxahachie. 1896.
J. Riely Gordon, architect.

1902. Perhaps because of his exposure to Eastern practice, Gordon became the most sensitive and successful interpreter of Richardson in Texas. Among Gordon's dozen surviving Texas courthouses, a single design parti was employed seven times: at Decatur, Sulphur Springs, Waxahachie (FIG. 2.02), New Braunfels, Giddings, Gonzales, and Marshall. The plan is highly innovative, and departs from the conventional cross-axial plan with corner pavilions that Dodson had used in the Second Empire mode, and that C. H. Page and Brother would retain in their early Victorian Classic exercises in the genre. Gordon employed corner entrance porches to bring the visitor diagonally into a central stair hall, culminating in a clock tower or cupola rising above the roof. The formula is without known precedent, and does not occur in Richardson's repertoire.

The first designs on this formula were variations on the Richardsonian Romanesque, however, with characteristic round arches and rock-faced ashlar. At the last of the series at Marshall, completed in 1900 (FIG. 2.03), the same plan and space configuration have been rendered in classical dress. A dome on octagonal drum has replaced the Romanesque tower, and classical orders have supplanted the rusticated detail. In less than ten years, the Richardsonian Romanesque had come and gone in the oeuvre of its most prolific practitioner in Texas. The same thing happened in America at large.[4]

Richardson's work appealed to his Victorian contemporaries because of its vigor and powerful effects. It seemed like the realization of Eugene Viollet-le-Duc's dictum that "only primitive sources can supply the energy for a long career."[5] But it has also been said that a generation in art is ten years. Tastes change because people tire of the same old thing. An alternative to the vigorous and powerful Richardsonian Romanesque had in fact originated with Richardson's former apprentices, Charles Follen McKim and Stanford White. Even during Richardson's lifetime, the firm of McKim, Mead and White had been the best-known exponent of the American Renaissance: a classical alternative to the Richardsonian Romanesque. Their Boston Public Library of 1886, directly across Copley Square from Richardson's Trinity Church, confirmed the dialectic opposition.[6] Richardson's death in 1886, and that of the talented Richardsonian interpreter John Wellborn Root five years later, cleared the way for the return of classicism as the mainstream of American architecture. Critics such as Russell Sturgis had begun to snipe at the Richardsonian Romanesque as "an unorganized, simple, unelaborated style . . . [rather than] a highly developed and learned style."[7] The great demonstration piece of the new learned classical style was the Chicago Columbian Exposition of 1893. Daniel H. Burnham of Chi-

FIG. 2.03
HARRISON COUNTY COURTHOUSE, Marshall. 1900.
Gordon and Lancaster, architects.

cago presided over a consortium of American designers who adopted the forms of Roman classicism for the main exhibition buildings flanking the Court of Honor. The Columbian Exposition had an enormous impact on American taste. Its consequences began to be felt in American architecture quite generally by 1895. Yet the conversion was less immediate than is sometimes assumed. Away from the major cities, principal architectural firms, and national periodicals, the practices of design and construction changed slowly. Henri Focillon expressed this problem of culture lag in the life of forms in art: "History is, in

FIG. 2.04
CROCKETT COUNTY COURTHOUSE,
Ozona. 1900.
Oscar Ruffini, architect.

FIG. 2.05
DENTON COUNTY COURTHOUSE,
Denton. 1895–1896.
W. C. Dodson, architect.

general, a conflict among what is precocious, actual, or merely delayed. . . . The history of art displays, juxtaposed within the same moment, survivals and anticipations, . . . slow, outmoded forms that are the contemporaries of bold and rapid forms."[8]

If the Richardsonian Romanesque had been a precocious form in Texas in 1887 when the Supervising Architect published his design for the San Antonio Federal Building, by 1895 it had become a delayed survival. But there are a large number of such delayed Richardsonian survivals in Texas, a circumstance traceable to several factors: the cultural solitude of Texas, the affinity between the Richardsonian Romanesque and vernacular building practice in Texas, and the possibility of

suggesting southwestern regionalism by manipulating its details.

The first of these was the cultural isolation of even the leading Texas architects and their clients. All had been trained in the apprenticeship system and continued to operate small offices on similar principles. They had converted to the Richardsonian Romanesque with varying degrees of finesse and conviction. Some continued to apply tried-and-true pre-Richardsonian styles as late as the mid-1890's. Oscar Ruffini, for example, repeated his brother, Frederick's, Second Empire design for the Concho County Courthouse in Paint Rock (1885–1886), again for the Sutton County Courthouse in Sonora in 1891–1893, and still employed the corner pavilions and curving mansard lantern of this extremely retarded style in his Crockett County Courthouse in Ozona of 1900 (FIG. 2.04). W. C. Dodson created a strange and unconvincing mixture of styles at his Denton County Courthouse in Denton of 1895–1896 (FIG. 2.05). This peculiar concoction retains the cross-axial plan, central clock tower, and mansarded corner pavilions of Dodson's standard Second Empire courthouse parti from the 1880's (Weatherford, Granbury, Hillsboro), while rusticating the wall surfaces sufficiently to persuade the commissioners that Dodson should replace his former apprentice, J. Riely Gordon, as designer.[9]

Not all Texas architects showed as much diffidence in adopting the Richardsonian Romanesque as Ruffini and Dodson. A. O. Watson of Austin and Eugene T. Heiner of Houston collaborated to produce a very credible Richardsonian courthouse for DeWitt County in Cuero

(1894–1896; FIG. 2.06), perhaps modeled on Richardson's Allegheny County Courthouse in Pittsburgh, Pennsylvania.[10] Watson and Heiner seem to have appreciated the more fundamental qualities of Richardson's example: respect for the proper scale of rusticated stone, for the integrity of the wall surface, and for carefully proportioned fenestration.

Practicing architects such as Gordon, Ruffini, Dodson, Heiner, and Watson designed only a small fraction of the buildings in Texas in the 1890's, however. By far the largest proportion of commercial and institutional construction was designed by either dilettantes or contractor-builders.

Considering the models for college architecture provided by Richardson at Harvard (Sever and Austin Halls) and the profusion of academic architecture in the Richardsonian Romanesque elsewhere in the United States, it seems strange that such work is so scarce in Texas. (There are no Richardsonian public libraries in Texas either). It seems that Southwestern University in Georgetown was one of the few universities in Texas to undertake a major building program in the 1890's, when the style was current.[11] Main Building at Southwestern, constructed in 1898, was planned by the school's president, Robert S. Hyer, and is an example of a dilettante design (FIG. 2.07). Hyer employed the common picturesque expedient of skewing the plan to a diagonal aspect by the asymmetrical placement of the tower on the salient western corner, balanced against a recessed eastern wing terminated in an octagonal corner turret. Hyer's command of picturesque composition shows considerable fi-

FIG. 2.06
DEWITT COUNTY COURTHOUSE,
Cuero. 1894–1896.
A. O. Watson and Eugene T. Heiner, architects.

nesse; his handling of the details is less successful. The construction is of rusticated stone, some of the principal window heads are round-arched, but the details are unconvincing. They betray an intention to be Romanesque without any careful study of Richardson's repertoire. Like most Richardsonian Romanesque constructions in Texas, the stonework is monochrome.[12]

Of the various Richardsonian interpreters in Texas, only J. Riely Gordon emulated the polychrome masonry that Richardson had introduced on Trinity Church (1872–1877), and even Gordon used this palette of dark trim on a light field only three times: at Decatur, Waxahachie, and Sulphur Springs. As Richardson himself began to move

FIG. 2.07
MAIN BUILDING,
Southwestern University,
Georgetown. 1898.
Robert S. Hyer, designer.

tractor-builders, who often functioned also as designers.

In 1900 the firm of Martin and Moodie, contractors, appears alone on the datestone of the McCullough County Courthouse in Brady, a very accomplished if somewhat simplified exercise in the Richardsonian Romanesque (FIG. 2.08).[13] It is significant that at the same time that Gordon was employing the classical idiom at Marshall, Martin and Moodie were still using the earlier mode. Culture lag is more pronounced among contractor-builders and their patrons than among professional architects and their clientele. Nevertheless, the courthouse in Brady is a fine piece of work, perhaps based on various devices from Gordon's work, if not taken directly from Richardson. The semicircular pavilions flanking the main entrance are a popular Richardsonian device, used by its inventor at Sever Hall, Austin Hall, and Allegheny Courthouse, and by Gordon at Waxahachie et al. The great segmental arch thrown between these pavilions was also very popular among the Richardsonians, Gordon included. The lantern marking the crossing of circulation axes seems like a simplified version of the Salamanca lantern Richardson had used at Trinity Church, rather than the more complicated clock towers that Gordon had employed. Round arches are used sparingly only for side entrances and axial windows. More impressive than the assemblage of Richardsonian elements is the character of the rusticated, monochrome stonework, which Martin and Moodie handled with a splendid simplicity not often found in the more complicated work of professional architects.[14]

away from these polychrome effects in his last buildings (Billings Library, Pittsburg Courthouse and Jail, and the Marshall Field Building were all executed in monochrome ashlar), this chromatic simplification in Texas might be viewed as further evidence of the master's influence. It seems more likely, however, that it was born of the need to economize in construction by using local stone to avoid transportation costs. The fact remains that rock-faced rustication was the easiest method of dressing the soft limestones of Central Texas and sandstones of West Texas, and had been used as field, if not as trim, on public buildings in the Second Empire mode before the Richardsonian Romanesque briefly became the national style in the 1890's. This convergence of a vernacular building tradition with the elite architectural style seems to be the second factor explaining the long survival of the Richardsonian Romanesque in Texas, even in the hands of con-

Another example of rusticated ashlar wielded with monumental simplicity is the First National Bank in Jacksboro of 1897 (FIG. 2.09).[15] Here the integrity of the monochrome wall surface stands without ornament, save for the dentillated cornice and parapet. The building mass is modulated by three slight offsets in the wall plane, defined in sunlight by crisp shadows, and by the varied rhythms of window placement in the five surfaces thus defined. All voids are square-headed except for the two entrances, which are framed by great Romanesque arches composed of massive, deep voussoirs. The aesthetic impact of fenestration, wall surface, and the nature of materials—Richardson's three contributions to modern architecture—have seldom achieved such splendid resolution.

The fact remains, however, that in the absence of specific stylistic detail, rusticated ashlar used with round arches tends to convey the image of the Richardsonian Romanesque, as seen in the P. H. Dimmit Building of Georgetown (1901; FIG. 2.10), whereas the brick-constructed Dr. Pepper Bottling Plant in Waco (now the Doctor Pepper Museum; FIG. 2.11) requires specific Richardsonian detail to make the connection. Thus, the rusticated voussoirs of the arches and the corbelled arcade at the eave line establish the definitive style of this extremely delayed manifestation of the Richardsonian Romanesque, designed by Glenn Allen and Milton W. Scott in 1906 for the Artesian Manufacturing and Bottling Company. But the original red-tile roof and squat tower of the Dr. Pepper Plant are not part of the Richardsonian repertoire. They suggest the cross-

FIG. 2.08
MCCULLOUGH COUNTY COURTHOUSE,
Brady. 1900.
Martin and Moodie, contractors.

FIG. 2.09
FIRST NATIONAL BANK,
Jacksboro. 1897.

FIG. 2.10
P. H. DIMMIT BUILDING,
Georgetown. 1901.

FIG. 2.11
DR. PEPPER BOTTLING PLANT,
Waco. 1906.
Glenn Allen and Milton W. Scott,
architects.

breeding of Richardson's style with devices evocative of the Spanish Colonial period in the American Southwest.[16]

This role of the Richardsonian Romanesque as mediator of southwestern regionalism in fact originated with Richardson's office shortly after the master's death. Shepley, Rutan and Coolidge, Richardson's corporate heirs, designed the Stanford University Quadrangle in Palo Alto, California, in 1888 (FIG. 2.12), generally accepted as the beginning of the Mission Revival.[17] Although the round arches and rusticated ashlar of the Stanford Quadrangle are Richardsonian mannerisms, the Spanish tile roofs have a regional connotation and the open arcades with exposed beam ceilings are deliberately suggestive of the California missions. Furthermore, the monochrome buff ashlar used at Stanford is consonant with the adobe and plaster construction of the original missions.

It is ironic that the Mission style should have originated in California and spread from there to Texas, because the Spanish missions in Texas were fifty years older than the California chain founded by Junípero Sera in the 1770's. Nevertheless, that is what transpired, and by the first decade of the twentieth century the Mission Revival had begun to appear in Texas. Although Chapter 5 discusses this phenomenon in more detail, the rapprochement between the Richardsonian Romanesque and the Mission style, as had happened at Stanford, is relevant here.

If the co-existence of Spanish tile roofs and Richardsonian detail signals such crossbreeding, then J. Riely Gordon's Nolte National Bank in Seguin of 1898 (FIG. 2.13) may be the earliest example in Texas. It is a far more ornamental design than the severely impressive Jacksboro bank, with a corner entrance defined by a salient pavilion picked out with some of Gordon's finest Richardsonian detail, while the generously scaled arches of the ground floor convey a monumentality appropriate to the quasi-institutional aspirations of the banking establishment. The plaster walls, overhanging eaves, and tile roofs are not found in Richardson's repertoire, however, and convey a sense of historical regionalism perhaps suggested by Stanford.[18]

Another prime example of the crossbreeding of styles is the University Methodist Church in Austin, designed by Frederick Mann in 1907 (FIG. 2.14). The monochrome rusticated ashlar is similar to that at Stanford, but the red-tile roofs and extensive eave bracketing are Mission details, the latter not found in Gordon's bank at Seguin. The round arches are ubiquitous to several historical periods, the Romanesque and Spanish Colonial among them.[19]

If the Richardsonian Romanesque could be evoked by rusticated ashlar and round arches, and crossbred with tile roofs and Spanish woodwork to create a regional expression, the Romanesque could also be used without specific Richardsonian or regional content. As hard-finished pressed brick became increasingly popular throughout the country in the first decade of the new century, architects applied it to all modes of design. One such designer was Elmer G. Withers of Stamford, who used the new medium for the First Methodist Church in Haskell in 1910 (FIG. 2.15). Although the forms are undeniably Romanesque, the re-

FIG. 2.12
STANFORD UNIVERSITY QUADRANGLE,
Palo Alto, Calif. 1888.
Shepley, Rutan and Coolidge, architects.

FIG. 2.13
NOLTE NATIONAL BANK,
Seguin. 1898.
J. Riely Gordon, architect.

FIG. 2.14
UNIVERSITY METHODIST CHURCH,
Austin. 1907.
Frederick Mann, architect.

FIG. 2.15
FIRST METHODIST CHURCH,
Haskell. 1910.
Elmer G. Withers, architect.

duction of rusticated stonework to trim on a hard-brick field deprived the building of any strong Richardsonian affinity. One might describe the church as post–Richardsonian Romanesque. On the other hand, the use of rusticated ashlar without specific Romanesque elements may give rise to a quasi-Richardsonian classicism if the stone is handled according to Richardson's design principles. An example of this development is Oscar Ruffini's Ozona High School of 1912 (FIG. 2.16), where the grouping of fenestration and large fields of unadorned stone wall—but not the details—suggest Richardson's influence.

Richardson's architecture not only affected institutional design, it also had a major impact on commercial building in the United States, largely through a single commission

of enormous importance: the Marshall Field Wholesale Store in Chicago of 1884–1886 (FIG. 2.17). At Marshall Field, Richardson had disciplined the eccentricities of Victorian commercial building into a single unified block seven stories high, divided into registers by arcades of diminishing scale into which the fenestration was grouped. Above the basement of segmentally arched windows, the next three floors were grouped vertically under great round arches, followed by the next two under smaller arches, and a final attic floor crowned by a massive lintel supported on colonnettes. Although Richardson's massive rusticated wall surfaces and sparse ornament were generically Romanesque, the principle of fenestration grouped under diminishing arcades transcended this narrow eclectic mode, and was widely imitated by American architects and builders for the next quarter century. Several examples from Texas must suffice to demonstrate this phenomenon.

On a small scale, the Richardsonian commercial formula is demonstrated by the Southwestern Telephone and Telegraph Building in Austin, whose facade was remodeled in 1898 by A. O. Watson (FIG. 2.18). The ground floor is divided into two large arches, while the second floor fenestration consists of a bank of five windows placed under round arches of smaller radius and supported on grouped colonnettes. The rock-faced ashlar and Romanesque details make the debt to Richardson unmistakable.

In addition to such main-street institutions as the Southwestern Telephone and Telegraph Building, architects also employed the Richardsonian formula of sequential arcades in their designs for commercial-loft structures in the warehousing and light-industry districts that were developing around the major commercial centers of midwestern cities. Leonard Eaton has analyzed this phenomenon in four "gateway cities" where the wholesale trade led to extensive districts of this kind. Although none of Eaton's examples are Texas cities, his observations seem applicable to the West End Historic District in Dallas, actually better preserved than the city's adjacent business district of 1895–1915, and recently adapted as an entertainment district. As Eaton has shown, the Richardsonian formula had a long life in such districts, and was eventually superseded only when reinforced-concrete construction began to replace heavy timber mill construction, obviating the need for frequent external piers. Several of the structures in the West End display this long Richardsonian survival—as long as 1911, when J. Riely Gordon and H. A. Overbeck designed the Southern Supply Company (FIG. 2.19). Although constructed of brick and devoid of any explicit Romanesque detail, the building's derivation from Marshall Field is apparent in the use of diminishing arcades. It is true that the Southern Supply Building is articulated by corner pavilions that interrupt the rhythm of the arcades in a different way from that of Richardson's example. In the course of twenty-five years, the model had been crossbred with other principles of design.[20]

More extreme departures from the Richardsonian model could be identified in office blocks within the business districts, in which only

FIG. 2.16
OZONA HIGH SCHOOL. 1912.
Oscar Ruffini, architect.

the vertical grouping of fenestration beneath tall arches remains, merging with other tendencies in American commercial architecture related to the expression of the steel frame or to a classical vocabulary of ornament. The former alternative is represented by H. A. Overbeck's MKT Building in Dallas of 1911 (FIG. 2.20), in which the arcades have been attenuated to five stories, the piers reduced to column fireproofing, and the basement and attic arcades replaced by trabeated forms. The observer is left to decide whether the more significant influence is Richardson or Sullivan, and whether the MKT Building should be classified a retarded survival or a progressive manifestation.

The Commercial National Bank Building at 116–120 Main Street in Houston, designed by Green and

FIG. 2.17
MARSHALL FIELD WHOLESALE STORE,
Chicago. 1884–1886.
Henry Hobson Richardson, architect.
*Photograph courtesy The Museum of Modern
Art, New York.*

FIG. 2.18
SOUTHWESTERN TELEPHONE
AND TELEGRAPH BUILDING,
Austin. 1898.
A. O. Watson, architect.

Svarz in 1904 (FIG. 2.21), is an example of the opposite tendency, in which the Richardsonian arcades become centerpieces of the facade, surrounded on all sides by wall areas fenestrated in conventional square-headed windows. Rather than being dissolved into an armature of piers and windows, the wall is reasserted as an artfully composed facade, despite the building's steel-frame construction.[21]

H. H. Richardson was the first great seminal personality in American architecture; he summed up the Victorian eclecticism of the nineteenth century and anticipated an authentically modern American architecture in the twentieth. His spiritual heirs were Louis Sullivan and Frank Lloyd Wright, whose impact on Texas architecture is discussed in the following chapter. But the Prairie School of Sullivan and Wright, the concept of a modern architecture not based on past historical styles, remained an avant-garde movement in the generation before World War I. Most American architects reverted to the habit of eclecticism, now disciplined into new modes of expression more academically correct and learned than the exuberant Synthetic Eclecticism of the Victorian age, which had culminated in Richardson. The Academic Eclectics also had something to learn from Richardson, however. As one of his admirers wrote in the great architect's obituary: "The qualities aimed at in Mr. Richardson's Romanesque work are the qualities that one must gain for success, whatever the style that he chooses: . . . reasonableness, sincerity, subordination of detail to mass, harmony. . . . There are Renaissance and Gothic offspring as well as Romanesque, to Trinity and Sever and the Quincy Library."[22]

FIG. 2.19
SOUTHERN SUPPLY COMPANY,
Dallas. 1911.
J. Riely Gordon and H. A. Overbeck,
architects.

FIG. 2.20
MKT BUILDING,
Dallas. 1911.
H. A. Overbeck, architect.

FIG. 2.21
COMMERCIAL NATIONAL BANK
BUILDING,
Houston. 1905.
Green and Svarz, architects.

FIG. 2.22
HUTCHINGS-SEALY BUILDING,
Galveston. 1895.
Nicholas J. Clayton, architect.

VICTORIAN CLASSICISM

The classical forms of architecture nurtured in the 1880's by McKim, Mead and White and a few other practitioners of the American Renaissance, which triumphed at the Columbian Exposition in 1893, were not a complete innovation to American architects of the Victorian era. Classical forms had served as the basis for the Second Empire and Italianate modes of Victorian design, although they had been subordinated to the aesthetic values of the period. Proportions had been distorted to conform to the contemporary will to form, striving for the vertical. Details had been applied out of historical context and surcharged with the ornamental exuberance that we identify with Victorian taste. The Victorian generation of Texas architects thus brought an archaic diction to the new turn-of-the-century classicism. Whereas the graduates of the Ecole des Beaux-Arts and alumni of the East Coast offices strove for harmony, proportion, and accurate detail, the old guard in Texas were accustomed to interpreting classical forms with greater liberty. Their residual Victorian rendering of such forms represents another survival of past traditions in Texas architecture at the turn of the century, as a selective survey of the work of established Texas designers will demonstrate.

The Hutchings-Sealy Building in Galveston (FIG. 2.22), designed in 1895 by Nicholas J. Clayton, is one example of this residual Victorian classicism. In response to the commercial demand for natural light, window surfaces dominate the two street facades, separated by giant pilasters rising through the second and third floors. The proportions of these structural bays are unclassically vertical, and the subtle rhythm toward the corner also belies the normal principle of symmetry in classical architecture. The Hutchings-Sealy Building is more Baroque than Renaissance, which merely confirms the fact that Victorian exuberance is closer to the Baroque pole of the classical continuum than to the Renaissance.[23]

W. C. Dodson was another old-guard Victorian architect in Texas, an accomplished practitioner of the Second Empire mode who was uncomfortable, as we have seen at Denton, with the Richardsonian Romanesque. His design for the Coryell County Courthouse at Gatesville of 1897 (FIG. 2.23) betrays all of the anomalies of a Victorian architect trying to come to terms with new values in design. Although the temple portico over the vaulted undercroft of the main entrance facade is well proportioned, it is applied to a building mass still rooted in the Second Empire. The tall crossing lantern is a compromise between dome and tower, and although the corner pavilions are capped with domes rather than mansards, they remain vestiges of the Second Empire. The entire composition reads as a restless assemblage of vertically proportioned parts, rather than as a harmoniously integrated classical entity. Dodson obviously tried to apply the new dispensation in design, but he could not shake his predilection for Victorian form conventions. Moreover, the rusticated polychromatic ashlar recalls Richardson's customary palette, although now pressed into the service of classical rather than Romanesque forms.[24]

Other Texas architects wrestled with this problem with varying degrees of success. We have seen Oscar Ruffini still adhering to the Second Empire in all essentials at the Crockett County Courthouse as late as 1900 (FIG. 2.04, discussed previously), whereas J. Riely Gordon seems to have mastered the new classical dispensation at the Harrison County Courthouse in Marshall during the same year (FIG. 2.03, discussed previously).[25] One controversial issue carried over from the Victorian era continued to plague designers at the turn of the century: Was the appropriate symbolic icon of county government the tower or the dome? Medieval styles tended to promote the tower, which represented communal independence. Classical styles suggested the dome, symbolic of Republican self-government. Residual Victorian designers tended to combine the two icons, resolving upon lanterns that could be Romanesque or classical, with variations in detail. Occasionally at the turn of the century a Texas architect did apply a true dome of classical proportions to the courthouse type, as when J. Riely Gordon designed the McLennan County Courthouse at Waco (1897–1901; FIG. 2.24).[26] The Waco courthouse seems more closely related to the morphology of the state capitol than to that of the county courthouse, however. It coincides with Gordon's design for the Arizona State Capitol in Phoenix, and reminds us that in both training (his apprenticeship with the Supervising Architect in Washington) and ambition (his relocation to New York in 1902), Gordon was somewhat different from the typical Victorian architect in Texas.

FIG. 2.23
CORYELL COUNTY COURTHOUSE,
Gatesville. 1897.
W. C. Dodson, architect.

FIG. 2.24
MCLENNAN COUNTY COURTHOUSE,
Waco. 1897–1901.
J. Riely Gordon, architect.

FIG. 2.25
FORT BEND COUNTY COURTHOUSE,
Richmond. 1908.
C. H. Page and Brother, architects.

FIG. 2.26
EDWARD EASTBURN BUILDING,
Jacksboro. 1898.

Even new firms like C. H. Page and Brother (formed in 1898) began their practice designing in the Victorian interpretations of the classical repertoire. The earliest courthouse they designed, in Richmond for Fort Bend County in 1908 (FIG. 2.25), retains such vestigial Victorian mannerisms as the prominent corner pavilions.[27] This tendency to subdivide the building form into discrete volumes is a distinctly Victorian attribute. It disappears as the Beaux-Arts propensity for modulated but integral forms progressively supplants Victorian form conventions in the generation before World War I. Moreover, at Richmond the central dome is insufficiently elevated to mark the crossing of axes properly. The architects presumably did not realize that the dome would be foreshortened when seen in perspective.

The classical vocabulary was the most canonical and sacrosanct means of expression at the turn of the century. Every pattern book and architectural treatise rehearsed the classical orders and their rules of application. It therefore is not surprising to find this classical vocabulary employed in the design of Texas buildings around 1900 by contractor-builders as well as professional architects. The Edward Eastburn Building in Jacksboro of 1898 (FIG. 2.26) is typical of this tendency. The use of rusticated limestone conveys a harmonious ambience with the Richardsonian forms of the adjacent First National Bank (FIG. 2.09 above) and the classical details are suitably simplified in consonance with the soft stone out of which they are carved. The Eastburn Building exemplifies the classical mode in the vernacular tradition, as the neighboring bank represents the Richardsonian Romanesque.

The corner bank as a small-town institution in Texas enjoyed an importance on the public square second only to the courthouse or occasional opera house. The bank as a building type underwent a transformation from Victorian to Beaux-Arts Classic forms and details, although the details tended to appear before formal maturity. Whereas Victorian design tended to emphasize the corner in such compositions, the Beaux-Arts Classic relied on axial symmetry. The corner bank in Ballinger of 1909 (FIG. 2.27) combines mature and retarded characteristics. The corner oriel and corner entrance are Victorian vestiges, as are the rusticated lintels. On the other hand, the hard-finished tan brick, the horizontally proportioned fenestration, and the elliptical arches with classicizing keystones are progressive features.

The opera house was a common but not universal institution in Texas towns of the nineteenth century. Those at Granbury and Columbus stand out as exemplary.[28] Although opera houses would gradually give way to the lodge hall, the motion-picture theater, and the civic auditorium in the course of the twentieth century, they continued to be erected in the nineteenth-century morphology until around World War I. The traditional form of the opera house had consisted of a high-ceilinged hall on the second floor above commercial retail space. The opera house at Anson, designed by its contractor, Thomas Vetch, in 1907 (FIG. 2.28), corresponds to the vaguely Romanesque post-Richardsonian idiom commonly found in commercial architecture at the turn

of the century. But because the opera house facade is symmetrical and because the round arch occurs in the Renaissance as well as in the Romanesque, the Anson facility has a classical character that is perhaps stronger than its Romanesque attributes. It falls somewhere between the Victorian and Beaux-Arts sensibilities, a not-uncommon stylistic compromise for its date.

Classical forms were ascendant in the 1900's, however, whereas Romanesque forms were in retreat. Most of the Victorian designers in Texas, as well as newcomers to the profession, would develop greater finesse and propriety in interpreting the new classicism, moving into the mainstream of the Beaux-Arts Classic design that dominated American architecture in the decade before World War I. This evolution is discussed in Chapter 4. But perhaps this classical idiom triumphed so quickly after the Chicago Columbian Exposition because the vocabulary, common to the classical revival before the Civil War, had

FIG. 2.27
CORNER BANK,
Ballinger. 1909.

FIG. 2.28
OPERA HOUSE,
Anson. 1907.
Thomas Vetch, builder.

FIG. 2.29
NEWPORT CASINO,
Newport, R.I. 1879–1881.
McKim, Mead and White, architects.

never been entirely lost over the Victorian interregnum. The peculiar Victorian rendition of classical forms bridged the gap and prepared the way for the Beaux-Arts Revival and the City Beautiful.

THE SHINGLE STYLE

The domestic vernacular has always been largely a separate matter from monumental or public architecture. The distinction between vernacular and elite forms of expression is valid for most periods of history, although it is rarely an absolute dichotomy. The vernacular building culture and the high architecture have normally interacted to some degree, if only because architects have had to rely on vernacular craftsmen to execute their designs. Throughout history, however—and in the United States during the nineteenth and twentieth centuries—the vast bulk of housing has been constructed without benefit of the architect as a learned professional. This does not mean that these buildings were constructed spontaneously without design; master craftsmen and contractor-builders were quite adept at interpreting the desires of their clients, which ranged from traditional building to fashionable design reflecting the changing vagaries of taste. In the nineteenth century, several factors led to the dominance of the contractor-builder over the master craftsman. The balloon frame, which used machine-cut lumber of standard sizes secured by wire nails, required less skill than traditional forms of braced frame construction. Stock forms of ornament, such as Victorian stickwork or "gingerbread," could be ordered from catalogs and simply nailed up by semi-

skilled workmen. The advent of the railroads made the transportation of mass-produced materials both economical and expeditious.

Nevertheless, the wealthy were increasingly prone to commission their houses from professional architects, and because the middle-class housing market tended to look to the upper classes for cultural models, the small percentage of professionally designed housing exercised a disproportionate influence on American architecture. Much of this prestige housing was simply a domestic expression of the dominant modes of design: Second Empire, Victorian Gothic, etc. Yet, the domestic vernacular of past historical periods was available for eclectic interpretation just as the high styles were, and professional architects therefore also tended to develop a domestic genre distinct from their public work. Andrew Jackson Downing pioneered this cultivation of a domestic pseudo-vernacular during the 1840's, and it was continued for fifty years in what Vincent Scully has defined as the Stick and Shingle styles.[29]

The Shingle style originated in England with the country houses of Richard Norman Shaw in the late 1860's: these freely composed eclectic pastiches were somewhat incongruously dubbed the Queen Anne style.[30] Its constituent ingredients were masonry ground floors, ornate brick Tudor chimneys, half-timbering with banks of leaded casement windows, and tile hanging as an exterior envelope on upper stories. When architects began to copy the style in the United States during the early 1870's, the tile hanging was translated into wooden shingles, as on McKim, Mead and White's Newport Casino (FIG. 2.29). As the style continued to develop in America, the skin of shingles increasingly became dominant over Shaw's other ingredients. The Shingle style was consciously developed by a coterie of professional architects on the East Coast, largely for the suburban villas or summer retreats of wealthy clients.

One of the earliest American renditions of Richard Norman Shaw's half-shingle Queen Anne was the Watts-Sherman House of 1874 in Newport, Rhode Island, designed by H. H. Richardson, under whom both Charles Follen McKim and Stanford White apprenticed. Although McKim left Richardson's atelier in 1872, White joined the office that year and remained until 1878, when he joined McKim and Rutherford Mead in practice. The firm of McKim, Mead and White would contribute significantly to the development of the Shingle style in America, as discussed below.

But as always, this elite Shingle style tended to trickle down to the middle class and their contractor-builders. Thus, by the late 1880's shingles were being widely used in American domestic (and occasionally institutional) architecture, even in Texas.

Except for the southern pine forests of East Texas, the state is not well endowed with timber resources. This has led some interpreters to conclude that the Shingle style was a rare phenomenon in Texas. It was certainly not indigenous. In fact, much of the decorative stickwork or "gingerbread" used in Victorian Texas came from the forests of Michigan, having been fabricated into stock items to be ordered from catalogs and shipped by rail to

FIG. 2.30
JOHN HICKMAN MILLER HOUSE,
Oaklawn/Turtle Creek area,
Dallas. 1904.

Texas. Shingles were equally amenable to such fabrication and shipment, and were used more widely in Texas than is often supposed, although for the most part they served as accessories to other materials. Many Victorian buildings constructed of masonry or sheathed in clapboards featured shingles in a subsidiary role on dormers, gables, or skirts between floors. Examples of Texas buildings totally clad in shingles are rare. Much more common is a formula previously mentioned, which might be called the half-shingled Queen Anne, with shingles used above a ground story of clapboards or masonry.[31]

A few totally shingled buildings in Texas do survive. The 1904 John Hickman Miller House in Dallas (FIG. 2.30)[32] recalls the grand seacoast villas of McKim, Mead and White et al. It is particularly close to the Low House in Bristol, Rhode Island, where all of the domestic functions are condensed in a compact unitary form beneath a single great roof gable.[33] Although the veranda and secondary gables on the Miller House lie outside the main roof volume, they too are totally

FIG. 2.31
HOUSE,
Seguin. N.D.

FIG. 2.32
HOUSE AT 116 CHURCH STREET,
Gainesville. N.D.

clad in shingles, even to the porch supports. There are no traces of antecedent stickwork, although the Palladian window on the second floor axis shows the influence of the Beaux-Arts Classic, perhaps suggested by Charles Follen McKim's use of classicizing details in his seacoast villas.[34]

A house in Seguin (FIG. 2.31) represents an alternative dispensation within the Shingle style, comparable to McKim, Mead and White's Isaac Bell House in Newport. Rather than condensing interior functions in a single unitary form, as with the Low and Miller houses, the Seguin example employs a flexible membrane wrapped around freely generated spaces of an organic plan. Panels of shingles alternate with clapboards to provide a texturally variegated wooden skin.

A third variant on the Shingle style is represented by a house in Gainesville (FIG. 2.32), which takes a middle position between the Dallas and Seguin examples. Again, a skin of shingles encapsulates all surfaces, including the porch supports. The plan does not ramble as much as at Seguin, and the formal geometry is not as insistent as at the Miller House.

The flaring lip between first and second stories is apparent at both Seguin and Gainesville; this is a vestige of the Queen Anne country houses of Richard Norman Shaw and of the half-shingled Queen Anne in general. The flaring lip would shed water without staining the masonry or clapboard story below. Because the Shingle style had a historical affinity to English vernacular building, it tended to be associated with more casual building types: country or suburban villas, carriage houses, and country churches. There are numerous half-shingled carriage houses in Texas, mostly on the grounds of mansions rendered in the more formal modes of design current in domestic architecture around the turn of the century (see Chapter 7). The Heard-Craig House in McKinney and its adjacent carriage house, designed by J. E. Flanders in 1901, will suffice to demonstrate the point (FIGS. 2.33, 2.34). The house proper uses shingles only as a skirt around the second story beneath the eaves and on the central dormer. The carriage house, however, has a fully shingled second story above a clapboarded ground floor. The use of the gambrel roof and corner tower are vernacular or picturesque gestures appropriate to the character of a grange barn or carriage house. The gambrel, or four-pitched, roof, of course, permits more usable space in the upper floor, where feed was stored.

The published literature on the Shingle style in America makes scant reference to churches, except for the work of Ernest Coxhead in California in the 1890's and of James Lyman Silsbee in Chicago.[35] It is possible that Coxhead influenced the designers of the several excellent examples of shingled churches in Texas, or that both illustrate a more widespread phenomenon that has not yet come to historical attention. The grandest of the shingled churches of Texas lies securely within the Victorian period: St. James Episcopal Church in La Grange of 1885, designed by the well-known East Coast architect, Richard M. Upjohn, Jr. As in much domestic work, panels of shingles alternate with stickwork and clapboarding at St. James, suggesting

FIG. 2.33
HEARD-CRAIG HOUSE,
McKinney. 1901.
J. E. Flanders, architect.

FIG. 2.34
HEARD-CRAIG CARRIAGE HOUSE,
McKinney. 1901.
J. E. Flanders, architect.

FIG. 2.35
FIRST BAPTIST CHURCH,
Kosse. N.D.

FIG. 2.36
CHURCH OF THE MERCIFUL SAVIOUR,
Kaufman. 1909.

that it should be considered a highly sophisticated variant of the Carpenter's Gothic. Nothing quite this exuberant occurs in Texas in the twentieth century, when the Arts and Crafts movement seems to have kept alive this pseudo-vernacular form of ecclesiastical expression.[36]

The shingled attic story of the First Baptist Church in Kosse (FIG. 2.35) suggests Coxhead at his most lyrical, with a tactile counterpoint between the clapboards below and the shingled gables and corner tower above. At the Kosse church, the shingles approximate a flexible skin that adjusts itself to an organic structure beneath. At the Church of the Merciful Saviour in Kaufman of 1909 (FIG. 2.36), however, shingles are applied pervasively to the angular surfaces of a Carpenter's Gothic church with central bell cote rather than full tower. Despite its late date, the Church of the Merciful Saviour seems to reproduce in shingles a common church type of the Ecclesiology movement, often preferred for smaller parishes of the Episcopalian communion.[37]

The evidence from the churches suggests that the use of shingles in American architecture was not strictly confined to a self-consciously created Shingle style. Shingles had been used to create variety of pattern and texture in Victorian architecture, and they would continue in such use in the twentieth century. The Bungalow and Chalet styles imported from California around 1900 frequently used shingled surfaces, although not the fluid membranes that one associates with the Shingle style of the 1880's in the East (see Chapter 7). The western Shingle style employed a more angular, hard-edged aesthetic, in which shingled surfaces were often constrained in precise planes and subordinated to overscaled half-timbering, rafters, and bracketing.

Unlike the Richardsonian Romanesque—with which it shared a common gestation in Richardson's office in the 1870's—the Shingle style was not particularly appropriate to the Texas environment. Its forms did not lend themselves to the vernacular tradition in much of Texas. Yet distinguished specimens of the Shingle style *were* built in Texas, demonstrating that regional ecology is only one of the factors in American architecture, and not necessarily the dominant consideration.

## THE ECCLESIASTICAL GOTHIC

Gothic forms have a long history in Western architecture, rivaled only by the classical forms, which originated in Greece and Rome. Although in the nineteenth century the Gothic was interpreted eclectically for a wide variety of building types, the style always retained a special appropriateness for church building. After all, the great Gothic monuments of the Middle Ages are Christian churches; the style is Christian by historical definition. Therefore, even when the High Victorian Gothic as an eclectic mode for civil architecture succumbed around 1880 to the taste for the Queen Anne and Richardsonian Romanesque, the Gothic remained somewhat in favor for church building. It is true that Romanesque architecture was also a Christian style used for church building in the eleventh and twelfth centuries, and some Richardsonian Romanesque churches were built in the 1880's

and early 1890's, but the eclectic use of these forms as interpreted by Richardson was a relatively brief phenomenon. The use of Gothic forms for church building in the nineteenth century is of much longer duration, going back to the Federal period around 1800, and continuing throughout the century. It lasted long enough to affect the vernacular tradition, and Carpenter's Gothic became a common style for country-church building for half a century. At the end of the century the Gothic style remained the principal vehicle for the representation of Christian values in church architecture, and would continue to be throughout the period covered in this book.

But as with other styles, the Gothic was susceptible to development and interpretation. The obvious distinguishing feature of the Gothic style is the pointed arch. Any church with pointed arches is by definition Gothic. Such pointed arches can be employed, however, on churches of a different plan, of different materials, for different sectarian liturgies, and with different degrees of finesse. I have selected a few examples to show the numerous permutations of the Ecclesiastical Gothic in Texas architecture around the turn of the century.

Sacred Heart Cathedral (now Santuario de Guadalupe) in Dallas (FIG. 2.37), attributed to Nicholas J. Clayton but supervised by J. Edward Overbeck (not to be confused with H. A. Overbeck) and erected between 1898 and 1902, represents the somewhat retarded High Victorian interpretation of the typical French Gothic cathedral for the Roman Catholic liturgy.[38] This typology had been canonized by James Ren-

FIG. 2.37
SACRED HEART CATHEDRAL
(now SANTUARIO DE GUADALUPE),
Dallas. 1898–1902.
Design attributed to Nicholas J. Clayton.
J. Edward Overbeck, supervising architect.

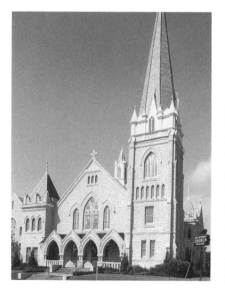

FIG. 2.38
FIRST METHODIST CHURCH,
Corsicana. 1896.

wick in his design for St. Patrick's Cathedral in New York (1858–1879), and had been replicated extensively in the nineteenth century. This French Gothic cathedral type consisted of a clerestory-lighted nave with side aisles, transepts, and choir. The west front was tripartite, with twin towers flanking the nave section, lighted by a rose window above the main portal. This formula of portal and rose window was normally repeated, with or without the towers, at each end of the transept. The Dallas cathedral faithfully reproduced this formula. The left front tower is taller than its right-hand neighbor, thus skewing the otherwise symmetrical composition to the salient corner in accordance with Victorian principles of picturesque design. The materials, red brick contrasting with smoothly dressed stone trim, were a common Victorian palette, and obeyed John Ruskin's dictum that color was essential to architecture. The interior has an exposed beam ceiling that approximates a ribbed vault. Sacred Heart Cathedral might easily be taken for a building constructed ten or fifteen years earlier than its actual date. It represents a lingering survival of Victorian habits of design.

The First Methodist Church in Corsicana of 1896 (FIG. 2.38) represents a plan configuration developed in the nineteenth century for Protestant worship. The shallow Greek-cross plan places the congregation in a compact, well-lit auditorium suitable to a liturgy of preaching, congregational singing, and common prayer. One enters the sanctuary through arcaded porches from each of the intersecting streets, and the communion service takes place in a shallow radial chancel. The reentrant angles of the Greek cross are occupied by square pavilions: low turrets left and right, with a dominant tower and spire at the salient corner—again, a common device in Victorian composition. An administrative block that also accommodates the social functions of the church is attached behind the sanctuary, and a semicircular baptistry at this point defines the connection between liturgical and service functions. The church is constructed of monochrome rusticated stone (actually cast stone) with pointed arches used pervasively. There is nothing particularly original about the Corsicana Methodist Church. The plan was commonplace for Protestant worship at the end of the nineteenth century, as that of Sacred Heart Cathedral in Dallas was traditional for the Catholic liturgy. The same spatial configuration was rendered elsewhere in Romanesque or classic forms with equal conviction. Indeed, the use of rusticated stone suggests the influence of Richardson, and one might almost describe the ensemble as Richardsonian Gothic.

A similar conclusion might be rendered on the First Baptist Church in Beaumont, designed by A. N. Dawson in 1903 (FIG. 2.39), where the Richardsonian character of the stonework and details is even more emphatic than at Corsicana.[39] Were two great Gothic windows not used to light the sanctuary, the Beaumont church could pass for Richardsonian Romanesque. But then, "there are Renaissance and Gothic offspring as well as Romanesque, to Trinity and Sever and the Quincy Library."[40]

FIG. 2.39
FIRST BAPTIST CHURCH
(now TYRRELL LIBRARY),
Beaumont. 1903.
A. N. Dawson, architect.

FIG. 2.40
CHRIST EPISCOPAL CHURCH,
Temple. 1905.
A. O. Watson, architect.

The Episcopal Church in America enjoyed a peculiar relationship to the Gothic Revival not shared by other Protestant sects. As an affiliate of the Church of England, the American Episcopal church before the Civil War had participated in the Ecclesiology movement, which sought to prescribe the appropriate architectural forms and liturgical dispensations for Anglican worship. The forms were those of the medieval English parish church; the liturgy was that of medieval Anglo-Catholic England.[41] Although the direct influence of the Ecclesiology movement had disappeared by the 1890's, the Anglican communion remained imbued with its spirit, reinforced by the participation of practitioners of the Arts and Crafts movement in the design of parish churches in Great Britain. Moreover, whereas the main-line American Protestant denominations sought to fill great preaching

auditoriums for their worship services, the Episcopal Church concentrated on the sacramental aspects of the liturgy, which led to the design of vestments, furnishings, and the communion plate in the Arts and Crafts manner. Episcopal churches tended to be small, cozy, and intimate; they were Gothic in a parochial rather than a cathedral sense.[42]

A. O. Watson of Austin designed several such parish churches for Episcopal congregations in Texas. Christ Episcopal Church in Temple of 1905 (FIG. 2.40) reflects his interpretation of the genre.[43] As was customary in Anglican churches, the entrance is indirectly reached through a side porch, in this case placed beneath the salient corner tower. Although Christ Episcopal has transepts (somewhat unusual in the English parish-church model), it also has the customary Anglican pronounced chancel, the focus of the vested choir and communion service. The church has a rather loose or casual assemblage of parts. Although the stonework is rusticated, Watson has avoided any vestigial allusion to the Richardsonian manner. The building has the homely character of a country parish church, which was the ambience Watson doubtless sought to convey.

The Gothic was probably imposed as a precondition on many designers by vestries and building committees: A church should be Gothic! Only the more avant-garde denominations, such as Unitarians and Christian Scientists, were willing to place themselves in the hands of progressive designers like Frank Lloyd Wright or Bernard Maybeck.[44] Progressive designers of lesser rank would have to compromise between the Gothic and the Modern. One such progressive intermediary was James E. Flanders of Dallas.

Flanders' First Methodist Church in Royse City of 1904 (FIG. 2.41) reflects his mediating position among several possible ecclesiastical forms of expression. First, the church is wood with pointed windows, relating it to the Carpenter's Gothic tradition, although the use of shingles on the foundation skirt, gable ends, and salient tower relate it to the Shingle style as well. The plan configuration, a shallow Greek cross with towers in the reentrant corners, recalls that of the First Methodist Church in Corsicana, although the forceful massing of these towers relative to the auditorium, and the extreme angularity of their roof forms, suggest an attempt at a progressive interpretation. Although Flanders was constrained to work in wood, he was hardly a typical Carpenter's Gothic builder. The narrow eave band placed between the clapboarded walls and roof, echoing the continuous sill line between clapboarding and foundation skirt, suggests the influence of Frank Lloyd Wright and the Prairie School. Flanders would go on to repeat this basic configuration several times for Methodist churches in Texas: at Trinity Methodist Church in Dallas (1904); at First Methodist in Pittsburg (1904–1905);[45] and at St. John's Methodist at Stamford (1910). These churches were built of brick, however, and the eave bands and towers were filled with Sullivanesque ornament, thus confirming the suggestive allusion of the Royse City church. It is a monument of transition, rooted in the historical tradition of the Carpenter's Gothic yet seduced by the modern age: a tentative vanguard of the Prairie School.

FIG. 2.41
FIRST METHODIST CHURCH,
Royse City. 1904.
J. E. Flanders, architect.

# III

# PROGRESSIVE MODES OF DESIGN

According to most histories, the Progressive Era in America stretched from the mid-1890's until World War I. The Progressive movement was born of a reaction against the laissez-faire politics and economics of the previous thirty years, and sought to reform the American body politic in the public interest. It embraced the presidencies of Theodore Roosevelt and Woodrow Wilson, and achieved such national reforms as the income tax, direct election of U.S. senators, and, ultimately, women's suffrage and prohibition. The Progressive movement was particularly vigorous in the sphere of municipal government, where it coincided with a fundamental change in the scale of American cities made possible by electric traction. The City Beautiful movement was the concomitant of the Progressive movement in the field of planning and urban design, as American cities sought both to reform their constitutions and to improve their public environment. It was inspired by the Chicago Columbian Exposition of 1893, and reinforced by the 1900 McMillan Commission Plan for Washington, D.C. Its ideals of urban improvement and beautification were embraced by several Texas cities. The Kessler Plan for Dallas (1911), the Houston Park Plan, the Seawall in Galveston, and the Broadway-Bluffs Improvement in Corpus Christi were all expressions of the City Beautiful.

There is an inherent ambiguity in the use of the term "progressive" when applied to American architecture of this period. The stylistic idiom of the City Beautiful was overwhelmingly classical and historicist; it disciplined and purified the eclectic tradition with new ideals of formality and monumental order. This body of American architecture until recently has been considered "regressive" by modern critics and historians. But the Progressive movement in American history also coincided with the development of a "progressive," avant-garde architecture that transcended the eclectic practices of the previous half-century and sought an architecture true to its own time; one that was not based on historical models. Thus, after H. H. Richardson, who was the last great Victorian eclectic, American architecture tended to bifurcate into two channels. On the one hand, there was the continued development of the eclectic tradition, to which the vast majority of American designers and their patrons gave allegiance. This Academic Eclecticism in Texas is considered in Chapter 4. The other channel might be called the progressive tradition: an architecture based loosely—if at all—on historical models. The two preeminent American architects to eschew historicism as a basis for design were Louis Sullivan and Frank Lloyd Wright. Their work, and that of others inspired by it, is known collectively as the Prairie School.[1]

The Prairie School may be defined as a body of American architecture derived from the ornamental conventions of Sullivan or from the form conventions of Wright, or from both. In addition to his role in the Chicago School of giving definitive form to the American skyscraper, Sullivan became the finest ornamentalist in the history of American architecture. His brilliant, original synthesis consisted of a complicated geometrical armature overlaid with naturalistic foliage. Sullivan's ornament was also commercially available, and is widely diffused throughout the Midwest and beyond, even to Texas.[2]

Frank Lloyd Wright did not follow the example of his *Liebermeister*, Sullivan, in developing either the American skyscraper or an organic system of ornament. Wright's practice in the Prairie School years (1892–1910) concentrated on domestic commissions, and involved an organic concept of architectural form. The Prairie School house was conceived as organically related to its site, with an emphasis on the horizontal extension of space into the landscape of the midwestern prairie. This was achieved by incorporating porches, terraces, and porte cocheres as intermediate spaces between the house and the landscape; by defining the interior as a sequence of connected spaces radiating out from a fireplace core; and by empha-

sizing the horizontal dimension through continuous eave-and-sill lines and continuous banks of casement windows. Wright eschewed Sullivan's ornamental system in favor of a more purely geometrical conception. His most successful ornament was frequently in art glass, the one medium whose refractory character had frustrated Sullivan's quest for lush naturalistic ornament. Conversely, Wright rarely used terracotta, the most characteristic medium for Sullivan's ornament.

Although the bulk of Wright's Prairie School practice was residential work, he did design several significant institutional and commercial buildings that influenced architecture in Texas. At the Larkin Building in Buffalo, New York, of 1904 (FIG. 3.01), Wright created an introverted business headquarters, expressed on the exterior by powerfully massed corner piers •articulated by a slot of fenestration and a minor pier. This slot-and-pier articulation, which also occurs on some of his Prairie School houses, would become one of the more influential of Wright's mannerisms among Prairie School practitioners in Texas. The Unity Temple in Oak Park (1906) also was conceived as an introverted interior whose corners are defined by slot-and-pier articulation. The sanctuary is top-lit by a clerestory consisting of closely spaced piers terminating in geometrically abstracted capitals. Such piers and capitals occur again in Wright's City National Bank and Hotel in Mason City, Iowa (1909), only now the capitals are formed by projecting and recessing the bricks. Such sculptural manipulation of the brick coursing would be widely imitated by progressive architects, and

FIG. 3.01
LARKIN BUILDING,
Buffalo, N.Y. 1904.
Exterior view from southwest.
Frank Lloyd Wright, architect.
*Photograph courtesy of*
*The Museum of Modern Art, New York.*

the closely spaced piers terminating in Prairie School capitals—either cast ornament or articulated brick coursing—became a Prairie School convention. It seems significant that Wright's three-dimensional ornament was usually cast cement, too coarse a medium for Sullivan's more naturalistic métier, which achieved its finest expression in terra-cotta.

After the demise of his partnership with Dankmar Adler in 1895, Louis Sullivan became an increasingly isolated figure, rescued from obscurity by the splendid series of small-town midwestern banks he designed between 1907 and 1919. The first and perhaps finest of these, in Owatonna, Minnesota (1907), was designed while George Grant Elmslie was still in Sullivan's employ. Elmslie left Sullivan shortly thereafter to form a partnership with William Gray Purcell, and the firm of Purcell (Feick) and Elmslie also developed the progressive small-town bank concurrently with Sullivan for the next decade.[3] Purcell and Elmslie sometimes combined the form conventions of Wright with the ornamental conventions of Sullivan, as in the Merchants Bank of Winona, Minnesota (1912), and the Woodbury County Courthouse in Sioux City, Iowa (1917; with William Steele). As their work was extensively published in the *Western Architect*, it probably exerted an independent influence on other progressive designers, in Texas as well as elsewhere.

If Sullivan was professionally isolated in his Prairie School years, Frank Lloyd Wright's practice became an important atelier for the training of younger designers between 1895, when he opened the Oak Park Studio, and 1910, when he fled to Europe. Among the young associates who accepted Wright's rather irregular terms of employment were two men who subsequently came to Texas, bringing the lessons of the Prairie School with them: George Willis and Charles Erwin Barglebaugh. Willis, who also worked for Walter Burley Griffin in Chicago, would work for J. Edward Overbeck in Dallas and for Atlee B. Ayres in San Antonio before establishing his own practice in 1917. Barglebaugh worked for Lang and Witchell in Dallas from 1907 until 1916, when he established a practice with Lloyd Whitson.[4]

The Texas to which Willis and Barglebaugh emigrated in the first decade of the new century was rapidly outgrowing the professional structure of the nineteenth century. J. Riely Gordon's departure for New York in 1902 may be taken as symbolic of the changing of the guard, because the new century would be characterized by new firms with extensive regional practices supplying designs of greater size and sophistication than ever before. Among the most important of these new firms were Trost and Trost of El Paso, Sanguinet and Staats of Fort Worth and Houston, Lang and Witchell of Dallas, and Atlee B. Ayres of San Antonio. Although all of these firms did stylistically diverse work both before and after World War I, in the Progressive Era before the war they all dabbled intermittently in the Prairie School. But Prairie School influences were not confined to these new firms, for occasionally an older, established architect would also turn to Sullivan or Wright for inspiration. One such architect was James E. Flanders of Dallas.

JAMES E. FLANDERS OF DALLAS

Chapter 2 has already introduced Flanders, the designer of the First Methodist Church in Royse City, which displays suggestive allusions to the Prairie School within the Carpenter's Gothic tradition. At Flanders' subsequent brick churches, these allusions become more explicit through the use of Sullivanesque ornament. The basic form conventions of Flanders' three known Prairie School Gothic churches are similar to those of Royse City: a shallow Greek-cross plan with aggressively modeled towers placed in reentrant corners, with entrance porches attached. The horizontal bands beneath the projecting eaves of each tower are retained, only now they are filled with decorative plaster rendered in Sullivanesque ornament. At Trinity Methodist Church in Dallas, which was destroyed by fire in 1985, the chancel was also bordered by concentric friezes of this ornament, in a manner somewhat suggestive of Sullivan's Transportation Building at the Chicago Columbian Exposition. The two surviving examples of Flanders' Prairie School Gothic are not identical, but both share the same fundamental composition. The First Methodist Church in Pittsburg, which Flanders designed in 1904 (FIG. 3.02), is constructed of hard-finished orange brick with red-tile roofs, and the dominant tower is shifted away from the street intersection. Prairie School ornament is also used to impanel the bell louvers and second-story window on this dominant tower.

At St. John's Methodist Church of Stamford (FIG. 3.03), erected in 1910 of the popular tan brick with a dark-shingled roof, the dominant tower

FIG. 3.02
FIRST METHODIST CHURCH,
Pittsburg. 1904–1905.
J. E. Flanders, architect.

FIG. 3.03
ST. JOHN'S METHODIST CHURCH,
Stamford. 1910.
J. E. Flanders, architect.

FIG. 3.04
NAVARRO COUNTY COURTHOUSE,
Corsicana. 1905.
J. E. Flanders, architect.

marks the street corner and is given an elaborated roof. Except for the ornament, there is nothing strongly Prairie School about any of Flanders' churches. For all their idiosyncracies, they remain fundamentally Ecclesiastical Gothic.[5]

A similar conclusion suggests itself in regard to the Navarro County Courthouse in Corsicana, which Flanders designed in 1905 (FIG. 3.04). The building is hard to classify: Flanders uses classical elements with the same idiosyncratic bravura as he had used Gothic on the churches, and the centerpiece seems to strike a compromise between tower and dome. The only explicit Prairie School features are again the Sullivanesque ornament, which is now confined to the interior, where it is used for bordering friezes within the crossing space beneath the tower.[6] The Prairie School, of course, includes the form conventions of Wright as well as Sullivan's ornament, and although some Texas designers drew only upon the former, others continued to use Sullivanesque detail in ways similar to Flanders.

TROST AND TROST OF EL PASO

Henry C. Trost established the family firm of Trost and Trost in Tucson about 1898. The firm opened a second office in El Paso in 1903, where Henry joined his brother, Gustavus. His other brother, Adolphus, and his nephew, George Ernest Trost, rounded out the firm, although Henry has always been regarded as the principal designer. The El Paso office quickly became the principal headquarters for an enormous regional practice in Arizona, New Mexico, and West Texas that endured even beyond Henry Trost's death in 1933.[7]

Although there is no conclusive evidence of any formal connection between Henry Trost and either Sullivan or Wright, before moving to Tucson, he had worked in Chicago as a designer for Winslow Brothers, who executed ornament for Sullivan. William Winslow was a client and friend for whom Wright designed the Winslow House in River Forest in 1893. Trost may have worked for Adler and Sullivan, or for Sullivan alone after the demise of their partnership. In any event, Henry Trost's personal interest in both the ornament of Louis Sullivan and the form conventions of Frank Lloyd Wright may be inferred from much of his work. His attempt to assimilate Sullivan's ornament into a southwestern regional expression is evident in his early work in Tucson, such as the Santa Rita Hotel and the First and Second Owls Clubs.

In El Paso, this aspect of Trost's Prairie School practice is best represented in the Douglas Gray House of 1906 (FIG. 3.05). The overall form of the house is bizarre in the extreme, with the broad hipped roof of the Prairie School negated by the blank plaster walls and idiosyncratic fenestration. The inset porch, however, is bordered by a frieze of finely detailed Sullivanesque ornament supported by two squat columns-in-antis of indeterminant derivation. The frieze recalls one that Sullivan had used on the Wainwright Tomb (1892), and that Wright had featured at the entrance to the Winslow House (1893), both of which Trost might be expected to have known.

If Henry Trost's interest in Sullivan's ornament is apparent in the Douglas Gray House, his affection for the domestic work of Frank Lloyd Wright is quite evident in his own house (1908) in El Paso, perhaps the finest Prairie School house in Texas (FIGS. 3.06 and 3.07). The Henry Trost House is a mature and thoroughly comprehended exercise in Wright's Prairie School manner, perhaps most closely resembling the Susan Dana House in Springfield, Illinois, of 1903 (FIG. 3.08), although the half-timbering seems derived from other Wright examples. The pier-and-slot articulation of Trost's house is a common attribute of Wright's work, although the heavy frieze under the eaves seems peculiar to Henry Trost's own design vocabulary. The house is approached from the side street by a steep flight of stairs into an arcaded entrance porch, thence into the vestibule. One thus enters the house in the middle of the cross-axial plan, with a fireplace inglenook opposite, the living room to one's right, and the dining room to the left. This planning formula is one that Wright used a number of times when building on a restricted site, as in the

FIG. 3.05
DOUGLAS GRAY HOUSE,
1205 North El Paso Street, El Paso. 1906.
Trost and Trost, architects.

MacArthur and Heller houses. In this case it permits the living room and master bedroom above it an unrestricted prospect over Yandell Drive to the (original) dramatic view beyond, whereas the less important spaces are grouped to the rear of the site. The living room opens through French doors to a walled terrace in front, and to porches on either side that support balconies off the master bedroom above. All of these transitional elements can be found in one or more of Wright's houses and shelter the important private spaces from the view of the public on the street. The Henry Trost House thus shares those qualities of prospect and refuge that have been shown to exist in Wright's domestic architecture. Much of the furniture was designed for the house by Henry Trost, and the leaded glass windows betray the influence of Wright's geometrical ornament.[8] This concern for the total furnished environment was not unique to the Prairie School, of course, but was shared with the Arts

FIG. 3.06
HENRY TROST HOUSE,
1011 North Mesa Street, El Paso. 1908.
Trost and Trost, architects.

FIG. 3.07
HENRY TROST HOUSE. Floor plans.
*Redrawn by author from working drawings
published by Engelbrecht,* Prairie School
Review *6 (1969). Reprinted by permission of
Lloyd C. Engelbrecht and* Prairie School
Review.

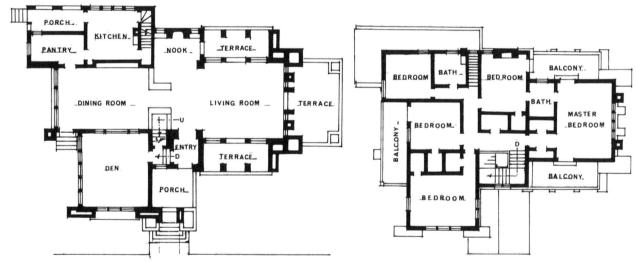

FIG. 3.08
SUSAN DANA HOUSE, Springfield, Ill.
1903. Frank Lloyd Wright, architect.

and Crafts movement in England and America.[9]

Other Prairie School manifestations in the work of Trost and Trost are less obviously derived from Wright's or Sullivan's examples. Mount Sinai Synagogue in El Paso of 1916 (FIG. 3.09) illustrates at best a diluted influence. For two centuries American designers had been challenged by the synagogue as a building type: an edifice expected to suggest a house of worship without looking like a church. Trost and Trost rose to this challenge in a curious amalgam of progressive and eclectic tendencies. The closed unitary form and soft tapestry brick with terra-cotta trim at Mount Sinai are suggestive of Sullivan's banks, whereas the slot window and suggestion of a corner pier recall Wright's institutional work. The ornament is not Sullivanesque, however, nor are the corner pier and slot very strongly articulated, and these Prairie School tendencies are combined with round arches and flamboyant Gothic window tracery.[10]

The commercial architecture of Trost and Trost in El Paso before World War I undeniably deserves to be called progressive, but lacks the obvious references to Sullivan and Wright found in the firm's residential and institutional work. One might expect the Chicago School of the 1880's and 1890's to have been Henry Trost's point of departure, but his commercial work in El Paso in the 1900's is distinguished from the earlier work in Chicago by a change in building technology. The Chicago architects developed the steel frame, which, because of a need for fireproofing, led to the development of terra-cotta sheathing,

FIG. 3.09
MOUNT SINAI SYNAGOGUE,
El Paso. 1916.
Trost and Trost, architects.

suggesting to Sullivan and others the possibilities of cast ornament. Adler and Sullivan's 1894 Guaranty Building in Buffalo, New York, (FIG. 3.10) is perhaps the Chicago School's tour de force: a steel frame fireproofed entirely in terra-cotta of minimal section, and totally impressed with Sullivan's original ornament.[11]

In El Paso, however, Henry Trost worked in an alternative technology: reinforced concrete. Between 1909 and 1916, he designed five concrete buildings in downtown El Paso, culminating in the twelve-story Mills Building of 1912–1916 (FIG. 3.11).[12] Although several of these had shown combinations of structure and fenestration reminiscent of various Chicago School experiments, none employed Sulli-

FIG. 3.10
GUARANTY BUILDING,
Buffalo, N.Y. 1894.
Adler and Sullivan, architects.

Pirie Scott Store, its real affinity to the Chicago School lies in the masterful synthesis of structure and technique. The facade expresses a rhythm of major and minor piers. The major piers, spaced twenty feet apart, articulate the building's structural grid, and alternate with two minor piers that correspond to its fenestration module and that also permit the flexible placement of interior partitions. Thus, the alternating rhythm of major and minor piers not only animates the facade but also resolves the conflict between a rational structural span and a functional space-planning module. Because the minor piers and spandrels were presumably poured with the columns and floor slabs, the exterior facade is integrated with the structure, unlike a steel-framed building, whose facade is fireproofing. Trost also articulated the building horizontally by establishing a base consisting of ground-floor shop space and a mezzanine, and by cantilevering a balcony with cast ornament at the tenth floor, defining the top two stories as a cap. This horizontal division recalls Sullivan's analysis of the tall office building as base, shaft, and capital. Despite such differences in structural technology and its expression, however, G. H. Edgell wrote in 1928 that "such a work as the Mills Building is designed in the spirit, and really in the letter, of Louis Sullivan's ideas."[13]

Unlike Sullivan and Wright, however, Henry Trost was not a stylistic ideologue. He was a capable and willing designer in historical styles when called upon, and his work will be encountered again in the following chapters.

vanesque ornament. Instead, Trost explored the possibilities of cast-in-place concrete ornament. The coarser technique used for this ornament calls for a more simplified morphology and a bolder scale than Sullivan's finely detailed work in terra-cotta. Although the Mills Building is sometimes compared superficially to Sullivan's Carson

FIG. 3.11
MILLS BUILDING,
El Paso. 1912–1916.
Remodeled.
Trost and Trost, architects.
*From El Paso Chapter AIA,* Portals at the Pass.
*Photograph, File No. 9063, Southwest*
*Collection, El Paso Public Library. Reprinted*
*by permission of El Paso Chapter AIA and*
*El Paso Public Library.*

FIG. 3.12
SANGER BROTHERS
DEPARTMENT STORE,
Dallas. 1910.
Lang and Witchell, architects.
Remodeled for El Centro Campus,
Dallas Community College.

FIG. 3.13
SANGER BROTHERS
DEPARTMENT STORE.
Detail.

## LANG AND WITCHELL OF DALLAS

The firm of Lang and Witchell was formed in 1905 by Otto H. Lang, who had worked as a structural engineer for the Texas and Pacific Railroad, and Frank O. Witchell, who had worked for J. Riely Gordon and for Sanguinet and Staats. In 1907, Lang and Witchell employed Charles Erwin Barglebaugh, who had recently come from Chicago, where he had worked for Frank Lloyd Wright and Walter Burley Griffin. Barglebaugh remained with the firm until about 1916, and is the presumptive designer of its Prairie School constructions. Barglebaugh's extremely diverse work during this period included residential, commercial and institutional buildings in Dallas and its surrounding communities, and drew upon both Sullivan and Wright for inspiration.[14]

Lang and Witchell designed a number of large commercial buildings in downtown Dallas before World War I, of which only the Sanger Brothers Department Store survives (FIGS. 3.12 and 3.13), albeit in altered state as part of the El Centro Campus of the Dallas County Community College District. This ten-story building has a clear affiliation with the Chicago School; it has a rigorously expressed steel frame fireproofed in brick and terracotta, which defines large horizontally proportioned windows for maximum light. Some of these are "Chicago windows"[15] with additional transoms; others consist of three double-hung sashes. As the building was designed for a department store, the influence of the Carson Pirie Scott Store is likely, although it has not been slavishly copied. The Sanger building exhibits a dynamic balance between horizontal and vertical proportions, with an alternating rhythm of major and minor piers on the narrow frontage. The piers are accentuated vertically by the modeling of their terra-cotta fireproofing, and terminate in foliate cartouches of Sullivanesque ornament at the cornice (since removed) and mezzanine. The shop windows at the ground floor were replaced by a recessed loggia in the El Centro remodeling, but the flat relief ornament on the ground floor piers remains. The surviving terra-cotta on the Sanger building represents a rather coarse interpretation of Sullivan's ornamental system (FIG. 3.13). The principles are obvious: the evolution of an increasingly complex geometrical armature of circles, arcs, and rotated squares, which slowly awakens to the animating power of naturalistic foliage. Unfortunately, whether through poor detailing in the drafting room or poor execution in the casting process, the organic foliage remains flat and mechanical. The firm would do much better work in Sullivan's manner elsewhere.[16]

Large commercial buildings by Lang and Witchell in downtown Dallas that did not survive included the twelve-story Commonwealth National Bank Building, the eight-story Cotton Exchange, and the sixteen-story Southwestern Life Building. The latter two made use of Sullivanesque ornament at mezzanine and cornice, although their patterns of fenestration differed from the Sanger Building. The Southwestern Life Building, erected between 1911 and 1913, must have been the most imposing skyscraper in Dallas during that decade.[17]

FIG. 3.14
RALEIGH HOTEL,
Waco. 1912.
Lang and Witchell, architects.

FIG. 3.15
RALEIGH HOTEL. Detail.

FIG. 3.16
FIRST NATIONAL BANK BUILDING,
Paris. 1916.
Griffith and Barglebaugh, architects.

After office buildings and department stores, the hotel was probably the most significant of downtown building types. Although Lang and Witchell were not invited to design the premier hotel constructed in Dallas during this period, they were commissioned in 1912 to design the Raleigh Hotel in Waco (FIGS. 3.14 and 3.15). This ten-story, red-brick block obeys a common formula: ground floor, mezzanine, uniform hotel floors, and a terminating cornice at the tenth floor. It is distinguished principally by eight splendid badges of Sullivanesque ornament in cream terra-cotta on the mezzanine corners. By now the firm had mastered Sullivan's ornamental repertoire. The luxuriant, high-relief foliage is convincingly rendered and the cartouche is seated on the pier by a saddle of brick strapwork formed by projecting certain courses beyond the wall line. It is one of the most satisfying Prairie School details in Texas.[18]

Somewhat akin to the Dallas skyscrapers and the Raleigh Hotel is the First National Bank Building in Paris (FIG. 3.16), designed about 1916 by Griffith and Barglebaugh (who had recently left Lang and Witchell). Six-stories tall, the First National Building dominated the High-Victorian fabric of this ambitious town in northeast Texas, a harbinger of the multistory bank building that became a prominent building type after World War I (see Chapter 4). It survived the fire of 1916, which gutted the business district. The palette of red brick and cream-glazed terra-cotta recalls that of the Raleigh Hotel, although it lacks the splendid ornament badges that distinguish the Waco building. The Prairie School content of the

Paris bank building is muted and allusive rather than explicit, yet the absence of historical detail and touches of Sullivanesque ornament on the overhanging cornice suggest that it belongs in the progressive camp rather than the Academic Eclectic one.[19]

Another genre of commercial architecture was found in the warehousing and light-industrial districts adjacent to the downtown areas of major American cities, as discussed in Chapter 2. In addition to generic loft space, these districts often included wholesale stores of major mail-order firms such as Montgomery Ward and Sears Roebuck, both of which had built huge depots in Chicago designed by progressive architects. Sears, Roebuck in particular cultivated a progressive image, with regional distribution centers in Chicago, Kansas City, and Seattle designed by the firm of Nimmons and Fellows.[20] For its Dallas distribution center in 1913, Sears Roebuck commissioned Lang and Witchell, probably because of the firm's reputation for progressive work.

The Sears Roebuck Wholesale Store on South Lamar Street in Dallas is an enormous structure nine stories high and one block long (FIG. 3.17). Faced with this vast bulk, the designers chose to emphasize the horizontal dimension. Horizontal window groups are constrained between a continuous header and a continuous sill, between which the horizontal brick spandrels run uninterrupted. In contrast to the previously constructed Sears Roebuck stores, the model for the Dallas facility seems to have been Schmidt and Garden's wholesale store for Montgomery Ward in Chicago,

FIG. 3.17
SEARS ROEBUCK WHOLESALE STORE,
Dallas. 1913.
Lang and Witchell, architects.

FIG. 3.18
SEARS ROEBUCK WHOLESALE STORE,
Dallas. Entrance detail.

where the inexorable horizontal character of the composition is expressed in similar fashion. The main entrance to the Dallas store combines traces of Sullivan and Wright: the narrow sidelights and foliate pier capitals are yet another example of the pier-and-slot articulation so common in the Prairie School (FIG. 3.18).[21]

Adjacent to the wholesale store, Lang and Witchell designed an employees' clubhouse for Sears Roebuck (FIG. 3.19) that was clearly based upon the Prairie School houses of Frank Lloyd Wright. This compact, one-and-a-half-story structure recalls some of Wright's smaller commissions, such as the Arthur Heurtley or Edwin Cheney houses in Oak Park. The building is encompassed by a single, hipped roof with a continuous, overhanging eave line. Stairs slotted into the corners and flanked by brick banisters

FIG. 3.19
SEARS ROEBUCK EMPLOYEES
CLUBHOUSE,
Dallas. 1913.
Lang and Witchell, architects.

FIG. 3.20
HIGGENBOTHAM HOUSE,
5002 Swiss Avenue, Dallas. 1913.
Lang and Witchell, architects.

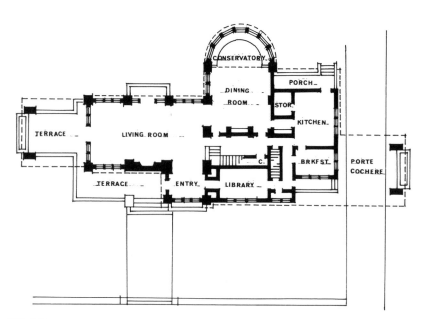

FIG. 3.21
HIGGENBOTHAM HOUSE. Floor plan.
*Redrawn by author from Henry et al.,*
Perspective *10 (1981).*

with stone copings and, originally, planting urns—all possibly inspired by Wright—lead to the entrance on the elevated main floor. The fenestration consists of regularly spaced double-hung windows divided by brick piers, terminated at the top by Prairie School capitals of projected and recessed brick, similar to Wright's handling of piers and windows at the Mason City Bank.[22]

Lang and Witchell further demonstrated their command of Wright's domestic idiom at the Higgenbotham House in Dallas, built in 1913 (FIGS. 3.20 and 3.21). This large house on an expansive lot combines features found on many of Wright's larger Prairie School houses. It most closely resembles the Darwin Martin House in Buffalo, New York, of 1904. The characteristic features of such a fully comprehended Prairie School house include the cross-axial floor plan, the hipped roof with overhanging eaves, the indirect or concealed entrances, the horizontal banks of windows constrained by continuous eave and sill lines, the separate roofs for first and second stories, and a lower floor that extends into the landscape through porches, terraces, porte cocheres, and conservatories. The use of continuous stone copings and the ubiquitous planting urns were common devices when Wright built in brick. The semicircular conservatory off the dining room was used by Wright at the Blossom, Winslow, and Dana houses. The geometric pattern of art glass in the first floor windows is also closely modeled on Wright's ornamental style.

On the other hand, certain aberrations from the master's work are also apparent. The main fireplace in the living room is placed on the front wall; it does not become the central core from which the plan radiates, as it would in a Wright house. The main entrance, although approached indirectly from the street, is not really tucked away as it would be in Wright's mature work, and the broad approach esplanade and front terrace, common to many houses on Swiss Avenue, had long been abandoned by Wright in favor of a more indirect involvement with the site. Moreover, the windows are double-hung rather than the casement sash preferred by Wright, and they lack the horizontal proportions that reinforce the integration of the house with the flat prairie in the master's oeuvre. Thus, the Higgenbotham House is not a perfect rendition of Wright's Prairie School example. It is, however, after the Henry Trost House in El Paso, probably the best Prairie School house in Texas.[23]

Sullivan's repertoire was primarily commercial; Wright's primarily domestic. Their occasional institutional commissions did not generate a ground swell of enthusiasm for public architecture in the Prairie School mode. Except for a number of Chicago schools by Dwight Perkins, the first important Prairie School public institution was Purcell and Elmslie's Woodbury County Courthouse in Sioux City, Iowa, of 1917, which came too late to save the Prairie School from the "return to normalcy" following World War I. It therefore is surprising to find manifestations of the Prairie School appearing in Texas courthouses, traditionally the most prestigious building type in Texas. Once again, one instrument of transmission is the firm of Lang and Witchell and, presumably, their associate, Charles

Erwin Barglebaugh. Lang and Witchell designed five courthouses in Texas between 1907 and 1917; manifestations of Sullivan and Wright's influence appear in two: the Cooke County Courthouse in Gainesville (1910) and the Johnson County Courthouse in Cleburne (1912).[24]

At first glance, the Cooke County Courthouse appears to conform to the standard idiom of Beaux-Arts Classic design, which by 1910 had become de rigueur for monumental public buildings in the United States (FIG. 3.22). It is cross shaped and biaxially symmetrical, with entrances facing the four sides of the public square. Access corridors meet in a central lobby, which rises through the full height of the three-story building and is crowned by a well-scaled lantern carrying clock faces. The ground floor and basement are constructed of stone; the main and upper floors are in hard-finished tan brick trimmed in terra-cotta. The entrance is on the ground floor, whence one ascends to the main floor internally; there are no monu-

FIG. 3.22
COOKE COUNTY COURTHOUSE,
Gainesville. 1910.
Lang and Witchell, architects.

FIG. 3.23
COOKE COUNTY COURTHOUSE.
Lobby detail.

FIG. 3.24
JOHNSON COUNTY COURTHOUSE,
Cleburne. 1912.
Lang and Witchell, architects.

FIG. 3.25
WOODBURY COUNTY COURTHOUSE,
Sioux City, Iowa. 1917.
Purcell and Elmslie, with William Steele,
architects.

mental exterior staircases. Each arm of the cross terminates with classical columns rising through main and upper floors set in antis: four columns on each of the broad fronts and two columns on the narrow. These columns serve to dignify the *piano nobile* where the principal ceremonial spaces— the courtroom and commissioner's court—are located. All of this is thoroughly conventional. It is only when examining the details carefully that suggestions of novelty can be perceived. Although recognizably Ionic, the capitals have been geometrically abstracted, as have the heraldic eagles and the central cartouche.

The central lobby is crowned by an art-glass skylight beneath the external lantern, supported on splayed corner piers. The ornament on these piers and around the lobby's attic is unmistakably derived from Sullivan and Wright (FIG. 3.23). The long stem on each corner pier is closer to Wright's geometrical ornament, but

the foliate cartouches at the cornice are pure Sullivanesque, combining naturalistic foliage over a geometric armature.

The Johnson County Courthouse at Cleburne of 1912 (FIG. 3.24) is similar in general organization to that at Gainesville, except that a tall central clock tower has replaced the domed lantern. At Cleburne, however, the form conventions and ornament of the Prairie School are manifest on the exterior. The piers that bracket the two broad fronts of the courthouse are pronounced and strongly modeled, with a slot of fenestration down the center, although not as powerfully articulated as in Wright's oeuvre or in that of Purcell and Elmslie. The ornament is a balance of Wright's repetitive geometry and Sullivan's naturalistic foliage over a geometric armature. The interior is also similar to Gainesville in that splayed piers with Sullivanesque ornament support an art-glass skylight over the central lobby.[25]

Both the Gainesville and Cleburne courthouses combine formal and ornamental elements of the Prairie School with a conventional idiom of public architecture. Neither is as radical as the commercial and residential work of Lang and Witchell discussed previously. Both courthouses are tame and conventional when compared with Purcell and Elmslie's courthouse in Sioux City, Iowa (FIG. 3.25). Their departure from the literal correctness of Academic Eclecticism qualifies these two buildings as progressive, however. The Cleburne edifice shares with Atlee B. Ayres' Jim Wells County Courthouse in Alice the distinction of being one of the two most remarkable courthouses of its generation in Texas.

SANGUINET AND STAATS OF
FORT WORTH AND HOUSTON

Not all progressive manifestations in American architecture were strongly related to the specific mannerisms of Sullivan or Wright. Other architects also attempted independently to avoid overt historicism. As Stephen Fox has observed, "while formal likenesses can be discerned, Sanguinet and Staats were far less Wrightian than such Texas contemporaries as Trost and Trost, Lang and Witchell, and George Willis."[26]

The firm of Sanguinet and Staats was formed in Fort Worth around 1900 by Marshall R. Sanguinet, formerly of Messer, Sanguinet and Messer, and Carl G. Staats, who had worked for J. Riely Gordon from 1891 until 1898. The firm opened a branch office in Houston in 1903, and quickly developed a reputation in both cities for the design of modern, steel-frame office buildings. One of their earliest exercises in this building type was the seven-story Flatiron Building in Fort Worth of 1907 (FIG. 3.26). Although one can recognize Sullivan's formula of ground floor, mezzanine, uniform office floors, and attic in this building, in general the structure has no strong affinity for anything in Chicago. Neither does it have the historical period detail with which Sanguinet and Staats dressed contemporary buildings in Houston. The ornament on the Flatiron Building is a rather awkward form of geometrical strapwork. The building might be termed progressive more by default than conviction.

Fourteen years later at the Neil P. Anderson Building in Fort Worth (1921; FIG. 3.27), Sanguinet and

FIG. 3.26
FLATIRON BUILDING,
Fort Worth. 1907.
Sanguinet and Staats, architects.

FIG. 3.27
NEIL P. ANDERSON BUILDING,
Fort Worth. 1921.
Sanguinet and Staats, architects.

FIG. 3.28
TARRANT COUNTY CRIMINAL
COURTS BUILDING,
Fort Worth. 1917.
Sanguinet and Staats, architects.

Staats once again returned to this rather neutral form of progressive architecture. Whereas the Flatiron Building is awkward, the Anderson building is a very mature and handsome piece of commercial design. Although the radial-corner treatment recalls Sullivan's Carson Pirie Scott Store, the Anderson building displays neither the dominant horizontal character of this model, nor the vertical emphasis of Sullivan's skyscrapers. Neither does it resemble Trost and Trost's Mills Building in El Paso, despite a similar site configuration on an obtuse angle facing a public square. The Mills Building had derived both structure and formal expression from reinforced concrete; the Neil P. Anderson Building—despite its concrete frame—is clad in brick trimmed in terra-cotta. The tenth floor, containing the executive suite and boardroom, is an interesting exercise in space planning adapted to

the obtuse angle of the site. A ten-story building in 1920 would no longer be considered a skyscraper in Fort Worth, of course (it had been surpassed by the firm's twelve-story Burk Burnett Building of 1914 and their twenty-story Waggoner Building of 1920). Neither the horizontal dimension nor the vertical one dominates the Anderson building, which has a fenestration pattern that reinforces this neutrality. Although the vertical piers carry through in front of the spandrels, they are neither widely nor narrowly spaced, and both piers and spandrels are faced in uniform brick. The effect is that of a neutral field, in which the horizontal and vertical proportions are held in ambiguous tension. Like much of Sanguinet and Staats' work, it is subtle rather than outstandingly original, and might arguably be assigned to the Academic Eclectic category.[27]

Something of the same subtle tension animates the Tarrant County Criminal Courts Building in Fort Worth of 1917 (FIG. 3.28). Although the narrow windows in the upper floors were doubtless dictated by the jail functions accommodated there, the effect is sufficiently similar to the pier-and-slot articulation of Frank Lloyd Wright to suggest Prairie School influence as well. This suggestion is reinforced by the corner pavilions, blank above the third floor except for a narrow window slot down the center. These features are combined with conventional classicizing elements, however, such as the rusticated base and conventional cornice. Moreover, the corners are defined by pavilions rather than articulated piers, and a true pier-and-slot articulation is not employed. As in the case of

FIG. 3.29
TRIMBLE HIGH SCHOOL,
Fort Worth. 1917.
Sanguinet and Staats, architects.

the Neil P. Anderson Building, it is a subtle judgment to call the Criminal Courts Building progressive rather than eclectic.

This same subtlety can be found in Sanguinet and Staat's school buildings of the period. Two Fort Worth high schools stand out: Trimble High School, completed in 1917, and North Fort Worth High School, completed in 1918. The American high school in its modern form was very much a product of the Progressive Era, because to the middle class eight years of elementary education no longer seemed adequate for the complexities of modern life. Electric traction made it possible for older students to travel greater distances to school; the interurban railways even permitted students from rural areas to commute to modern high schools in towns and cities. The diversified curriculum and practice of changing classes required an efficient plan of no more than three or four floors, with frequent stairways, commodious hallways, gymnasiums, auditoriums, laboratories, etc. The large, relatively low buildings resulting from this program required new approaches to architectural composition. Above all, classrooms and laboratories required good natural light, placing demands on the ingenuity of the designer comparable to those faced by commercial architects. Academic Eclectics tended to seek out those historical styles characterized by large window areas; the Gothic and Elizabethan were favored over classical and Renaissance modes for this reason.[28]

There is a recognizably Gothic flavor to Trimble High School (FIG. 3.29), just as there was a classic flavor to the Criminal Courts Building. The only overtly Gothic details, however, are those in terra-cotta at the main entrance. All other details are suggestive, rather than literal.

FIG. 3.30
NORTH FORT WORTH
HIGH SCHOOL. 1918.
Sanguinet and Staats, architects.

The leitmotif of the Gothic at Trimble High School is the flat, four-centered arch, typical of late Gothic. This arch is repeated, without other Gothic detailing, over each of the window groups on the main facade. Within each of these window groups an alternation of major and minor piers occurs, analogous to the slot-and-pier articulation of the Prairie School. On the sides of the building the arches are omitted, although the asymmetrical rhythm of the piers continues. Terra-cotta trim is used sparingly to enhance the verticality of these minor piers, and to counteract the inherent horizontal character of the building. The handsome tapestry brick is laid in a variety of patterns to enrich the ensemble.

If the progressive modernity of Trimble High School is somewhat diluted by its allusive Gothicism,

the same cannot be said of Sanguinet and Staats' North Fort Worth High School of 1918 (FIG. 3.30), which is about as close as the firm ever approached to a pure expression of the Prairie School.[29] The main facade consists of a dominant central block flanked by recessive wings. The paired main entrances are placed in slots between the central block and each wing, rather as Wright had handled the entrance at the Larkin Building, although the slot is not as dramatic at North Fort Worth. The corner pavilions that flank the central block are more forcefully modeled than those on the Criminal Courts Building, and the heavy attic above the continuous cornice is anticlassical in spirit and emphasizes mass over detail. But the regularly spaced piers between the classroom windows are the most overt evidence of the Prairie School. Even though the capitals are purely geometric rather than Sullivanesque, they have the proportions of Prairie School capitals.[30]

Sanguinet and Staats were capable of traditional ecclesiastical design of high quality: their St. Andrew's Episcopal Church in Fort Worth of 1909 was a manifestation of the continued use of the Gothic style for church building and the continued use of the medieval as a paradigm for worship in the Anglican communion. Other denominations were not as conservative, however. As I noted, the Methodist Church patronized J. E. Flanders during this period (FIGS. 3.02, 3.03) and although Flanders' churches were overtly Gothic in their use of pointed arches, the plans were nontraditional auditorium forms, and Flanders employed extensive Sullivanesque ornament. The First Methodist Church in Temple (FIG. 3.31), designed by Sanguinet and Staats in 1912, seems related to Flanders' churches in spirit, if not in form. The plan is unconventional, although not original: a semicircular auditorium and balcony converges upon the chancel, with a block of service functions behind the chancel wall.[31] The stylistic idiom is allusive rather than specific, but the round arches seem to draw upon the Lombard Romanesque, with a touch of Spanish Mission added in the paired towers and tiled roofs. Several colors of brick are used in various course patterns to create a rich ensemble. As in much of Sanguinet and Staats' work, one must weigh historical allusion against originality in design to determine whether to assign the Temple Methodist Church to the progressive or eclectic camp.

FIG. 3.31
FIRST METHODIST CHURCH,
Temple. 1912.
Sanguinet and Staats, architects.

## ATLEE B. AYRES AND GEORGE WILLIS OF SAN ANTONIO

Atlee B. Ayres practiced with C. A. Coughlin until 1905, when he launched his independent practice in San Antonio, perhaps filling the void left by J. Riely Gordon's departure for New York. In 1910 George Willis joined Ayres' office, and remained there until 1917, when he set up his own practice in San Antonio. Willis had worked for Frank Lloyd Wright in Oak Park from 1898 until 1902, and then had moved to Dallas, where he was associated with H. A. Overbeck. As in the case of Barglebaugh's association with Lang and Witchell, Willis may be assumed to be the designer of the occasional Prairie School work coming from the Ayres office between 1910 and 1917. Both he and Ayres continued to operate productive

FIG. 3.32
JIM WELLS COUNTY COURTHOUSE,
Alice. 1912.
Atlee B. Ayres, architect.

FIG. 3.33
CAMERON COUNTY COURTHOUSE,
Brownsville, 1912. Interior detail.
Atlee B. Ayres, architect.

practices in San Antonio throughout the 1920's and beyond, and will be encountered again in subsequent chapters.[32]

Ayres designed five courthouses and remodeled two in this period; all show some degree of Prairie School influence.[33] This effect is most apparent in the first two of the series, the Jim Wells County Courthouse in Alice (FIG. 3.32) and the Cameron County Courthouse in Brownsville, both of 1912. The plans of none of Ayres' courthouses are remarkable; indeed, they are typical of cross-axial Beaux-Arts planning already encountered in work of the same genre by Lang and Witchell. The closely set brick piers of the Alice courthouse are its most obvious distinguishing attribute, and although the ornamental capitals are not strongly Sullivanesque, they defy other historical classification. The ornamental detail at Alice is cast cement. As I have previously described, the coarse texture of cast cement inhibited the achievement of truly convincing Sullivanesque effects. By their proportions they may be called Prairie School capitals. The closely set columns-in-antis in the entry porch also approximate the common pier-and-slot articulation of the Prairie School, being perhaps closer to the work of George W. Maher than to that of either Sullivan or Wright.[34]

Whereas at Alice the exterior form denotes the Prairie School, at Brownsville the progressive elements are internalized. The exterior appears to be a conventional piece of cross-axial Beaux-Arts design, but as in Lang and Witchell's Gainesville and Cleburne courthouses, an art-glass skylight over the rotunda is supported on a frieze of Sullivan-

FIG. 3.34
KLEBERG COUNTY COURTHOUSE,
Kingsville. 1914.
Atlee B. Ayres, architect.

esque ornament (FIG. 3.33), which is also employed elsewhere within the central space. Moreover, all ornament at Brownsville is cast terracotta, Sullivan's natural medium.[35]

At the Kleberg County Courthouse in Kingsville of 1914 (FIG. 3.34) Ayres employed a column-in-antis entrance porch similar to that at Alice, but without the vigorously rendered piers on the main body of the courthouse. At Kingsville the capitals look like abstractions of classical detail, but the central cartouche appears to be Sullivanesque in character, and as with Brownsville, cast in terra-cotta. The porch is the only remarkable feature of the Kingsville courthouse; in other aspects it is typical of its period.

The entrance porch is again the

significant progressive feature of the Refugio County Courthouse in Refugio (FIG. 3.35), which Ayres designed in 1917. Here the pier-and-slot articulation so typical of the Prairie School is reinforced by the use of brick piers. Refugio has art-glass ceilings over the second-floor stair lobby, but reverts to cast-cement ornament. The Refugio courthouse is more horizontally proportioned than the earlier ones, an effect enhanced by the darker-brick basement and the heavy attic, although the latter appears to have been altered when the courthouse was expanded at a later date.

The office of Atlee B. Ayres designed several significant Prairie School houses that invite comparison to Henry Trost's residence (FIG.

FIG. 3.35
REFUGIO COUNTY COURTHOUSE,
Refugio. 1917.
Atlee B. Ayres, architect.

3.07) or to the Higgenbotham House of Lang and Witchell (FIG. 3.20). Although his name does not appear on the drawings, it is customary to assume that George Willis was the designer. The first of these, the L. T. Wright House in San Antonio (FIG. 3.36), was designed in 1914 but not completed until 1917. It shows Willis' skill in adapting the Prairie School repertoire to a difficult problem. The one-story house is built close to the ground on a small lot, like a typical bungalow of its generation, and hence lacks the more involved site integration of Wright's best work. The wall construction of plastered masonry and the absence of a dominant fireplace core further tend to dilute the Prairie School character of this house, which is U-shaped, with a patio in the center. This suggests Wright's tendency after 1910 to surround and enclose exterior space. It is not unreasonable to assume that Willis had kept up with the master's work after leaving the Oak Park studio. The intersecting hipped roofs that establish a consistent horizontal eave line, sheltering the porch, porte cochere, and various conditions of wall and window, show Willis' allegiance to Wright's principles.

Another Willis-designed house, for Dr. Lenma Young in San Antonio (FIG. 3.37), is much closer to explicit Wright models, recalling the George Barton House in Buffalo of 1903; hence it is a less adventurous design than that of the L. D. Wright House. It is significant that the younger designers of the Prairie School tended after 1910 to reinterpret Wright's earlier corpus of work, rather than the most current exam-

FIG. 3.36
L. T. WRIGHT HOUSE,
342 Wilkins Avenue, San Antonio. 1917.
George Willis, architect.

ples. Wright constantly worked on the cutting edge of design innovation, whereas his younger associates from the Oak Park years, including Willis and Barglebaugh, remained more conservative and eventually reverted to eclecticism after World War I. A remaining Prairie School house by Ayres' office, the Williams-Tarbutton House of 1912–1914 in San Marcos, is disappointing as a completed ensemble, although all ingredients of Wright's style have been carefully followed.[36]

FIG. 3.37
DR. LENMA YOUNG HOUSE,
828 Cambridge Oval,
San Antonio. C. 1918.
George Willis, architect.

FIG. 3.38
JOHN DEERE CO. (later TEXAS
IMPLEMENTS) BUILDING,
Dallas. 1902.
Hubbell and Greene, architects.

OTHER PROGRESSIVE
MANIFESTATIONS

The examples of the Chicago and Prairie schools were widely diffused in American architecture, not only through direct discipleship of men like Barglebaugh and Willis, but also through word of mouth and publication in the architectural journals. Sometimes an adventurous client would seek out a progressive architect, as had happened with Sears Roebuck and Lang and Witchell. Another such progressive client was the John Deere Company, as Leon-

ard Eaton has shown.[37] For its Dallas facility of 1902 (FIG. 3.38, also known from a later owner as the Texas Implements Building) John Deere engaged the services of Hubbell and Greene. The result was a starkly modeled building in red brick, with windows deeply set behind vertical piers and exaggerated blank corners. The separation of ground and top floors by string courses suggests Sullivan's Wainwright Building as a possible model, although because the John Deere Building is a warehouse distribution facility rather than an office building, Hubbell and Greene were free to exaggerate the breadth of the corners without concern for diminishing the natural light. The ornament on the ground floor is cut brick rather than terra-cotta, and despite its intricate geometric interlace, shows no traces of Sullivanesque foliage.[38]

In 1919 Barglebaugh, who had left the employ of Lang and Witchell around 1916, formed a partnership with Lloyd R. Whitson. Although some of their work was quite conventional—a response to the conservatism of American culture after World War I—they did produce a progressive masterpiece in the Armor Building (now known as the Hogg Building) in Houston of 1919 (FIG. 3.39). The eight-story building was constructed as an auto showroom and office space. Its reinforced concrete frame permitted extremely long spans between minimal brick-faced piers, infilled with metal industrial sash. The ratio of fenestration to brickwork is extreme. Both piers and spandrels are extremely attenuated, and the horizontal and vertical proportions are held in ambiguous tension. The building is unornamented except for badges of Sullivanesque ornament defining each pier at mezzanine and attic levels. The Hogg Building is Barglebaugh's last homage to Sullivan and his experiences in Chicago.[39]

As a building designed, at least in part, for the automobile trade, the Hogg Building was not unique in its use of Sullivanesque ornament. As a new building type for which no historical models existed, the automobile showroom/service garage in the 1910's and early 1920's was often decorated in Prairie School ornament selected from the catalogs of the American or Midland Terra Cotta companies. An outstanding example of this is found at 906 Austin Street in Waco (FIG. 3.40). The sales showroom is placed in front, with large display windows on the street and a transom of industrial glazing above. Two automobile ramps at either side connect to an extensive two-story, concrete-frame parking and service garage behind the showroom, which extends the full depth of a city block and exploits a change in street grade. One can also enter the garage through a lower level from the rear street. The main facade is tied together by a deep brick parapet, punctuated above each entrance by a cartouche of Sullivanesque ornament in terracotta, which is also used for the linear moldings and arch springings. The cartouches are also used on the rear facade. This particular badge of ornament is found throughout the Midwest in buildings constructed during the 1910's and early 1920's, because it was available from the catalog of the Midland Terra Cotta Company until the mid-1920's.[40]

Ingenious as the Waco building is, its formal composition owes nothing, beyond its ornamental detail, to either Sullivan or Wright. The same cannot be said of a comparable building for the automobile trade at 2210 Commerce Street in Dallas (FIG. 3.41). Here not only the ornament but the facade composition comes from the Prairie School, with Wright's pier-and-slot articulation within a defining frame. Sullivanesque ornament is employed in the cartouches placed in the upper corners of the facade, as well as on the pier capitals.[41]

Although all buildings discussed so far in this chapter were designed by Texas architects, occasionally an out-of-state firm would be brought in for a prestige commission, usually of an eclectic character. Although none of the well-known Prairie School architects from the Midwest were invited to design any-

FIG. 3.39
ARMOR BUILDING
(now HOGG BUILDING),
Houston. 1919.
Barglebaugh and Whitson, architects.

FIG. 3.40
AUTOMOBILE SHOWROOM/GARAGE,
906 Austin Street, Waco. N.D.

FIG. 3.41
AUTOMOBILE SHOWROOM/GARAGE,
2210 Commerce Street, Dallas. N.D.

FIG. 3.42
SANTA FE RAILROAD STATION,
Snyder. 1911.
Louis Curtiss, architect.

thing in Texas, Louis Curtiss, a Kansas City designer with a reputation for progressive, if not idiosyncratic, architecture, did considerable work in the state, much of it for the Atchison, Topeka, and Santa Fe Railroad. Curtiss' Santa Fe Station in Snyder of about 1911 (FIG. 3.42) is the best surviving example of this body of work. His powerfully articulated forms combine details from the Prairie School with suggestions of the Mission Revival, which was more or less the corporate idiom of Santa Fe Railroad buildings.[42]

Several discernibly new commercial building types emerged in the Progressive Era in larger Texas towns. These are normally rather neutral stylistically, but on occasion exhibit pronounced eclectic or progressive features. Mercantile interests in many towns actively promoted modern hotels as social gathering places and as accommodation for commercial travelers. These buildings, which frequently comprised four or five stories, usually had to be designed to resolve the competing architectural requirements of private guest rooms and public spaces. This genre includes the Rogers Hotel in Waxahachie and the Redlands Hotel in Palestine, but the most remarkable for its progressive-form characteristics is the Plaza Hotel in Seguin, designed in 1916 by Leo M. J. Deilmann (FIG. 3.43). The narrow block of guest rooms rises from a laterally extended ground floor and mezzanine, in which lobby, offices, concession spaces, and dining room are located. The guest room slab is articulated by a rhythm of wide and narrow bays, and a subtle tripartite division of the long facade. The sculptural quality of the building is enhanced by the application of pilaster strips to the piers, with major piers demarcated at the cornice by badges of cast-cement ornament suggestive of the Prairie School. Although the coarser scale of cast cement usually precludes the degree of clarity and detail achievable in terra-cotta or plaster, Sullivan's system of ornament seems to be the basis for Dielmann's pier finials at Seguin. The broader two-story base is divided into thirds, with a main entrance leading to a double-height central lobby, overlooked by a balcony at mezzanine level and joined by a side passage leading to the building's secondary entrance facing the courthouse square. The smaller public and administrative functions are placed on ground floor and mezzanine to the left of the lobby, with separate street access for retail concessions. The dining room is a

FIG. 3.43
PLAZA HOTEL,
Seguin. 1916.
Leo M. J. Dielmann, architect.

handsomely proportioned space of double height to the right of the lobby, denoted by a subtle shift in fenestration pattern.[43]

Another new building type that originated in the twentieth century was a novel form of commercial-business block known as the modern broad-front. In the nineteenth century, commercial blocks along main street and surrounding the public square normally had been long and narrow, with one storeroom on the ground floor and warehousing or office functions above. Even when larger units were built, they normally reflected the narrow windows and limited joist spans dictated by masonry-bearing wall construction and the vertical propor-

FIG. 3.44
BROAD-FRONT,
Pecos. C. 1915.

ware store beneath its four banks of horizontally grouped windows.[44]

At the other end of the functional spectrum from the automobile trade and modern broad-front was church architecture: the great example of progressive design in this genre was Frank Lloyd Wright's 1906 Unity Temple in Oak Park (FIG. 3.45). Unity Temple was not widely influential among more conservative sects accustomed to traditional form and symbolism in their houses of worship. A partial exception among mainline Protestant denominations were the Methodists, who commissioned the First Methodist Church of Cameron, designed by Waller, Silber and Company in 1921 (FIG. 3.46). The plan is hardly unconventional, consisting of a shallow Greek cross with circulation and service functions placed in the re-entrant corners. The familiar Prairie School pier-and-slot articulation is apparent on each arm of the Greek cross, and Sullivan's characteristic ornament appears somewhat timidly on the pier capitals. A continuous string course above the second-story windows establishes a heavy attic, another common Prairie School device that reinforces the geometrical character of the composition.

Sullivan's ornament and Wright's form conventions were adapted to a variety of contexts, from church architecture to the commercial vernacular. If details of Sullivan's or Wright's style begin to appear in the commercial vernacular, it is not surprising to find that trace elements of Frank Lloyd Wright's domestic repertoire were also widely diffused. Hipped roofs with continuous horizontal eaves, continu-

tions of the Victorian aesthetic. In the new century, the broad-front incorporating several ground-floor storerooms became more common, and the use of steel shelf angles to carry masonry over voids made larger, horizontally proportioned window groups on the upper floors possible. Such horizontally proportioned broad-fronts, often constructed of the ubiquitous hard-finished tan brick of the period, might be picked out in ornamental detail derived from the Prairie School, Academic Eclecticism, or Mission Revival. Without such specific stylistic detail, the modern broad-front conveys a formal neutrality that might be considered progressive by default, as the straightforward, unaffected expression of modern building technology. Hundreds of examples of this type of building exist, but FIG. 3.44 from Pecos provides a good study, because it accommodates both a furniture and a hard-

ous second-floor sill lines, separate roofs for first and second floors (with the former extended to porches and porte cocheres), grouped and banked windows, and planting urns occur frequently in neighborhoods of Texas towns and cities under development before World War I. Occasionally, Wright-inspired patterns of art glass or friezes and badges of Sullivanesque ornament are to be seen as well. The T. W. Newsome House in Dallas (FIG. 3.47), just down the street from Lang and Witchell's Higgenbotham House, was designed in 1914 by C. P. Sites and is often cited as an example of Prairie School influence. When examined carefully, however, the Newsome House proves to have little fundamentally in common with Wright's work.[45] The plans of such houses are usually conventional, without the flow and penetration of internal space characteristic of Wright's planning. Porches and porte cocheres are not transitional spaces between house and site, but additional spaces added onto the house. Such houses usually have a foursquare formality and directness of approach that is foreign to Wright's mature Prairie School work. Some authors use the term "Prairie style" to describe this body of work. This term is unfortunate, because it promotes confusion between the fully comprehended work of a school of designers pursuing commonly understood objectives, and the ephemeral employment of a few trace elements by architects or building contractors trying to stay current. Such houses, which will be discussed in Chapter 7, are better described as variants on the foursquare mode.[46]

FIG. 3.45
UNITY TEMPLE,
Oak Park, Ill. 1906.
Frank Lloyd Wright, architect.

FIG. 3.46
FIRST METHODIST CHURCH,
Cameron. 1921.
Waller, Silber and Company, architects.

FIG. 3.47
T. W. NEWSOME HOUSE,
4930 Swiss Avenue, Dallas. 1914.
C. P. Sites, architect.

## PROGRESSIVE SURVIVALS IN THE 1920'S

It is axiomatic that World War I put an end to progressivism in American culture and politics, as Warren Harding and Calvin Coolidge replaced Theodore Roosevelt and Woodrow Wilson and presided over a "return to normalcy." Like all such axioms, this one is only approximately correct. Old habits die hard—good ones as well as bad—and just as the ornament of Louis Sullivan remained in commercial production beyond the master's death in 1924, so also the quest for modernity, rather than literal historicism, survived as an undercurrent of American design culture and gradually emerged as a new modernistic style. Wright, of course, remained committed to his own vision of an organic architecture, which was no longer recognizably Prairie School. Some of his younger Prairie School associates, notably Barry Byrne and Alfonso Ianelli,

drew upon European Expressionism as a vehicle to bridge the gap between the Prairie School and the modernistic style. Bertram Goodhue and Paul Philippe Cret began to abstract and stylize the eclectic forms they had deployed in the teens. But direct links between the Prairie School and the modernistic tradition are elusive and few.

One that might be identified is the Garza County Courthouse in Post (FIG. 3.48), designed by Guy A. Carlander of Amarillo in 1923, which almost seems to have descended from the courthouses of Ayres and Willis. The Post courthouse is a rectangular block enclosing a conventional cross-axial plan, but the axes are articulated only by one-story entrance porches and a change in fenestration on the front stair—there are neither pavilions nor a centralizing lantern. The character of this simple building prism is conveyed by regularly spaced brick piers, continuous through three stories, each with a simplified cubical capital and supporting a continuous frieze and shallow brick attic. These regular brick piers can be construed either as survivals of Wright's Prairie School conventions (although somewhat more widely spaced), or as simplified abstractions of classical orders. They thus anticipate the Modern Classicism of Paul Philippe Cret, while maintaining a certain integrity in the expression of brick construction that seems appropriate to an evolving American culture on the South Plains of Texas.

## CONCLUSION

During the 1920's, Frank Lloyd Wright was probably better known and more influential in Europe than in the United States. Richard Neutra left Vienna after the Austrian defeat to seek the sources of modern architecture in America, and met Wright at Sullivan's funeral in 1924. In 1926, *Wendingen*, the journal of the Amsterdam School, devoted seven consecutive issues to Wright's work; they were reissued as a monograph in 1927. Sullivan lived long enough to publish a favorable review of Eliel Saarinen's Tribune Tower Design of 1922, the same year that Bertram Grosvenor Goodhue completed the Nebraska State Capitol, drawing upon Saarinen's Helsinki Railroad Station (finished in 1914) for inspiration. Saarinen's Tribune Tower Design and Goodhue's Nebraska Capitol would become two of the most influential sources for a new expression of modern American architecture in the late 1920's (see Chapter 6), and new interpretations of international and regional modernism would begin to appear by the mid-1930's (Chapter 8). In the meantime, however, the United States declined to participate in the Exposition of Modern Decorative and Industrial Arts held in Paris in 1925 because, as Secretary of Commerce Herbert Hoover explained, there was no *modern* American decorative art. The triumph of eclecticism seemed complete in 1925; the avant-garde alternative had been driven underground, if not extirpated.

The modernists' revenge came in the 1940's and 1950's, when a modern architecture of largely European derivation took root in the United States, and when the adherents of that international modernism rewrote the history of twentieth-century architecture. This time it was

FIG. 3.48
GARZA COUNTY COURTHOUSE,
Post. 1923.
Guy A. Carlander, architect.

the eclectics' turn to be driven underground and virtually written out of history. More recently, however, a more catholic spirit has permeated historical scholarship on American architecture. Rather than a single mainstream of "constituent facts" from which "transient phenomena" can be arbitrarily excluded, as Sigfried Giedion has expressed it,[47] modern architecture is increasingly viewed as a complex matrix of styles and movements, from which not even the eclectic tradition legitimately can be excluded. All aspects of human history are viewed as intrinsically interesting and worthy of study. This is fortunate, because without this ecumenical spirit of tolerance this book would never have been written. The fact remains that the vast majority of Texan architecture constructed between 1900 and 1940 is a component of the eclectic tradition, the subject of the next two chapters.

IV

# ACADEMIC ECLECTICISM
# 1900–1940

Meanwhile the virus of the World's Fair, after a period of incubation in the architectural profession and in the population at large . . . began to show unmistakeable signs of the nature of the contagion. There came a violent outbreak of the Classic and the Renaissance in the East, which slowly spread westward, contaminating all that it touched. . . . The damage wrought by the World's Fair will last for half a century from its date, if not longer. It has penetrated deep into the constitution of the American mind. . . . We now have the abounding freedom of Eclecticism, the winning smile of taste, but no architecture. For Architecture, be it known, is dead.[1]

Thus Louis Sullivan described the state of American architecture in 1924, thirty years after the Chicago Columbian Exposition of 1893 to which he traced the origins of the problem. Most of Sullivan's contemporaries would have agreed that the Chicago fair had rejuvenated the eclectic tradition in America. Few would have accepted his acerbic description of the consequences.

"Eclecticism" defines a method of selection or choice from among various systems, with freedom of combination in constructing a composite system. Applied to architecture, it aptly describes the styles of

the nineteenth century, where new building types for the needs of modern life were composed by assembling elements from past styles in new combinations. Thus, the various Victorian modes of design—Second Empire, Victorian Gothic, Queen Anne, Richardsonian Romanesque—would never be confused with the authentic historical styles of the Baroque era or the Middle Ages. Not only were many of the building types unprecedented and the combination of elements original, but the fundamental principles of architectural form were unique to the nineteenth century: variety, movement, irregularity, intricacy, roughness. According to Carroll L. V. Meeks, these characteristics define an authentic nineteenth-century style that transcends the individual modes of expression, and that can be distinguished from the Baroque on one hand and from modern architecture on the other. Meeks called this style, which spanned from 1790 until 1914, Picturesque Eclecticism. Obviously no body of work remains constant for 125 years, and so to accommodate the concept of evolutionary change Meeks divided Picturesque Eclecticism into three phases: Symbolic (1790–1860), Synthetic (1860–90), and Creative (1890–1914). Meeks saw verticality in proportion as the dominant form conception of the style, and traced an evolutionary curve in which proportions rise during the Symbolic phase, crest during the Synthetic, and subside during the Creative. It is obvious that Meeks' Creative Eclectic phase closely coincides with the Columbian Exposition and its aftermath so much deplored by Sullivan.[2]

It was never clear what was uniquely "creative" about the last phase of Meeks' cycle, and so a more appropriate term was sought to describe this third phase of Picturesque Eclecticism, which overlaps the progressive tradition discussed in Chapter 3. Richard Longstreth has proposed "Academic Eclecticism,"[3] which seems to conform to both the formal sources and the professional habits of American architects during this period. Not only did the verticality of proportions subside after 1890, but Meeks' other formal characteristics became less pronounced as well. Order tended to replace variety, repose supplanted movement, symmetry was favored over irregularity and monumentality over intricacy, and smooth surfaces replaced rustication. In a broad generic sense, American architecture became more classical, and in a narrow stylistic sense it did, as well. Although American architects still chose their preferred modes of expression, the classical styles—either Roman or Renaissance—by far predominated after 1890, as the Richardsonian Romanesque waned in popularity. Architects became more careful and more correct in their usage; although they lost some eclectic freedom, they could exercise a greater erudition when choosing among the growing number of

historical examples that scholarship presented for their selection. Some have called this phase of the eclectic tradition "the revival of Revivalism,"[4] and, indeed, the term "revival" is increasingly appended to these modes of design.

The classicizing of American architecture also reflects changes in the profession, or perhaps the gradual emergence of architecture as a learned profession in the United States. The vast majority of nineteenth-century architects were trained in the apprentice system, and this continued to be the case, at least until World War I. In fact, the ideals of the Arts and Crafts movement, which denigrated the distinction between fine and applied arts and considered the craftsman a true artist, retarded the tendency toward professional education in architecture. Nevertheless, the trend developed. The most prestigious school of architecture in the world was the Ecole des Beaux-Arts in Paris, to which the best and brightest prospective American architects were drawn. Beginning with Richard Morris Hunt in the 1850's, H. H. Richardson in the 1860's, and Charles Follen McKim in the 1870's (not to mention Louis Sullivan, who left without completing the curriculum), a swelling tide of aspirants from the United States attended the Ecole. They returned with certain habits of design, including a predilection for classical forms and monumental composition, which began to be felt in the United States with the American Renaissance of the 1880's. This spirit of Beaux-Arts design would animate the Chicago Columbian Exposition, whence it "penetrated deep into the constitution of the American mind."[5] The ideals of classical composition and formal order made an enormous impact on visitors, and laid the basis for the City Beautiful movement (see Chapter 2). The term Beaux-Arts Classic seems to be the most appropriate generalization for the various nuances of classicism used by late-eclectic American architects, and has been used to describe much of the work discussed in this chapter.

The Ecole des Beaux-Arts represented more than a method of design; it was a system of education. The atelier system of teaching design was emulated when returning students set up their own offices in the United States. Hunt and Richardson both modeled their offices on the Beaux-Arts atelier,[6] so that even apprentices who could not matriculate in Paris were exposed to the system. As American schools of architecture were gradually established, beginning with that at the Massachusetts Institute of Technology in 1869, architects trained at the Ecole or indirectly in professional ateliers eventually infiltrated the professorships. Thus, by 1900 the ideals and methods of the Ecole des Beaux-Arts were perhaps the dominant influence on American architecture of the conservative, eclectic strain, and the term Academic Eclecticism seems more appropriate than Meeks' original Creative Eclecticism.

Eclecticism, of course, implies choice, and the choice need not be classical. As in the Victorian period, styles continued to be chosen for the appropriate images that they conveyed. Gothic remained popular for churches and sometimes for collegiate architecture, and the Gothic Eclectic mode continued its own internal development. But styles could also be selected for their regional associations, and in the southwestern United States a sequence of eclectic modes was developed that evoked the Spanish heritage of the region: the Mission Revival, the Pueblo Revival, the Spanish Colonial, even the Meso-American. In an effort to bring some organization to an overwhelming body of data, these "Regional Eclectic" modes have been relegated somewhat arbitrarily to a separate chapter. The present chapter considers only that body of work which shares its modes of expression with other American regions: styles applied equally in Texas as in the Midwest or New England. The title of this chapter, therefore, may be somewhat misleading, for the regional modes are just as creative, if perhaps not as academic, as the rest. Indeed, a case may be made that after World War I—in the 1920's in particular—the various expressions of the Spanish heritage of the Southwest were more interesting and vital than the Beaux-Arts tradition, which seems to have been running out of energy. The problem is further complicated by attempts of various designers to *regionalize* classical architecture by the selective application of Spanish or Mediterranean details. Chapter 5 considers this phenomenon as well.

Both this chapter and the following consider the period from 1900 to 1940 as a single unit, although both describe the internal evolution of the eclectic tradition. I have divided the present chapter into building types, in order, once again, to render comprehensible a vast amount of information, and to avoid a narrative of pure stylistic analysis. Because as many of these building types are also common to the Regional Eclectic modes and eventually to the modernistic style as well, much of the discussion of program and function will also apply to Chapters 5 and 6, where it will be treated in a more summary manner.

Many of the Academic Eclectic modes considered in this chapter, as well as the regional styles in Chapter 5, were applied to both public and domestic architecture. The latter of these includes a much broader range of formal expression, because it draws on both the elite and vernacular buildings of various historical periods. In addition, about the time of World War I a fundamental change in domestic composition occurred that eschewed formal values in design to return to picturesque forms. Domestic architecture really seems a thing apart, and for this reason has been treated exclusively in Chapter 7, which will consider academic, regional, vernacular, and modernistic expressions of American housing in Texas.

Although it is more apparent in domestic than in public architecture, World War I serves as something of a dividing line between two periods of American design. The progressive tradition virtually ends with the war; the modernistic tradition emerges sometime after. The eclectic tradition continues beyond the war, transformed in subtle but significant ways. Although I contemplated dividing these two chapters into chronological periods before and after World War I—rather than stylistically into academic and regional manifestations—I eventually rejected such a schema in favor of the present organization.

## THE ACADEMIC ECLECTIC COURTHOUSE

The county courthouse remained the dominant institutional building type in Texas throughout the period of this book, as it had been during the Victorian period. Even so, commercial architecture outstripped it in size and value of construction, and other public institutions came to compete with it for cultural significance. Of 254 extant courthouses in Texas, approximately 100 were constructed in classical styles between 1900 and 1940, including those discussed as Victorian survivals and progressive manifestations in preceding chapters.[7] Of these one hundred, two-thirds were constructed before World War I. In general, the dome was retained as the icon of county government before the war, at least on the larger structures, and omitted after 1920. Plans after World War I became less centralized, and less emphatically crossaxial, and the courthouses tended to be larger.

I have described in Chapter 2 the way in which the classical dome gradually replaced the Romanesque clock tower in the course of the 1890's. J. Riely Gordon's conversion to the classical idiom is symptomatic of this transition. Gordon's McLennan County Courthouse in Waco of 1897 (FIG. 2.24) is not typical of Texas courthouses before or since; in size and monumentality it more closely anticipates the Beaux-Arts state capitol, corresponding to Gordon's own concurrent Arizona capitol. Gordon and Lancaster's Harrison County Courthouse in Marshall of 1900 (FIG. 2.03) is more typical than Waco of the emerging Beaux-Arts courthouse type. The plan is identical to that Gordon had

FIG. 4.01
ANDERSON COUNTY COURTHOUSE,
Palestine. 1914.
C. H. Page and Brother, architects.

used on so many of his Richardsonian Romanesque courthouses, but classical details have replaced Romanesque, and a dome on octagonal lantern has supplanted the medieval clock tower as symbolic icon. The plan worked well in either style. In the Romanesque idiom, it had permitted a picturesque ascent of masses to the central tower. In classical dress, the emphasis is on the cross-axiality of the plan, with columnar porticos terminating the ends of the cross, and recessive circular forms in the reentrant corners. Viewed on axis, the arms of the cross do foreshorten one's perception of the dome. Viewed obliquely, however, the recessive corner volumes permit a satisfactory view of dome and lantern.

Other architects did not handle the problem of foreshortening the dome as well. C. H. Page and Brother struggled with this problem on their first three courthouses, all versions of the Fort Bend County Courthouse in Richmond of 1908

(FIG. 2.25).[8] The vertical, elaborately crested corner pavilions are vestiges of Victorian sensibility rather than of Beaux-Arts principles of design. The building mass is handled as a rectangular block with no receding corner volumes to permit oblique views of the dome, which thus is foreshortened from any angle. The dome itself is semicircular on a low, blank drum, relieved only by the lantern and statue at the crown. It is neither the broad, shallow dome of the Pantheon nor the tall, pointed Baroque dome of Michelangelo and Mansart. Lang and Witchell handled the new classical dispensation much more satisfactorily at Gainesville in 1910 (FIG. 3.22), even as they introduced progressive details into the composition.

C. H. Page and Brother fully mastered the Beaux-Arts Classic idiom only at the Anderson County Courthouse in Palestine of 1914 (FIG. 4.01). The corner pavilions are eliminated and the vertical proportions have subsided. The plan remains cross-axial but is no longer four-square. The Ionic order is used to define the main and second floor only, resting upon a plain, ground-floor podium and supporting a correct entablature and balustrade, all of which tend to emphasize the horizontal proportion. Moreover, the orders are paired at the corners, a common Baroque detail retained in Beaux-Arts design. Most important, perhaps, the dome marking the crossing of the axes is raised on a tall drum with windows, although the dome itself is still a bit awkwardly proportioned. Finally, the Palestine courthouse is sited grandly on a hill overlooking the town, rather than in the center of a level public square so common to county seats in Texas. It is perhaps the finest of the pre-war Beaux-Arts Classic courthouses of Texas.[9]

A larger and more grandiose expression of Beaux-Arts planning and design is the (Old) Nueces County Courthouse in Corpus Christi, designed in 1913–1914 by Harvey L. Page of Washington, D.C. (FIG. 4.02). Sited on an expansive tract overlooking the city and the Gulf of Mexico, this courthouse represents the flexibility of the Beaux-Arts system in handling large modern buildings of unusual plan. Including the basement, the building's central block is six stories high, taller than any historical models within the recurring classical tradition. This uncomfortable bulk is accommodated by placing one floor in the basement, grouping the next three floors within a giant order, placing the fifth floor in an attic above this, and squeezing the sixth floor into the level of pediment and cornice. The plan is cross-axial, with extremely long arms, needed to accommodate the bureaucratic functions of a large, predominantly urban county. There is no domed crossing. Instead, Page has emphasized the termination of each of the arms. One contains the main entrance, approached by a broad esplanade, monumental staircase, and giant columnar porch. The crossarms of the plan are only four stories high. The order is reduced to two stories above the common basement; the fourth floor is placed in an attic, and the cornice level internal space is eliminated. These crossarms are terminated by pavilions at right angles, each with columnar orders and pediment. The effect when approaching the courthouse is to perceive a sequence of three classical porticos: the central

FIG. 4.02
(OLD) NUECES COUNTY COURTHOUSE,
Corpus Christi. 1913–1914.
Harvey L. Page, architect.

entrance and two receding in the wings. It is an extremely skillful parti that shows Harvey Page well versed in the nuances of Beaux-Arts composition. He was not, of course, a Texas architect.[10]

The Corpus Christi courthouse had no direct influence in Texas. No other courthouses of such size were attempted until the new modernistic idiom of the 1930's permitted indefinite height without compromising the classical system of proportions and scale. Academic Eclectic courthouses in Texas of the 1920's did change in subtle ways, however, varying with the size of the site available. Three have been selected to illustrate this tendency.

The Dallam County Courthouse in Dalhart (FIG. 4.03) was designed by Smith and Townes in 1922. Its vintage is immediately suggested by the use of soft, red tapestry brick, which increasingly supplanted the hard-finished tan brick so popular before 1917. Light terra-cotta trim is used sparingly to render the col-

FIG. 4.03
DALLAM COUNTY COURTHOUSE,
Dalhart. 1922.
Smith and Townes, architects.

FIG. 4.04
STEPHENS COUNTY COURTHOUSE,
Breckenridge. 1926.
David S. Castle, architect.

umns and other bits of classical detail. The application of this classical detail is somewhat suggestive of Page's formula at Corpus Christi: a half-sunken ground floor with exterior stairs to the columnar porch at the main-floor level, two floors grouped under classical orders, and a top floor placed in an attic above the primary cornice. Perhaps the top floor was adopted to provide necessary office space without further intruding on the limited courthouse park. At Palestine, C. H. Page and Brother had to cope with only three stories, and the formula of ground-floor base and double-height orders worked admirably. Faced with a fourth floor at Dalhart, Smith and Townes chose to use an attic instead of increasing the order to three stories. The result is less than completely satisfying: a composition of too many parts for such a modest building. The cross-axial plan seems to call for some central terminating feature, but there is no dome at Dalhart.

The Stephens County Courthouse at Breckenridge, designed in 1926 by David S. Castle (FIG. 4.04), employs the same formula of a ground-floor base, double-story orders, and attic, but achieves a more coherent and monumental expression than Dalhart. The Breckenridge courthouse is constructed of uniform light terra-cotta simulating stone, and the cross-axial plan requiring a central terminus has been avoided. Like most extant Texas courthouses, the Breckenridge facility replaced an earlier structure on the same site. A much larger building, it crowds the park somewhat, but presents a monumental facade to the commercial frontage across Main Street. The central axis is marked only by the down-played triple entrance on the ground floor. Otherwise, symmetry is enforced by bracketing the main facade between end pavilions, and an unbroken sequence of ten Corinthian half-columns defines the second and third floors between them. The idiom seems related to contemporary Beaux-Arts Classic architecture for the federal government in Washington (FIG. 4.05), or that of the numerous City Beautiful civic centers created in American cities before World War I. If the Breckenridge courthouse would be commonplace in the federal capital or in Burnham's Chicago, it is nonetheless significant if not unique in Texas: it is one of the most satisfactory solutions within the Beaux-Arts Classic tradition to the problem of the growing size of public buildings.[11]

The same problem of increasing size and the crowding of the courthouse square is demonstrated with a less happy result at the Hunt County Courthouse in Greenville (FIG. 4.06), designed by Page Brothers in 1928, with William R. Ragsdale of Greenville as associate architect. At Greenville the courthouse consumes virtually the entire public square, and presides over a sea of parking and circulating traffic. The increasing bulk of the building has been accommodated uneasily within the classical idiom by a number of strategies. The base is elevated to a story and a half, squeezing the orders into an uncomfortably narrow band between the high base and the simplified cornice. Fifth and sixth floors are accommodated in stepped-back masses over the center of the courthouse only, and the lower floors project forward in a pair of wings on the

FIG. 4.05
HOUSE OFFICE BUILDING,
Washington, D.C. 1908.
Carrere and Hastings, architects.

FIG. 4.06
HUNT COUNTY COURTHOUSE,
Greenville. 1928.
Page Brothers, architects. William R. Ragsdale, associate architect.

front and rear facades, creating an I-shaped floor plan. The Greenville courthouse seems to anticipate the step-back massing of the modernistic style, which had appeared the same year elsewhere in Texas (see Chapter 6), but the accurately detailed Ionic columns used at Greenville belie modernistic abstraction. Nevertheless, it is probably best viewed as a monument to the transition from Beaux-Arts Classicism to the modernistic style.[12]

FIG. 4.07
U.S. POST OFFICE,
Palestine. 1910.
James Knox Taylor, supervising architect.

POST OFFICES AND LIBRARIES

In the nineteenth century, court-houses, county jails, and federal buildings were very nearly the only significant public institutions in Texas towns and cities.[13] The proliferation of other public institutions, in both number and diversity, is another aspect of the American commonwealth's increasing maturity during the Progressive Era.

Between 1865 and 1895 the U.S. government erected several hundred new buildings in the large and small cities of the nation. Normally these accommodated the three instruments of federal authority—the postal service, the customs service, and the federal courts—on three successive floors. These buildings were designed in the Office of the Supervising Architect of the Treasury in Washington, through which passed nine incumbents between 1863 and 1897, when James Knox Taylor assumed the office.[14] Taylor

would remain in office until 1914, presiding over the expansion of the federal presence into the smaller towns of the United States and confirming the Beaux-Arts Classic style as the appropriate idiom for governmental architecture.

Under Taylor's superintendence, dozens of Texas towns received new post offices. As in the Victorian period, the Supervising Architect was expected to create variety from an essentially repetitive plan: a centralized entrance to the postal lobby, the mail room behind, and boxes or offices on either side. Depending on the size of the town, a second floor of offices might be provided over the side spaces or over the entire ground floor. All were symmetrical and classical, although Taylor's command of the classical repertoire was rich and varied. Most are either Roman or Renaissance in inspiration, and use the classical orders or the round arch as a leitmotif, with a varying degree of regional connotation suggested by tile roofs and eave brackets in some of the buildings. The post offices at Palestine of 1910 (FIG. 4.07) and Mineral Wells of 1912 (FIG. 4.08) are representative of these two strands of classicism in Taylor's oeuvre.[15]

It also fell to the Supervising Architect to design the occasional large federal government building, such as the U.S. Customhouse in Houston of 1912 (FIG. 4.09). James Knox Taylor's design shows him capable of composing on a large scale within the classical idiom. The Houston customhouse is neither Renaissance nor Roman, but closer to Baroque, reflecting the modulation and nuance of the Beaux-Arts Classic mode at its most effective.[16]

Taylor was succeeded briefly as Supervising Architect by Oscar

Wendroth in 1914, and then by James A. Wetmore as Acting Supervising Architect in 1915. Wetmore remained in this post into the 1930's; hence, his tenure coincides with the second, post-war phase of Beaux-Arts Classicism. This phase was affected by two developments. First was the increasing use by the federal government of private architectural firms, under the general management of the Supervising Architect. The other was the increasing influence of the Beaux-Arts system of architectural education in the United States, and the personal influence of Paul Philippe Cret on classical American architecture. Cret, a French designer, was educated at the Ecole des Beaux-Arts, and held the position of professor of architecture at the University of Pennsylvania from 1903 until 1937. Under his aegis, the university became the best known American school of architecture following the Beaux-Arts system. Cret also developed an extensive practice as a consulting architect, which began with his winning design in the competition for the Pan American Union in Washington of 1907, and was reinforced by the designs for the Indianapolis Public Library in 1914 and the Detroit Institute of Arts in 1922. These influential buildings represent an "aesthetic of the facade [reflecting] plan and section . . . ;" embodying the "hierarchy, compactness, and processional axiality characteristic of Beaux-Arts design."[17] Apart from Cret's work as a consulting architect to the University of Texas at Austin, discussed in Chapter 5, these values of Beaux-Arts design also characterize the U.S. Post Office and Courthouse in San Antonio of 1937, for which Cret

FIG. 4.08
U.S. POST OFFICE,
Mineral Wells. 1912.
James Knox Taylor, supervising architect.

FIG. 4.09
U.S. CUSTOMHOUSE,
Houston. 1912.
James Knox Taylor, supervising architect.

FIG. 4.10
U.S. POST OFFICE AND COURTHOUSE,
San Antonio. 1937.
Ralph Cameron, architect.
Paul Philippe Cret, consulting architect.

FIG. 4.11
U.S. POST OFFICE,
Wichita Falls. 1931.
Voelcker and Dixon, architects.
James Wetmore, acting supervising
architect.

was consulting architect to Ralph Cameron (FIG. 4.10). Here Cret accommodated five floors of office space by skillfully manipulating the classical repertoire. Classical orders as such are employed only on the main facade facing Alamo Plaza. The rear and sides are soberly composed of modulated masses and simplified classical moldings, a simplification that Cret had increasingly developed since the late 1920's.

By 1937 the Beaux-Arts Classic style was no longer the unchallenged mode of expression for federal architecture. The modernistic idiom had largely supplanted it, and Cret himself had done much to develop this style, variously called Modern Classic, Stripped Classic, or Starved Classic, by his experiments in abstracting and simplifying the classical vocabulary. Such a simplified classical style, probably reflecting Cret's influence, may be seen in the U.S. Post Office in Wichita Falls (FIG. 4.11), designed in 1931 by the local firm of Voelcker and Dixon, with James Wetmore as the supervising architect. Although the moldings are correctly classical, the orders are suppressed in favor of a three-story sequence of piers between base and cornice, similar to the pilastrades that Cret had begun to use in the 1920's.[18]

The public library in Texas is closely related in formal morphology to the typical Beaux-Arts post office, many of which, in fact, have been converted to libraries when abandoned by the postal service. As a building type, this American institution emerged in the 1870's and 1880's with the series of public libraries designed for small New England towns by H. H. Richardson. Most of these bear the name of a donor: the public library in the United States is a monument not only to universal literacy in America, but also to private philanthropy. There are no Richardsonian Romanesque libraries in Texas, however. By the time the institution reached Texas in the late 1890's, the Romanesque had succumbed to classical modes of expression, but the philanthropic tradition remained. The 1899 Dr. Eugene Clark Library in Lockhart was named for its donor (FIG. 4.12). Designed by a local contractor, T. S. Hodges, this library is a somewhat ingenuous Greek-cross plan with an entrance in one of the reentrant corners and a domed rotunda over the crossing. Particularly noteworthy is the alternation of wide and narrow bays defined by brick pilasters on each end of the cross and the arched window placed in the wide bay on the main facade. It is doubtful if Hodges knew Alberti's San Andrea in Mantua, where this motif was first used, but he must have had access to an architectural library in order to create this remarkably sophisticated treatment.[19]

If the library in Lockhart combines naiveté with sophistication, the Rosenberg Library in Galveston (FIG. 4.13), similarly named for its donor and designed in 1902 by Eames and Young of St. Louis, is a highly accomplished piece of Beaux-Arts Classicism. Eschewing the obvious use of the classical orders, the architects relied on a Renaissance combination of giant arches between horizontally rusticated piers, and smaller pedimented aediculae to demarcate the main floor. The Rosenberg Library is constructed of the hard-finished tan brick that occurs so frequently in the generation before World War I.[20]

FIG. 4.12
DR. EUGENE CLARK LIBRARY,
Lockhart. 1899.
T. S. Hodges, designing contractor.

FIG. 4.13
ROSENBERG LIBRARY,
Galveston. 1902.
Eames and Young, architects.

FIG. 4.14
CARNEGIE LIBRARY (now the BELL
COUNTY MUSEUM),
Belton. 1904.
Smith and Moore, architects.

FIG. 4.15
CARNEGIE LIBRARY,
Franklin. 1914.

The public library in Texas came to maturity in the 1900's with the nationwide philanthropy of Andrew Carnegie. Thirty-one Carnegie libraries were endowed in Texas between 1898 and 1915, of which twelve or more survive. Many of these are slightly modified versions of the same Beaux-Arts Classic design, although after 1908 a less pretentious formula was enforced, upon recommendation of the Carnegie Corporation. The Carnegie Library at Belton represents the earlier, more monumental genre; that at Franklin, the later, more modest model.

The Carnegie Library at Belton, designed by Smith and Moore in 1904, reflects the earlier, more monumental parti (FIG. 4.14). Such libraries are two full stories in height, and are symmetrical about a central pavilion that contains the main entrance. Giant orders are used to monumentalize this central pavilion, which is crowned by a triangular pediment. A centralized entrance foyer conducts the visitor to a sequence of reading rooms on the first floor (not distinguished from stack areas) and to a staircase leading to a large lecture hall with stage on the second.

The Carnegie Library at Franklin (FIG. 4.15) of 1914 represents the later, more modest genre: a T-shaped single story above an elevated basement, to which the lecture hall has been relegated. The main floor is defined on the front facade by five equal arches of noble scale, rising from the basement water table to a string course near the eave line. The hipped roof is bracketed beyond the wall line to form deep overhanging eaves. The central arcade accommodates the main entrance, which leads to an entrance foyer from which three separate reading rooms have access.[21]

Taken together, the small-town post offices and public libraries represent the smallest scale of public institutional architecture in Texas during the period of discussion, just as the county courthouse was the largest and most significant. Between these two extremes lay a range of other public and private architecture, which drew upon the diverse historical sources available to the Academic Eclectic designer.

CITY HALLS AND FIRE STATIONS

If the county courthouse, post office, and public library were resolved easily into a series of design typologies within the Beaux-Arts Classic vocabulary, the same cannot be said of the city hall and fire station, which presented a typological and stylistic conundrum to the eclectic designer. At smaller scale, the city hall and fire station tended to be combined in a single structure. In larger towns, particularly after 1920, the city hall tended to incorporate a civic auditorium, which inflated its scale. Both of these combinations created problems of composition not found in previous building types.

The fire station was particularly difficult to resolve. The simplest solution was to treat the facility as an equipment garage with two or three garage doors opening directly onto the street, and a second floor above to be used as city offices or as living quarters for the fire crews. This formula was difficult to resolve within the various eclectic modes. Most fire stations of this genre were built before World War I and tended to

avoid specific historical detail. The San Marcos City Hall and Fire Station, designed in 1915 by Roy L. Thomas, is representative of this genre (FIG. 4.16).[22] Because the fire-fighting function dominated the composition, such buildings did not adequately represent or symbolize the functions of city government.

A more hierarchically satisfactory solution involved treating a corner building as an elongated block. In such a case the narrow face of the building would contain the monumental entrance to the city hall, and the fire department would be placed toward the rear so that its equipment bays could open on to the side street. The Stamford City Hall of 1917 (FIG. 4.17) is an example of this design strategy. Its main facade is defined by giant orders and classical window consoles, but the side facade is much more plainly treated, with no finesse shown in resolving the equipment garage.[23]

FIG. 4.17
STAMFORD CITY HALL. 1917.

FIG. 4.18
CITY HALL AND FIRE STATION,
Paris. 1920.
Curtis and Lightfoot, architects.

FIG. 4.19
TOWN HALL AND FIRE STATION,
University Park. 1924.
Harry M. Burnet, architect.
Expanded and remodeled, C. 1938.
Grayson Gill, architect.

A more sophisticated version of this format is seen at the Paris City Hall and Fire Station (FIG. 4.18), designed by Curtis and Lightfoot in 1920. The long elevation is treated as a range of equipment stalls, bracketed between projecting pavilions that accommodate city hall and fire department offices, respectively. The treatment of the two wings is not quite identical, nor is the side elevation exactly symmetrical about the center line, but the adjustments are so subtle that they mask this incongruity. The city hall end of the ensemble is treated more monumentally, with simplified pilasters or antae, and has a central entrance on the short front, as does the Stamford City Hall. It is the graceful treatment of the equipment garage, however, that distinguishes the Paris facility.[24]

In the course of the 1920's, historical modes other than Roman or Renaissance Classicism were revived as architects and their patrons sought to infuse novelty into the eclectic tradition. Perhaps a majority of the 1920's city halls in Texas employed the Spanish Colonial style, which will be discussed in Chapter 5, whereas on the East Coast the English Colonial or American Georgian style appealed to historical sensibilities. Nevertheless, the American Georgian had its partisans in Texas as well. Two Dallas suburbs, Highland Park and University Park, both built combined city halls and fire stations in the 1920's. Highland Park adopted the Spanish Colonial style, but University Park chose the American Georgian, probably because Southern Methodist University had employed this mode for its campus buildings. The University Park Town Hall and Fire Station (FIG. 4.19), originally designed in 1924 by Harry M. Burnet, was expanded and remodeled around 1938 by Grayson Gill. In its final form, the town hall received a steeply pitched roof with dormers and cupola, based upon Early Georgian models from the Williamsburg restoration initiated in 1927. An additional wing on the north was added in the 1950's. In its final form, the University Park town hall managed to be both formal and picturesque at the same time. The fire department is placed in the rear wing of the T-shaped plan, facing away from the city hall. There is a picturesque quality to the University Park town hall, however, that is foreign to the symmetrical formality of the authentic American Georgian style, but that is found frequently in architecture of the 1920's and 1930's. Although the main entrance is centralized and lined up with the

FIG. 4.20
CITY HALL,
Dallas. 1912.
C. D. Hill and Co., architects.
Mauran, Russell and Crowell, associate
architects.

lantern on axis, the left and right sides of the facade are not identical. Three large windows on the south half denote the second-floor council chamber, whereas to the north of the entrance a large round-headed window lights the landing of a monumental front stair. This form of picturesque, asymmetrical composition is found frequently in the domestic architecture of the 1920's, but it is totally without precedent in the eighteenth century.[25]

Expenditure on both public and private architecture tended to dry up after 1929 owing to the Depression, only to revive in the public sphere later in the 1930's as a result of subsidies from the federal government through the Public Works Administration or other agencies.[26] Although a majority of PWA projects were carried out in the modernistic style, and will be discussed in Chapter 6, the New Deal adminis-

trators were not modern ideologues, and both modernistic and eclectic architecture was subsidized.

All of the city halls and fire stations considered thus far, from San Marcos to University Park, have been composite facilities for fairly small towns, where economy of scale dictated that the city government and its fire department be lodged together. But larger cities also built new city halls in this period, in which monumentality became the predominant objective. Perhaps the most monumental Beaux-Arts Classic city hall in Texas was one in Dallas, designed in 1912 by C. D. Hill and Co. in association with Mauran, Russell and Crowell of St. Louis (FIG. 4.20).[27]

In everything but its situation, the Dallas city hall is larger and more imposing than most contemporary Texas courthouses. Its cramped downtown site, however,

FIG. 4.21
CITY HALL AND AUDITORIUM,
Beaumont. 1927.
F. W. and D. E. Steinman, architects.

On the long Harwood Street elevation, a series of nine engaged half-columns recede slightly behind the corner pavilions, and the attic story is masked by a balustrade. On the short facades, a central pavilion projects slightly and carries through the attic story, while full columns-in-antis flank the entrance. The corner pavilions are severely plain, except for the smaller scale of window detail set within the nobly proportioned arches. In all respects, the Dallas city hall is a superb rendition of the Beaux-Arts Classic style.

After World War I, the functions of the city hall were frequently combined with a municipal auditorium in towns large enough to support such a facility. As in the case of the smaller town halls and fire stations, the majority of these in Texas were executed in the Spanish Colonial style in the 1920's and the modernistic style in the 1930's. The exceptions are worthy of note, however. The normal formula for such a city hall and municipal auditorium was to provide a main entrance leading to a central lobby, with the auditorium opening off to the rear of the lobby. The functions of city government would be located on several floors stretching laterally on either side of the lobby and above it. If a fire station was also included in the program, it would most likely be placed behind the auditorium, facing toward a rear street. This formula was used for the Beaumont City Hall and Auditorium (FIG. 4.21), designed in the Beaux-Arts Classic mode by F. W. and D. E. Steinman in 1927. Here a landscaped esplanade in the best City Beautiful tradition leads to a monumental Corinthian portico crowned by a low attic, with the wings of the

belies its formal grandeur. Most Beaux-Arts Classic buildings of this generation in the United States were conceived as part of a City Beautiful civic center, a grouping of public buildings about a formally landscaped plaza. The 1911 Kessler Plan for Dallas had proposed such a civic center, to adjoin the Union Railroad Terminal south of downtown. Although the terminal was completed and a block reserved for a monumental plaza (Ferris Plaza), the other elements of the civic center were sprinkled throughout the downtown area. Nevertheless, the Dallas city hall is indeed imposing (Hill's Galveston city hall of 1914–1915 is pedestrian in comparison). The architects skillfully manipulated the classical repertoire, with low base, giant three-story Corinthian orders, an attic floor above the cornice, and an exposed tile roof that gives the edifice a French flavor. The building is set back from the street just enough on each frontage to permit monumental staircases to ascend to the main floor.

city hall set back slightly on either side, overlooking a modest park of grass and trees. The Beaumont situation reconciles the best qualities of City Beautiful formality with the American park tradition.

In general, the most effective examples of Beaux-Arts Classicism occurred before World War I. In the 1920's the eclectic tradition maintained its vitality through the discovery of new historical styles to manipulate, such as Spanish Colonial or American Georgian, and through an increasing dependence on picturesque composition. The 1920's also saw a greater tendency to simplify the classical vocabulary, which led to the Modern Classic style or modernistic mode that prevailed in the 1930's as the eclectic tradition began to run out of energy.

MISCELLANEOUS PUBLIC
BUILDINGS

The ideal image of the City Beautiful and of Beaux-Arts Classicism was white. The Chicago Columbian Exposition had been white; the Classical Revival and Beaux-Arts Classic buildings of the McMillan Plan for Washington were white. The ultimate medium of expression was stone. But stone was also heavy and expensive. Brick and terra-cotta were not only cheaper, but also more rational materials for fireproofing a steel frame. Many of the courthouses, post offices, libraries, and city halls considered previously in this book were constructed of brick with stone or terra-cotta trim. And although hard-finished tan or orange brick became a popular medium before the war in both progressive and eclectic styles, the traditional red brick of the Victorian

FIG. 4.22
DALLAS COUNTY CRIMINAL COURTS
AND JAIL BUILDING,
Dallas. 1910.
H. A. Overbeck, architect.

period never totally disappeared. Contrasting three Texas government buildings of the 1910's, diverse in purpose and in formal composition but all constructed of red brick, shows how large the range of possibilities within Beaux-Arts Classicism had become. A concluding comparison to a later, stone-built exercise in Beaux-Arts Classicism in the grand manner, by a distinguished firm of Eastern architects, completes the range of possibilities.

The Criminal Courts and Jail Building in Dallas (FIG. 4.22), de-

FIG. 4.23
PARKLAND (WOODLAWN) HOSPITAL,
Dallas. 1913.
H. M. Greene Co., architects.

signed in 1910 by H. A. Overbeck and constructed just north of the Romanesque courthouse, exemplifies the public needs of a major metropolis.[28] The functional organization is similar to one that Sanguinet and Staats would employ in Fort Worth at the Tarrant County Criminal Courts Building (FIG. 3.28): three floors of offices and courtroom space at the bottom; six floors of detention facilities at the top. Unlike the Tarrant County building, however, the facade of the Dallas structure gives no indication of the detention function. Instead, the building resembles—in both morphology and style—the Edwardian Baroque hotels that were becoming popular in the teens, such as Trost and Trost's Paso del Norte Hotel in El Paso of 1913 (FIG. 4.73). Above a high base with the courtrooms occupying a *piano nobile,* the deten-

tion floors conform to a U-shaped plan grouped around a light court. The handsomely grouped windows of the criminal courts building do not light individual rooms, however, but a peripheral guards' corridor at each floor. As was common in penal design of the period, the cell blocks are completely internalized within each wing, consisting of barred enclosures that borrow light from the guards' corridor but permit the prisoners no view to the outside. The top floor is treated as an elaborately ornamented attic that terminates the composition.

Ironically, Woodlawn Hospital in Dallas is now used as a minimum-security detention facility (FIG. 4.23). Designed by H. M. Greene Co. and built in 1913, it was the second facility of Parkland Hospital in the Oak Lawn district of Dallas. As befits its neighborhood location,

Woodlawn Hospital is a low, sprawling structure of two stories set behind a spacious lawn planted with trees. A low basement of variable depth adjusts to the sloping terrain. The long, low facade is articulated into five pavilions in hierarchical progression: A-B-C-B-A. The only use of orders is on the two-story entrance porch appended to the central pavilion. All of the other classical detail is done in variations of the Renaissance vocabulary. Corners of the pavilions are defined by brick quoins. Although all window heads are flat, relieving arches and stone dressings convey the suggestion of Renaissance detail. This is particularly apparent on the end pavilions, where the main floor windows are defined by the Palladian motif, highly abstracted but still recognizable. These details in light terracotta trim on a red brick field suggest the English Baroque or its American Colonial derivative as the presumptive influence, although no close model suggests itself.[29]

In 1917, Atlee B. Ayres designed the State Office Building, located on one corner opposite the capitol square in Austin (FIG. 4.24). The formula is by now familiar: a rusticated stone base adjusting to the sloping site, and giant orders rising three stories on both street facades, set between corner pavilions. However, the top floor is squeezed into the entablature, rather than placed in an attic. The corner entrances inflect diagonally across the intersection toward the dominant capitol. The windows are unclassically large, grouped in threes with transoms, and tend to compete with the Ionic half columns for dominance of the two uniform facades. The corner pavilions above the basement

FIG. 4.24
STATE OFFICE BUILDING,
Austin. 1917.
Atlee B. Ayres, architect.

are of red brick, but are further overlaid by simplified pilasters at the edges, which have the effect of trivializing the pavilions rather than visually strengthening them. The State Office Building, in short, is not an inspired exercise in the Beaux-Arts Classic mode. It uses brick without exploiting its architectonic possibilities.[30]

The great public museum had been one of the archetypical buildings of the classical revival around the turn of the eighteenth century: a new building type for which the purity of Greek architecture seemed ideally suited. For one thing, most museums were top-lighted, relieving the architect of the need for accommodating windows in a historically windowless style. The museum could thus be a paradigm of Greek purity and classical perfection. These same conditions held

FIG. 4.25
HOUSTON MUSEUM OF
FINE ARTS. 1924.
William Ward Watkin, architect.
Cram and Ferguson, associate architects.

The side walls have projecting six-column porches at the rear corners. All wall surfaces are plain except for blank window frames in very shallow relief. The detailing is impeccable and very Greek. The museum is splendid and very austere; an ideal companion to Mies van der Rohe's 1958 addition to the rear. But it avoids the problem of reconciling classical design with modern fenestration, with which Ayres had wrestled without complete success on the State Office Building.

SCHOOL BUILDINGS

The problem of fenestration was particularly acute in school design, which placed a premium on natural light. The classroom unit tended to generate fenestration patterns, and large banks of grouped windows normally dominated school buildings. "Style" often became a matter of applying a few recognizable details to salient parts of the facade. Gothic arches or Mission style gable parapets were often used in this way. As a result, although high schools are among the largest American buildings designed over this forty-year period, school design is not particularly noteworthy. The extensive school design practice of Trost and Trost over three states, for example, is not the firm's most interesting body of work. An exception must be made for their El Paso High School of 1914–1916 (FIG. 4.26), one of the most imposing monuments of Beaux-Arts Classicism in Texas. The architects cannot be accused of ignoring the architectonic possibilities of brick; except for the Corinthian entrance porch, the character of the hard-finished tan brick is expressed ev-

true of most museum design in the Academic Eclectic period. Perhaps in no other building type did Beaux-Arts Classicism come so close to being a revival of Revivalism. This characteristic is certainly apparent in the Houston Museum of Fine Arts (FIG. 4.25), designed as the first public art museum in Texas in 1924 by William Ward Watkin in association with Cram and Ferguson.[31] The museum is situated at the head of South Main Street on a triangular site resulting from the convergence of boulevards in George Kessler's Plan for the South Park System.[32] It thus epitomizes the objectives of the City Beautiful movement better than any other building in Texas, with the possible exception of Jarvis Hunt's Union Station in Dallas (FIG. 4.52). The museum itself is trapezoidal in plan, with a small landscaped park taking up the front corner of the site. The main facade consists of eight giant Ionic columns contained between end pavilions canted slightly to the center.

erywhere, and fused with a severe classical sensibility. Recognizing the inherent horizontality of a building over 500 feet long, Trost and Trost emphasized the horizontal dimension by dividing the four-story building into three parallel bands: a low basement story, two floors incorporated within an order of giant antae, and a fourth-floor attic above the cornice. The use of antae freed the architects somewhat from the normal proportions of the classical orders, and permitted the insertion of paired window groups between each. The simplified terracotta bases and capitals are subordinated to the tectonic expression of a sequence of brick piers, deeply modeled by shadow in the bright El Paso sunshine. The classroom unit does not directly generate the fenestration pattern, however. Most classrooms correspond to two pier modules; some spaces are two and a half, with the partition falling on the mullion line. The planning seems like an inversion of that Henry Trost was using concurrently on the Mills Building (FIG. 3.11). There the widely spaced piers corresponded to rational structure; the smaller planning module was accommodated by partitions at the intermediate mullions. At El Paso High School, the pier spacing seems dictated by the classical ordonnance, and the intermediate mullions provide flexibility in the arrangement of interior spaces.[33]

The school's monumental entrance, placed diagonally in the re-entrant angle, leads to the offices, thence to a radial main hall connecting the classroom corridors in each wing, and finally to a wedge-shaped auditorium in the outside corner of the L-shaped plan. The

FIG. 4.26
EL PASO HIGH SCHOOL. 1914–1916.
Trost and Trost, architects.

FIG. 4.27
EL PASO HIGH SCHOOL. Main hall.

detailing of the main hall is particularly handsome (FIG. 4.27), with original improvisation based on classical motifs. The ornamental collars placed beneath the Doric capitals are particularly noteworthy examples of Henry Trost's virtuosity as a designer.

The situation of the El Paso High School is one of the grandest in

FIG. 4.28
NORTH DALLAS HIGH
SCHOOL. C. 1920'S.
William B. Ittner, architect.

Texas. Placed on one of El Paso's steep hillsides, the monumental building commands an expansive vista of the athletic fields below and the city beyond. It is perhaps El Paso's finest evocation of the City Beautiful movement; an exercise worthy of Daniel H. Burnham or McKim, Mead and White.

After World War I, growing cities like Dallas were faced with the need to expand their school systems, and specifically to build additional high schools in different districts of the city. Rather than relying on local architects, however, Dallas employed the services of a prominent school architect of national reputation, William B. Ittner. Ittner's North Dallas High School (FIG. 4.28) is typical of his work. The height is reduced to three stories, with a grand-entrance stair to the intermediate main floor. Ittner decreased the apparent length of the building through his use of a compact, U-shaped plan. Long banks of windows characterize the facade, which is broken up by center and end

pavilions. Ittner also employed some rather delicate Renaissance-inspired ornament: an arcaded main-entrance porch, brick quoins on the corners, broken pediments to strengthen corner windows, etc. The result is an eclectic pastiche that lacks the solemn grandeur of El Paso High School or the inventive abstraction of Woodlawn Hospital, suggesting once again that by the 1920's the eclectic tradition was running out of energy.[34]

Elementary schools were, of course, smaller and more closely spaced than junior or senior high schools. Before World War I they tended to be two stories high, and were less monumentally designed. In the 1920's and 1930's they more often were only one story, usually with some form of centralized entrance as focal point. The Raymondville School (FIG. 4.29), designed in 1924 by Elwing and Mulhausen, is a particularly compelling example of this tendency. The Raymondville School falls somewhere between progressive and eclectic. The conception of linking classroom blocks to a central activities room by open loggias seems advanced for its date. The vocabulary of round arches in brick is vaguely Romanesque, but is handled with originality and a fine sense of the tectonic possibilities of brickwork, which avoids the obvious eclectic details such as arcaded corbel tables and pilaster strips. It is not an easy task to give a public character to a small building, but Elwing and Mulhausen succeeded admirably at Raymondville. Other architects grappling with this problem tended to apply Spanish Colonial detail to the salient features (see Chapter 5).

FIG. 4.29
RAYMONDVILLE SCHOOL. 1924.
Elwing and Mulhausen, architects.

## COLLEGIATE ARCHITECTURE

Collegiate architecture in nineteenth-century Texas consisted largely of a series of "Old Mains": Frederick Ruffini's for the University of Texas at Austin, Larmour and Watson's for Baylor, Nicholas J. Clayton's for the Medical School at Galveston, Robert S. Hyer's for Southwestern University at Georgetown. Designed variously in Victorian Gothic, Second Empire, and Richardsonian Romanesque, these Old Mains originally accommodated all the teaching and administrative functions of these institutions. As schools grew in enrollment and curricular diversity, however, these original main buildings proved inadequate, and as additional buildings were added, the concept of a "campus" as a uniquely American environment for higher education came to Texas.[35] Thus, the Carroll Science Hall supplemented Old Main at Baylor in 1901, and in 1906 C. H. Page and Brother were commissioned to design Mood Hall as a student dormitory at Southwestern (FIG. 4.30), to supplement the picturesque Richardsonian main building that its president had designed a decade before. Mood Hall is a curious and belated monument to the transition between picturesque and formal values in design. The rusticated ashlar has been carried over from the earlier building, and the pitched roofs, simplified cornice, and baldly arcaded ground-floor windows seem like Romanesque vestiges. Unlike Hyer's asymmetrical, picturesque massing of the Old Main, however, Mood Hall is biaxially symmetrical and approached on axis to a central arcaded porch that fronts an open courtyard (since enclosed). The windows on the upper two floors are square-headed and rhythmically grouped, neither overtly classical nor medieval in character.[36]

An earlier but more convincing exercise in the new classical dispensation is the Old Main for Texas State College for Women (now Texas Woman's University) in Den-

FIG. 4.30
MOOD HALL,
Southwestern University,
Georgetown. 1906.
C. H. Page and Brother, architects.

FIG. 4.31
OLD MAIN,
Texas State College for Women
(now Texas Woman's University),
Denton. 1902.
Dodson and Scott, architects.

ton (FIG. 4.31), designed by Dodson and Scott in 1902. Only the rusticated base course and lintels suggest a lingering archaism. The ubiquitous hard-finished brick is now in evidence, and axial symmetry is marked not only by a classical temple portico but also by a small dome. The original building was quite small; in 1916 wings were constructed on either side, expanding Old Main to its present size.

The construction of a single building does not necessarily imply a direction in the further development of a campus, but the execution of several buildings in a short period may influence future development. This seems to have occurred at the Agricultural and Mechanical College of Texas (now Texas A&M University) at College Station in 1909, when F. E. Geisecke launched his tenure as campus architect for the university. Geisecke's Nagle Hall of 1909 was a fairly modest piece of architecture, but acquired significance as part of a campus plan when his Academic Building was erected nearby in 1912 (FIG. 4.32). Together the two buildings define a Beaux-Arts system of axis and cross-axis, with the (original) main western entrance to the campus drawn upon the Academic Building's portico and dome. Except for its rather diminutive dome, the Academic Building was the most imposing piece of collegiate work in the classical idiom to that date in Texas. It established the basis for further expansion of the campus under Geisecke's design up to the new eastward-facing Administration Building that redirected the principal entrance in 1932.

There were numerous precedents for Geisecke's work at A&M, of

FIG. 4.32
ACADEMIC BUILDING,
Agricultural and Mechanical
College of Texas
(now Texas A&M University),
College Station. 1912.
F. E. Giesecke, architect.

course. The university campus had been one of the principal arenas for Beaux-Arts planning concepts during the City Beautiful period. New master plans had reorganized the campuses at Columbia and Berkeley along classical lines, and new universities had been established with master plans at Stanford, the University of Chicago, and Rice University in Houston.[37] The master plans for pre-existing campuses usually stressed the addition of new buildings on a Beaux-Arts system of axes and cross-axes, as Geisecke implemented at Texas A&M. The plans for new campuses instead tended to develop the closed quadrangle, in the Spanish Romanesque, Gothic, or Spanish Byzantine modes. There was one hallowed model for American university planning that stood apart from these two tendencies: Thomas Jefferson's plan for the University of Virginia in Charlottesville (FIG. 4.33). Although there are suggestions of Jefferson's Great Lawn

at Texas A&M, the strongest impression of Jeffersonian influence is found in Texas at a new university founded without a master plan: Southern Methodist University in Dallas.

Southern Methodist University began, as many such schools had done for half a century, by building an Old Main on the highest point of ground in the tract donated by the developers of Highland Park. The institution did, however, commission a distinguished firm of national reputation, Shepley, Rutan and Coolidge, to design Dallas Hall, completed in 1915 (FIG. 4.34).[38] This structure resolves the problem of the dome that had troubled the Page brothers, Dodson and Scott, and Geisecke. In place of the semicircular dome or the pointed Baroque dome, Dallas Hall employs a shallow Roman dome on an octagonal base, preceded by a giant temple portico. This formula derives ultimately from the Pantheon in Rome

FIG. 4.33
LIBRARY AND GREAT LAWN,
University of Virginia, C. early 1800's.
Thomas Jefferson, architect.

FIG. 4.34
DALLAS HALL,
Southern Methodist University,
Dallas. 1915.
Shepley, Rutan and Coolidge, architects.

of the 2nd century A.D.; it was mediated through Palladio's Villa Rotunda in Vicenza of the sixteenth century, and adapted by Jefferson for the library at the University of Virginia. As such, it had appropriate associations with collegiate architecture, and had been used previously in somewhat altered guise by McKim, Mead and White for the Low Library at Columbia. Moreover, Jefferson's usage had been in red brick with white trim, which sanctioned this palette of materials at SMU. Unlike the Jefferson Library at Virginia, however, the domed rotunda and portico at SMU do not stand alone, but serve as the centerpiece of a three-story academic building, with wings that terminate at the ends of the cross-axial corridor in semicircular columnar porches.

The establishment of Bishop Boulevard on axis with Dallas Hall as the main approach to the SMU campus seems to have accompanied the

building's design, and today the central lawnstrip bordered by trees suggests a somewhat narrower version of Jefferson's Great Lawn at Virginia. A master plan for the campus was not commissioned until 1924, however, when Bremer W. Pond, a landscape architect from Boston, performed this service. Meanwhile, several additional buildings had been constructed in red brick with white classical trim, beginning with Atkins (now Clements) Hall, a Dallas Hall companion designed by Shepley, Rutan and Coolidge in 1915 (FIG. 4.35). Atkins Hall drew upon the American Georgian idiom rather than Jeffersonian neo-classicism, and this style was preserved into the 1950's in later campus additions by various architects. As a result, SMU is one of the most stylistically coherent and impressive campuses in the United States. Purists may distinguish subtle variations in the sources of period detail. Most of it evokes the American Georgian rather than the Beaux-Arts Classic or the classical revival, but all of these combine a fundamentally classical vocabulary of detail in red brick and white trim. The total impression of the ensemble is greater than the sum of its parts.

The American Georgian idiom became a popular vehicle of expression in American collegiate architecture in the 1920's and 1930's, perhaps rivaled only by the Collegiate Gothic. Surprisingly, there are few specimens of Collegiate Gothic in Texas, but the American Georgian found its way to Baylor University at Waco in the 1930's. Despite an earlier flirtation with modernistic styles and the absence of any compatible tradition, Baylor adopted the

FIG. 4.35
ATKINS (now CLEMENTS) HALL,
Southern Methodist University. 1915.
Shepley, Rutan and Coolidge, architects.

FIG. 4.36
ADMINISTRATION BUILDING
(now PAT NEFF HALL),
Baylor University,
Waco. 1938.
Birch D. Easterwood and Son, architects.

American Georgian style for its new Administration Building in 1938 (later named Pat Neff Hall; FIG. 4.36), designed by the local Waco architects Birch D. Easterwood and Son. Here the troublesome dome is replaced by a tall lantern tower—reminiscent of Independence Hall in Philadelphia—which serves as a vertical reference point for the campus. The American Georgian was only the latest in a series of styles on the Waco campus, however, and not part of a thematically consistent campus plan, as at SMU, Rice, or UT at Austin.

FIG. 4.37
ST. JAMES CATHOLIC CHURCH,
Seguin. 1914.

FIG. 4.38
ST. STEPHEN'S EPISCOPAL CHURCH,
Sherman. 1909.

ECCLESIASTICAL ARCHITECTURE

Church architecture is the most prominent exception to the dominance of Beaux-Arts Classicism within the Academic Eclectic tradition. Although the Beaux-Arts Classic was adopted for many churches, particularly by Baptist and Presbyterian congregations, the Gothic style never went out of fashion for ecclesiastical architecture, as I described in Chapter 2. It was reinvigorated by new experiments in eclectic adaptation in England by the Arts and Crafts architects (Prior, Lethaby, Seddon, et al.), and in America by Henry Vaughan in the 1890's and Ralph Adams Cram in the 1900's.[39]

Gothic church architecture took on a pronounced sectarian flavor in certain denominations. Catholic churches remained the most conser-

vative, with the central tower porch preceding a longitudinal nave remaining the most common form into the 1920's. Such churches were normally built of red brick. They frequently had piers dividing the central nave from side aisles, but were rarely basilican in section. St. James Catholic Church in Seguin of 1914 (FIG. 4.37) is typical of this formula, which had remained commonplace throughout the nineteenth century. Occasionally a Romanesque vocabulary of round arches and arcaded corbel tables would be substituted for the Gothic without basically altering the composition.

Episcopalian churches also assumed a distinct sectarian character, traceable to their affiliation with the Ecclesiology movement in the nineteenth century and the contemporary Arts and Crafts movement in England (see Chapter 2). Episcopal churches are normally small and look to the medieval English parish church rather than to the Gothic cathedral for models. They are traditionally entered through a side porch, and have a spatially distinct chancel. St. Stephen's Episcopal Church in Sherman of 1909 (FIG. 4.38) is one of the finest of this generation. Constructed of the ubiquitous hard-finished tan brick with stone trim, St. Stephen's abstracts medieval precedent rather than slavishly copying it. The buttresses along the low side wall recall the Gothic, but the windows between them have segmental arches, rather than pointed ones, and their tracery is suggestive of Gothic, not a literal transcription. The side entrance, asymmetrically placed tower, and roof dormers create a low-keyed, picturesque composition.

The shallow Greek-cross plan incorporating a compact preaching auditorium, which had been such a common form for Protestant worship in the Victorian period, remained popular during the prewar era. The same ubiquitous tan pressed brick trimmed in glazed terra-cotta, which was used to render Beaux-Arts Classic designs, was also widely adapted to the Gothic idiom. Oak Lawn Methodist Church in Dallas, designed by C. D. Hill in 1912 (FIG. 4.39), is typical of this genre. The resuscitation of the Late English Perpendicular Gothic, considered degenerate by Ruskin and the Ecclesiologists, had provided an especially apt model for the large windows filling the ends of the cross. Perpendicular tracery also lent itself to casting in terra-cotta; hence such churches also typify the

FIG. 4.39
OAK LAWN METHODIST CHURCH,
Dallas. 1912.
C. D. Hill, architect.

FIG. 4.40
TRINITY EPISCOPAL CHURCH,
Houston. 1919.
Cram and Ferguson, architects.
William Ward Watkin, associate architect.

great age of terra-cotta in American design. As in earlier Victorian Gothic churches of the same plan, towers were placed in the reentrant corners, with the one at the street intersection dominant. At Oak Lawn Methodist, however, the main entrance is not placed beneath this corner tower, but is centralized on the Cedar Springs elevation, perhaps as a concession to the more formal design habits of the Beaux-Arts generation. More significant of developing tendencies in Protestant church design, Oak Lawn Methodist has an extensive block of offices and Sunday school rooms to the rear. Such extensive educational wings would come to dominate church planning after World War I.[40]

Ralph Adams Cram remained the preeminent American Ecclesiastical Gothicist of the twentieth century. The campus plan for Rice University of 1910 (see Chapter 5) had given Cram and Ferguson their entry to practice in Houston, as well as their relationship with William

Ward Watkin, who was the associate architect for the Rice University plan. Watkin was a former employee of the firm and now dean of architecture at Rice and a frequent collaborator with the New York architects. Cram's design for Trinity Episcopal Church in Houston of 1919 (FIG. 4.40) reflects the architect's personal commitment to providing an appropriate ambience for the High Episcopalian liturgy. The tall, narrow lancets on the west front and south clerestory are somewhat out of character with Cram and Ferguson's more customary perpendicular forms, and the latter seem to have been more influential on subsequent ecclesiastical architecture in America and in Texas.[41]

The conjunction of the perpendicular Gothic with the need for Sunday school and office space occurs frequently in the design of Texas churches between the world wars. St. Paul's Methodist Church in Houston (FIG. 4.41), designed by Alfred C. Finn in 1930, is typical of this genre of ecclesiastical work. A single large window replaces Cram's narrow lancets, and windows of similar proportions light the nave. Moreover, the tower, which Cram had placed adjacent to the south wall of the sanctuary, has now been shifted some distance away, where it becomes a secondary focus for the large educational wing. As Cram did for his Trinity Episcopal, Finn designed St. Paul's Methodist in limestone. Other architects working in the genre, however, would frequently substitute cream-colored brick. Churches of this provenance continued to be built into the 1950's.[42]

Occasionally, however, a particular congregation would desire an exception to the norm, as several had done in employing progressive architects or would do in seeking out modernistic designs. Vestries and building committees were normally conservative, however, and so the exception to the norm might imply a more faithful return to historical models for a grander or purer conception of the Gothic. Wiley G. Clarkson seems to have followed this approach in his design for the First Methodist Church in Fort Worth of 1928 (FIG. 4.42), which seems like a reasonably accurate transcription of a French Gothic cathedral facade. The horizontal and vertical tripartite division; the triple portals with colonnettes and archivolts; the blind gallery; the asymmetrical disposition of the paired towers—all testify to thirteenth-century French sources. Only the replacement of the rose window by triple lancets and the more English detailing of the towers suggests Cram's influence. Fort Worth Methodist represents one alternative to the imperative for continual novelty within the eclectic tradition, by returning to authentic Gothic sources for models. Other eclectic designers would diverge from the Gothic in their search for new forms of ecclesiastical expression.[43]

The eclectic tradition had to be renewed periodically with new sources or combinations. The Gothic style survived throughout the period because it did change through internal development. But Gothic was not the only historical style derived fundamentally from Christian church architecture; the same could be said of Byzantine and Romanesque, both of which enjoyed a revival of enthusiasm about the time of World War I. One of the con-

FIG. 4.41
ST. PAUL'S METHODIST CHURCH,
Houston. 1930.
Alfred C. Finn, architect.

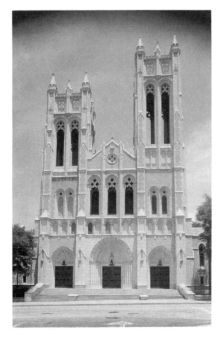

FIG. 4.42
FIRST METHODIST CHURCH,
Fort Worth. 1928.
Wiley G. Clarkson, architect.

FIG. 4.43
ST. MICHAEL'S CHURCH,
Cuero. 1930.
F. B. Gaenslen, architect.

FIG. 4.44
FIRST BAPTIST CHURCH,
Amarillo. 1929.
Guy A. Carlander, architect.

sistent interpreters of the Roman-esque as an ecclesiastical alternative to Gothic in Texas was F. B. Gaenslen, whose work for the Catholic Church in Texas stretches from the Chapel at Incarnate Word College in San Antonio of 1907 to St. Michael's Church in Cuero of 1930 (FIG. 4.43). Gaenslen's early work owes nothing at all to Richardson; it is a brickbuilder's idiom of round-headed windows and arcaded corbel tables.[44] By 1930, his command of the Romanesque had become more learned, with stone trim and a convincing reproduction of the Lombard style. When done in light brick with red-tile roofs, this rejuvenated Lombard Romanesque took on a regional aspect. The extensive work in Texas in this regionalized Romanesque is discussed in Chapter 5.

The Byzantine style had over-lapped the Romanesque in medieval Europe, and the two styles influenced each other at several points. There had been attempts to crossbreed Byzantine ornament with the Richardsonian Romanesque, and comparable attempts continued in the Academic Eclectic period. Cram, Goodhue and Ferguson had achieved something of this cross-fertilization in the quadrangle for Rice University (see Chapter 5), and in ecclesiastical architecture at St. Bartholomew's Church in New York of 1914–1919.[45] The First Baptist Church at Amarillo (FIG. 4.44), designed by Guy A. Carlander in 1929, suggests such a crossbreeding, and it also epitomizes the prominence that the educational wing played in church designs during the 1920's. Yet, just as Carlander extended the Prairie School in anticipation of modernistic effects at the

Garza County Courthouse in Post of 1923, (FIG. 3.48), it is not surprising to find a similar abstraction and simplification in the medieval forms and ornament of the Amarillo Baptist church. As an ensemble, it resembles Finn's St. Paul's Methodist in Houston and many other contemporary church plants in its studied balance between sanctuary and Sunday school wing, with the tower serving as fulcrum between the two functions.[46]

The shallow Greek-cross plan so commonly used for Protestant worship before World War I was equally susceptible to rendering in the Beaux-Arts Classic mode, usually for Baptist, Presbyterian, or Congregational denominations. There seem to have been two main variants. The first of these is represented by the First Baptist Church in Stamford of 1908 (FIG. 4.45). Entrance vestibules are placed in the reentrant corners of the Greek cross, and a square attic rises above the central portion of the auditorium. In the Stamford church the ordonnance is quite severe; simplified antae and entablature support the front pediment. The church is built of hard-finished orange brick over a purple basement, and the attic is shingled.[47]

The second classical variant on the Greek-cross plan is represented by the First Presbyterian Church in Orange of 1912 (FIG. 4.46), designed by James Oliver Hogg of Kansas City.[48] Here a full temple portico is placed on one arm of the cross, and the crossing of axes is marked by a dome on a raised drum. Such churches are extremely common in this period, although the size and shape of the dome varies considerably. Such domes usually seem like

FIG. 4.45
FIRST BAPTIST CHURCH,
Stamford. 1908.

FIG. 4.46
FIRST PRESBYTERIAN CHURCH,
Orange. 1912.
James Oliver Hogg, architect.

FIG. 4.47
FIRST BAPTIST CHURCH,
Wichita Falls. 1919–1922.
Stanley W. Field, architect.

arbitrary roof ornaments that, unlike the attics of the first variant, do not accurately reflect the dominant space of the congregational auditorium. As with the frequently troublesome contemporary courthouse domes, they tend to be eliminated in later churches of the Beaux-Arts Classic mode.

The most common form of classical church plan after World War I was a binuclear, U-shaped composition with extensive provision of Sunday school and office space, not unlike those in Houston and Amarillo, which were encountered in different modes. The First Baptist Church in Wichita Falls of 1919–1922 (FIG. 4.47), designed by Stanley W. Field, is typical. The dome is now eliminated, just as it so often was in Beaux-Arts Classic courthouses after World War I, and a second temple portico is placed on the educational wing.

Just as Wiley G. Clarkson moved beyond the norm in his response to the desire for a grand and note-worthy expression of the Gothic for the First Methodist Church in Fort Worth, so the First Methodist Church in Paris (FIG. 4.48) sought an exceptional design within the classical repertoire. The church was built in 1919–1924, and designed by Van Slyke and Woodruff.[49] One can discern the Greek-cross sanctuary within the building mass, but now the educational facilities have been packed into the corners and extended front and back. The classical details are more Palladian than Beaux-Arts, and the attic above the congregational auditorium has a vaguely Byzantine flavor. Unlike Clarkson's return to pure and authentic sources, the designers of the Paris Methodist Church improvised and combined freely among various species of classicism, creating an eclectic tour de force.

As in the case of institutional or collegiate architecture, the American Georgian enjoyed widespread popularity for church design in the 1920's and beyond. Its popularity in Texas was probably diluted by competition from the Spanish Colonial mode, but even so, English Colonial churches were built in Texas into the 1950's. This usage comes very close to literal revivalism rather than eclecticism, because the formal dispensation of the eighteenth-century churches on the Eastern Seaboard was taken over virtually intact. Ultimately these churches derive from the London city churches of Christopher Wren, designed after the Great Fire of 1666, which provided the great model for the Protestant parish church in the English-speaking world. Wren's model was further developed in the eighteenth century by succeeding generations of architects, of whom

James Gibbs was the most influential in America through his widely circulated *Book of Architecture.* Gibbs' most influential church was St. Martin-in-the-Fields, at which he applied a giant temple portico to Wren's prototypical tower-porch church. Both Wren and Gibbs had used a classical vocabulary based on the work of Andrea Palladio, which was also transmitted to the American colonies by way of pattern books. The combination of classical porch from Gibbs, graceful spire from Wren, and chancel window from Palladio composed the basic model of the American Georgian church, which was taken over virtually intact by eclectic architects in the 1930's. Maurice J. Sullivan's First Presbyterian Church in Houston (FIG. 4.49), designed with Hobart Upjohn in 1939 but completed only ten years later, is typical of both the style and the tardy popularity of this mode of church design. The separate classical portico has been omitted.[50]

Churches built between 1900 and 1940 comprise the most diverse stylistic range of any building type from the period in Texas. In addition to those just discussed, the Mission Revival and the Spanish Colonial were popular modes of ecclesiastical design, respectively before and after World War I (see Chapter 5). The prevalence of religious architecture in most cultures until the Renaissance, and of persuasive examples for church design in more recent historical periods, had supplied an unusually rich repertoire of models for architects and their patrons to draw upon: copying, combining, improvising, and abstracting within the Academic Eclectic tradition.

FIG. 4.48
FIRST METHODIST CHURCH,
Paris. 1919–1924.
Van Slyke and Woodruff, architects.

FIG. 4.49
FIRST PRESBYTERIAN CHURCH,
Houston. 1939–1949.
Maurice J. Sullivan and Hobart Upjohn,
architects.

FIG. 4.50
UNION STATION,
Washington, D.C. 1907.
Daniel H. Burnham and Co., architects.

SEMIPUBLIC INSTITUTIONS:
RAILROAD STATIONS, BANKS,
AND LODGE HALLS

When the railroads came to Texas in the 1870's, it became the practice for each railroad to acquire its own rights of way through or around existing towns and cities, and to erect its own passenger and freight stations. When additional lines built into a city, they purchased their own rights of way with minimum municipal interference and erected their own competitive terminals. This had the effect of strangling the larger cities in a maze of railroad lines. Dallas, the largest city in Texas at that time, was served by eight railroads in 1890.[51]

Individual railroads continued to build and operate their own stations in Texas throughout the fifty years covered by this book. Even San Antonio, which temporarily supplanted Dallas as largest Texas city in 1900, never acquired a Union Station, but continued to be served by separate depots for the Southern Pacific and the Missouri, Kansas, and

Texas. The Southern Pacific and the Santa Fe were the two transcontinental railroads serving Texas, and by adopting the Mission Revival style for their architecture, they were prime movers in introducing the Regional Eclectic styles to Texas (see Chapter 5).

Controlling the municipal environment in the public interest was one of the objectives of the Progressive movement and its aesthetic counterpart, the City Beautiful movement. Control over railroad rights of way and the channeling of competing lines into a single station had been a significant feature of the McMillan Plan for Washington, D.C., and Daniel H. Burnham's Union Station (FIG. 4.50), opened in 1907, became one of the most successful examples of Beaux-Arts Classic architecture and City Beautiful planning. Subsequent city plans by Burnham—for Cleveland in 1903, San Francisco in 1906, and Chicago in 1909—gave a prominent role to the channeling of competing railroads into either a civic center (Cleveland) or a focal point in a system of boulevards (Washington, San Francisco).[52] In addition to Burnham's work, Grand Central Station by Warren and Wetmore and Pennsylvania Station by McKim, Mead and White, both in New York, provided examples of complex functional planning within the Beaux-Arts Classic style. Significantly, both D. H. Burnham and Co. and Warren and Wetmore were invited to design union stations in Texas: Burnham for El Paso in 1905 (FIG. 4.51) and Warren and Wetmore for Houston in 1910. Neither of these stations were part of a significant City Beautiful plan (New York's Grand Central Terminal and Penn

Station had not been either); nor were they as impressive architecturally or urbanistically as Burham's Washington station. The El Paso Union Station contains a great concourse modeled on the frigidaria of Roman baths, similar to those at Penn Station and in Washington, but its grandeur is diminished by its red-brick construction and routine fenestration. The classical vocabulary is restricted to the appended porte cochere, and the asymmetrically placed tower seems like a vestige of the iconography of Victorian railroad depots. The El Paso station has no purposeful relationship to the city plan, but is isolated on the edge of the center city.[53]

In 1900, the nearest larger city to Dallas outside Texas was Kansas City, to which it was bound by the Missouri, Kansas, and Texas Railroad (MKT). Kansas City was in the process of implementing and extending George Kessler's plan of 1893, which included a provision for a new union station, designed by Jarvis Hunt in the Beaux-Arts Classic manner in 1910 and completed in 1914. Not only did Dallas employ George Kessler as planner for its comprehensive City Beautiful plan in 1911, but it also secured the services of Jarvis Hunt to design the station. The latter strategy was recommended by Kessler to ameliorate the stranglehold that competing rail lines had imposed on Dallas. Hunt's Dallas Union Station of 1914–1916 (FIG. 4.52) was intended as the monumental gateway to the city; part of a civic center of classically ordered public buildings similar to those being proposed for many American cities. Like most other features of the Kessler plan for Dallas, the civic center never material-

FIG. 4.51
EL PASO UNION STATION. 1905.
Daniel H. Burnham and Co., architects.

FIG. 4.52
DALLAS UNION STATION. 1914–1916.
Jarvis Hunt, architect.

FIG. 4.53
MKT DEPOT, Denison. 1909.
Henry T. Phelps, architect.

ized, and only Union Station and Ferris Plaza across the street reflect Kessler's proposals. Although constructed of white-glazed brick with matching terra-cotta trim, Union Station approximates its stone-built exemplars. The main entrance to the building is through a low undercroft, whence stairs in a side lobby ascend to the grand vaulted waiting room on the *piano nobile*. This space is lighted by three large windows set between piers on the front of the building, and dignified on the exterior by giant Ionic columns-in-antis cast in terra-cotta sections. In addition to the city hall (FIG. 4.20) (inappropriately located elsewhere in the city), the station is the most imposing monument to Beaux-Arts Classicism in Dallas, and to the frustrated ideals of the City Beautiful movement.[54]

In building terminals for their own exclusive use, the railroad companies serving Texas normally used standard repetitive designs, which evolved from Richardsonian

to Mission detail around 1900, but otherwise changed little. An exception was the MKT Depot at Denison (FIG. 4.53), the Texas railroad town par excellence.[55] As was appropriate for its threshold to Texas and division headquarters, the "Katy" railroad constructed a handsome station that, despite its red brick and natural terra-cotta trim, expressed the monumentality of its Beaux-Arts Classic sources. It was designed by Henry T. Phelps of San Antonio and opened in 1909. The concourse is expressed as a giant arched portal filled with glass, set between piers defined by paired pilasters, and crowned by entablature and parapet. This imposing central block is flanked on either side by lower wings, each two stories in height; its service functions are on the main floor and railroad offices are on the upper, acting as a mezzanine overlooking the central concourse. The ground-floor windows are arched and fan-lighted; the upper floor has modern triple-window groups. A side entrance is denoted by a slightly projecting pavilion, with coupled brick pilasters and a classical console in terra-cotta above the door. The structure adjoins a block of railroad offices, set back from the main front and paralleling the tracks. The station is set back from the street by a landscaped plaza in the best City Beautiful manner. Because Denison is not a county seat, there is no single civic institution to compete with the MKT station as the city's preeminent monument.[56]

The small-town bank underwent a cultural metamorphosis in the Progressive Era, as bankers sought to counteract their negative populist image and cultivate their role as community leaders.⁵⁷ The nine-teenth-century bank had little to distinguish it from other commercial enterprises facing the public square of a Texas town. If occupying a corner location, the entrance normally would be placed on the corner, splayed diagonally in conformity to the Victorian preference for oblique perspective. Sometimes a corner oriel would be placed above the entrance to further skew the composition to the diagonal prospect. The corner bank at Ballinger of 1909 (FIG. 2.27) has been seen as a transitional monument, whose ubiquitous tan brick, horizontally proportioned windows, and classical details coexist with the corner oriel and rusticated stone trim, survivals of Victorian composition.

Although certain progressive bankers in the midwest turned to Louis Sullivan or Purcell and Elmslie for Prairie School design, there are no Prairie School banks in Texas. At first impression, the First National Bank in Mineola of 1912 (FIG. 4.54) suggests a Prairie School derivation, but on closer inspection it proves to be merely idiosyncratic. The exuberant ornament beneath the eaves is not really based on Sullivan's system, and the splayed corner entrance is a vestige of an earlier day, found in neither Sullivan's banks nor in the more traditional Beaux-Arts Classic institutions. Both bodies of work are invariably symmetrical. Nevertheless, the Mineola Bank (now occupied by the Chamber of Commerce) is the most original exercise of the type in Texas.

Bankers tended to avoid originality, however, and to adopt the Beaux-Arts Classic style because of the images of stability and order it

FIG. 4.54
FIRST NATIONAL BANK,
Mineola. 1912.

conveyed. The actual size of such banks varied with the size of the town and the existence of competing banks. Many were only one story high, and monumentalized by inflating the scale and enriching the classical detail. The First National Bank of Kaufmann (FIG. 4.55) represents this type. Despite its corner location, the bank is entered symmetrically on axis through a classical porch of four Ionic columns, crowned with entablature and pediment that are set within a low attic. The modillion cornice is unusually heavy and adds to the monumental character of the bank. The entablature is carried around the side, but the orders are replaced by simplified brick antae between the regularly spaced windows. The front columns rest on a low plinth, which is also carried around the side. A rear entrance is acknowledged by a very slight cross pavilion with its own pediment. The small size of the Kaufmann bank is offset by its unusually grand classical vocabulary.

FIG. 4.55
FIRST NATIONAL BANK,
Kaufmann. N.D.

FIG. 4.56
NATIONAL BANK,
Denton. N.D.

FIG. 4.57
NATIONAL BANK,
Waxahachie. 1905.

Many banks were built on narrow lots, which necessitated a second story above the banking lobby for offices. In such cases a tall, vertically proportioned main facade did not permit a full temple porch, and giant orders in antis were used to monumentalize the banking institution. The National Bank in Denton (FIG. 4.56) is typical of this composition. The attenuated Roman Doric columns are set on a high base, and crowned by a deep entablature, dentillated cornice, and balustrade. The main entrance is further dignified by an elaborate door console. The two stories of the Denton bank rise half again as high as the contiguous two-story commercial frontage to provide a nobly proportioned main banking room.

An even larger configuration for a corner bank is seen at the National Bank in Waxahachie of 1905 (FIG. 4.57). Here the classical orders are suppressed in favor of a more Renaissance dispensation of arcades and string courses. The nobly proportioned main banking room is dignified by large, fan-lighted windows, above which a top floor of office space is located. Horizontal registers are established by a granite plinth, a string course at the upper sill line, and a simplified cornice at the roof line. The Waxahachie bank is faced in white-glazed terra-cotta, already noted as a popular architectural medium of a period that was equally susceptible to the casting of classical detail or Sullivanesque ornament.[58]

As the value of their prestigious corner sites rose in the larger towns and cities, Texas banks sought to capitalize on the demand for commercial office space. Thus, even before World War I the bank-office building had emerged as a distinct type. The First National Bank Building in Paris of 1916 (FIG. 3.16) is, as I have discussed, an early expression of this tendency. As a six-story structure, the functions of an office building have come to dominate those of the bank, whose public lobby occupies the high ground floor. The classical vocabulary has been suppressed at Paris in favor of a stylistically neutral combination of red brick and cream-glazed terra-cotta with touches of Prairie School ornament on the cornice. It is as close as anyone came to a Prairie School bank in Texas.

The bank-office building as a type in Texas architecture continued to burgeon after World War I. Typologically the National Bank Building in San Angelo (FIG. 4.58), designed by Anton C. Korn of Dallas in 1927, is very similar to the earlier edifice at Paris, only now the parti has been

FIG. 4.58
NATIONAL BANK BUILDING,
San Angelo. 1927.
Anton C. Korn, architect.

FIG. 4.59
KNIGHTS OF PYTHIAS LODGE HALL,
Fort Worth. 1901.
Sanguinet and Staats, architects.

stretched to eight stories and the details are recognizably eclectic.[59] The same combination of elements can be found in contemporary hotels and office buildings, which relative to the size of the community often take on the character of skyscrapers.[60] The uniquely monumental character of the bank as a semipublic institution has been lost, although smaller banks retained this quality throughout the 1920's and beyond as the modernistic idiom became widely adopted in the 1930's.

Like the railroad terminal and the bank, the lodge hall had a peculiar, quasi-institutional status. It shares with the Victorian opera house and post-war theater the need to provide for large assemblies of people. As did the opera house before it, the assembly room normally occupied the upper floors of the lodge hall, and the ground floor was rented out to the retail trade to produce revenue. Because meetings required a large, free-span room, placing such a space

on the top floor meant the structure had to support the roof load only. Because large meeting rooms also required higher than normal ceilings, the lodge hall took on a subtly different appearance from its commercial neighbors in that the top floor was usually taller, and frequently two floors were provided above the street, corresponding to main and balcony levels of the assembly room. Lodge halls in Texas covered an unusually wide range of styles, and relied less on the Beaux-Arts Classic mode than did most contemporary building types. Several lodge halls from before World War I show at least trace elements of the Prairie School; others similarly lean toward the Mission style. Finally, several of those from the 1920's seem to serve as a transition between the Regional Eclectic modes and the modernistic idiom, and will be discussed in Chapter 6.[61]

The Knights of Pythias Lodge Hall in Fort Worth (FIG. 4.59), designed by Sanguinet and Staats in 1901, was explicitly modeled on Northern Renaissance civic architecture, and evokes the guild halls of Germany and the Low Countries rather than the Beaux-Arts Classic or the Italian Renaissance. The tall vertical proportions are quite unclassical, as are the steeply pitched roof, the stepped-gable facade, and the side gables. This steep roof and tall third-floor windows accommodate the assembly hall, which is reached by a very classical entrance at the rear corner. The oriel on the front corner is a vestigial Victorian element. Although the lodge hall might be read as a belated expression of the Queen Anne mode, the combination of classical detail within an intrinsically medieval form is equally typical of the early sixteenth century north of the Alps, which seems more likely to have been Sanguinet and Staats' eclectic source. The Fort Worth lodge hall is one of the most unusual buildings of its date in Texas.[62]

The lodge hall at Llano (FIG. 4.60) represents a more common expression of the genre. The materials of red sandstone trimmed in gray granite were doubtless selected to match those on the courthouse across the street. Unlike A. O. Watson's Llano County Courthouse of 1892, which is one of the rare asymmetrical courthouses in Texas, the Llano lodge hall was undoubtedly intended to reflect the new four-square classical dispensation. The corner quoins, the horizontal water table, and the bull's-eye window in the attic all testify to this classical predilection, although they are rendered in indigenous West Texas materials and are devoid of the more difficult elements such as orders. Unfortunately, the designer's command of the new vocabulary and syntax failed him in the handling of the side stair, which throws the windows on the upper floor out of symmetrical balance. The Llano lodge hall should probably be construed as a naive attempt by a regional builder to incorporate the Beaux-Arts Classic tradition within an indigenous context of rough-faced West Texas stonework.

When occasionally relieved of its ground-floor commercial functions, the Texas lodge hall became much easier to compose and imbue with institutional significance. This can be seen at the Abilene Elks Lodge of 1913 (FIG. 4.61), where a graceful sequence of double-story Renaissance arches defines the classical style,

FIG. 4.60
MASONIC LODGE HALL,
Llano. N.D.

FIG. 4.61
ELKS LODGE HALL,
Abilene. 1913.

FIG. 4.62
SCOTTISH RITE TEMPLE,
El Paso. 1921.
Herbert M. Greene, architect.

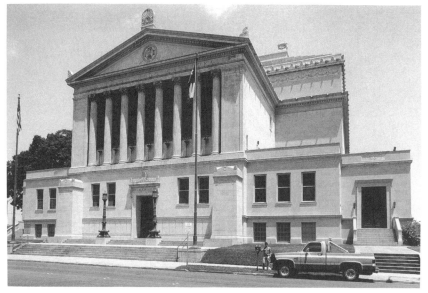

FIG. 4.63
SCOTTISH RITE CATHEDRAL,
San Antonio. 1924.
Herbert M. Greene, architect.

complete with spring-line moldings and rondels. The tiled visor roof seems like a Mission Revival device, but in other respects the Elks Lodge is an exemplary exercise in Academic Eclecticism on a small scale, invested with the grace of the Early Renaissance rather than the grandeur of Roman classicism.

In the course of the first three decades of the twentieth century, the lodge hall tended to evolve into the grandiose Masonic temple, at least in larger cities. The most significant Texas designer of such temples, or Scottish Rite cathedrals, was Herbert M. Greene, whose repertoire ranges from a straightforward application of classical syntax in brick and terra-cotta at Dallas in 1907 (Hubbell and Greene) to the frozen white-stone grandeur of the Scottish Rite temple in San Antonio of 1924. Between these two monuments falls his most interesting exercise in the genre, the El Paso Scottish Rite Temple of 1921 (FIG. 4.62).[63] Interesting but not original, for it is an almost literal transcription of Paul Philippe Cret's Pan American Union in Washington of 1913, and the first evidence in Texas of Cret's considerable influence on American architecture between the world wars (see Chapters 5 and 6). The Pan American Union, and Herbert M. Greene's gloss on it in El Paso, exhibit an architecture of discretely modulated forms, which reflect the functional plan and the hierarchy of spaces within the buildings. The El Paso temple is monumental without being grandiose, a reticence abandoned in 1924 when Greene, in association with Ralph Cameron, designed the Scottish Rite Cathedral in San Antonio (FIG. 4.63).[64]

The extremes of Academic Eclecticism can be summarized in the Pythian castle in Fort Worth on one hand, and the Scottish Rite temple in San Antonio on the other. The former is the more interesting and creative exercise; the latter the more academically proper, justifying the designation "revival of Revivalism," which for many American architects had become a cultural straitjacket in the 1920's.

THEATERS AND RETAIL ARCHITECTURE

Opera houses, lodge halls, and, later, civic and high school auditoriums satisfied the needs of smaller Texas communities for periodic ceremony and entertainment. Only the advent of motion pictures in the 1910's and 1920's altered this pattern in smaller towns, whereas in the larger cities vaudeville led to the erection of new commercial theaters that could accommodate either stage performances or motion pictures. The principal distinction between a theater and an opera house or lodge hall was that one entered the former at street level, rather than on an upper floor. If commercial retail functions were incorporated in the design, they were located on either side of the entrance vestibule. Since the auditorium was usually placed behind a public lobby on one or more levels, the street facade might provide several floors of offices or service functions, thus masking the bulk of the theater proper. These characteristics can be seen in a theater on the public square in McKinney (FIG. 4.64). Its handsomely proportioned but stylistically neutral main facade and blank

side elevation clearly express this dichotomy between headhouse and auditorium.[65]

From the beginning of the century, however, commercial theaters that catered to vaudeville or motion pictures had frequently sought to attract an audience by creating an exotic environment suggestive of entertainment. The Alhambra Theater in El Paso, designed in 1914 by Trost and Trost (FIG. 5.69), would draw upon the Islamic style for both its ornamental repertoire and its allusion to the pleasure gardens of Moorish Spain. The Hippodrome Theater in Dallas, named for the Byzantine racetrack in Constantinople, was designed by Lang and Witchell in an Egyptian mode (although traces of the Prairie School were also apparent).[66] In the 1920's, the Spanish Colonial became a popular mode for theaters in Texas, followed in the 1930's by the modernistic idiom of neon and colored glass. Many earlier theaters were remodeled into Spanish Colonial designs in the 1920's and into Moderne movie houses in the 1930's. The commercial theater, therefore, was not a prime subject for the Beaux-Arts Classic style, and is characterized more by the exotic choice of eclectic styles.

Theater design was also a highly specialized proposition, requiring knowledge of acoustics and sight lines that lay beyond the average architect's expertise. Thus, it is not surprising to find John Eberson of New York, principal architect for the Interstate Theater chain, associated with the design of several Texas theaters. Eberson, Fugard and Knapp's Paramount Theater in Austin of 1915 (FIG. 4.65) is one of the

FIG. 4.64
THEATER,
McKinney. N.D.

FIG. 4.65
PARAMOUNT THEATER,
Austin. 1915.
Eberson, Fugard and Knapp, architects.

FIG. 4.66
MAJESTIC THEATER,
Dallas. 1922.
John Eberson, architect.

handsomest theaters in Texas. The design vocabulary is vaguely Palladian rather than Beaux-Arts Classic, but the materials are handled with extraordinarily rich chromatic effect. The horizontal rustication of the brickwork is reinforced by varying the color of the recessed courses, and the deep-purple hue of the brick contrasts dramatically with the green tile roof.[67]

Eberson's Majestic Theater in Dallas of 1922 (FIG. 4.66), designed in association with Lang and Witchell, is more grandiose, but less original, than the Paramount in Austin. A five-story, highly Baroque headhouse masks the block-deep auditorium and stage house at the Dallas Majestic. Eberson also designed the Majestic Theater in San Antonio in 1929. This structure recalls an older tradition of theater design, going back to the great auditorium theaters of Dankmar Adler and Louis Sullivan of the Chicago School, and culminating in the Chicago Auditorium of 1886–1889.[68] At the Majestic in San Antonio, a narrow eighteen-story office slab fronts on Houston Street, and the auditorium fills out the block to the rear. A similar and common relationship of a theater to a tall office building is demonstrated by the Yucca Theater in Midland (FIG. 4.67), designed in 1927 by Wyatt C. Hedrick and Co. of Fort Worth as an adjunct to the Petroleum Building. Against all economic necessity the Petroleum Building self-consciously proclaimed itself a skyscraper: an icon of urban progress brought to the Permian Basin by the oil boom. The theater sits on the lot next to the Petroleum Building, with which it shares the stylistic vocabulary of the commercial Gothic, although the interior of the former is decorated in the theatrically popular Egyptian mode. At the Yucca Theater the relationship between the headhouse and the auditorium is frankly apparent, for the foyer and its flanking shops are only one-story high, with nothing to mask the auditorium rising behind. The blank, unfinished party wall of the contiguous skyscraper suggests, like many other such endeavors of the 1920's, that the theater headhouse was conceived as a temporary arrangement, to be replaced when another tall structure was erected adjacent to the Petroleum Building. The temporary completion of the ensemble occurred in 1929, however, the year of the stock market crash that precipitated the Depression, and the next stage was never undertaken.

In the smaller towns of Texas, the glitz and glamour of the great metropolitan movie houses would have to wait for the 1930's, when the modernistic theater with its colored glass and neon lights became a universal American phenomenon. Most small-town Texas movie theaters that survive from the 1920's do so in dilapidated or altered states, and those seem to draw upon Spanish regional sources. Several theaters from the late 1920's do survive in smaller Texas cities, however, such as the Plaza Theater in Paris and the Texas Theater in Seguin. The latter anticipates the commercial-advertising style of the 1930's, and is discussed in Chapter 6.

In the larger cities the vaudeville and movie palace became part of the downtown culture during the 1920's. The electrification of the street railways, which occurred in the 1890's, had made possible a

greatly expanded radius of urbanization, extending the benefits of suburban residence even to the lower middle class. Except in great cities where cross-town lines were feasible, all streetcar lines converged on the downtown area. Although the street railways did lead to the nodal suburbanization of certain commercial functions at transfer points and neighborhood termini, they also supported the concurrent concentration of a different scale of commercial retail activity in the downtown area. "Downtown" became subtly diversified into separate areas for hotels and restaurants, shopping, business offices and banking, and entertainment. People came downtown for shopping and entertainment on the streetcar lines from the suburban neighborhoods and, at least in North Texas, on the interurban railways from neighboring communities in the region to Dallas or Fort Worth. First-run movie houses normally lay within

FIG. 4.67
YUCCA THEATER,
Midland. 1927.
Wyatt C. Hedrick and Co., architect.

FIG. 4.68
NEIMAN MARCUS
DEPARTMENT STORE,
Dallas. 1928.
Greene, LaRoche and Dahl, architects.

FIG. 4.68
NEIMAN MARCUS
DEPARTMENT STORE,
Dallas. 1928.
Greene, LaRoche and Dahl, architects.

FIG. 4.69
TICHE GOETTINGER
DEPARTMENT STORE,
Dallas. 1929.
Greene, LaRoche and Dahl, architects.

one or two blocks of one another, after talking pictures gave the coup de grace to vaudeville and forced the conversion of the stage theaters to motion pictures. The major department stores, chain stores, and hotels were also found within a block or two of one another.[69]

Even more than the motion picture theater, the department store epitomized downtown attractions in the heyday of the streetcar. Unfortunately, department stores from the 1910's and 1920's are not well preserved in Texas, because many were rebuilt in more contemporary styles in the 1930's and later. An earlier vintage of department store is represented by the Sanger Brothers Store in Dallas (FIG. 3.12), designed by Lang and Witchell in 1910 and discussed in Chapter 3. Four years later Herbert M. Greene designed a competing facility for the Neiman Marcus Company seven blocks east on Main Street, which his firm enlarged and renovated in 1928. The presumptive designer of the enlarged Neiman Marcus Store was George L. Dahl, an architectural graduate of Harvard who had joined Greene's firm as a partner in 1926. Dahl was an example of the new blood that was transfused into Texas architecture during the 1920's, as established firms took on younger associates and as junior partners established their own practices. Greene, LaRoche and Dahl's design for the Neiman Marcus Store (FIG. 4.68; since expanded) is a curious mixture of structural rationalism and Beaux-Arts aesthetics. The column grid can be read in the spacing of the show windows at street level, and alternates in an A-B-B-A rhythm on each of the original street facades. The narrower corner

bays take on the character of classical pavilions, however, as continuous pilaster strips and paired window groupings set them off from the intervening field of six uniformly spaced windows. Similar moldings running horizontally set off the ground and top floors, creating the impression of base and attic. The pilaster strips and entablatures are reduced to linear moldings in very shallow relief, thus simplifying the traditional classical detail.

As an example of classical rationalism, the Neiman Marcus Store stands in marked contrast to Greene, LaRoche and Dahl's design for its competing rival, the Tiche Goettinger Company, completed in 1929 just two blocks away (FIG. 4.69; later Joske's, now Dallas Area Rapid Transit headquarters). The Tiche Goettinger Store is a frankly eclectic exercise in Beaux-Arts Classicism, with which Dahl was familiar not only from his student days at Harvard, but also from his apprenticeship with Myron Hunt in California before joining Greene and LaRoche. The eight-story block is treated as a Renaissance palazzo; the lower three floors are contained within a rusticated base and the top floor is treated as an attic of Venetian windows. All windows are regularly spaced and conventionally proportioned, with no indication of the structural frame behind.[70]

The downtown department store, which might contain seven or eight floors of retail space serviced by elevators, represents a distinct typology of commercial architecture. This typological clarity is not found in other buildings used for retail trade, in which shopping normally occupies only the street floor, and offices, apartments, or general warehousing fill the upper stories. It is these superincumbent functions that give buildings in the larger cities their character; the ground floor retail space is incidental. Even in smaller towns, the upper floor(s) of the commercial row were used for other purposes, and the architecture is normally stylistically neutral, if not positively nondescript. The emergence of the broad-front commercial block in the twentieth century has been discussed in Chapter 3, of which many normative examples in Texas could be identified. Occasionally, however, a small-town retail building stands out as noteworthy. One such is the Scott Building in Paris of 1917, designed by local architect J. L. Wees (FIG. 4.70), a rare example of the Commercial Gothic style on such a small scale. Unlike its neighbors around the public square, the Scott Building seems intended to provide two floors of retail space, with the uncharacteristically large second-floor windows admitting light. The suspended marquee shelters window-shoppers and merchandise displays from the sun. As in the occasional use of the Gothic for school buildings, the style seems to have been selected because it was compatible with large window areas. The Scott Building appears to have been designed as a small department store or furniture store, and represents the great age of terra-cotta in American architecture.[71] As in ecclesiastical usage, the attenuated forms of late-Gothic tracery were ideally suited to casting in this highly flexible medium.

The Commercial Gothic in cast terra-cotta was also exploited by the burgeoning automobile trade in the 1920's. In particular, the Magnolia

FIG. 4.70
SCOTT BUILDING,
Paris. 1917.
J. L. Wees, architect.

Petroleum Company, headquartered in Dallas, constructed a series of Gothic service stations in the major cities of Texas. That on East Commerce Street in Dallas, designed by Lang and Witchell, survives (FIG. 4.71). Similar facilities were constructed in Amarillo, San Antonio, Fort Worth, and Houston within the transitional service zone around the central business district, which had previously accommodated applications of Prairie School ornament to the needs of the automobile trade (see Chapter 3). All of these Magnolia stations were two-story structures, with the second floor extended over an open bay that sheltered the pump islands—a morphology subsequently extended to the smaller towns of Texas without the second floor. Thus, the integrity of the street frontage was maintained, at least temporarily, as the automobile invaded the American city after World War I.[72]

FIG. 4.71
MAGNOLIA PETROLEUM CO.
SERVICE STATION,
East Commerce Street, Dallas. C. 1920's.
Lang and Witchell, architects.

Not all commercial retail buildings were necessarily located downtown, of course. The streetcar network promoted the suburbanization of certain retail functions at the nodal points in the system, and with implementation of the National Highway Act of 1923, Texas cities and towns experienced a further stimulus to commercial dispersion. Although the two forms of traffic co-existed on certain radial arteries, the commercial highway strip gradually supplanted the streetcar node in importance, and those streets selected to carry the new highways through town were quickly lined with new retail shops and service establishments. The Beaux-Arts Classic mode was not generally amenable to such strip de-

velopment. In the late 1920's most of it was designed in the Spanish Colonial style, joined in the 1930's by the newer idiom often described as Depression Modern. These aspects will be discussed in Chapters 5 and 6.[73]

The development of the suburban strip occasionally emulated the forms of the historical vernacular used for contemporaneous residential architecture. The Spanish Colonial style is the most common example of this tendency, but such strips were sometimes built in the English Tudor mode, particularly when they were intended to serve adjacent residential neighborhoods. This usage had a long ancestry, with common origins in the Shingle style. The domestic vernacular shopping center can probably be traced back to McKim, Mead and White's Newport Casino of 1879; English Tudor half-timbering replaced the shingled upper story at Wyatt and Nolting's Roland Park Shopping Center in Baltimore of 1896. Although the English Tudor idiom was employed as early as 1898 by Frost and Granger for the city hall in Lake Forest, the shopping center for that railroad suburb north of Chicago was not designed until 1916 by Howard van Doren Shaw. The commercial strip at Davis and Edgefield Streets in the Winnetka Heights neighborhood of Dallas (FIG. 4.72), with its steeply pitched roofs and half-timbering above a ground floor of brick, descends from this tradition. Other examples include the Park Hill Shopping Center in Fort Worth, and that at the intersection of Ninth and Van Buren Streets in Wichita Falls, which serves the Morningside neighborhood.[74]

FIG. 4.72
WINNETKA HEIGHTS
SHOPPING CENTER,
Davis and Edgefield Streets, Dallas. N.D.

## HOTEL DESIGN

Although inns and taverns accommodated travelers by stagecoach in Texas before the advent of the railroads in the 1870's, the modern hotel was a product of railroad travel. Of the great Victorian hotels of Texas, only the Driskill in Austin survives. Most other extant hotels in Texas date from the early twentieth century, when improved and expanded accommodations for travelers were seen as a competitive commercial necessity in the greater and smaller cities of the state. This development has been discussed in Chapter 3, which identified the Plaza Hotel in Seguin as a particularly noteworthy example of small-

town hotels during the Progressive Era. The modern urban hotel was the result of the same technological factors as the large office building: the safety elevator; modern water supply and plumbing; central heating; the telephone and electricity; and the structural frame, either steel or concrete, which had replaced bearing-wall construction for buildings of any height by 1900. With these innovations, hotels with hundreds of rooms could be erected on restricted urban sites. There were several problems unique to hotel design that were not common to office buildings, however. One was providing window space to each of the hundreds of small guest rooms. The other was the accommodation of public functions in the form of lobbies, dining rooms, ballrooms,

FIG. 4.73
PASO DEL NORTE HOTEL,
El Paso. 1912.
Trost and Trost, architects.
Mauran, Russell and Crowell, associate
architects.

barber shops, and the necessary kitchen and housekeeping space. The requirement that all guest rooms have outside exposure tended to dictate a vertical slab with two rows of rooms opening from a center corridor, which could be bent to a U-plan for restricted sites. The public spaces required lateral extension on one or two levels. The unique morphology of the hotel resulted from the resolution of these two kinds of space: the narrow and high guest room slab and the broad and low public spaces.

An extremely common resolution of these disparate functions is that adopted for the Paso del Norte Hotel in El Paso of 1912, designed by Trost and Trost in association with Mauran, Russell and Crowell of St. Louis, prominent hotel specialists (FIG. 4.73). The guest room slab is U-shaped, with a light court between the wings, insuring that every room has natural light and ventilation. The public functions are located in a tall base, with the grandly scaled lobby placed below the light court and skylighted from above. The main dining room, placed beneath the west wing, is equal in height to the lobby and equally defined by tall, fan-lighted windows. The opposite wing to the east is divided into a ground floor and mezzanine, and is bisected by a passageway leading from the lobby to a side entrance on El Paso Street. The double-height podium is clad in white terra-cotta; the guest room floors are red brick, with the terra-cotta appearing again on the top floor, ornamentally treated to give the hotel a sense of vertical termination. The ornamentation is generically classical, but without the use of orders, and is used with a lavish hand. The lobby interior is a highly ornate ensemble of simulated marbles, gilding, mirrors, and art glass, including the lobby's domical skylight, executed by Tiffany Studios. The ambiance is Baroque rather than either Renaissance or Roman. The inspiration for this genre of hotel design is the eclectic usage of Baroque forms in England around the turn of the century, dubbed Edwardian Baroque after the reigning sovereign. Both the plan configuration and the formal parti were very common expedients for hotel design, and remained common until late in the 1920's.[75]

An even grander expression of the Edwardian Baroque is the Adolphus Hotel in Dallas (FIG. 4.74), designed in 1912 by Barnett, Hayes and Barnett of St. Louis, and built by Adolphus Busch. Busch's patronage explains the rather Germanic character of the Adolphus, especially its exposed slate roof and ornate dormers. Except for its over-wrought roofline, however, the Adolphus follows the same formula as the Paso del Norte: a tall base of white stone with an arcaded *piano nobile,* uniform floors of guest rooms in red brick, and an elaborate Baroque cornice and attic. Its functional configuration varies somewhat from the Paso del Norte, in that it is taller at sixteen stories and tucks its light well inside the L-shaped plan, rather than turning it to the street. It is an atypical expression of the common Edwardian Baroque style of hotel design.[76]

Hotels such as the Paso del Norte and the Adolphus were joined after World War I by a new generation of small-town hotels, successors to the Plaza Hotel in Seguin (FIG. 3.43). Such hotels catered largely to

FIG. 4.74
ADOLPHUS HOTEL,
Dallas. 1912.
Barnett, Hayes and Barnett, architects.

FIG. 4.75
BAKER HOTEL,
Mineral Wells. 1926–1929.
Wyatt C. Hedrick and Co., architects.

the needs of commercial travelers, among them the traveling salesman, who has become part of American folklore. An extension of the wholesale market of the larger cities, these salesmen traveled by train during the 1910's and 1920's, and a proper commercial hotel was important both to them and to the town's retail merchants who were their customers. Another class of hotel catering to vacationers might be found in seacoast cities such as Galveston or in the health spas that had grown up around mineral springs. A health resort such as Mineral Wells is dominated by several large hotels, of which the Baker Hotel (FIG. 4.75), designed in 1926 and completed in 1929 by Wyatt C. Hedrick and Co., is the most imposing.[77] Despite a certain attempt to monumentalize and regionalize the genre, the Baker is essentially a slab of guest rooms with public spaces at the base. In this establishment the slab is indented and splayed to provide a diagonal main front bracketed by wings, and features such as the main-floor veranda and rooftop solarium obviously cater to a clientele taking its leisure. With ten floors of guest rooms, the Baker Hotel exemplifies the greater height and scale typical of hotel design in the 1920's.

The competing mineral springs resort at Marlin seems to have been less successful than Mineral Wells. Nevertheless, it was sufficiently promising for the young hotel entrepreneur Conrad Hilton to construct the eight-story Falls Hotel in 1930. More typical of the growing trend toward skyscraper hotels was the Hilton (later Cactus) Hotel in San Angelo (FIG. 4.76), designed in 1928 by Anton F. Korn of Dallas.[78] At fourteen stories, the hotel dominates the skyline of San Angelo even today. The formula of composition is the customary base, shaft, and terminating cornice, and the unbroken expanse of guest rooms is alleviated by string courses above the fourth and twelfth floors. The need for a grand ballroom is accommodated by a wing to the rear, where a tall *piano nobile* is provided above street-level shops. This ballroom wing also provides a buffer to isolate the guest room slab from adjacent property. The stylistic vocabulary of classical devices such as rustication, quoins, and fan-lighted windows is rather weak and unconvincing. Conrad Hilton would shortly convert to the modernistic idiom in his great hotel for El Paso, which is discussed in Chapter 5.[79]

Hotels such as the San Angelo Hilton were also intended to cater to the increasing numbers of vacationers traveling by automobile in the 1920's. Prior to World War I, the automobile had been largely a rich man's toy, although the popular sport of touring had prompted the adventurous onto the nation's very uncertain network of rural roads. Touring clubs had been founded, private highway systems had been organized, and in 1912 Emily Post demonstrated that it was possible to motor from coast to coast. It was World War I, however, that forced the government to pay attention to the state of the nation's rural highways. Tested by wartime mobilization, the nationalized railroad system proved inadequate to the task, and the War Department organized truck convoys to move matériel to East Coast ports of embarkation.

FIG. 4.76
HILTON (now CACTUS) HOTEL,
San Angelo. 1928.
Anton F. Korn, architect.

FIG. 4.77
GAGE HOTEL,
Marathon. 1926.
Trost and Trost, architects.

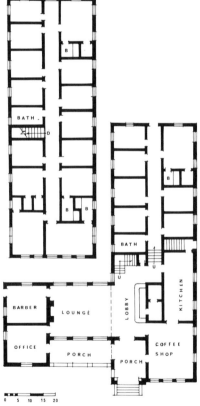

FIG. 4.78
GAGE HOTEL. Floor plans.
*Courtesy of Southwest Collection,*
*El Paso Public Library. Reprinted by permission.*

These convoys demonstrated both the feasibility of motor transport and also the shortcomings of the nation's rural highways. As a result of this experience, Congress passed the National Highway Act in 1923, which provided for a national system of public highways. The 1920's also saw a three-fold increase in the number of automobiles registered in the United States, and the appearance of forty thousand buses on the nation's streets and highways. People traveling by car needed overnight accommodations, and since the national highways for the most part followed existing rights of way through cities and towns, such automobile travelers augmented the clientele of commercial hotels like the San Angelo Hilton. A day's driving did not always coincide with the interval between towns large enough to possess a commercial hotel, however, and some of the most attractive scenic locations for motor journeys were in sparsely settled territory with no significant towns,

such as the approaches to the Big Bend country in West Texas. Therefore, a new class of small-town hotels catering to the motoring public emerged in the 1920's.

In the American Southwest, the most prolific designers of such hotels were Trost and Trost, who built a considerable number in Arizona, New Mexico, and West Texas. Most of these hotels were in either the Pueblo Revival or the Spanish Colonial modes, including El Capitan in Van Horn and El Paisano in Marfa. These will be discussed in Chapter 5.[80] The Gage Hotel in Marathon of 1926 (FIGS. 4.77 and 4.78), however, is stylistically neutral and illustrates the potential inherent in the genre. The Gage Hotel is L-shaped in plan and asymmetrical in massing, giving it a picturesque aspect found in most of the firm's small hotels. The soft tan brick and arcaded porches give a faint regional flavor that, nevertheless, lacks the specific stylistic attributes of the Pueblo or Spanish Colonial styles. Twenty-one guest rooms are provided; fourteen on the second floor and seven to the rear below, with kitchen, coffee shop, and lobby placed beneath the second-floor guestrooms at the front of the building. The lounge with adjoining porch, barbershop, and office are placed in the one-story wing to the west. Like all Trost and Trost hotels, it is an ingenious plan that is reflected in the three-dimensional massing of the building.[81]

In the 1930's hotels encountered competition from the more economical motor courts, and with the lack of finance capital, the construction of new full-service hotels in Texas virtually ceased. A few skyscraper hotels were erected in the modernistic idiom around 1930. These are discussed in Chapter 6. Apartment hotels of various sizes, ranging from two-story walk-ups to tall elevator buildings, were built in the larger Texas cities from the 1910's onward. These tended to occur in suburban neighborhoods, which were beyond the downtown area but well served by streetcars and commercial shopping, and were therefore undergoing an intensification of land use and property values. Particularly prestigious apartment hotels were often located in proximity to park space, and represented a new development in the urban geography of Texas cities, although architecturally they differed little from commercial hotels. Although most of these were designed in the Spanish Colonial style, the Aurora Apartments overlooking Crockett Park in San Antonio, designed in 1930 by Richard van der Stratten and Herf and Jones, employed Gothic detail (FIG. 4.79).[82]

THE OFFICE BUILDING

The office building is not a pure type; it was usually combined with retail space on the ground floor and sometimes on the mezzanine. In larger cities during the nineteenth century, such commercial buildings might reach eight or ten stories in height even with bearing-wall construction, and the development of the steel frame and of reinforced concrete construction soon obviated any technical barriers to unlimited height. In the twentieth century, the earliest immediate change was in style, as a Beaux-Arts Classic vocabulary replaced the Richardsonian Romanesque. For the space on the upper floors to be

FIG. 4.79
AURORA APARTMENTS,
San Antonio. 1930.
Richard van Stratten and Herf and Jones,
architects.

FIG. 4.80
WILSON BUILDING,
Dallas. 1903.
Sanguinet and Staats, architects.

high ground floor of display windows and transoms separated by marble columns (subsequently obliterated in a modernization by H. L. Green and Co., the present tenant of this prestige location). Above this, the mezzanine consists of large horizontally proportioned windows set in a deeply rusticated field. Windows on the next three floors are grouped under giant arches, spanning from pier to pier, but are subdivided by mullions into narrower window units. The sixth- and seventh-floor windows are grouped under arches of smaller span, each corresponding to the width of a single window. Finally, above an intervening cornice, an attic of square-headed windows occurs. The rhythm is interrupted to turn the radial corner in three equal bays of intermediate span, and again at the western edge on Main Street, where the access to the upper floors of office space is located. Here, the treatment on the lower three registers is varied to emphasize the change in function, with an elaborate sequence of classical details. The influence of both Richardson's Marshall Field Building and Sullivan's Carson Pirie Scott Store is likely; yet the Wilson Building looks like neither of these paradigms, for it has been rendered in Beaux-Arts Classic ornament used with almost Baroque intensity.[83] Its ornamental exuberance might be viewed as a vestige of the Victorian sensibility.

Although the Wilson Building is steel framed, it would hardly be considered a skyscraper in the normal usage of the term. It is broader than it is tall, and hence does not "scrape the sky," nor dwarf contemporary neighbors. One might propose these

readily leased for office purposes, however, it was necessary to provide natural light to all parts of the plan. This tended to conflict with the needs of retailers for large unbroken floor areas on the ground and mezzanine levels. A common solution was to divide the upper floor areas by light wells, similar to those used in hotel design. This formula was used by Sanguinet and Staats for the Wilson Building in Dallas of 1903 (FIG. 4.80), which occupies an important intersection acknowledged by a radial corner. The long facade is broken up by two light wells above the ground-floor retail frontage. The Wilson Building is an ornate and contrived composition. The eight-story elevation is subdivided horizontally into no fewer than five registers. First comes a

as the two definitive characteristics of a skyscraper: that it be uncharacteristically tall, and that the vertical dimension dominate over the horizontal. It need not necessarily be an office building, since the technological advances that made the large office building possible also permitted the modern hotel and department store, with no necessary change in formal expression.

The twentieth century has seen the corner bank transformed into the bank building in the smaller cities in Texas, which established the fact that the tall office building is not exclusively a function of commercial concentration and land values in the larger American cities. Frank Lloyd Wright did not originate the concept of the skyscraper commanding the skyline of a prairie town, for many such skyscrapers had been built for office or hotel purposes before Wright's Broadacre City project of the 1930's. The skyscraper had become an icon of progress in America by the 1920's.

The definition of a skyscraper was relative to time and place. Ten- and twelve-story corporate office towers using conventional bearing-wall construction had been built in New York in the 1870's. Taller than they were broad, this first generation of American skyscrapers had elaborate mansard roofs and clocktowers as visual symbols of corporate enterprise. Such obvious roof forms tended to disappear in the second generation—during the 1880's in Chicago. Ten-story office buildings such as Burnham and Root's Rookery or Adler and Sullivan's Auditorium were broader than they were tall, and hence, except for the sixteen-story Auditorium tower, they did not appear to scrape the

sky. Moreover, although they used some iron to support interior floors, the exteriors of both the Rookery and the Auditorium were masonry-bearing walls. Of the first true skyscrapers of the 1890's, Burnham and Root's Monadnock Building at sixteen stories was still masonry bearing-wall construction, whereas Adler and Sullivan's Guaranty Building was steel frame, but was only twelve stories.

By the 1900's, however, the steel frame had become a standard part of American construction technology, permitting indefinite height. Reinforced concrete was less widely diffused, although it had its partisans, such as Henry Trost. By 1911 Lang and Witchell's Southwestern Life Building was rising to sixteen stories in Dallas, and Sanguinet and Staats' twenty-story Amicable Building (FIG. 4.81), the tallest skyscraper of its date in Texas, was under construction in Waco. Thus, by the time the United States entered World War I in 1917, the taller buildings in selected Texas cities stood as follows:

FIG. 4.81
AMICABLE BUILDING,
Waco. 1911.
Sanguinet and Staats, architects.

| Waco | Amicable Building | 20 | 1911 |
| Dallas | Southwestern Life Building | 16 | 1911 |
| Dallas | Praetorian Building | 14 | 1909 |
| Dallas | Adolphus Hotel | 16 | 1912 |
| Dallas | Busch Building | 16 | 1913 |
| Fort Worth | Burk Burnett Building | 13 | 1914 |
| El Paso | Mills Building | 12 | 1912 |

It is obvious that neither land values nor competitive pressures induced the Amicable Insurance Company to build a twenty-story corporate headquarters in Waco. The building was frankly intended to advertise the corporation and the city, establishing a tendency that

FIG. 4.82
BUSCH (now KIRBY) BUILDING,
Dallas. 1913.
Barnett, Hayes and Barnett, architects.

would spread widely in Texas after the war.

Both the Amicable and the Southwestern Life buildings employed a common design morphology. Both are rectangular slabs narrow enough to permit natural light to all office spaces, obviating the need for light wells. The structural frame of widely spaced columns can be read in each, but the continuous pier-and-mullion lines on the Southwestern Life emphasized the verticality, whereas on the Amicable it is the horizontal spandrels whose continuity is expressed. On both buildings the uniformity of the office floors is interrupted several stories above ground to create a base, and several stories below the roof to create a capital, with an elaborately ornamented attic floor. The Southwestern Life Building used Prairie School ornament, which, combined with the vertical emphasis of the piers and mullions, made it appear more Sullivanesque, but both are very close in formal expression, and both are fireproofed in brick and terra-cotta. An examination of the drawings for the Amicable Life Building reveals that using terra-cotta ornament was not just a matter of applying detail. The overhanging ornamental forms of the penthouse had to be supported by a subsidiary structure of steel struts and braces, bracketed off the main structural frame. Certain panels of the Amicable Building's frame were also diagonally braced against wind shear.[84]

The Busch (now Kirby) Building in Dallas (FIG. 4.82), designed in 1913 by Barnett, Hayes and Barnett of St. Louis in association with Lang and Witchell, stands apart from the Southwestern Life and Amicable buildings in several respects. First, despite its sixteen stories, the Busch Building presents very nearly equal frontages to the two streets of the intersection, and thus presents itself as a block rather than a slab. Second, the steel frame on the two street facades is entirely fireproofed in glazed terra-cotta, which permits smaller sections and more finely scaled detail than brickwork. Finally, the terra-cotta ornament is cast in the Commercial Gothic style, making the Busch Building the earliest Gothic skyscraper in Texas. The emphasis on the ground floor and mezzanine as a base and on the top floor as a vertical terminus is retained; only now, Gothic tracery and finials replace the Prairie School and classical ornament.[85]

After 1900, as American skyscrapers pushed beyond twenty stories, designers began undertaking various experiments in formal configuration. The only historical models for structures of such height were towers of various kinds, but the proportions of a tower such as the Campanile of St. Mark in Venice did not permit sufficient rentable space on each floor. Some architects experimented with the formula of a tower upon a base, in which the narrower penthouse tower rested upon a broader, more economical base. Ernest Flagg's Singer Building in New York of 1909 proved to be an influential model for this formula, with its tower crowned by a Baroque dome. Far more important, however, was Cass Gilbert's Woolworth Building in New York of 1913 (FIG. 4.83), which was, at sixty stories, the tallest building in the world. Gilbert employed the same formula of tower upon a base, but he adopted the Gothic style for his ornamental

FIG. 4.83
WOOLWORTH BUILDING,
New York. 1913.
Cass Gilbert, architect.
*Photograph courtesy of Richard A. Scherr.*

FIG. 4.84
STATE NATIONAL BANK BUILDING,
Corsicana. 1926.
C. D. Hill and Co., architects.
H. O. Blanding, associate architect.

vocabulary. The Gothic had the great advantage of being the only historical style that had been inherently vertical, and it lent itself admirably to the expression of a tall building. The intricate forms of Gothic ornament also were ideally suited to casting in glazed terracotta, which for lightness and minimum bulk was the optimum material for fireproofing a steel-framed skyscraper. The Woolworth Building confirmed the Gothic as the dominant mode for skyscraper construction for the next ten years in the East and fifteen in Texas, a notion reinforced by John Howells' and Raymond Hood's successful Gothic entry to Chicago's Tribune Tower competition in 1922. Gothic skyscrapers were built widely in Texas after World War I.

The State National Bank Building in Corsicana (FIG. 4.84), designed in 1926 by C. D. Hill and Co. in association with H. O. Blanding, demonstrates how widely the skyscraper as icon of progress had spread in Texas. Although only eight stories high, the building was clearly intended to dominate the skyline of Corsicana, and by that criterion deserves to be called a skyscraper. Perhaps to compensate for the building's small size, its terracotta piers are unusually heavy and spaced more closely together than on the Busch Building, and the roof cresting is unusually florid. The polychrome glazed patterns used on the spandrels make it one of the more colorful terra-cotta facades in Texas. As with so many contemporaneous skyscrapers, the Gothic forms are confined to the two street facades. The party walls along adjacent lot lines are conventional masonry without ornamental embellishment.[86]

The Petroleum Building in Midland (FIG. 4.85), designed in 1928 by Wyatt C. Hedrick and Co., performs a similar role in advertising Midland's role as emporium of the oil boom in the Permian Basin. Although considerably larger at twelve stories than the Corsicana building, the Midland skyscraper nevertheless reads as a diminished version of the fifteen-story Medical Arts Building in Houston, designed in 1926 by Sanguinet, Staats, Hedrick and Gottlieb before Hedrick bought out his partners. Both of these buildings are L-shaped structures that present broad frontages to the two intersecting streets, and both are faced with Gothic detail only on these public facades. Rear and party walls are brick. As seen previously, the Yucca Theater (FIG. 4.67) was designed in conjunction with the Petroleum Building. Compared to the earlier Busch Building in Dallas, the design of the Midland Petroleum Building lacks animation. The subtle alternation of pier spacing and window size is ignored in favor of a uniform grid of widely spaced piers. The rooftop belvedere on the corner of the Busch Building might have relieved the incipient monotony of Hedrick's repetitive block.[87]

Hedrick and Co.'s skyscrapers appeared to be flat-topped, with rooflines broken only by the repeated Gothic finials at each pier line. The elevator penthouse tucked into the back corner virtually disappears when viewed from street level. Both the Woolworth Building and the Tribune Tower had been stepped-back toward the top to create a more sculptural termination, as had Eliel

FIG. 4.85
PETROLEUM BUILDING,
Midland. 1928.
Wyatt C. Hedrick and Co., architects.

FIG. 4.86
NORWOOD TOWER,
Austin. 1929.
Geisecke and Harris, architects.

Saarinen's great prototypical modernistic entry in the Tribune Tower competition (see Chapter 6). More adventurous designers in Texas attempted the same. The Norwood Tower in Austin (FIG. 4.86), designed in 1929 by Geisecke and Harris, not only completes the terra-cotta detail on all three faces visible from the street, but also breaks the roofline with a cruciform penthouse floor converging on the elevator crossing tower. The Santa Fe Building in Amarillo similarly employs a set-back penthouse floor to break the skyline, but the ornament on the base and roofline is more drastically simplified than the Norwood Tower.[88]

FIG. 4.87
MEDICAL ARTS BUILDING (now EMILY
MORGAN HOTEL),
San Antonio. 1926.
Ralph Cameron, architect.

Medical-arts buildings were a common skyscraper specialization in the 1920's, as physicians found it advantageous to practice together in facilities designed for their specific needs. The Medical Arts Building (now the Emily Morgan Hotel) in San Antonio (FIG. 4.87) is actually a flatiron building designed by Ralph Cameron in 1926 to fill an acutely angled site. Here, the suggestion of Gothic verticality is enhanced by the forced angle of the perspective. The corner tower with its flying buttresses seems inspired by the roofline of the Chicago Tribune Tower, and the terminating cornice is made more interesting by the use of dormers in a mansard roof. Like Hedrick and Co.'s two Gothic skyscrapers in Midland and Houston, the San Antonio Medical Arts Building is incomplete, with unfinished party walls awaiting a continuation that never occurred. The structure occupies an unusually propitious site, however, on one corner of Alamo Plaza, where it can be seen from a picturesque vantage point without being hemmed in by other buildings.[89]

San Antonio is unusually well endowed with such propitious sites, owing to the interweaving of the street pattern with the river. One such irregular site between St. Mary's Street and the river became the location for the Smith-Young Tower (FIG. 4.88), San Antonio's tallest skyscraper, designed by Atlee B. and Robert M. Ayres in 1929. Unlike the unfinished flatiron configuration that Cameron had given to the triangular site of the Medical Arts Building, the Smith-Young wedge-shaped site was treated as a six-story pedestal for an irregular six-sided tower, which can be perceived in the round from numerous vantage points on the streets and river in downtown San Antonio. The building's two-story base, and the copings at the set-backs at the sixth, twentieth, twenty-fourth, and top floors, feature Gothic ornament in glazed terra-cotta. The rest of the building is clad in brick, with continuous major and minor piers reinforcing the tower's verticality. The Smith-Young Tower is perhaps the most successful application of the tower-and-base formula for skyscrapers in Texas, and the step-back massing of the tower coincides with a similar treatment in the modernistic skyscrapers, which were beginning to appear by this date on the urban scene (see Chapter 6).[90]

Despite its peculiar affinity for the vertical expression of the skyscraper, however, the Gothic was not the only stylistic alternative for skyscraper design in the 1920's. If ornament were to be confined simply to base and attic, then other forms worked just as well: Spanish Colonial, classical, or modernistic. The architectonic properties of ornament—its placement, pattern, scale, color, etc.—became more important than its historical accuracy, particularly when placed too high on a building to be examined in detail.

The step-back massing that gave the best of the Gothic skyscrapers their special skyline is usually traced to the influence of the New York Zoning Ordinance of 1916, which had mandated a cone of space from centerline of street to cornice. The 1916 ordinance had been precipitated not by the Woolworth Building, which was congenially

sited in relation to open space in lower Manhattan, but by the Equitable Building of 1915. The Equitable Building was the ultimate result of rising land values and urban congestion: 1,200,000 square feet of floor space, thirty times the area of the site.[91] This was achieved by compressing the U-shaped plan with front light court to its ultimate dimensions, depriving adjacent streets and property of sunlight. Despite these problems, the Equitable Building was quite influential. Both the Waggoner Building in Fort Worth, designed by Sanguinet and Staats in 1920,[92] and the Magnolia Oil Building in Dallas of 1921 (FIG. 4.89) derive from the New York example.

Prior to World War I, Dallas had three sixteen-story buildings, including the Adolphus Hotel across Akard Street from the site of the Magnolia Building, which at twenty-five stories—plus eight more in the set-back penthouse—became the tallest building in Dallas. The Magnolia Building owes more than its inspiration to New York, for it was designed by Alfred C. Bossom of New York and London, who went on to do considerable work in Texas. The Magnolia Building differs in several respects from the Equitable, however. The continuous pier lines that Graham, Anderson, Probst and White (successors to D. H. Burnham and Co.) had run from mezzanine to attic on the Equitable are interrupted twice on the Magnolia by pairs of intermediate string courses, and the light well between the two wings is spanned by a giant arch at the seventeenth floor. Bossom also clad the Magnolia Building in limestone,

FIG. 4.88
SMITH-YOUNG TOWER,
San Antonio. 1929.
Atlee B. and Robert M. Ayres, architects.

FIG. 4.89
MAGNOLIA OIL BUILDING,
Dallas. 1921.
Alfred C. Bossom, architect.

FIG. 4.90
NIELS ESPERSON BUILDING,
Houston. 1927.
John Eberson, architect.

hardly the most rational material for fireproofing a steel frame, but a presumptive concession to academic propriety.[93]

The Equitable and Magnolia Buildings both had penthouses at the rear of the light court that rose considerably higher than the wings. If the entire building could not be modeled on a classical tower, then at least the penthouse could receive such treatment. This idea seems to have originated with McKim, Mead and White's Municipal Building in New York of 1907–1916,[94] and occurs frequently in the 1920's in various locations. John Eberson drew on this formula for the Niels Esperson Building in Houston of 1927 (FIG. 4.90), which is crowned by a choragic monument somewhere between that of Lysicrates and Mausolus. The wings of the Esperson Building project into the block rather than toward the street, and the composition builds in set-back masses toward the classical tholos at the pinnacle. It could just as easily have been rendered in Gothic or modernistic or even Spanish Colonial dress. The classical idiom was a conscious stylistic choice, reflective of the prevailing habit of Academic Eclecticism.[95]

The classical, Spanish, and Gothic skyscrapers of the late 1920's in Texas are actually delayed manifestations of an outmoded style; in the East the modernistic skyscraper had supplanted eclectic forms by the mid-1920's. Yet one must look carefully at the Smith-Young Tower, for example, to discern that it is Gothic and not modernistic, for the individual character of skyscraper ornament was less important than its architectonic function. As Henry-Russell Hitchcock wrote in 1929, "Skyscrapers . . . dependent on the New Tradition are generally very little more excellent than many of those which in their ornamentation imitate the styles of the past. . . . The skyscraper['s] . . . size after all makes detail, however intrinsically interesting, of minor importance."[96]

In the modernistic period of the late 1920's and 1930's, moreover, in Texas the skyscraper would cease to be exclusively a commercial entity. Following the example of Bertram Goodhue's Nebraska State Capitol, the skyscraper form would be adopted as the appropriate symbol for local government by several counties and cities in Texas. Virtually the entire range of building types, which since the turn of the century had been rendered in Academic or Regional Eclectic modes, would now be reinterpreted in the various nuances of the modernistic idiom. Before considering this transformation, however, it is necessary to return to the turn of the century to consider historically explicit manifestations of southwestern regionalism in Texas architecture.

# V

## REGIONAL ECLECTICISM
## 1900–1940

Attempts to create a historically appropriate eclectic mode for the Spanish borderlands of the United States began in the 1880's with the commissions of Eastern firms in New Mexico, Florida, and California. McKim, Mead and White's design for Ramona School in Santa Fe featured a Spanish tile roof and plaster walls trimmed in brick. Carrere and Hastings' design for the Ponce de Leon Hotel in St. Augustine (1885–1887) crossbred the popular Richardsonian Romanesque with Spanish tile roofs and bracketed eaves and porches. Shepley, Rutan and Coolidge's design for Stanford University (1887–1891; FIG. 2.12) also combined the Richardsonian Romanesque with an appropriate evocation of the California missions. There was no equivalent commission for Texas, however, which would borrow its Regional Eclecticism from New Mexico, Florida, and especially California.[1]

The Stanford plan is generally regarded as the starting point for the Mission Revival.[2] By the 1890's, the Mission style in California had shed its most Richardsonian attribute, rusticated stonework, in favor of wall surfaces of plaster, or even brick. It was also adopted by the two southwestern transcontinental rail-

roads, the Southern Pacific and the Atchison, Topeka, and Santa Fe, as the corporate style for their stations.[3] In 1894 the AT&SF erected the Castenada Hotel in Las Vegas, New Mexico (FIG. 5.01), in the Mission style. This hotel was one of the railroad company's earliest Harvey Houses, intended to improve the quality of travel across the Southwest.

In 1898, the United States acquired by conquest a Spanish-speaking empire, whose disparate parts (the Philippines and Cuba) would be tied together by construction of the Panama Canal. American architects now had the opportunity to design for this new empire, which led to a cross-fertilization of the Beaux-Arts Classic and City Beautiful with an old and sophisticated Spanish Colonial tradition. Daniel H. Burnham's plans for Manila and Baguio, and Cram, Goodhue and Ferguson's work in Havana and Panama laid the basis for what might be called a Regional Classical style.[4] The Mission Revival had been based very loosely on a provincial extension of the Spanish Baroque culture. In comparison to the authentic Renaissance and Baroque monuments of Spain, Mexico, Cuba, and the Philippines, it seemed increasingly crude and unsophisticated as the new century progressed into its sec-

FIG. 5.01
CASTENADA HOTEL,
Las Vegas, N. Mex. 1894.
Atchison, Topeka, and Santa Fe Railroad.

FIG. 5.02
CALIFORNIA BUILDING,
Panama-Pacific Exposition,
San Diego. 1915.
Bertram Grosvenor Goodhue, architect.

ond decade. Bertram Goodhue's intervention at the Panama-Pacific Exposition of 1915 in San Diego (FIG. 5.02) was crucial in replacing the Mission Revival with the Spanish Colonial or Baroque, although other designers, such as Myron Hunt in his First Congregational Church at Riverside (1915), had reached the same transformation. The Baroque in Spain and its American colonies had been characterized by extreme ornamental exuberance concentrated on salient parts of a building, such as doors and windows. This style, introduced by Goodhue and Hunt in 1915, became the dominant mode of southwestern Regional Eclecticism after World War I. Now, for the first time, the Texas missions, earlier and finer provincial Baroque monuments than those of California, began to be appreciated.

Long before the effective Spanish settlement of Texas in the 1720's or of California in the 1770's, however, Santa Fe had been the extreme frontier outpost of New Spain. Founded in 1594 among an indigenous Indian culture living in permanent settlements or towns (*pueblos* in Spanish), the Spanish province of New Mexico was too remote from the viceroy's court in Mexico City to import the forms of Spanish architecture. The Spanish in New Mexico necessarily adopted the indigenous adobe construction of the native pueblos. This style also attracted the interest of twentieth-century architects seeking appropriate sources of regional expression. Although the Pueblo Revival of the 1910's and 1920's was largely confined to New Mexico, it did occasionally infiltrate into West Texas. One of the most successful practitioners of the Pueblo Revival was the firm of Trost and Trost, headquartered in El Paso. Their Franciscan Hotel in Albuquerque of 1921 (FIG. 5.03) was probably the most important work in the style; their El Capitan Hotel in Van Horn (FIG. 5.37) was the finest example in Texas. But if the fully comprehended Pueblo Revival is rare in Texas, occasional trace elements occur in work falling between the Spanish Colonial and modernistic styles.[5]

In California, Irving Gill and a few other practitioners would bridge the gap between the indigenous Spanish style of the region and a modern regionalism of flat, unadorned plaster walls and stark window voids. Occasionally, such a modern regionalism also was expressed in experimentation with the new technology of reinforced concrete, as at Myron Hunt's addition to the Mission Inn at Riverside or Irving Gill's precast Hispanic portales at the La Jolla Women's Club. In Texas, however, the great experimenter in concrete technology was Henry Trost, whose innovative structures, culminating in the Mills Building (FIG. 3.11), show no reference to historical form conventions. Although Trost was an accomplished eclectic who worked in both the Mission and Spanish Colonial revivals, this aspect of his practice seems divorced from the concrete experiments, and it provided no bridge in Texas between a historical regionalism and an environmental regionalism. In Texas, the breakthrough to a modern (as opposed to eclectic) regionalism would not occur until the 1930's, and then would be based largely on non-Hispanic sources (see Chapter 8).

All of the southwestern styles, like other eclectic modes not spe-cifically regional, fed upon increasingly accurate archaeology and scholarship. Early in the century, the artifacts of the pre-Columbian civilizations of Meso-America had come under scholarly investigation. The Meso-American styles influenced Frank Lloyd Wright in the 1920's, and in the 1930's they would form the inspiration for a native style of modern architecture in Mexico. Generally, however, Meso-American influence on architecture in the United States and Texas was limited to two tendencies. One was the substitution of Meso-American ornament for the Spanish Baroque or the Islamic, particularly on buildings such as theaters, where the cultivation of the bizarre and exotic was expected. The other tendency was to incorporate certain Meso-American form conventions into the modernistic idiom of the late 1920's. The *talud-tablero* motif was one such convention, in which the heavy shelf or frieze of ornament (*tablero*) supported a high, sloping attic (*talud*). Another common modernistic motif deriving from Meso-American sources was the stepped arch. The Meso-American "pyramids," which actually were stepped platforms closer to Mesopotamian ziggurats than to true pyramids, played a subordinate role in influencing the step-back massing of many public buildings and skyscrapers in the late 1920's.[6] Just as a tendency toward simplification and abstraction was observed in the Beaux-Arts Classic style of the 1920's, so also in the Regional Eclectic modes, a modernistic stylization can be seen in certain monuments of transition. Implicit in the eclectic habit was the readiness to invent new combinations of historical styles.

FIG. 5.03
FRANCISCAN HOTEL (now demolished), Albuquerque. 1921.
Trost and Trost, architects.
*Photograph courtesy of Southwest Collection, El Paso Public Library. Reprinted by permission.*

FIG. 5.04
SOUTHERN PACIFIC RAILROAD STATION,
San Antonio. 1902.
J. D. Isaacs and D. J. Patterson, architects.

FIG. 5.05
SANTA FE RAILROAD STATION,
Gainesville. 1901.
C. W. Felt, chief engineer.

## THE MISSION REVIVAL IN TEXAS

The Mission Revival, as it developed during the 1890's in California, consisted of a simplified repertoire of vaguely Spanish motifs: the tile roof; the wooden bracketed eaves; the tower, either hip roofed or domical; the arcaded porch or *portales*; and the curved gable parapet. Occasional touches of Baroque ornament were applied frequently, of which the quatrefoil window was the most common. The California missions had been constructed of plastered adobe; those in Texas employed plastered rubble with dressed stone trim. In either case, it was light-colored stucco that carried the greatest historical authenticity. Mission Revival constructions, however, frequently used brick instead of plaster, or contained brick as a complementary material.

The transcontinental railroads serving Texas seem to have been the prime movers in introducing the Mission Revival to the state. San Antonio was a principal stop on the Southern Pacific's "Sunset Route" from New Orleans to Los Angeles. The railroad's architect and engineer in San Francisco, J. D. Isaacs and D. J. Patterson, respectively, designed one of the more extravagant Mission Revival stations for the Alamo city in 1902 (FIG. 5.04). The curved gable parapet set between flanking towers established the regional style, with both Spanish Baroque detail and brick arcading used for ornamental effect against the plaster wall surfaces. The curved gable parapet also occurred on the Alamo, and the widespread use of this motif in Texas led to the occasional designation "Alamo Revival" or "Texian Style" for the Mission Revival.[7]

The curved gable parapet also became a common feature on stations of the rival Santa Fe line. For many of the Santa Fe's smaller stations, the Mission Revival involved no change in fundamental morphology from previous, vaguely Richardsonian stations. Merely substituting the curved parapet on end walls, accompanied by the company's trademark, was sufficient to establish regional identity. The Santa Fe station at Gainesville (FIG. 5.05), built of red brick, is representative of this simplified Mission style. It was designed in 1901 by C. W. Felt, the chief engineer for the railroad. Since Gainesville was a layover point, the station included a Harvey House restaurant, with quarters for the waitresses upstairs.[8] In the 1930's, the basic trademark and corporate style of the Santa Fe Railroad was sometimes subjected to modernistic abstraction.

For its main-line station at Temple (FIG. 5.06), the Santa Fe employed an alternative parti in which the obvious leitmotifs of the Mission Revival are less apparent. There are no scroll parapets, towers, or Baroque ornament at the Temple station. The regional content is conveyed by the hipped tile roof and white plaster, augmented by brown brick for base and trim. This use of brick to ornament plaster wall surfaces seems to have been introduced to the regional vocabulary by McKim, Mead and White in their 1886 design for the Ramona School, as an attempt to regionalize the American Renaissance style. Its application to the Santa Fe station at Temple suggests a similar intent to

FIG. 5.06
SANTA FE RAILROAD STATION,
Temple. N.D.

regionalize a basic Beaux-Arts Classic parti. In this case, the Santa Fe trademark of a cross within a circle is worked into the brick ornament.

Smaller railroads also tended to employ the Mission Revival, occasionally using Texas architects rather than the in-house design staffs employed by the major lines. An outstanding example is the Quanah, Acme and Pacific Railroad Depot in Quanah, designed in 1909 by C. H. Page and Brother of Austin (FIG. 5.07). It demonstrates the facility with which this prominent firm, which was discussed in Chapter 4 as designing classic courthouses, could manipulate the regional idiom. Because the building also incorporated the railroad offices, it departs from the normal morphology. The inclusion of twin towers and the peaked pinnacles on the corners of the gable parapets make this an unusually flamboyant pastiche.[9]

FIG. 5.07
QUANAH, ACME, AND PACIFIC
RAILROAD DEPOT,
Quanah. 1909.
C. H. Page and Brother, architects.

FIG. 5.08
HOTEL GALVEZ,
Galveston. 1912.
Mauran, Russell and Crowell, architects.

Both the Santa Fe and the Southern Pacific promoted tourism along their routes, particularly in New Mexico, Arizona, and California, which joined Florida as prime vacation attractions. The resort hotel was a necessary adjunct to the promotion of tourism. The Ponce de Leon and Alhambra Hotels in St. Augustine, designed by Carrere and Hastings before 1890, were joined by the Castenada in Las Vegas in 1894 and by the Mission Inn in Riverside, which was originally designed by Arthur Benton and constructed in 1902, with later additions by Hunt and Grey. Although Texas was primarily an obstacle to be crossed en route to more scenic attractions, it did have a short seacoast and a deteriorating port at Galveston. As Galveston declined in commercial importance relative to Houston, its potential as a vacation resort rose to prominence. The Hotel Galvez (FIG. 5.08), located on the Seawall in Galveston, was designed in 1912 by the prominent firm of hotel architects, Mauran, Russell and Crowell of St. Louis. Like most resort hotels of this generation, the Galvez rambles over a landscaped site. The building mass reduces from an eight-story central block to six-story lateral wings to five-story wings framing the front lawn. The hipped and bracketed tile roofs are punctuated by dwarf gables, reentrant towers, and corner turrets. The curved parapet form is used sparingly.[10]

If the Mission Revival rarely was used on commercial hotels in Texas, it proliferated widely on apartment houses, largely because of the ease with which the style could be suggested by the selective application of isolated details. An apartment

FIG. 5.09
APARTMENT HOUSE,
El Paso. N.D.

house in El Paso (FIG. 5.09) is typical of this usage. There is little below the top floor to suggest regional character. At the top floor, however, the red brick gives way to white plaster, and tiled visor roofs are supported on extensive eave bracketing, which is interrupted periodically by curved parapets.

The iconography of the Mission Revival as symbol of southwestern regionalism suggested its propriety for certain types of enterprises. Cattle ranching in Texas was part of the Spanish cultural heritage, and it is therefore not surprising to find that the Mission Revival was selected shortly after the turn of the century for the development of the Fort Worth Stockyards. The earliest of the stockyards facilities was the Fort Worth Livestock Exchange (FIG. 5.10), erected in 1902. The Livestock Exchange is a characteristic rendition of the Mission Revival, in that a U-shaped plan de-

FIG. 5.10
LIVESTOCK EXCHANGE,
Fort Worth. 1902.

FIG. 5.11
STOCKYARDS NATIONAL BANK,
Fort Worth. 1910.

fining an entrance forecourt is set off behind an arcaded *portales*. The plaster walls and tile roofs echo the familiar palette of materials, and the curved "Alamo" parapet recurs three times.

The Livestock Exchange was supplemented in 1908 by the North Fort Worth Coliseum, essentially a large barn where cattle shows and rodeos could be held. Identical Mission Revival commercial buildings were erected flanking Exchange Avenue, which leads to the exchange and the coliseum. The Stockyards National Bank (FIG. 5.11), built in 1910, repeats the same familiar vocabulary: plaster walls, tile roofs, arcaded window voids, and curved parapets. Versions of this sort of commercial application of Spanish details would be repeated many times in Texas well into the 1920's, long after the Mission Revival was abandoned for more prestigious commissions in favor of the more sophisticated Spanish Colonial Revival.[11]

As seen in Chapters 3 and 4, schools represented a peculiar challenge to eclectic architects, since their need for large windows was difficult to resolve within most academic modes of design. The high school, in many cases, was the largest building in the town. The Mission Revival proved quite popular for school design, again, because it lacked strict rules and could be signified stylistically by the application of a few recognizable motifs. The King High School in Kingsville of 1909 (FIG. 5.12), attributed to Jules Leffland, is one of the more elaborate Mission Revival school buildings in Texas. The curved gable in the center of the main front is flanked by paired towers, whose dissimilar treatment above the second floor skews the otherwise symmetrical plan into a picturesque composition. The King High School is constructed of the same hard-finished tan brick that has been used so often in progressive and academic designs of this generation. Although the round-arched windows and entrances are stylistically unspecific and the eave lines project only slightly without bracketing, the red-tile hipped roofs and curved parapets, repeated on the roof dormers, are sufficient to evoke the regional connotations of the Mission style.[12] Other Texas schools of this generation that make similar use of the stylistic shorthand of the Mission Revival include the Alice High School of 1905 and the Denison High School of 1913–1914.

Although commonly known as the Mission Revival, the style was in fact highly eclectic, consisting of the free and unhistorical application of a few selected details. Nothing makes this clearer than the Mission Revival churches, which look nothing like the eighteenth-century provincial Baroque sources of the style. An abandoned church in Rockwall (FIG. 5.13) illustrates this freedom from precedent. The plan is the typical shallow Greek-cross configuration encountered so often in Gothic and classical churches. At Rockwall, however, the end walls of the cross have been crowned with curved parapets, and the tower porches inserted in the reentrant angles have been capped with overhanging hipped roofs on heavy eave brackets. The round-headed arches are not particularly Spanish, nor does the brown brick convey any regional connotation. The church could have been rendered in Gothic

FIG. 5.12
KING SCHOOL,
Kingsville. 1909.
Attributed to Jules Leffland.

FIG. 5.13
ABANDONED CHURCH,
Rockwall. N.D.

FIG. 5.14
WESTMINSTER PRESBYTERIAN CHURCH
(now ST. GEORGE ORTHODOX CHURCH),
El Paso. 1910.
Trost and Trost, architects.

faces. Thus, plaster, rather than brick, carried the greatest authenticity within the Regional Eclectic styles. Henry Trost must have realized this when he designed the Westminster Presbyterian Church in El Paso in 1910 (FIG. 5.14). Although the large arched windows in the sanctuary have been walled over in the subsequent remodeling for St. George's Orthodox Church, as it is now known, the character of the original Mission Revival design is still impressively evident. At Westminster Presbyterian, Trost eschewed the obvious symbolism of the curved parapet in favor of an emphasis upon the wooden eave brackets, which support a variety of gabled-and-hipped tile roofs. The dramatic contrast among the tile roof, wooden bracketing, and plaster walls, along with the asymmetrical placement of the tower porch, makes Westminster Presbyterian one of the most picturesque and evocative Texas specimens of the Mission Revival.[13] In composition, it resembles Frederick Mann's University Methodist Church in Austin (FIG. 2.14), although the latter's construction of rock-faced stone suggested its inclusion in Chapter 2 as a delayed example of cross-fertilization between the Richardsonian Romanesque and the Mission Revival.

Compared to the wealth of architecture designed in the Beaux-Arts Classic and other academic modes between the turn of the century and the World War, the Mission Revival made relatively little impact on Texas. Except for schools, very few public institutions were designed in this style, although there were occasional attempts to regionalize the Beaux-Arts Classic mode through the introduction of tile roofs and

dress just as easily with a substitution of detail.

Brick is not a common building material in post-Islamic Spain or in Spanish America. Because the Spanish appropriated a stone-building culture from the Aztecs and their pre-Columbian predecessors, the transfer of the Spanish styles of stone architecture to Mexico was relatively easy. When pressing beyond the areas of Meso-American high culture into northern Mexico, Texas, and California, the Spanish necessarily simplified the forms of Renaissance and Baroque architecture for the remote provincial context and used plastered rubble stonework or adobe for wall sur-

FIG. 5.15
ATASCOSA COUNTY COURTHOUSE,
Jourdanton. 1912.
Henry T. Phelps, architect.

eave bracketing. The style does not seem to have been taken seriously as an academic alternative to the Beaux-Arts Classic, although much of what was constructed no longer survives. Only one Texas courthouse was designed in the Mission Revival: Henry T. Phelps' Atascosa County Courthouse in Jourdanton (FIG. 5.15) of 1912, which disports a full repertoire of curved parapets, tiled visors, and towered pavilions, although built of brick. It did not establish a trend, for Phelps' considerable subsequent courthouse practice was in the Beaux-Arts Classic mode. The plan of the Jourdanton courthouse is cross-axially symmetrical, as so many contemporaneous classical courthouses are, but instead of emphasizing the crossing with a dome, Phelps has emphasized the corners with towers. Like Henry Trost before him, Phelps has used Sullivanesque ornament on the balcony brackets, further emphasizing the stylistic liberties possible within this loosely defined and suggestive mode.

Although no college building in Texas was designed in an obvious Mission Revival manner—with similar towers and curved parapets—three Texas campuses of distinctly regional character had their inception in the period before World War I, contemporaneous with the Mission Revival.

FIG. 5.16
OLD MAIN,
Texas School of Mines and Metallurgy
(now University of Texas at El Paso). 1917.
Trost and Trost, architects.

REGIONAL CAMPUS DESIGN

The University of Texas at El Paso has one of the most unusual campuses of any school in the United States. The idiom of design for many of the campus buildings derives from the original Old Main for the Texas School of Mines and Metallurgy (FIG. 5.16), designed in 1917 by Henry Trost. The plaster walls trimmed in brick have something in common with certain species of the Mission Revival, whereas the sloping batter recalls somewhat the forms of the Pueblo Revival so popular in nearby New Mexico. The bands of windows under the widely spreading eaves might be derived from the Prairie School. One's immediate impression of the El Paso campus is of a highly original attempt to create an autonomous regional style based upon historical and environmental conditions of the Southwest. In point of fact, however, the style was imposed on Henry Trost by the school's admin-

istration, and was explicitly derived not from the American Southwest, but from the Himalayan country of Bhutan. This Bhutanese Revival, and the image of a Buddhist lamasery in the Himalayas, were thought to convey the appropriate character of a mining college set among the sere hillsides above El Paso. Despite the exotic derivation, the architecture is strangely compelling. The battered wall surfaces obviously provide good insulation from the heat, and the broad eaves shelter the walls from direct sunlight through much of the day. If the style of the El Paso campus was not based directly upon conditions of the Southwest, its choice was at least a happy accident.[14]

The William M. Rice Institute (now University) in Houston was one of a number of new, endowed private schools of higher learning, including Stanford and the University of Chicago, that were founded between 1885 and World War I. Like Stanford and Chicago, Rice began with a master plan commissioned in 1909 from a distinguished architectural firm of national reputation, in this case, Cram, Goodhue and Ferguson of Boston and New York. Despite his reputation as the leading Gothicist of the new design generation, with work at Princeton and the U.S. Military Academy at West Point recently completed, Ralph Adams Cram considered the Collegiate Gothic inappropriate for Texas. Instead, he invented a Mediterranean synthesis, incorporating "all the elements I could from Southern France and Italy, Dalmatia, the Peloponnesus, Byzantium, Anatolia, Syria, Sicily and Spain,"[15] generically a crossbreeding of Byzantine and Romanesque forms with

Mediterranean overtones. Although the extensive master plan was not carried out in its entirety, the main academic quadrangle as finally completed after World War II reflects reasonably well both Cram's master plan and his Regional Eclectic parti (FIG. 5.17).

Lovett Hall (FIGS. 5.18 and 5.19), the first unit of the quadrangle, was erected between 1909 and 1912 to Cram's design. Initially conceived as the Institute's administration building, library, and great hall, the building closes the eastern end of the quadrangle and incorporates an arched portal or sally port on axis, which frames a view of the library at the west end. Lovett Hall has two facades: an outside one facing east and an inside one bounding the quadrangle to the west. The modulation of the two facades is quite different. The east front is orchestrated into five increments, with the vertical dimension emphasized and tall loggias opening off the library and great hall on the *piano nobile.* The inner, west facade is much more horizontally proportioned, with ground-floor loggias providing continuous sheltered walkways connecting to those on the north and south sides of the quadrangle. The ground floor contains lecture halls and business offices, and corresponds to the single-story height of the inward-facing cloister, all roofed in Guastavino vaults. The outer facade is a monumental frontispiece through which one enters the institute; the inner facade is part of a serene landscaped cloister for academic retreat. The shallow-pitched roof is masked by a parapet. Lovett Hall, for all of its lovely mixture of pink brick, white stone, and Romanesque motifs with Byzantine details, avoids

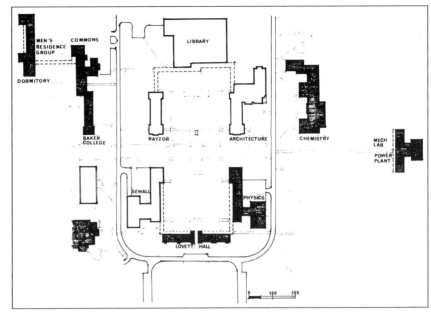

FIG. 5.17
MAIN QUADRANGLE AND ENVIRONS, Rice Institute (now Rice University), Houston. Site plan. 1910+.
Cram, Goodhue and Ferguson and William Ward Watkin et al., architects.
*Adapted from Fox,* General Plan.

FIG. 5.18
LOVETT HALL, Rice, east front.
1909–1912.
Cram, Goodhue and Ferguson, architects.

FIG. 5.19
LOVETT HALL. West front facing
quadrangle.

FIG. 5.20
PHYSICS LABORATORIES,
Rice. 1914.
Cram, Goodhue and Ferguson, architects.

FIG. 5.21
CHEMISTRY LABORATORY,
Rice. 1925.
Cram and Ferguson, with William Ward
Watkin, architects.

any of the obvious Regional Eclectic mannerisms of the Mission Revival.

When Cram designed the second unit on the quadrangle, the physics laboratories of 1914 (FIG. 5.20), he reduced the building's height to two stories and crowned it with a Spanish tile roof, although he continued the Byzantine/Romanesque detail. This building is also asymmetrical, inflecting toward the cross-axis through the quadrangle, which would connect the residential colleges on the south to engineering laboratories on the north. This cross-axis terminates on the mechanical laboratory and power house, also by Cram, constructed at the same time as Lovett Hall, with the power house chimney masquerading as a Romanesque campanile.

Further construction on the quadrangle was postponed until 1945, while work proceeded to the north and south. William Ward Watkin, Rice's dean of architecture and Houston associate of Cram, Goodhue and Ferguson, became associate designer for the chemistry laboratory north of the quadrangle in 1925 (FIG. 5.21). Although it retains the same pink and white palette with tile roofing, the design is consciously more picturesque, being organized about a Romanesque tower. Watkin also designed the faculty club in 1927.

South of the quadrangle, Cram designed a men's residence group consisting of a dormitory and student commons—buildings later expanded into three residential colleges: Will Rice, Hanzen, and Baker (FIG. 5.22). Here, the perceived effect is less formal and more vernacular. The proportion of pink brick to stone has been reduced, and large surfaces of light plaster predomi-

FIG. 5.22
BAKER COLLEGE,
Rice. 1914.
Cram, Goodhue and Ferguson, architects.

nate. Arcades, which spring from points closer to the ground, more closely resemble Spanish *portales*. Tower forms, inserted at picturesque junctures, are capped with overhanging hipped tile roofs suggestive of the Mission Revival. Projecting wooden window bays and iron balcony railings further reinforce the Spanish character. Cram presumably sought a more informal, domestic character for the residential buildings.

William Ward Watkin emerged from his association with Cram, Goodhue and Ferguson as the most experienced campus planner and university architect in Texas. This doubtless led to his appointment as associate architect for Texas Technological College (now Texas Tech University) in Lubbock, founded by the legislature in 1923. Owing perhaps to Amon G. Carter's chairmanship of the board of governors, the principal architects for the new Administration Building were Sanguinet, Staats and Hedrick of Fort Worth. Wyatt C. Hedrick (who

FIG. 5.23
ADMINISTRATION BUILDING,
Texas Technological College
(now Texas Tech University),
Lubbock. 1924.
Sanguinet, Staats and Hedrick, architects.
William Ward Watkin, associate architect.

FIG. 5.24
CHEMISTRY BUILDING,
Texas Tech. 1928.
Wyatt C. Hedrick and Co., architects.
William Ward Watkin, associate architect.

bought out his partners in the same year) and Watkin would continue their role as designers of the Texas Tech campus until World War II.

The idiom selected for the new Administration Building (FIG. 5.23) was a species of Spanish Renaissance quite different from both the Mission Revival and from the Mediterranean, Romanesque, and Byzantine styles of the Rice campus—a vast U-shaped plan with an entrance passageway through an axis. This is perhaps a reflection of Lovett Hall at Rice, although less grandly treated. The ground floor is white limestone, supporting two additional floors of light-yellow brick and a hipped Spanish tile roof. Two points of detail seem to be based upon specific historical models. The centerpiece of the main facade, executed entirely in stone, resembles the sixteenth-century university in Alcala de Henares in Spain, which Watkin, Cram, and Ferguson had already used on the Houston Public Library (discussed at a later point in this chapter). The paired towers that break the two sides resemble the minaret/belltower of the Great Mosque of Cordoba, which was converted to Christian use during the sixteenth century. This erudite quoting of specific sources is quite different from the simplified regional shorthand of the Mission Revival, although it lacks the eclectic virtuosity of Cram's work at Rice.

The Administration Building at Texas Tech became the focal point of a cross-axial plan of much greater dimensions than the quadrangle at Rice; Hedrick and Watkin designed further groups of buildings along three of these axes. The Chemistry Building (FIG. 5.24; 1928), which was the first one done for the group of buildings devoted to the sciences, must suffice to illustrate their development of the Spanish idiom. The detail here is more specifically Baroque than the Administration Building, but less explicitly borrowed from obvious sources. Because the building was intended to close one side of a quadrangle, it is asymmetrical about its long axis, inflecting toward the central axis of the quadrangle, which was closed only in 1950 when the building group was finally completed. The arcaded passageway recalls the Rice campus, but differs in basic idiom. Rice was Mediterranean Romanesque and Byzantine, for which combinations of brick and stone were historically authentic materials. The Chemistry Building at Texas Tech was ostensibly Spanish Baroque, but its execution in brick deprives it of comparable historical authenticity. The Texas Tech campus, despite its cross-axial armature and its stylistically compatible buildings, hardly rivals SMU, Rice, or the University of Texas at Austin as an exercise in campus planning on Beaux-Arts principles. Not only is the scale uncomfortably vast, but the architecture of the Spanish Colonial Revival in brick is somewhat bland and unconvincing.

The Regional Romanesque was much easier to render with conviction in brick. This style became very popular for institutional building in the 1920's, stimulated in part by the building of a new campus for the University of California at Los Angeles. George W. Kelham laid out the master plan for the Westwood campus in 1925–1926, with ten buildings in variations of the Regional Romanesque, by Kelham and others, following by 1932. Royce

Hall, designed by Allison and Allison in 1928, is modeled on San Ambrogio in Milan (FIG. 5.25).[16] Although the specific sources at UCLA are Lombard rather than Spanish, during the Romanesque period a common vocabulary of forms and details in brick was widely diffused along the Mediterranean, from northern Spain to northern Italy. Pilaster strips, blind arcades, arcaded corbel tables, and low-pitched tile roofs are indigenous to this brick-building culture and much easier to reproduce with eclectic conviction than the stone-and-plaster forms of the Spanish Baroque. I will consider some individual examples of this Regional Romanesque idiom later in this chapter, but one entire campus in Texas planned in this style requires discussion here.

The Hardin Administration Building for Midwestern University in Wichita Falls (FIG. 5.26) was designed in 1936 by Voelcker and Dixon of that city, who adopted the Regional Romanesque style subsequently extended to other campus buildings. The main entrance seems based on San Ambrogio, Kelham's model at UCLA, although the single tower combines with the frontispiece in a picturesque fashion less faithful to the original than Kelham's paired towers. The tower also helps to identify the center of the low, sprawling structure of only two stories spread out behind a lawn thickly planted in trees. The vocabulary of brick details picked out with stone trim seems historically authentic, and the broken massing of brick-and-tile forms is composed for fine picturesque effect. Although by 1936 Voelcker and Dixon had adopted the modernistic idiom for

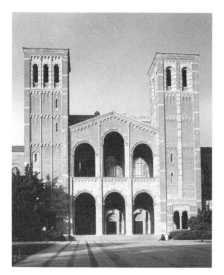

FIG. 5.25
ROYCE HALL,
University of California
at Los Angeles. 1928.
Allison and Allison, architects.

FIG. 5.26
HARDIN ADMINISTRATION BUILDING,
Midwestern University,
Wichita Falls. 1936.
Voelcker and Dixon, architects.

most of their institutional work, they could still improvise from historical models with great panache.

Southern Methodist University (see Chapter 4), the University of Texas at El Paso, Rice, Texas Tech, and Midwestern State each received its definitive character from the first building designed for its new campus. At the University of Texas at Austin, however, the character of an old campus was gradually transformed into a Regional Eclectic ensemble through a series of interventions over a quarter of a century. The original Old Main, designed in 1882 by Frederick Ruffini in the Victorian Gothic style, had been located on the highest point of ground on campus, facing the State Capitol a mile away. Other buildings were added, and in 1909, Cass Gilbert of Minneapolis was commissioned to design a new library (now Battle Hall; FIG. 5.27). Gilbert's library was the first step toward a regional mode of expression for the University of Texas campus.[17]

Gilbert described the style of his library as "modified Spanish Renaissance."[18] Although a preliminary study showed engaged orders defining the reading room on the *piano nobile*, these were omitted in the final design in favor of arcades resting on broad piers, with terra-cotta rondels suggestive of the Foundling Hospital in Florence. The arcades are filled with Palladian fanlighted windows bordered by polychrome terra-cotta. These arcaded windows extend to the floor line and contain iron railings for safety. The library is crowned by a simple hipped roof in red tile, supported by elaborately painted wooden eave bracketing. It is a restrained and impeccably classical building; the tile

roof, eave bracketing, glazed tile, and ironwork allude to Spanish sources, but have none of the obvious mannerisms of the Mission Revival.

It was Gilbert's second building for the university, however, that in the 1920's established the style for the campus. The Education Building, now Sutton Hall (FIG. 5.28), which Gilbert designed in 1918, was less auspiciously sited than the library and contained more prosaic functions. Although Gilbert retained the hipped tile roof on elaborate eave brackets, he constructed the body of the building with brick, rather than limestone, and two floors of teaching space replaced the monumentally scaled *piano nobile* of the library reading room. Gilbert's Education Building established the norm for subsequent additions to the campus by Herbert M. Greene and his partners, LaRoche and Dahl: Garrison Hall (1925), Waggener Hall (1931), and Hogg Hall (1932) are all variations on the parti Gilbert had created.

In 1933, the University of Texas employed Paul Philippe Cret to design a master plan for the campus, and to serve as consulting architect on a continuing basis. It is to Cret's "elastic formal plan"[19] that the campus owes its present character, with its axial approaches to the main building from all four directions. Since Gilbert's library was already too small, Cret proposed replacing the Victorian Gothic Old Main with a new library that would serve as the campus focal point. Cret's work in the Beaux-Arts Classic mode during the 1920's had progressed through a series of simplifying steps, culminating in what he called "Modern Classic" at the Folger Library in

1929, which is recognized as one of the seminal sources of the modernistic idiom of the 1930's.

Although Cret proposed several alternative schemes for the new library—one of which resembled the "Modern Classic" of the Folger Library—in the end the regents selected a formal Beaux-Arts Classic parti with tile roofs and restrained regional characteristics, thus continuing and confirming the regionalized classical idiom that Gilbert had established for the old library two decades before. In the final design (FIG. 5.29), the new library became the base for the Administration Tower, which was indirectly inspired by Goodhue's skyscraper capitol for Nebraska and its numerous progeny.[20]

The library/administration building, fronting on a paved terrace and facing south, became the focal point of a cross-axial development plan with distinct and varied approaches from the four directions (FIG. 5.30). Although many aspects of Cret's development plan were not carried out, the four axes were implemented essentially as proposed, and gave the Austin campus its formal character. The most imposing of these is South Mall, planted as a lawn bordered in trees and flanked by six virtually uniform buildings. The mall rises in a moderate slope from the Littlefield Fountain at the pedestrian entrance on Twenty-first Street to a flight of stairs ascending to the main terrace. This south axis is visually the most important of the four, because it reinforces the reciprocity between Administration Tower and the State Capitol a mile away.

East and west of the main terrace, Cret proposed a subtle shift of axes. Gilbert's old library (now Battle

FIG. 5.27
LIBRARY (now BATTLE HALL),
University of Texas,
Austin. 1909.
Cass Gilbert, architect.

Hall) was centered on the terrace to the west, necessitating a corner entrance to the terrace when approached from Guadalupe Street, the principal urban edge of the campus. The projecting corner pavilions of Cret's new library line up with this west axis, which was developed as a fairly narrow pedestrian avenue. Drawn toward the colonnaded pavilion on axis, the pedestrian is squeezed between the corner of the new library and Battle Hall, only to experience the terrace that is shifted to the south. Cret acknowledged the Guadalupe Street entrance to the campus by the design of two buildings flanking the west axis: Goldsmith Hall for the School of Architecture on the south, and the Texas Union on the north. Although these two buildings differ greatly in plan and function, they present similar and balanced facades to the west mall, and both main entrances in-

FIG. 5.28
EDUCATION BUILDING
(now SUTTON HALL),
University of Texas,
Austin. 1918.
Cass Gilbert, architect.

FIG. 5.29
LIBRARY/ADMINISTRATION BUILDING,
University of Texas,
Austin. 1933–1936.
Paul Philippe Cret, consulting architect.

flect toward the corner on Guadalupe Street. The Texas Union (FIG. 5.31), with its bracketed eaves and arcaded *piano nobile*, is perhaps Cret's most overtly Spanish building for the Austin campus.

East of the main terrace, Cret proposed additions to Garrison and Hogg halls. These would have redirected the main front of Garrison to the west, where it would have balanced Battle Hall on axis across the main terrace. The two proposed additions would also have narrowed the eastern axis of approach, which would have then been focused upon the new library pavilion just as the western one is. The additions were never built, so that today the steep eastern ascent to the main terrace

is more diffused than Cret had intended.

North of the Library/Administration Building, Cret projected the north/south axis as a service road to Twenty-fourth Street, beyond which the "Women's Residence Group" was proposed around a college green on axis. Because the Home Economics Department was the centerpiece of women's studies in the 1930's, it became the focal point of this northern area. Cret's Home Economics Building (now Mary Gearing Hall; FIG. 5.32) is one of his most subtle exercises in Beaux-Arts planning and regional character. Gearing Hall was located astride the axis, with its principal access from the north. Approaching across the green (today

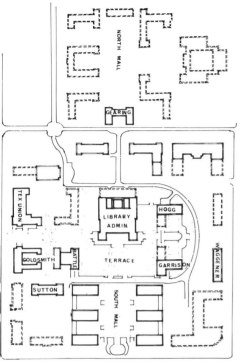

FIG. 5.30
UNIVERSITY OF TEXAS, AUSTIN.
Master plan. 1933.
Paul Philippe Cret, consulting architect.
Adapted by the author.

FIG. 5.31
TEXAS UNION,
University of Texas,
Austin. 1933.
Paul Philippe Cret, consulting architect.

the University Avenue mall), one sees the administration tower rising behind the main facade. Other than the Library/Administration Building, this is the only Cret building on the Austin campus that blocks a main axis, forcing one to pass through or around it when approaching from any direction. All four facades are different, responding to different conditions of approach, and although each facade is biaxially symmetrical in elevation, as one moves around the building, the shifting masses take on a spatial dynamic that seems more picturesque than classical. Two towers mediate between the main four-story block and the flanking three-story wings, which frame a raised

FIG. 5.32
HOME ECONOMICS BUILDING
(now MARY GEARING HALL),
University of Texas,
Austin. 1933.
Paul Philippe Cret, consulting architect.

FIG. 5.33
OZONA HIGH SCHOOL
AUDITORIUM. 1931.

FIG. 5.34
CENTRAL CHRISTIAN CHURCH,
Austin. 1928.
Robert Leon White, architect.
Ralph Cameron and Samuel Vosper,
associate architects.

## REGIONAL ROMANESQUE AND MEDITERRANEAN STYLES

The most obvious attribute signifying Spanish or Mediterranean style was the low-pitched tile roof, a regional characteristic widely distributed around the Mediterranean since Greek and Roman times. Such roofs had been adapted to the Romanesque style in Spain, southern France, and Italy, where they coincided with a certain repertoire of details easily adapted to brick construction. Pilaster strips, blind arcades, and arcaded corbel tables, easily rendered in brick and combined with tile roofs, comprised in the 1920's a Regional Romanesque alternative to the Spanish Colonial mode. It had the great advantage in that the forms and details seemed indigenous to brick construction, which always was cheaper than stone and more durable than plaster, whereas the Spanish Colonial done in brick frequently seemed to lack authenticity. And because the prominent historical models were churches, the style lent itself to large primary spaces such as gymnasiums and auditoriums. The Gregory Gymnasium discussed in the previous section thus was ideally suited to the Regional Romanesque style, as was the Ozona High School Auditorium of 1931 (FIG. 5.33).

The style could provide the vehicle for an extremely flexible eclecticism, however, as can be seen in two churches. The earlier of these is the Central Christian Church in Austin (FIG. 5.34), designed in 1928 by Robert Leon White with Ralph Cameron and Samuel Vosper.[22] The second is the Third Church of Christ Scientist in Dallas (FIG. 5.35), de-

and somewhat cloistered patio on the south approach: a private space in contrast to the more public main entrance on the north. Although the tile roofs and iron balconies establish the building's Spanish character, the absence of specific classical or Baroque detail gives Gearing Hall a vernacular and even domestic aspect appropriate to its function. As Carol McMichael has written, "In Home Economics, Cret created a rational and symmetrical plan with a true expression of the masses on traditional Beaux Arts principles; at the same time he produced the effect of an almost provincial and vernacular air of relaxed and varied massing that has grown through the process of accretion."[21]

Between Cass Gilbert's library in 1916 and Paul Cret's decisive intervention in 1933, the Austin campus had been placed largely in the hands of Greene, LaRoche and Dahl, whose academic buildings I have described as derivative of Gilbert's Sutton Hall. In 1930, Greene's firm also designed the Gregory Gymnasium for the Austin campus, but in the widely popular idiom best described as Regional Romanesque.

signed in 1932 by Mark Lemmon.[23] In both cases it is the red-tile roof that signifies regional content, and the handsome detailing in brick with restrained stone trim that establishes the Romanesque idiom. Lemmon, who was also an adept manipulator of Ecclesiastical Gothic, created a particularly engaging ensemble, which, because it cannot be attributed to any single historical model, is appropriate for a modern Protestant denomination that has no pronounced theological or liturgical roots in Christian history.

The eclectic freedom to combine various regionalist sources in a single composition is demonstrated superbly at Loretto Academy in El Paso (FIG. 5.36), designed in 1923 by Trost and Trost.[24] Two wings devoted to school and convent functions converge upon the dominant chapel, which is set diagonally and linked to the wings by curving loggias. The buff plaster walls and red-tile roofs unite school and chapel in a common regional sensibility that belies the separate sources of the parts. The wings are a rather neutral Mediterranean Classicism, except for touches of Spanish Baroque detail at the entrances. The curving loggias strongly suggest Baroque sources, although not specifically Spanish ones. The exuberant two-story chapel portal is decisively Spanish Baroque, but the chapel form to which it is applied is stylistically indeterminant, and the single asymmetrically placed tower is derived from the Italian Romanesque. In short, Loretto Academy is a composite of various sources, and a tour de force of regional eclecticism.

FIG. 5.35
THIRD CHURCH OF CHRIST SCIENTIST,
Dallas. 1932.
Mark Lemmon, architect.

FIG. 5.36
LORETTO ACADEMY,
El Paso. 1923.
Trost and Trost, architects.

FIG. 5.37
EL CAPITAN HOTEL (now VAN HORN
STATE BANK),
Van Horn. 1926.
Trost and Trost, architects.

### THE PUEBLO AND
### MESO-AMERICAN REVIVALS

Although the Pueblo Revival in the 1910's and 1920's was largely confined to New Mexico, it figured prominently in the extensive regional practice of Trost and Trost. Their Franciscan Hotel in Albuquerque (FIG. 5.03) was one of the principal monuments of the revival, and the style was used for several of the firm's small-town hotels built to accommodate automobile touring in the 1920's (see Chapter 4). Of three such Texas hotels designed by the firm, the El Capitan in Van Horn (now the Van Horn State Bank; FIG. 5.37) is probably the finest specimen of the Pueblo Revival in Texas.

Unlike other manifestations of southwestern regionalism, which depended on tile roofs for Spanish character, the New Mexico pueblos had flat roofs protected by parapets. Roofs were framed in roughly

shaped logs that projected through the adobe walls (*vigas*). Wall openings were also framed with wooden lintels, and wooden pergolas were sometimes used, but arcaded forms were impossible to construct in the adobe technique. Surfaces and edges were soft and amorphous, unlike the more precise, plastered masonry surfaces of the Spanish Colonial architecture of Texas. The larger openings of Pueblo Revival structures often featured lintels supported on corbeled haunches. Sometimes called "flat arches," these approximate the parabolic arches found so often in progressive architecture as an alternative to more historical shapes. All of these characteristics, derived from primitive techniques of adobe construction in the seventeenth century, of course became strictly stylistic or ornamental devices in the Pueblo Revival. All are found on the El Capitan Hotel, which is organized as a U-shaped block of public spaces about a front patio, not unlike the firm's El Paisano Hotel in Marfa, rendered in the Spanish Colonial mode (see the next section).

Such fully comprehended examples of the Pueblo Revival are rare in Texas, particularly in nonresidential structures. One can occasionally discern some trace elements, however. The Masonic temple in Gainesville (FIG. 5.38), designed in 1926 by F. E. Robertson, displays such suggestive trace elements. Although executed in exposed brick, the soft curve of the parapet and window profiles suggests the Pueblo style, and the *vigas* have been abstracted as a row of ornamental bosses. The Gainesville temple might almost be interpreted as a modernistic abstraction of the Pueblo Revival style. Similarly, at the West Texas Utility Company Office in Ozona (FIG. 5.39), the treatment of the show window, doorway, and porch seem like abstractions of Pueblo Revival details.

In the 1920's, the Pueblo Revival seemed to some observers to be not only another historical style, but also a point of departure for a truly modern architecture. Trost and Trost's Franciscan Hotel in Albuquerque was recognized in Europe as a provocative new form with affinities to Cubism and Expressionism, and, prior to his move to California, Rudolf Schindler showed a strong interest in the New Mexico pueblos, which is well documented.[25] Progressive modernists were drawn to the similarities between pueblo construction and reinforced concrete, both of which were seen as generating blank-wall surfaces and flat roofs. Irving Gill and Schindler had both experimented (Gill before World War I and Schindler soon after) with new techniques of reinforced concrete construction, which was believed to be regionally appropriate to California. In fact, identical forms can be produced by casting concrete or plastering masonry, and, occasionally, starkly modeled forms with flat roofs lying somewhere between Regional Eclecticism and modern regionalism were constructed. A rare example of this ambiguity in Texas is the First Christian Church in Marfa of 1926 (FIG. 5.40). Only minor details, such as the scalloped parapet, bell portal, and tiled porch roofs, separate the Marfa church from Irving Gill's Christian Science Church at Coronado of 1929.

FIG. 5.38
MASONIC TEMPLE,
Gainesville. 1926.
F. E. Robertson, architect.

FIG. 5.39
WEST TEXAS UTILITY
COMPANY OFFICE,
Ozona. N.D.

FIG. 5.40
FIRST CHRISTIAN CHURCH,
Marfa. 1926.

FIG. 5.41
AZTEC HOTEL,
Monrovia, Calif. 1925.
Walter Stacy-Judd, architect.

The Meso-American styles were very different from the New Mexico pueblos. As the stone-built, monumental architecture of an advanced civilization, the pre-Columbian temples differed profoundly from the indigenous vernacular forms of the pueblo villages. Yet, in comparison to the evolving stone architecture that the Spanish transported to Mexico, the pre-Columbian monuments were technically conservative. Unlike Western European architecture since the Roman Empire, they were primarily ensembles of mass, with relatively insignificant interior spaces. The structural technique of corbel vaulting limited the size of interior rooms and also led to a characteristic proportion in which a tall, frequently sloping attic enclosed and stabilized the corbel vault within. This tall attic, often separated from the lower story by a frieze of ornament, became the most commonly imitated form convention of the Meso-American Revival, and influenced the modernistic idiom of the 1930's as well. The Meso-American arch—derived from the corbeling technique whether stepped or slope-sided—was superficially similar to the approximately parabolic flat arch of the Pueblo Revival, and some designers combined the two influences. The leading interpreter of the Meso-American Revival in the United States was probably Walter Stacy-Judd of Los Angeles. His Aztec Hotel of 1925 in Monrovia, Calif. (FIG. 5.41), is heavily encrusted in Meso-American ornament that, if stripped away, would leave a building mass essentially compatible with the Pueblo style. Similarly, Walter Burley Grif-

fin's design for the Chemistry Building at the University of New Mexico in Albuquerque (1914) is
variously interpreted as Prairie
School, Pueblo Revival, or Meso-
American. It doubtless combines all
three influences.[26]

Meso-American ornament was
perhaps more easily translated to
contemporary use than were the
larger forms or proportions of the
style. As a style of geometrically abstracted but recognizable iconography primarily confined to full face
and profile, it was fundamentally
architectonic in origin and hence
easier to adapt to contemporary architecture than such concurrent artistic stimuli as African sculpture
or Native American art. It also conveyed the impression of being applied in *horror vacui*, which suited
it to such lavish (tasteless, to some
critics) decorative programs as those
applied to movie theaters, where it
represented an equally exotic alternative to the Egyptian, the Oriental,
or the Islamic. Aztec and Mayan
Theaters joined the Alhambras and
Majestics all over America in the
late 1920's.

The most important example of
this minor mode in Texas is the Casino Club Building in San Antonio
(FIG. 5.42), designed in 1926 by the
Kelwood Company.[27] The stepped-
pyramidal treatment of the salient
tower seems derived from Meso-
American sources, as does the sloping profile of the attic. The unusual
depth and ponderous elaboration of
the top floor, although related to
many such penthouse floors in
more conventionally styled buildings, nevertheless suggests the
heavy attic of Meso-American ar-

FIG. 5.42
CASINO CLUB BUILDING,
San Antonio. 1926.
The Kelwood Company, architects.

FIG. 5.43
AZTEC THEATER,
Eagle Pass. 1915.
Leonard F. Sneed, designer.

chitecture; yet no specific source can be identified. It is the carved ornament on the top and bottom floors, however, that unmistakably establishes the Meso-American character of the Casino Club, although whether this should be considered a species of Regional Eclecticism, rather than part of the modernistic idiom, is subject to interpretation.

The earliest use of the Meso-American style in the United States may have been the Aztec Theater in Eagle Pass (FIG. 5.43), designed by Leonard F. Sneed in 1915.[28] Despite its name, the Aztec Theater is actually a bizarre and fanciful mixture of Islamic and Egyptian elements, and the patterns of diaper ornament might be just as easily derived from Islamic as from Meso-American sources. In the spirit of theatrical fantasy, it is closer to the Alhambra in El Paso or the (demolished) Hippodrome in Dallas than to the later and more archaeologically convincing work of Walter Stacy Judd or the Kelwood Company.[29]

None of these styles—Pueblo Revival, Meso-American, or Regional Romanesque—was the true successor to the Mission Revival, however. That role fell to the Spanish Colonial Revival, which rose to supplant the earlier phase of Regional Eclecticism about the time of World War I. Of all the Regional Eclectic modes, it was the most significant in the history of Texas architecture.

## THE SPANISH COLONIAL REVIVAL

Spanish conquest and colonization in North and South America (and the Philippines) coincided with the Renaissance in Europe. Columbus' discovery of America in 1492 in the name of Ferdinand and Isabella coincided with the conquest of Granada by the Catholic sovereigns and the final expulsion of the Moors from Spain, leaving a residual content of Islamic or "Mudejar" style in the arts of design that was frequently drawn upon by Spanish Colonial Revivalists of the twentieth century. The *Mudejar* style of geometric surface ornament (Islam had discouraged any form of figural iconography), executed by converted Muslim craftsmen for Christian patrons, coincided with the importation of Italian Renaissance design and with the influx of gold and silver bullion from the New World. The increased supply of precious metals caused the metalsmith's craft to flourish and to influence the other arts of design. The term "Plateresque" (from *platero*, silversmith) is applied to the first phase of Renaissance design in Spain. It is characterized by the incorporation of Renaissance motifs into a style of overall surface ornament in shallow relief that was influenced by the techniques of the metalsmith. The Plateresque phase in Spain lasted from the 1480's until the mid-1550's, roughly coinciding with the retirement (1556) and death (1559) of the king of Spain and Holy Roman Emperor, Charles V, Ferdinand and Isabella's grandson.

Under the austere influence of Charles' son, Phillip II, Spanish architecture and design experienced a reaction against the decorative exu-

berance of the Plateresque. George Kubler has described this phase, which lasted for nearly a century, as the Purist style; the Escorial is its transcendent monument, but also erected in this phase were great works in Mexico and Peru, including the Cathedral of Mexico, begun in the 1570's.[30] The establishment of Spanish control over the New Mexican pueblos occurred during this time, but Santa Fe was so remote from the viceroy's court in Mexico City that the Spanish necessarily adopted the indigenous adobe construction of the natives. Between Santa Fe and the Valley of Mexico stretched a thousand miles of wilderness valued only for its occasional mineral wealth and for the souls of the nomadic Indian tribes who inhabited it. Claimed by Spain and explored in the sixteenth century by Coronado and others, these vast tracts of wilderness were only slowly and imperfectly integrated into the Spanish Colonial system. Except in New Mexico, within the Spanish borderlands of the present United States effective conversion of the natives and settlement of Spanish subjects occurred only in the eighteenth century, as earlier attempts to found missions in Texas and Arizona had failed.

Meanwhile, in about 1650, Spanish architecture experienced a reaction against the Purist style, giving rise to the Spanish Baroque. The Baroque in Spain and Spanish America was characterized by an intense concentration of ornament on certain salient building parts, especially doors and windows, and, in church architecture, by a preference for the twin-towered facade. These attributes can be seen in the Texas missions of the Alamo chain, particularly in the masterpiece of the series, Mission San Jose y San Miguel de Aguayo in San Antonio. The two-story sculptural main portal is typical of Spanish Baroque design, with its fusion of architectural membering, statuary, and foliate ornament. The great sacristy window at Mission San Jose is one of the finest specimens of the style anywhere in Spanish America. The Spanish Baroque was translated, with provincial adaptations, in Texas beginning in the 1720's, Arizona in the 1760's, and California in the 1770's.

Ironically, the Mission Revival originated in California and not in Texas, and the California missions were better known, if not more accurately understood, than the Texas missions for some thirty years. The Mission Revival in Texas was largely an importation from California, as has been seen, and consisted largely of a few suggestive motifs: the tile roof, the curved parapet, the bracketed eave line, the arcaded *portales.* This style began to seem banal and unsophisticated in comparison to the Beaux-Arts Classic or the Ecclesiastical Gothic, and once again it was the intervention of an Eastern architect that led to a stylistic transformation in Regional Eclecticism. The architect was Bertram Grosvenor Goodhue, and the occasion was the Panama-Pacific Exposition in San Diego in 1915 (FIG. 5.02). Earlier plans for the exposition had been drawn up in the Mission Style by Irving Gill of San Diego. Goodhue persuaded the board to substitute a more academically learned and ornamentally elaborate parti based on the Spanish Baroque.[31] This new mode of regional expression became widely popular after World War I, in Texas and throughout the Southwest, in contrast to the rather tepid reception that the Mission Revival had received in Texas.

Perhaps the new mode should be called the Spanish Baroque Revival, but designers were not always stylistically scrupulous in their choice of models. Both Plateresque and Baroque ornament were employed, and Plateresque was frequently mixed with Islamic and even late-Gothic details. Various permutations of vernacular architecture, generically Mediterranean or Andalusian, were also employed on less formal building types. Therefore, the general term Spanish Colonial Revival seems more appropriate than Spanish Baroque. The new phase, like the Mission Revival before it, of course was highly eclectic, so the term "revival" is something of a misnomer, retained for customary convenience. Only rarely were specific historical monuments replicated with the fidelity of a true revival.

The distinction between Mission Revival and Spanish Colonial is both stylistic and chronological. The later, post–World War I work tended to be more sophisticated and more learned in its sources, if not more accurate in application. Nevertheless, the leitmotifs of the Mission style recur frequently in the Spanish Colonial Revival, just as Baroque ornament occasionally figures in the Mission Revival. I have maintained a chronological distinction in view of this ambiguity. Most examples of Spanish Colonial influence occurring before 1917 I have considered Mission; those after World War I are classified as Spanish Colonial.

Since the most significant monuments of Catholic Spain in the New World were churches, the ecclesiastical architecture of the Spanish Colonial Revival seems like an appropriate point at which to begin the discussion. At the one extreme of literal revivalism, St. Francis Catholic Church in Waco (FIG. 5.44), designed in 1931 by Roy E. Lane, is an almost exact copy of Mission San Jose, complete with the famous sacristy window but without the domed crossing. The bell stage of one of the twin towers, left incomplete at Mission San Jose, is similarly omitted at St. Francis.[32] Most architects used the Spanish Colonial Revival as a vehicle for a more creative eclecticism, however.

One of the earliest and most influential Spanish Colonial Revival churches in Texas is University Baptist Church in Austin (FIG. 5.45), on Guadalupe Street facing the University of Texas campus. It was designed in 1921 by Albert Kelsey of Philadelphia, sometime partner of Paul Philippe Cret.[33] There is nothing particularly Spanish about the configuration of the church, which is basilican in section, has deep transepts, and is raised above a high basement. Neither a domed crossing nor twin front towers, which might be found on most eighteenth-century Spanish Baroque churches, are employed at University Baptist, and the soft tan brick is hardly a historically authentic material. It is the red-tile roof and Spanish Baroque ornament, on the transept windows and particularly on the three-story entrance portal, that signify regional character. One enters the building through a ground-story vestibule at street level, passing

FIG. 5.44
ST. FRANCIS CATHOLIC CHURCH,
Waco. 1931.
Roy E. Lane, architect.

FIG. 5.45
UNIVERSITY BAPTIST CHURCH,
Austin. 1921.
Albert Kelsey, architect.

FIG. 5.46
EPISCOPAL CHURCH OF THE ADVENT,
Brownsville. 1927.
McLaren and Bliss, architects.

through side stairs to the sanctuary level, expressed as a *piano nobile* with three high-arched windows. This is a departure from the more commonly equal height of main floor and choir loft found in the Spanish Baroque, and reflects the different liturgical character of a Baptist church. The figure sculpture used so profusely on Spanish Baroque churches is avoided on a Baptist church, but the ornamental vocabulary of scrolls, shells, finials, and spirally fluted columns is interpreted authentically.

A more picturesque and vernacular character was achieved by McLaren and Bliss on their Episcopal Church of the Advent in Brownsville of 1927 (FIG. 5.46), which might be interpreted as an attempt to regionalize the comfortable informality of the English parish church. The forms of the sanctuary, parish house, and Sunday school are kept low, spread out behind lawns and hedges, and anchored to the site by the picturesquely situated tower in the reentrant angle, a placement frequently used in the Ecclesiastical Gothic as well. The entrance to the sanctuary is through a side vestibule, which is balanced by a baptistry on the opposite wall. The end wall of the sanctuary is treated as a curved parapet and set with an elegantly framed window, the most overtly Baroque feature of the church. Although the red-tile roofs project slightly beyond the plastered walls, the elaborate eave bracketing of the Mission Revival is avoided.[34]

The most obvious model of a Spanish Baroque church, with twin towers, aisle-less nave, shallow chancel and transepts, and domed crossing, seems to have been imitated rarely in the church architecture of the Spanish Colonial Revival in Texas. Derived ultimately from Il Gesu and other Counter-Reformation churches in Rome, the type was perhaps too closely identified with Catholic worship to provide a comfortable model for Protestant churches. Except for St. Francis in Waco, the Catholic Church in Texas also did not use Spanish Baroque, but instead clung to Romanesque and Gothic styles. The twin-towered Spanish Baroque facade was, however, quite influential on institutional architecture, particularly on the civic auditoriums that were built in so many Texas towns and cities in the 1920's.

It seems strange that, of the surviving courthouses of Texas constructed between World War I and the Depression, only the one for Hudspeth County in Sierra Blanca (1919) was designed in the Spanish Colonial mode. However, the style was widely employed for city halls and auditoriums, sometimes jointly in the same building and sometimes as separate facilities. The San Antonio Municipal Auditorium of 1926 (FIG. 5.47), designed by the consortium of Atlee B. and Robert M. Ayres, George Willis, and E. T. Jackson, represents a common Spanish Colonial parti. The broad, low, paired towers, crowned by glazed ceramic-tile domes and enclosing an art gallery and a lecture hall respectively, flank a tall arcaded entrance loggia leading to the main lobby. The auditorium itself is an irregular octagon that encloses a horseshoe of seating on two levels about the arena, with a rear stage for more theatrical spectacles balancing the lobby on the front. The monumental entrance faces an urban plaza. The composition resolves a triangu-

FIG. 5.47
SAN ANTONIO MUNICIPAL
AUDITORIUM. 1926.
Atlee B. and Robert M. Ayres,
George Willis, E. T. Jackson, architects.

lar site resulting from the city's irregular street system, and manages to be both formal when viewed frontally and picturesque when approached on a diagonal. This ability to resolve both formal and picturesque values in design seems to have been one of the principal attractions of the Spanish Colonial Revival.[35] The San Antonio Municipal Auditorium was quite similar to the State Fair Music Hall in Dallas, which has, however, been extensively altered. Together, the San Antonio and Dallas facilities comprise the largest genre of Spanish Colonial Revival auditoriums in Texas.[36]

The smaller cities of Texas could not afford the luxury of separate facilities for government and culture. Page Brothers designed several composite facilities in which the functions of city hall and municipal auditorium were placed side by side. That for Sweetwater in 1926 (FIG. 5.48) features a conventional audi-

FIG. 5.48
CITY HALL AND MUNICIPAL
AUDITORIUM,
Sweetwater. 1926.
Page Brothers, architects.

FIG. 5.49
CITY HALL AND MUNICIPAL
AUDITORIUM,
Mexia. 1927.
Page Brothers, architects.

torium—an arcaded loggia flanked by twin towers. The city hall is appended as a separate mass to one side. The elaborate Baroque side entrance to the city hall does not really correct the impression of an unresolved dichotomy between unequal functions.[37] Page Brothers handled this problem much more successfully at Mexia in 1927 (FIG. 5.49). Here, a single low tower of conventional Spanish character is placed on the corner of the town hall, where it tends to balance the greater mass of the auditorium. The Mexia City Hall and Auditorium is a very skillful exercise in picturesque composition; it is one of the most successful designs in the Spanish Colonial Revival in Texas. It should be noted that considered alone, the auditorium would be taken for Regional Romanesque, with its blind arcade above the entrance loggia and arcaded corbel table along the roofline. When combined with the Spanish Baroque details of the city hall, however, a harmonious regional eclectic ensemble was produced.

An alternative to the side-by-side parti was to place the city hall functions in front of the auditorium. A central entrance lobby could serve both the public auditorium and, through lateral corridors on several floors, the spreading wings of government offices. This parti had been employed in the Beaux-Arts Classic mode at Beaumont (FIG. 4.21), and was adapted to Spanish Colonial guise for the City Hall and Auditorium in Wichita Falls (FIG. 5.50), designed in 1927 by Lang and Witchell in association with the local firm of Voelcker and Dixon.[38] Paired towers are situated at the outer corners of the auditorium, but they tend to diminish, through foreshortening, behind the mass of the city hall as one approaches the main entrance. This centralized, triple-arched entrance loggia, and the three prominently framed windows above, are the building's principal vehicles of Spanish Colonial character. The ornament on the triple entrance is an exuberant applique of the Spanish Baroque; the window frames above are somewhat more restrained. This detail is done in natural terra-cotta, which matches the soft buff brick against which it is set. As a result, the design loses the sense of historical authenticity that stone and plaster would convey, and the ornamental conventions appear arbitrary rather than intrinsic to a fully comprehended style.

The potential of the Spanish Colonial Revival for picturesque and historically authentic composition is demonstrated superbly, however, by Lang and Witchell's Highland Park City Hall of 1924 (FIG. 5.51). It was designed as a companion to an earlier Mission Revival fire station by the same firm, which was demolished when the city hall was later expanded to incorporate public-safety functions. The single, asymmetrically placed tower, along with the elaborate two-story Baroque portal, provides a superb picturesque and ornamental focal point for the small building of blank plaster walls and tile roofs. Additional ornament is concentrated on the (present) library windows at the rear of the building. Although the main entrance is unquestionably Baroque, with its spirally fluted columns, the ornament on the library windows seems more Plateresque. But such distinctions hardly matter in Regional Eclecticism,

FIG. 5.50
CITY HALL AND MUNICIPAL
AUDITORIUM,
Wichita Falls. 1927.
Lang and Witchell, architects.
Voelcker and Dixon, associate architects.

where character and sensibility are more important than scholarly accuracy.[39]

The exotic but effective blend of Mediterranean, Romanesque, and Byzantine sources that Ralph Adams Cram created for Rice Institute in 1910 never became a widespread institutional style, despite the continued influence of Cram and Ferguson on Houston architecture (Goodhue dropped out of the partnership in 1914). The firm's subsequent work in Houston, all done in association with William Ward Watkin, represents a potpourri of fashionable eclectic modes: Ecclesiastical Gothic for Trinity Episcopal Church in 1919 (FIG. 4.40); Beaux-Arts Classic for the Museum of Fine Arts in 1924 (FIG. 4.25); and finally, Spanish Colonial Revival for the Houston Public Library in 1926 (FIG. 5.52; now the Julia Ideson Building). The Houston library is an L-shaped,

FIG. 5.51
HIGHLAND PARK CITY HALL. 1924.
Lang and Witchell, architects.

FIG. 5.52
HOUSTON PUBLIC LIBRARY
(now JULIA IDESON BUILDING). 1926.
Cram and Ferguson, architects.
William Ward Watkin, associate architect.

complexly modeled building constructed partly of brick and partly of stone, with a subtle shift of scales at the main floor or *piano nobile,* which contains the main reading rooms. The limestone centerpiece of the main facade suggests a careful study of Spanish sources—in this case, Plateresque rather than Baroque, resembling the university in Alcala de Henares of 1537–1553. It is perhaps the most academically learned monument of the Spanish Colonial Revival in Texas, and yet, like Cram's work at Rice, it had little influence. Perhaps it was too scholarly and accurate, too subtle and mannered, lacking in the more obvious symbols of Regional Eclecticism.[40]

The Spanish Colonial Revival was commonly used in the 1920's for other public buildings, such as schools, usually with rather indifferent effect. School design usually consisted of tiled parapets and

touches of Spanish Baroque ornament applied to entrances and prominent windows. The form and fenestration patterns of the schools were generated by modern educational planning, which had little to do with the forms and rhythms of eighteenth-century Spain. The result was an arbitrary ornamental style that may have lacked both historical authenticity and true regional character, but that usually did not impose preconceived forms on school design.

The modern elementary school evolved in the 1920's and 1930's toward a lateral expansion to ever-larger sites with extensive playground space. The compact two-story blocks of the pre–World War I period tended to be replaced by single-story schools, which gave greater prominence to activity rooms. This development has been demonstrated at the Raymondville School of 1924 (FIG. 4.29). Page Brothers became one of the most prolific firms of school designers in Texas during this period. Their High and Ward School in Refugio of 1933 illustrates these tendencies toward dispersion (FIG. 5.53). Here, the architects have created an asymmetrical, picturesque composition by projecting the assembly room forward on the right, which balances a long expanse of classrooms on the left. The main entrance, placed as a fulcrum between these two elements, is faintly Spanish in character, with its arcaded porch and squat reentrant tower. The details are evocative rather than historically specific: the suggestion of *vigas,* a wrought-iron medallion rather than Baroque carving, round arches, an arcaded corbel table with tile coping. Roofs are flat. It is a modern school discretely decorated in Regional Eclectic allusions. By this date, other designers were applying modernistic detail to similar features of schools planned around modern conceptions of education.

If elementary school design became more dispersed after World War I, high schools became, if anything, even larger and more prominent as cultural institutions. Because of their large size, they remained multistory structures of enormous bulk and considerable functional diversity, posing a challenge to designers in terms of formal composition. The renewed tendency toward picturesque design of the 1920's, more amenable to Spanish Colonial than to more canonical Academic Eclectic modes, invited architects to experiment with a modulated articulation of the building mass coupled with a Regional Eclectic interpretation of the details and ornament. Two examples stand out: Lubbock High School, and Thomas Jefferson High School in San Antonio.

Lubbock High School (FIG. 5.54) was designed by the local firm of Peters, Strange and Bradshaw in 1929. The enormous and diversified bulk, which was given several additions, has been broken down into a U-shaped sequence of one-, two-, and three-story forms, constructed of buff brick with Spanish tile roofs and minimal regionalist detail, including pilaster strips and an arcaded corbel table that are more Romanesque than Spanish Colonial. The auditorium has been projected forward in the center of this U, connected to the extremities by arcaded *portales* that enclose landscaped courtyards. Although the basic disposition of the plan is sym-

FIG. 5.53
HIGH AND WARD SCHOOL,
Refugio. 1933.
Page Brothers, architects.

metrical, the auditorium has been fronted with an offset main entrance and Spanish Baroque tower. The total effect of Lubbock High School is that of a picturesque assemblage of forms and details, in which pictorial effect masks but does not impede the orderly and efficient planning of the institution. The use of a pointed arch for the main entrance demonstrates the extreme eclectic flexibility of the Spanish Colonial mode, which, in a search for evocative details, can be extended backward even to the Isabelline period of the late-fifteenth century.[41]

Thomas Jefferson High School in San Antonio (FIG. 5.55), designed in 1932 by Adams and Adams, has much in common with Lubbock High School, including the projection of the auditorium and the use of an arcaded *portales* to enclose landscaped courtyards. The main entrance is located in the reentrant

FIG. 5.54
LUBBOCK HIGH SCHOOL. 1929.
Peters, Strange and Bradshaw, architects.

FIG. 5.55
THOMAS JEFFERSON HIGH SCHOOL,
San Antonio. 1932.
Adams and Adams, architects.

FIG. 5.56
SCOTTISH RITE CATHEDRAL,
Galveston. 1929.
Alfred C. Finn, architect.

corner between the projecting auditorium and the classroom block, rather as Page Brothers had done at Refugio. Now, however, the entrance becomes an exuberant Baroque portal flanked by two domed towers of unequal size, the larger of which occupies the reentrant corner of the auditorium. The diagonal approach to this entrance enhances the picturesque aspect of the tower as a visual reference point. Seen from a distance across the extensive campus park, it becomes a vertical anchor for the sprawling wings of this modern high school. Although the ornamentation on the entrance is a rather heavy-handed Baroque, that on the projecting auditorium wing seems abstracted into art deco. By 1932 the modernistic idiom was well established, and it is not surprising to find Regional Eclectic design being crossbred with the new style. The same eclectic habits of design that could combine Gothic, Islamic, Plateresque, Baroque, and Meso-American into a single southwestern regional sensibility could also absorb elements of the modernistic idiom.[42]

Just as Robertson at the Gainesville Masonic Temple (FIG. 5.38) had abstracted and modernized the forms of the Pueblo Revival, so Alfred C. Finn at the Galveston Scottish Rite Cathedral of 1929 (FIG. 5.56) seems to have designed a modernistic abstraction of the generalized regional idiom. The studied asymmetry of the building in both mass and elevation unites it to the picturesque composition of much Spanish Colonial work, as does the obvious arcaded loggia. The unorthodox fenestration and the simplified cornice betray modernistic tendencies, although there are no clear quotations from Saarinen, Goodhue, or Cret, the seminal formgivers of the modernistic style.[43]

Although Texas railroad stations are primarily associated with the Mission Revival prior to World War I, several were built in the Spanish Colonial Revival in the 1920's. The Southern Pacific Depot in Brownsville (FIG. 5.57) was designed in 1928 by Ray W. Barnes, the railroad's chief engineer. As might be expected from an in-house company design, the Brownsville station retains a strong flavor of the Mission Revival, although combined with Renaissance and Baroque details. As a highly picturesque assemblage of forms in plaster and Spanish tile, it invites comparison with Wyatt C. Hedrick and Co.'s symmetrical but superbly detailed stone station for the Fort Worth and Denver South Plains Railroad in Lubbock of the same year (FIG. 5.58). The two stations represent alternative interpretations of the Spanish Colonial Revival.[44]

Even more than as a vehicle for institutional design, however, the Spanish Colonial Revival flourished as a commercial medium. Its commercial application ranged from hotels and office buildings to shopping centers and service stations; the last of these began springing up in the 1920's among the new building types of the automobile age. The El Paisano Hotel in Marfa of 1926 (FIGS. 5.59 and 5.60), like the Gage in Marathon and the El Capitan in Van Horn, was designed by Trost and Trost to cater to the motoring public on the fringes of the Big Bend country. The parti of El Paisano is similar to that of El Capitan; both

FIG. 5.57
SOUTHERN PACIFIC DEPOT,
Brownsville, 1928.
Ray W. Barnes, designer.

FIG. 5.58
FORT WORTH AND DENVER
SOUTH PLAINS RAILROAD STATION,
Lubbock. 1928.
Wyatt C. Hedrick and Co., architects.

FIG. 5.59
EL PAISANO HOTEL,
Marfa. 1926.
Trost and Trost, architects.

FIG. 5.60
EL PAISANO HOTEL. Lobby.

are U-shaped in plan and are organized about a front patio framed by
wings. The plaster wall surfaces are
more precise than the deliberately
amorphous Pueblo Revival forms,
however, and are capped with a tile
coping. The ornamental vocabulary
is Spanish Baroque, applied at a
number of salient points on the
building. The hotel is situated on
the southwest corner of Marfa's
main street, which leads from the
railroad (and parallel national highway) to the courthouse on the north.
The ground level of this main-street
frontage is lined with shops, interrupted by a two-story Baroque entrance portal that connects to a passage leading to the lobby. Since this
monumental portal is not centered
on the long street facade, a pavilion
has been created on the salient corner to visually minimize this dis-
crepancy, and also to inflect toward
the dominant intersection. This
corner pavilion consists of elaborately framed windows with projecting iron balconies, rusticated pilaster strips, and finials. The lobby
can also be entered from the side
street through the patio. The lunch-
room, parlor, and dining room are
placed in the wing west of the patio,
balancing the shops and other services in the east wing. The interior
of El Paisano, like all of Trost and
Trost's small hotels, is executed in a
generalized regional idiom of tiled
floors and wainscots, exposed beam
ceilings, roughcast plaster walls,
and carved woodwork. Parabolic
arches are used to frame main openings, and the parlor fireplace is
carved with Meso-American ornament. Taken together with the Gage
and El Capitan, and with the firm's
other hotels in New Mexico and Arizona, El Paisano is a remarkable ex-

FIG. 5.61
LAS LOMAS HOTEL,
Junction. 1926.

ercise in both functional planning
and regional character.[45]

Not all Spanish Colonial–style
hotels built in the 1920's for the motoring public in Texas were as elaborately provided with specifically Baroque ornament. Las Lomas Hotel
in Junction (FIG. 5.61), built in 1926,
is a more vernacular conception relying on plaster, tiled roofs, and an
arcaded *portales* for regional character. The L-shaped building is composed about a low tower in the reentrant angle and an arcaded porch
off the lobby and dining room, supporting a second-floor terrace above.
A similar vernacular Spanish idiom
was used for the Yacht Club Hotel
in Port Isabel and for La Posada
Hotel in McAllen, which brought
tourist facilities to the Rio Grande
valley.

By the 1930's, the first motor
courts had appeared to compete
with hotels for the allegiance of
the motoring public and to provide
cheap lodgings for the dispossessed
during the Depression. In Texas and

FIG. 5.62
CORTEZ HOTEL,
El Paso. 1926.
Trost and Trost, architects.

the Southwest these tended to draw upon the Spanish Colonial Revival. Some people claim that the Casa Grande Motor Lodge in El Paso was the first motel in Texas. In Dallas, Fooshee and Cheek designed the Grande Court Tourist Lodge in 1931. Neither of these motor courts survive, but the genre endured even beyond World War II. Alamo Plaza motels were built as late as 1948 in both Houston and Dallas.[46]

If small-town hotels and motor courts lent themselves to the picturesque and historical character that the Spanish Colonial Revival seemed to engender, the Cortez Hotel in El Paso (FIG. 5.62; also known as the Orndorf) demonstrated the problems inherent in applying historical styles to buildings of unprecedented type and scale.[47] Designed by Trost and Trost in 1926, the Cortez occupies one side of Main Plaza in El Paso, a typical location for large urban hotels in the 1920's. At street level, the dense Plateresque ornament in terra-cotta applied to the ground floor and *piano nobile* is reasonably effective, but above the second floor the application of ornament seems spotty and arbitrary, lacking sharp contrast in either depth or color from the soft brick wall surfaces. The Cortez also seems to lack a satisfactory vertical termination. Other designers tended to put Spanish roofs on such buildings or to apply arcades to the penthouse floor. When applied to tall buildings, historical ornament of any derivation seemed to require a certain architectonic abstraction, just as wall surfaces called for some articulation beyond the regular placement of uniform windows. An extreme case of the use of Spanish Baroque ornament to define a skyscraper is the Southwestern Bell Telephone Building in San Antonio (FIG. 5.63), designed by I. R. Timlin in 1931.[48] By this date most designers of skyscrapers had adopted the modernistic idiom; hence, the exuberant Baroque ornament used for the entrances at Southwestern Bell is doubly anachronistic. It seems both chronologically *retardataire* and stylistically unassimilated to the articulated verticality of the rest of the building.

The automobile made the single greatest impact on American culture in the 1920's. Still largely a sportsman's toy before World War I, or confined to intracity deliveries as a commercial vehicle, the automobile and truck became integral parts of American life after the war; by 1932 automobile registration in the United States had risen to 26.5 million vehicles. As I have described in Chapters 3 and 4, both Prairie School ornament and the Commercial Gothic were used to give character to automobile trade buildings as they found their place in the service zone of transition around the urban business district. Stimulated by the National Highway System, however, a new form of commercial architecture became prevalent along the highway margins and the corridor streets that carried the new routes through towns and into and out of the cities: the commercial strip. The most common design idiom for these new commercial strips in the 1920's was the Spanish Colonial Revival.[49] And the most prominent and radical of these were structures built for servicing the vehicles themselves, ranging from simple service stations to full-scale automobile dealerships. Before the war, a gasoline pump at curbside

FIG. 5.63
SOUTHWESTERN BELL
TELEPHONE BUILDING,
San Antonio. 1931.
I. R. Timlin, architect.

FIG. 5.64
MICHIE BUILDING,
Childress. 1926.

nize with its main street neighbors. The Michie Building in Childress of 1926 (FIG. 5.64) is one of the elaborate specimens of this type in Texas. The handsomely proportioned segmental arches and the discrete detail in brick stand out as exceptional. This type was sometimes taken over and expanded in the 1930's, when the major tire companies augmented their marketing efforts by opening "super stations," which not only sold tires and accessories but also competed with independent garages to provide mechanical services.

With the onset of the Depression, service stations could no longer expect to make a profit merely by dispensing gasoline. Led by Shell Oil Company, the major chains embarked on an aggressive campaign for the gasoline market by building new and larger stations, and for the first time began to compete with independent garages in tires, batteries, lubrication, washing, and minor repairs. In functional terms, this entailed the addition of one or more service bays to the original office pavilion, and often the addition of a second pump island. The service station was now treated as a freestanding entity, detached from any contiguous street facade, and was normally built along the highway margin beyond the main street. Initially, at least in the Southwest, these were often executed in a recognizably Spanish idiom, with plastered walls and tiled visors. Many of these survive, although only a few are still in use as gasoline stations. The one in Palo Pinto (FIG. 5.65) is typical of the genre. In the course of the 1930's such stations would take on a modernistic stylization, but the practice in the West of providing

had been added to many livery stables and general stores, anticipating the automobile service garage, which remained the primary dispenser of gasoline, despite the proliferation of gasoline filling stations in the 1920's, until the Depression.[50]

The simplest form of service garage was built into a main street intersection, with a diagonal drive-through and pump island sheltered by a canopy that was an extension of the street facade. Service bays or parts departments might be provided on one or both street frontages adjacent to the sheltered pump island. This morphology is not unlike that rendered in Gothic dress for the Magnolia Petroleum Co. (FIG. 4.71), except that in small towns and suburbs a second floor was usually omitted. Numerous examples of this common morphology survive in Texas towns, most of which are nondescript structures with no pretensions to design. Occasionally, however, the type might be subjected to studied design to harmo-

a canopy to shelter the pump island was retained.

The most elaborate of the Spanish Colonial service stations in Texas were those built by the Magnolia Oil Company. The surviving Magnolia (now Mobil) station at the intersection of Broadway and the Austin Highway in San Antonio (FIG. 5.66) is typical of these stations, which were probably intended to be compatible with the residential communities that surrounded them, such as Alamo Heights (the neon sign of the flying red horse was added later when Mobil acquired Magnolia Oil). The idiom is vernacular rather than Baroque, with tile roofs, white plaster walls, and exposed beams and brackets—not unlike the repertoire of materials widely used on residential architecture in Texas during the 1920's.[51]

The automobile was not the only technical innovation in American life to leave an impact on Texas architecture. The telephone, electricity, and natural gas did not become widespread as utility services in rural areas until after World War I, although all were perfected during the 1870's and 1880's. The West Texas Utility Company adopted the Spanish Colonial Revival for its offices and retail appliance outlets. Although the company did sell domestic appliances, for which a large show window was required, its use of the Spanish Colonial transcended mere commercial retailing, taking on an institutional character consistent with the utility's emerging public importance. There was no single prototype. A wide variety of designs was employed, although a consistent graphic style for the company's name served as a corporate trademark. The Ozona facility (FIG. 5.39)

FIG. 5.65
ABANDONED SERVICE STATION,
Palo Pinto. N.D.

FIG. 5.66
MAGNOLIA (now MOBIL)
SERVICE STATION,
San Antonio. N.D.

FIG. 5.67
WEST TEXAS UTILITY
COMPANY OUTLET,
Anson. N.D.

FIG. 5.68
BRYANT-LINK BUILDING,
Stamford. 1928.

has been seen as showing trace elements of the Pueblo Revival. The company's outlet in Anson (FIG. 5.67) is a free-standing building with two carefully designed facades of plastered masonry, inflected toward the corner with a dwarf tower and shallow tile roof. Not all facilities occupied by the West Texas Utility Company today were built in the corporate style, however. Some occupy main street frontage of varying character and date. Of these, the facility at Stamford is one of the grandest specimens of Spanish Colonial Revival storefront architecture in Texas (FIG. 5.68). In Stamford the WTU shares space in the Bryant-Link Building, constructed in 1928 with a facade of precast concrete panels comprising a pervasive pattern of Plateresque ornament. Like terra-cotta, concrete units are amenable to the replication of historic forms, although they do not permit the same sharp resolution of detail as the denser medium.[52]

The Bryant-Link Building is an exception. Most commercial architecture in the Spanish Colonial Revival made rather perfunctory use of a few standard features, little changed from the earlier phase of the Mission Revival: tiled parapets or visors, curved gable parapets, ornamental woodwork and ironwork, tiled floors and wainscots, and occasional touches of Baroque detail. The most exuberant specimens of commercial design in the style are the theaters, which tend to draw upon a wider range of historical expression, including Islamic and Meso-American models. An early example of this theatrical exoticism is the Alhambra Theater in El Paso (FIG. 5.69), designed in 1914 by Trost and Trost. As the name indicates, the design is based on Islamic models. The street end of the theater proper is fronted with a three-story facade of finely scaled and pervasive ornament, including calligraphic inscriptions and Sullivanesque traces. Tall, stilted, slightly pointed arches define the top story, while the round arches on the middle floor seem to spring from behind the pier in an arbitrary decorative fashion quite unorthodox from a Western standpoint. The ground floor was originally paneled in a manner similar to Trost and Trost's porch at the Douglas Gray House (FIG. 3.05). The flanking two-story wings, which contain the customary ground-floor shops, are the most obviously Spanish elements of the design, with their tiled visor roofs carried on heavy wooden bracketing.[53]

The Ritz Theater in Corpus Christi (FIG. 5.70) represents the frequent Spanish Colonial theaters built in Texas in the 1920's. Although the street level has been subsequently remodeled and the Spanish detail on the upper levels somewhat obscured by paint, enough survives of the Ritz to demonstrate its regional character. The basis of design for the facade is the Spanish twin-towered church facade, in this case vertically exaggerated with dissimilar towers for picturesque effect. The curved gable between the two towers and the quatrefoil windows seem to be carried over from the Mission Revival.[54]

In fact, much commercial design in the 1920's seems to be carried over from the Mission Revival. The Aziz Brothers Building in Brownsville (FIG. 5.71), designed in 1927 by Page Brothers, is typical of a large body of such work.[55] The corner

FIG. 5.69
ALHAMBRA THEATER,
El Paso. 1914.
Trost and Trost, architects.

FIG. 5.70
RITZ THEATER,
Corpus Christi. C. 1920's.

FIG. 5.71
AZIZ BROTHERS BUILDING,
Brownsville. 1927.
Page Brothers, architects.

FIG. 5.72
BRITE BUILDING AND
MARFA NATIONAL BANK,
Marfa. 1931.

towers with hipped roof and broadly projecting eaves, the curved gables, and the tiled visors were commonplace Mission-style devices. Occasionally, however, the Regional Eclectic modes of expression, rather than being ornamentally elaborated, were simplified and abstracted along the lines of Irving Gill's work in California. The Brite Building and Marfa National Bank of 1931 (FIG. 5.72) illustrates this tendency. The ornament used here seems based on American Indian forms in pottery and textiles rather than on anything introduced by the Spanish.

The most extensive commercial use of the Spanish Colonial Revival in Texas was doubtless the Highland Park Shopping Village (FIGS. 5.73 and 5.74), a suburban shopping center in Dallas designed by Fooshee and Cheek and constructed between 1930 and 1935, with subsequent additions.[56] Although the creation of the National Highway System, which channeled automo-

bile traffic through the major cities, had led to extensive commercial-strip development, frequently in the Spanish style, a shopping center with self-contained off-street parking was a relatively new concept in 1928. In that year, Hugh Prather and Edgar Flippen, the developers of Highland Park, opened a new addition to the elite North Dallas suburb that their father-in-law, John Armstrong, had laid out in 1907. Highland Park had originally excluded any form of commercial development, forcing such essential services as the Highland Park Pharmacy over the city line into Dallas. Prather and Flippen realized that excessive distance from shopping would deter development of their new addition west of Preston Road; the shopping center was seen as the alternative to unregulated strip development. The obvious model for such a shopping center was Country Club Plaza in Kansas City, developed from 1922 onward.[57] Prather and his architect, James Cheek, visited Country Club Plaza, and Fooshee and Cheek later incorporated a number of planning ideas from the Kansas City center, but Highland Park Village was not closely modeled on Country Club Plaza in either planning or style. For example, the shops at Highland Park Village face inward toward the central parking area, buffering the adjacent residence streets from traffic. This was a significant change from Country Club Plaza, where the shops faced onto peripheral streets.

Prather and Cheek also visited California, the heartland of the Spanish Colonial Revival in the 1920's, as it had been of the Mission Revival twenty years before. They might have seen such contemporaneous developments as the Lunda Bay Plaza at Palos Verdes Estates (1923+) or the rebuilding of Santa Barbara in the Spanish Colonial style after the earthquake of 1925. Their decision to develop the shopping center in the Spanish idiom hardly seems noteworthy, for the style had been extensively employed for the fine houses of Highland Park in the previous decade, many of which were designed by Fooshee and Cheek (see Chapter 7). What is surprising is the depth of their design research: in 1929 Prather and Cheek traveled to Spain to attend the Barcelona World Exposition. Although this showcase is best known for Mies van der Rohe's German Pavilion—one of the seminal monuments of the International style—most of its buildings were eclectic renditions of Spanish historical architecture. These ranged from essays on the Escorial to the vernacular forms of a Spanish village, which greatly impressed Cheek. They also visited Seville and Granada before returning home. Thus Cheek, sketching and photographing as he traveled, was exposed first-hand to a broad range of Spanish architecture, from the Islamic and Gothic, through the Plateresque, Purist, and Baroque phases of the Spanish Renaissance, to the Andalusian vernacular. This experience helps to explain the extremes of picturesque variety and ornamental richness of Highland Park Village. Intricately patterned arabesques and cusped forms suggestive of Islamic design coexist with Romanesque arches and Baroque details. Despite this variety, the shopping center has an overall unity achieved through a consistent use of appropriate materials: light-plaster walls, cast-stone ornament and trim, ex-

FIG. 5.73
HIGHLAND PARK SHOPPING VILLAGE,
Dallas. 1930–1935.
Fooshee and Cheek, architects.

FIG. 5.74
HIGHLAND PARK SHOPPING VILLAGE.

FIG. 5.75
BUNGALOW COURT,
San Angelo. N.D.

Although I will discuss the frequent use of the Spanish Colonial Revival for domestic architecture in Chapter 7, several new collective housing types seem more appropriate for consideration in the present context. Several forms of residential court originated in California and were emulated occasionally in Texas. The bungalow court is the most familiar of these, and consists of a series of three- or four-room bungalow flats that share common party walls and are grouped about a common yard. Intended largely for retired pensioners, these bungalow courts might be executed in either the Bungalow style or the Spanish Colonial idiom. One in San Angelo (FIG. 5.75) is typical of the genre. Three rows of joined bungalows set perpendicular to the street provide maximum lot coverage, while narrow lawnstrips carry the walkways to the individual unit entrances. The archway between street and lawnstrip signifies the separation of public right of way from tenants' domain. The walls are white plaster with flat roofs and parapets; however, tiled visors are tacked onto the facade, seemingly to denote Spanish character. They do not seem designed to shelter the windows from the sun.[59]

posed wooden balconies, tile roofs, and decorative ironwork. These materials convey the sense of historical authenticity often lacking in the Spanish Colonial Revival. Fooshee and Cheek have avoided monotony by breaking up the long shopping facades into changing increments of design, a strategy that climaxes at the Village Theater (opened in 1935) at the head of the parking lot. The asymmetrically placed tower and the elaborate Baroque lobby cresting make the Village one of the finest theaters in the Spanish Colonial mode in Texas, splendidly capturing the style's potential for picturesque expression. By 1935, however, Regional Eclecticism had succumbed to the modernistic idiom for most motion picture theaters, as for commercial design in general. The Highland Park Village is both the climax and the swan song of the Spanish Colonial Revival in commercial architecture in Texas.[58]

Other forms of courtyard apartments—sometimes intended as summer quarters for vacationers at beach resorts—were developed in California. Both Irving Gill's Horatio West Courts in Santa Monica (1912) and Rudolf Schindler's Pueblo Ribera Courts in La Jolla (1922) are walk-up apartments grouped about a landscaped court, although both eschew the Spanish Colonial idiom. In Los Angeles, the apartment court frequently achieved a considerable density; it often was adapted to steep terrain, and sometimes incorporated commercial shop space on the ground floor. Although progressive designers also developed this type, most were done in variations of the Spanish Colonial Revival,[60] and it is in this form that the Isabella Courts (FIG. 5.76) were built in Houston in 1928.[61] The Isabella Courts consist of two floors of apartment units grouped around a central courtyard, above a ground floor of commercial shops. The composition is deliberately asymmetrical to the point of being casual; vernacular rather than Baroque, although the tile copings, white plaster, and iron balconies connote Spanish character. The architectural drawings bear the seal of William Bordeaux, an architect from Miami, Florida, which suggests that Florida, rather than California, may have been the source of inspiration.

A more representative housing typology is that of the Mirasol Courts Apartments in Dallas (FIG. 5.77), which in this case combine the typical Spanish tile roof on heavy eave brackets with elements drawn from elsewhere in the Mediterranean. The windows, which consist of a paired sash set in a pointed arch, are suggestive of Venice. Such Venetian character is more commonly associated with the Regional Eclecticism of Florida in the 1920's, where it occurs in the architecture of Addison Mizner.[62] The maritime context of most of Florida's resort towns doubtless suggested this allusion to the Queen of the Adriatic. The Venetian character is also found in Venice, California, consciously laid out as a resort

FIG. 5.76
ISABELLA COURTS,
Houston. 1928.
William Bordeaux, architect.

FIG. 5.77
MIRASOL COURTS APARTMENTS,
Dallas. N.D.

FIG. 5.78
GATEHOUSE,
Loma Linda Residential Development,
Dallas. 1924.
David R. Williams, architect.

community of canals. Such allusions are rare in Texas, which employs the Islamic horseshoe arch more frequently than the Gothic pointed one. The gatehouses to Loma Linda residential development in Dallas (FIG. 5.78), designed by David R. Williams in 1924, provide a prime example.[63] Like the adjacent Highland Park Village, they allude to the rich and varied Spanish historical context that Regional Eclectic designers could draw upon for associative reference.

The symbolic propriety of the Spanish Colonial Revival for architecture in the Southwest is also demonstrated by the adoption of this mode of design by the Department of the Army for military installations in Texas. Both Fort Bliss in El Paso and Fort Sam Houston in San Antonio contain officer housing in a generically Hispanic idiom of plaster walls and tiled roofs and copings.[64] The most extensive exercise in the Spanish Colonial Revival in Texas by the federal government was Randolph Field (now Randolph Air Force Base) near San Antonio, dedicated in 1930 as one of a series of flying bases for the Army Air Corps. Like other bases in the series, such as March Field near Riverside, California; Langley Field, Virginia; and Wright Field near Dayton, Ohio, Randolph Field contained an eclectically designed neighborhood of officer housing. Whereas these areas at Langley and Wright Fields were done in the American Colonial and English Tudor modes, respectively,

those at March and Randolph, lying within the Spanish borderlands of the United States, employed the Spanish Colonial, not only for housing, but also for the headquarters and chapel. The original headquarters building at Randolph (FIG. 5.79), designed by Atlee B. and Robert M. Ayres following preliminary planning by an engineering officer, dominates the base plan with a dramatic Baroque tower that actually conceals the installation's water tank.[65] Randolph Field is perhaps the greatest single planned ensemble in the Spanish Colonial Revival in Texas.

The Spanish Colonial Revival was certainly the dominant expression of regionalism in Texas in the 1920's; in many respects it was a more flexible and appropriate medium of design than the Beaux-Arts Classic in its various permutations. By the late 1920's, however, both Regional and Academic Eclecticism were being challenged by new directions in design. David Williams himself, with his young protégé, O'Neil Ford, would seek a valid regional expression for the Texas house in a somewhat later, post-Spanish phase of the state's history: the ranch houses of the nineteenth century (see Chapter 7). For institutional and commercial work, and eventually for some residential design as well, a new style or family of styles rapidly would gain popularity after 1929. Collectively identified as modernistic modes of design, they comprise the subject of the following chapter.

FIG. 5.79
HEADQUARTERS BUILDING,
Randolph Air Force Base,
San Antonio. 1930.
Atlee B. and Robert M. Ayres, architects.

# VI

# MODERNISTIC MODES OF DESIGN
# 1928–1940

Most histories of post–World War I modern architecture focus primarily on Europe, except for passing mention of Frank Lloyd Wright and transplanted Europeans such as Schindler and Neutra in California during the 1920's. These studies usually describe the progressive influence associated with Sullivan and Wright before World War I as succumbing to the "return to normalcy" in the 1920's, only to re-emerge in the 1930's with a new wave of European émigrés. Behind this interpretation lies a conception of modern architecture as a reform movement, a total rejection of historicism, and the search for a radically new building culture based on modern functions, modern technology, and a heroic liberation from ornament—an International style.[1] In fact, this conception of a constituent mainstream of modern architecture excludes more than just the evolving Academic and Regional Eclectic traditions. Progressive tendencies before World War I had not rejected ornament per se, nor had they invariably stressed modern technology to the exclusion of traditional construction. The Art Nouveau in Europe, the Arts and Crafts in England and America, the Prairie School in the United States,

National Romanticism in Scandinavia, the Jugendstil in Germany, the Secession and the Wagnerschule in Eastern Europe—all retained John Ruskin's conception of architecture as decorated construction while searching out new combinations of form and new varieties of ornament. After the war in Europe, the Expressionist interlude in Holland and Germany continued the quest for modern expression in conventional materials and for a modern vocabulary of ornament. The International style did not really crystallize as a movement much before 1927, the year of the Weissenhof Siedlung and the League of Nations Competition, which led to the founding of the Congrès International de l'Architecture Moderne (CIAM) in 1928. From that point onward, a small band of avant-garde apologists promulgated a narrow definition of modern architecture, variously called Functionalism, the Neu Sachlichkeit, or the International style. Because this avant-garde definition of modern architecture was predicated on function, technology, and the repudiation of ornament, an alternative terminology was needed to define an architecture that, although not overtly historicist, sought contemporary expression of the traditional conception of architecture as decorated construction.

The term most commonly used by the lay public for both radical and conventional modern architecture was "modernistic." As American architecture progressively assimilated aspects of European modern design in the 1930's, this term acquired pejorative connotations. Modernistic came to mean a superficial modernism based on facile stylistic concerns rather than on fundamental principles. As modern architecture of largely European derivation triumphed in America after World War II, the modernistic alternatives of the 1920's and 1930's were denigrated and ignored. But by the 1960's, historians and aficionados alike had begun to rediscover this body of work, and the problem of terminology once again arose. Initially, the seminal event in the creation of this modernistic style seemed to have been the Exposition des Arts Decoratifs et Industrielles Modernes, held in Paris in 1925. The two most common terms for defining the style derive from this exposition: Art Deco and Moderne. Both are somewhat unsatisfactory in that they exaggerate the significance of the Paris exposition to the exclusion of other sources of the modernistic sensibility. Therefore, I will describe the contents of this chapter as modernistic rather than Art Deco or Moderne, without intending any pejorative implications.

As in the case of Academic or Regional Eclecticism, the modernistic style was really a sequence of three or four somewhat overlapping phases. David Gebhard has identi-

fied three such phases, which he terms the Zig-Zag, the Streamlined, and the PWA Moderne.[2] The first two terms describe the ornamental features of each phase, whereas the last one derives from the Public Works Administration (sometimes confused with the Works Progress Administration), which subsidized a large amount of public architecture during the Depression. Because the rudiments of the style were well established before the PWA's intervention, and since not all PWA-subsidized architecture was modernistic, this seems like a questionable term. Other terms have been proposed: Stripped Classic, Starved Classic, Cret Classic, Modern Classic. The last seems like the most appropriate, and has been adopted for this chapter. Finally, because the skyscraper is the quintessential American building type, partaking to some degree of all three phases, I have considered it in a separate section. I have thus divided institutional from commercial design, each of which is presented as a historical continuum combining to various degrees strands of Modern Classic, Zig-Zag, and Streamlined design.

MODERNISTIC
INSTITUTIONAL DESIGN

The three great formgivers of Modern Classicism were Eliel Saarinen, Bertram Grosvenor Goodhue, and Paul Philippe Cret. Goodhue was American born and trained; Saarinen and Cret emigrated to the United States from Europe. But despite its ultimate European roots—and a certain affinity with tenden-

FIG. 6.01
HELSINKI RAILROAD STATION.
1904–1914.
Eliel Saarinen, architect.

FIG. 6.02
NEBRASKA STATE CAPITOL,
Lincoln. 1920.
Bertram Grosvenor Goodhue, architect.

cies toward classical abstraction in Nazi Germany and Fascist Italy in the 1930's—American Modern Classicism seems largely a self-contained development.

The premise of a Modern Classicism rests on the abstraction and stylization of classical forms and details. This is found in several of the early modern components of European architecture before World War I, notably in the work of Otto Wagner and his students and associates in Vienna, and in the work of Peter Behrens in Germany. The influence of the Wagnerschule or the Werkbund on the development of an American Modern Classicism after the war is problematical, however.[3] That of Eliel Saarinen and the Finnish Jugendstil is more direct and obvious. Saarinen designed several buildings for Helsinki that seem to be direct models for American developments after the war. The best known of these is the Helsinki Railroad Station (FIG. 6.01). Saarinen's design for this building won the

competition in 1904, but he transformed it radically in the course of construction, which was completed in 1914. Although the modernistic clock tower would have considerable influence on American architecture, it was the architectonically abstracted figure sculpture that provided the greatest impetus. The heads and torsos that seem to emerge from the building mass recur frequently in the United States in the late 1920's. In addition to the Helsinki Station, however, Saarinen's unexecuted design of 1908 for the Finnish Parliament (FIG. 6.07), repeated in his second-place entry to the Canberra competition of 1913, provided an often unacknowledged model for American public buildings of the late 1920's and early 1930's. The Saarinen designs appear to be the first appearance of set-back massing, which would figure so prominently in the American modernistic idiom. They conveyed the impression of massive stability, monumental grandeur, and symbolic representation found in classical architecture, without copying the academic vocabulary or syntax.[4]

In 1920, Bertram Grosvenor Goodhue won the competition for the Nebraska State Capitol at Lincoln (FIG. 6.02). The architectonically abstracted figures emerging from the building mass derive directly from Saarinen's Helsinki station, which Goodhue is known to have admired, whereas other elements of the design seem like simplified abstractions of classical elements. Goodhue's classicism is arcuated rather than trabeated, however, and critics found a subtle Byzantine sensibility in his arcaded openings and in the flat relief sculpture contributed by Lee Lawrie. Yet

Goodhue's most influential innovation was the substitution of a skyscraper tower for the typical imagery of the capitol dome. The office or library tower would provide a new image for public buildings, beginning with the Los Angeles City Hall of 1924–1926, because it accommodated expanding bureaucracies more comfortably than academically correct classical buildings with their traditional proportions. Although there was some cross-fertilization between the commercial skyscraper and the institutional tower as icon of government, the two concepts seem relatively autonomous.[5]

In 1920 Paul Philippe Cret was still firmly entrenched in the Beaux-Arts Classic style, as seen in his fourth-place entry in the Nebraska Capitol Competition.[6] In the course of the following decade, he gradually simplified and abstracted this classicism until, in 1929, at the Folger Shakespeare Library in Washington, D.C. (FIG. 6.03), he achieved a definitive expression of Modern Classicism that would be highly influential on American architecture in the 1930's. Cret's design for the Folger Library retained the building mass as a closed block, articulating the wall plane horizontally by a basement and attic defined by moldings, and treating the main floor as an alternation of windows and fluted piers. It was these fluted piers separating basement and attic, with the allusion to classic orders resting on a base and supporting an entablature, that proved to be Cret's most influential innovation. Such fluted piers were used countless times in American Modern Classicism in the 1930's. Cret himself used them on the Texas Memorial Museum on

FIG. 6.03
FOLGER SHAKESPEARE LIBRARY,
Washington, D.C. 1929.
Paul Philippe Cret, architect.

the University of Texas at Austin campus, completed in 1937 (FIG. 6.04).[7]

Several prominent Texas firms seized on the examples of Saarinen and Goodhue for modernistic architecture in 1928. That year, Trost and Trost designed the San Angelo City Hall (FIG. 6.05), and Lang and Witchell of Dallas produced the Eastland County Courthouse in Eastland (FIG. 6.06), although Dudley Green has been identified as their Art Deco designer.[8] Both buildings seem derived from Saarinen's Finnish Parliament project of twenty years before (FIG. 6.07), with step-back masses rising to a dominant central block. It is true that this massing could have been derived from the New Mexico pueblos (Trost and Trost's Franciscan Hotel in Albuquerque is close in massing but not in detail; FIG. 5.03) or even from Meso-American temple platforms or Assyrian ziggurats, but the Saarinen model seems the most exact. The great planning advantage was that four or

FIG. 6.04
TEXAS MEMORIAL MUSEUM,
University of Texas,
Austin. 1937.
Paul Philippe Cret, consulting architect.
John F. Staub, associate architect.

FIG. 6.05
SAN ANGELO CITY HALL. 1928.
Trost and Trost, architects.

five floors of office, courtroom, or detention space could be accommodated in this model, whereas such height would be difficult to resolve within classical rules of design.[9] Both the San Angelo City Hall and the Eastland courthouse employ architectonically abstracted ornament comparable to Saarinen's at the Helsinki Station and Goodhue's at the Nebraska Capitol, although understandably less extensive. The entrance and interiors at San Angelo are quite conventional, however, almost conforming to a Regional Eclectic idiom, whereas the details of the Eastland courthouse are somewhat more advanced, with great heraldic eagles decorating the corners of the central block.[10]

The modernistic idiom proved to be the new monumental style for public architecture in Texas in the 1930's. Some forty-five new courthouses were erected between 1929 and 1941, with a hiatus between 1932, when the Depression precluded the planning of new facilities, and 1935, when the PWA began to supply construction subsidies. The earlier series are generally more interesting than the latter. Voelcker and Dixon of Wichita Falls, who proved to be the most prolific firm of courthouse designers in Texas, were responsible for eight of these. Their Cottle County Courthouse in Paducah of 1930 (FIG. 6.08) is perhaps the most interesting of the series. Not only does the step-back massing of the building seem derived from Saarinen's Finnish Parliament, but the symbolic figures of mercy and justice that emerge from the modeled piers flanking the main entrance seem explicitly based upon those at the Helsinki station.

FIG. 6.06
EASTLAND COUNTY COURTHOUSE,
Eastland. 1928.
Lang and Witchell, architects.

FIG. 6.07
PROJECT FOR FINNISH
PARLIAMENT. 1907.
Eliel Saarinen, architect.
*Photograph reproduced by permission of the
Museum of Finnish Architecture, Helsinki.*

The dramatically articulated massing seen in the Paducah courthouse tends to diminish in subsequent work by Voelcker and Dixon. At the Rockwall County Courthouse in Rockwall of 1941 (FIG. 6.09), the building form is reduced to a single mass with a slightly defined attic. It might be said that the influence of Paul Philippe Cret has supplanted that of Saarinen and Goodhue. The vertically banked windows separated by piers seem derived from Cret's Folger library, although the fluting of the piers is deleted.[11]

The four- and five-story central blocks at San Angelo, Eastland, and Paducah suitably accommodated the functions of those governments, but the great advantage of the modernistic style was that it was not constrained by canonical proportions. The step-back massing

FIG. 6.08
COTTLE COUNTY COURTHOUSE,
Paducah. 1930.
Voelcker and Dixon, architects.

FIG. 6.09
ROCKWALL COUNTY COURTHOUSE,
Rockwall. 1941.
Voelcker and Dixon, architects.

FIG. 6.10
POTTER COUNTY COURTHOUSE,
Amarillo. 1931.
Townes, Lightfoot and Funk, architects.

could be stretched to any height. The best example of this principle is the Potter County Courthouse at Amarillo (FIG. 6.10), designed in 1931 by Townes, Lightfoot and Funk. The central block is extended to eight stories, with five-story side wings and four-story corner pavilions. The terra-cotta sculpture includes such regional allusions as an American Indian in feathered war bonnet, doubtless inspired by similar themes at the Nebraska Capitol. The location of the Amarillo courthouse also differs from the typical cross-axial situation in a central square. A main axis passes through the courthouse, but there is no well-defined cross-axis, and the building is not centralized on its tract. Instead, the building is shifted to one edge of its site, giving it one street facade and one park exposure. The park is developed as a formally landscaped esplanade, rather than as a naturalistic park space characteristic of Texas courthouse squares that have not been designated for parking.[12] The street and park entrance porches at Amarillo employ round arches, as Goodhue had used at the Nebraska Capitol, and as occurred at San Angelo, Eastland, and Paducah. Later courthouses in the PWA sequence omit arcuated forms.

For all of its greater bulk, the Amarillo courthouse, at eight stories, is not a true skyscraper. The ultimate potential of the skyscraper to serve as an icon of Texas government was demonstrated in Beaumont in 1931, when associated architects Stone and Babin designed the Jefferson County Courthouse (FIG. 6.11). In this building, the central block is stretched to twelve stories, and towers above the lateral wings. The detailing is skillfully handled to em-

FIG. 6.11
JEFFERSON COUNTY COURTHOUSE,
Beaumont. 1931.
Stone and Babin, associated architects.

phasize the vertical proportions, but this courthouse seems more related to commercial skyscrapers of the late 1920's than to Goodhue's Nebraska capitol.[13]

The round arches found in Goodhue's paradigm occur in many early exercises in the modernistic style. Herbert S. Green's San Antonio Public Library of 1930 (FIG. 6.12, now housing the Hertzberg Circus Collection) is an excellent example of the idiom applied to a smaller but spatially complex building type. The symmetrical main facade on West Market Street is the most obvious quotation from Goodhue's capitol, with architectonically abstracted figures emerging from the piers that flank the monumental entrance arch. The asymmetrical prospect from the side is equally interesting, however, as the dominant volumes of the arcuated reading room and monolithic stacks rise above the ancillary spaces placed within the lower corner pavilions. It is a skillful marriage of Beaux-Arts planning with the step-back massing and abstracted classical details of the new style.[14]

Another example of Goodhue's abstracted classical idiom applied to a complex institutional program is Waco Hall at Baylor University of 1929 (FIG. 6.13), designed by the firm of Lang and Witchell. Waco Hall is a cross-axial building with three virtually identical main entrances. On each, massive corner piers shoulder a higher central mass, containing a triple ground-floor en-

FIG. 6.12
SAN ANTONIO PUBLIC LIBRARY. 1930.
Herbert S. Green, architect.

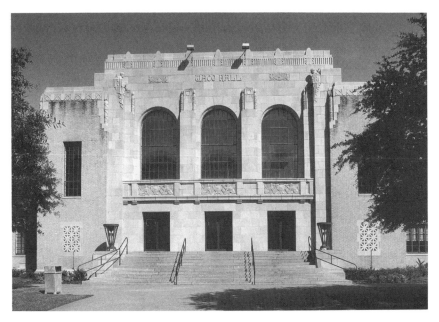

FIG. 6.13
WACO HALL,
Baylor University,
Waco. 1929.
Lang and Witchell, architects.

FIG. 6.14
WILL ROGERS MEMORIAL COLISEUM
AND AUDITORIUM,
Fort Worth. 1936.
Wyatt C. Hedrick and Co., architects.
Elmer G. Withers Architectural Co.,
associate architect.

trance and triple arched windows on the *piano nobile* above. Once again, the familiar architectonic sculpture in terra-cotta emerges from the corners of the piers and buttresses.[15]

The great arched portal and stylized symbolic figures may be traced back to Goodhue's own source, Eliel Saarinen's Helsinki station of 1904–1914. The station also deployed an asymmetrically placed clock tower, which was an influential source of inspiration in its own right. It was the ultimate model for the tower of the Will Rogers Memorial Coliseum and Auditorium in Fort Worth, designed to commemorate the 1936 centennial of Texas independence (FIG. 6.14). Architects were Wyatt C. Hedrick and Co. and Elmer G. Withers.[16]

Modernistic architecture of the first phase before 1932, although deriving primarily from Saarinen and Goodhue, was also influenced by the Zig-Zag mode, just as the second phase after 1935, heavily indebted to Paul Philippe Cret, was crossfertilized with the Streamlined sensibility. The influence of the Zig-Zag line is particularly evident in the work of Wyatt C. Hedrick and Co. of Fort Worth, and of their chief designer, Herman Paul Koeppe. Hedrick's firm was, as Chapter 4 discussed, the designer of Commercial Gothic skyscrapers in the late 1920's. Their familiarity with the Gothic seems to have colored their approach to the modernistic idiom, for the arcuated forms and architectonic sculpture Goodhue had popularized are not found in their modernistic work. Rather, they seem to have quickly assimilated the Zig-Zag vocabulary of ornament demonstrated so forcefully at the Paris Exposition des Arts Decoratifs in

1925 (FIG. 6.15). Their Fort Worth Central Fire Station of 1930 (FIG. 6.16) demonstrates this predilection. Despite the hipped tile roof over the central block, there is little suggestion of step-back massing or volumetric articulation. It is the structural bay that is emphasized, rather than the composition of masses. Segmental arches span the equipment bays, but vertical mullions on the floor above are emphasized in lieu of the round arches preferred by Goodhue and his followers. This emphasis on structure and the vertical line has a decidedly Gothic connotation, reinforced by the finials that cap each pier and give a broken, serrated profile to the roof cornice. One might almost describe the Central Fire Station as Modern Gothic, in contrast to previous examples of Modern Classic.

Another example of crossbreeding between the Zig-Zag and Modern Classic modes of modernistic expression is the State Highway Building in Austin (FIG. 6.17), completed in 1933 to the design of Adams and Adams, with Lang and Witchell as associate architects.[17] Doubtless Lang and Witchell were involved because of their familiarity with the modernistic idiom, not only at the Eastland courthouse and Baylor, but also on commercial skyscrapers in Dallas (see the section in this chapter on the modernistic skyscraper). At eight stories, the State Highway Building invites comparison with the Amarillo courthouse (FIG. 6.10). Although composed of set-back masses, the form of the Austin building is more compact, with a less dramatic hierarchy of forms ascending toward a central block. The tendency to articulate the masses by strengthen-

FIG. 6.15
GALERIES LAFAYETTE PAVILION,
Exposition des Arts Decoratifs,
Paris. 1925.
*From* Art Deco, *by Victor Arwas.*
*Reproduced by permission of Academy*
*Editions, London.*

FIG. 6.16
FORT WORTH CENTRAL
FIRE STATION. 1930.
Wyatt C. Hedrick and Co., architects.

FIG. 6.17
STATE HIGHWAY BUILDING,
Austin. 1933.
Adams and Adams, architects.
Lang and Witchell, associate architects.

ing the corners is suppressed in favor of a more pervasive emphasis on the vertical piers, which pass through the cornice to create a serrated or zig-zag roofline. Most significantly, the arcuated entrance at Amarillo is replaced by one closely derived from the Paris Exposition des Arts Decoratifs. The fluted piers crowned by sculpture that flank the main entrance appear to be modeled upon the Galeries Lafayette Pavilion at the Paris Exposition of 1925, or upon intervening examples of these forms by other American architects. All in all, the State Highway Building resembles a modernistic equivalent of the Commercial Gothic Norwood Tower a few blocks away.

The influence of Paul Philippe Cret on Texas public architecture in the 1930's was profound. By this time, Cret practiced only as a consulting architect, being responsible for the design of each building while local architects of record were charged with producing working drawings and supervising construction. He participated with Ralph Cameron in the 1936 design of the San Antonio Federal Courthouse (FIG. 4.10) in the Beaux-Arts Classic mode, and with Wiley G. Clarkson in the 1933 Fort Worth Federal Courthouse in the Modern Classic. As consulting architect for the University of Texas at Austin, he worked with Greene, LaRoche and Dahl to design buildings in a subtle and varied Regional Classicism. He also collaborated with John F. Staub for the Texas Memorial Museum (FIG. 6.04), designing in the Modern Classic idiom he had developed for the Folger Library in 1929. Above all, he would serve as consulting architect to the Texas Centennial

Exposition in Dallas in 1936. His work, particularly that for the Folger Library, was perhaps the single most potent influence when public building resumed under the sponsorship of the PWA around 1935.

The earliest building in Texas that appears to have been influenced by Cret's Folger Library is the Panhandle-Plains Historical Museum on the campus of West Texas State Teachers College (now West Texas State University) in Canyon, designed in 1932 by Rittenberry and Carder of Amarillo (FIG. 6.18). Here, both the arcuated forms of Goodhue and the serrated pier lines of the Zig-Zag tradition are suppressed in favor of a strictly trabeated abstraction of classical form. As Cret had done at the Folger, vertically proportioned windows alternate with piers, but they were not fluted, except for pilaster strips flanking the main entrance. The sculptured relief panels beneath each window seem to derive from the Folger, as does the heavy horizontal attic interrupted only by portrait rondels of Texas animals.[18]

If the Panhandle Plains Museum is the earliest Texas example of Cret's influence on the 1930's, the Houston City Hall (FIG. 6.19), designed by Joseph Finger and completed in 1939, is an excellent example of Cret's later influence.[19] Although conforming to the stepback massing prevalent at the beginning of the decade, with a ten-story central block shouldered by four-story wings that in turn rest upon a broad ground floor, the profiles of the masses have been clarified. Gone are both the arcuated portals and sculpturally modeled piers of Goodhue and the serrated verticality of the Paris Exposition. Al-

FIG. 6.18
PANHANDLE-PLAINS
HISTORICAL MUSEUM,
West Texas State Teachers College
(now West Texas State University),
Canyon. 1932.
Rittenberry and Carder, architects.

FIG. 6.19
HOUSTON CITY HALL. 1939.
Joseph Finger, architect.

FIG. 6.20
HALL OF STATE,
Texas Centennial Exposition,
Dallas. 1936.
Paul Philippe Cret, design consultant.
Associated architects.

though the windows are grouped vertically between continuous piers, these do not penetrate the cornice or fragment the profiles of the building's component masses. The influence of Cret's Folger Library is most apparent on the ground floor, where a sequence of large windows are separated by fluted piers. The suggestion is of a classical pilastrade rather than the insistently vertical grouped colonnettes of a Gothic pier. The same clarification and simplicity are found at smaller scale in the later modernistic courthouses of Voelcker and Dixon, although in their work the piers are not fluted. The site location of the Houston City Hall, which faces an axially landscaped park with a reflecting basin, typifies the survival of Beaux-Arts planning principles in the modernistic period. These principles are supremely evident at the Texas Centennial Exposition of 1936.

The greatest specimen of Cret's influence in Texas is the Hall of State at the Centennial Exposition (FIG. 6.20), for which Cret was design

consultant to an extensive consortium of Texas architects.[20] In this hall, reeded rather than fluted piers establish the classical allusion, defining the great exedra that terminates the Esplanade of State. These reeded piers, without bases or capitals, are repeated inside the hall. The exedra is flanked by lower lateral wings with a simplified classical peristyle and moldings, including a frieze inscribing the names of heroes of Texas history. Majestic as it is—almost Baroque in conception—the Hall of State was intended to enhance a larger plan: the most significant display of 1930's modernistic design in Texas, which illustrated the various nuances and possibilities open to architects within the new style.[21]

The site selected for the exposition was the State Fair Grounds in Dallas, at that time consisting of a polyglot assembly of Mission and Spanish Colonial Revival buildings. These included Lang and Witchell's Music Hall, the only structure that survived the centennial rebuilding. George L. Dahl was appointed Centennial Architect after leading a civic campaign to secure the exposition for Dallas against competing proposals from San Antonio and Houston. Dahl was responsible for coordinating the work of the various associated architects and designers, including Cret as consultant. Except for the Hall of State, most of the buildings at the exposition do not appear to be in Cret's personal style, and George Dahl should probably be credited as designer of some eight of them, although Cret's influence was doubtless felt. Dahl had worked with Cret on the plan for the University of Texas at Austin, and was well versed in the principles of Beaux-Arts planning from previous experience with Myron Hunt in California in the 1920's. Cret had also been consultant to the Chicago Century of Progress Exposition of 1933–1934, which Dahl had visited and from which he recruited many of the collaborating artists who were to enrich the Texas Centennial Exposition. The Dallas exposition differs greatly from that in Chicago, however. Faced with the onset of the Depression, the Chicago planners had scrapped plans for a highly formal plan with elaborately decorated buildings. They substituted a frankly temporary ensemble of bright colors, simplified forms, electric light, and dynamic composition—a crystallization of the commercial Streamlined style then beginning to emerge in the United States.

Dahl rejected this conception for Dallas. All of the principal buildings were to be permanently constructed, and the site planning returned to principles of Beaux-Arts formality. Dahl's final plan was organized about six building groups, five of them axial in composition (FIG. 6.21). He placed the Administration Building to the north of the main entrance gates on Parry Avenue, approximately balancing the existing Music Hall to the south. From the entrance, one could proceed along the fair's main axis to the Esplanade of State, developed as a pool with fountains, lined with shrubbery and statuary, visually terminated by the Hall of State at the far end, and flanked by the Hall of Transportation on one side and Hall of Varied Industries on the other.

The Esplanade of State (FIG. 6.22) reflected Dahl's conception of the new modernistic idiom. He treated

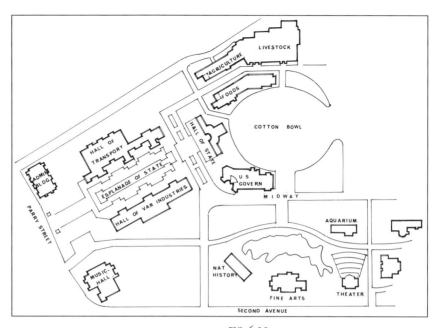

FIG. 6.21
TEXAS CENTENNIAL EXPOSITION.
Site plan. 1936.
George L. Dahl, centennial architect.
Paul Philippe Cret, consulting architect.

the halls of Transportation and Varied Industries as broad, simple masses; each was articulated with three monumental pavilions but was devoid of architectural detail. These broad, simple forms became the neutral foil for the work of collaborating artists whom Dahl recruited. The allegorical statues lining the esplanade, representing the six historical cultures of Texas, were executed by Lawrence Tenny Stephens and Raoul Josset. Pierre Bourdelle contributed the bas-reliefs on the two immense buildings, using a technique of low-relief sculpture in cement to "combine the machines and instruments of science with figures of allegorical significance,"[22] in the best tradition of Art Deco iconography. Bourdelle also designed the pylon fountains that flank the Esplanade of State. It is this program of applied art that gives the Art Deco character to the esplanade, which was recently restored to its 1936 situation.

The esplanade vista is arrested by the Hall of State, which masks the

FIG. 6.22
ESPLANADE OF STATE,
Texas Centennial Exposition. 1936.
George L. Dahl, centennial architect.

FIG. 6.23
HALL OF AGRICULTURE AND
HALL OF FOODS,
Texas Centennial Exposition. 1936.
George L. Dahl, Centennial Architect.

bulk of the Cotton Bowl behind and fronts upon a transverse Court of Honor leading to further activity areas to the north and south. North of the Cotton Bowl, Dahl placed the agricultural and livestock group, approached on an axis that passes between two inflected porticos on the halls of Agriculture and Foods (FIG. 6.23). Although this use of the Baroque principle of inflection shows the sophistication of Cret's and Dahl's Beaux-Arts planning, the two porticos are as stark and devoid of detail as those flanking the Esplanade of State. Again, they were relieved by applied art, in this case, murals by Carlo Ciampaglia, who had also designed the mural behind Jossett's statue on the Administration Building.

At the south end of the Court of Honor a shift of axes occurs, resulting from the irregular trapezoidal site of the fairgrounds. The main axis of the esplanade and the Hall of State had been generated as perpendicular to Parry Street, which was the main entrance to the exposition. Secondary entrances were placed along Second Avenue, which diverged from Parry Street at an obtuse angle. Both the Midway and the cultural group were aligned with Second Avenue, necessitating an oblique axial shift from the Court of Honor. Cret and Dahl skillfully marked this change with the insertion of the U.S. Government Building (FIG. 6.24), designed by Donald Nelson. The building's monumental triangular pylon—fluted on its leading edge and crowned by a stylized American eagle—bisects the obtuse angle. At its base, the pylon divides the concave arms of an exedra, which expands the awkward intersection of three approaching ave-

FIG. 6.24
U.S. GOVERNMENT BUILDING,
Texas Centennial Exposition. 1936.
Donald Nelson, architect.

FIG. 6.25
HALL OF AQUATIC LIFE,
Texas Centennial Exposition. 1936.
Fooshee and Cheek, Flint and Broad,
and H. B. Thompson, architects.

created some of the most interesting modernistic architecture at the exposition.

Mark Lemmon and Clyde Greisenbeck designed the Museum of Natural History, perhaps the least interesting of the cultural buildings. The monolithic, virtually windowless stone building is articulated into panels by reeded pilasters crowned with Art Deco sunburst capitals, both highly conventional and uninspired devices by 1936. The Museum of Natural History has none of the bold simplicity of Dahl's exhibition buildings, nor the applied art of the associated artists. The Museum of Fine Arts, despite its picturesque aspect when seen from across the lagoon, is also a somewhat tepid exercise in the Modern Classic style. It was designed by a consortium of LaRoche and Dahl, DeWitt and Washburn, Coke Knight, and Ralph Bryan. The interior betrays a strong regional character, with carved and painted beamed ceilings and elaborate metalwork.

By contrast, the Hall of Aquatic Life (FIG. 6.25) is one of the most interesting modernistic buildings of its date in Texas. It was designed by Fooshee and Cheek, Flint and Broad, and H. B. Thompson. Whereas the two museums were built of limestone, the Hall of Aquatic Life was constructed of brick with stone trim, reflecting a more pragmatic aesthetic. In response to its informal site, the building was made asymmetrical in composition, with an entrance pavilion placed between two subordinate wings of unequal size. These wings are devoid of windows, but are divided into a sequence of broad piers and shallow recessed panels, constrained be-

nues into a monumental space. The U.S. Government Building (now known as the Tower Building) became the fulcrum about which the diverging avenues pivoted. As in the other buildings for the exposition, the U.S. Government Building was composed in stark masses, relieved by the contributions of collaborating artists. In this case it was Julian Garnsey who designed both the abstracted American eagle and the bas-reliefs at the base of the building, which depict the history of the United States. Garnsey also designed similar bas-reliefs for the main entrance on Parry Street.

South of the Midway lay the cultural group, consisting of museums and an outdoor theater. As a counterpoint, no doubt, to the axial formality of the rest of the plan, these buildings were distributed informally around a picturesque lagoon. As a result, the designers were free of formal constraints and

neath a deep attic. This ordonnance seems derived from Cret's Folger Library, although the piers are not fluted. The building's composition reflects the familiar step-back massing, ascending from lateral wings to corner pavilions to central block, with certain innovations and refinements. The face of the central block is curved on a broad convex radius, and the piers that divide the entrance porch and attic above were given a teardrop shape, suggesting a fluidity in modeling possibly influenced by Streamlining. The serrated motif carved into the coping and the stepped profile on the entrance doors are vestiges of the Zig-Zag. In combining the Modern Classic with such vestiges, and with suggestions of Streamlining as well, the hall defines a position midway in the evolution of the modernistic style.

Christiansen and Christiansen defined a more extreme position in their Outdoor Theater (FIG. 6.26; often inaccurately called the amphitheater), firmly within the Streamlined idiom that had been developing during the course of the 1930's. The concentric arches of the bandshell recall the forms of Fellheimer and Wagner's Cincinnati Union Terminal (FIG. 6.27), which also may have supplied the model for the lighting pylons.[23] The rounded corners and horizontally banded curves have a much wider popular source in the commercial architecture of the 1930's, however. The theater was also constructed of exposed and painted concrete, and much of the streamlined detailing seems to respond to the exigencies of reinforced concrete construction. Linear banding could be constructed into the formwork before the concrete was poured, resulting in an integral ex-

FIG. 6.26
OUTDOOR THEATER,
Texas Centennial Exposition. 1936.
Christiansen and Christiansen, architects.

FIG. 6.27
CINCINNATI UNION TERMINAL. 1933.
Fellheimer and Wagner, architects.
Roland Wank, designer.

FIG. 6.28
COMMERCIAL STORE,
Oslo. 1933.
Eric Mendelsohn and R. E. Jacobsen,
architects.

FIG. 6.29
CENTRAL FIRE STATION,
Austin. 1938.
Kreisle and Brooks, architects.

admired in its time than subsequently. It certainly was a potent source of influence in America in the 1930's. Mendelsohn's influence coincided with that of the industrial designers—Norman Bel Geddes, Walter Dorwin Teague, Raymond Loewy, and others—whose concern for the streamlined packaging of machinery also affected architecture. Finally, modern architecture of the International style, however bastardized in transmission, contributed certain motifs and details such as flat roofs and roof terraces, bull-nosed curves, and glass block. All of these influences were most prominent in commercial architecture, and as such will be discussed in a later section of this chapter, but they are also perceptible to a degree in institutional architecture of the later 1930's, usually mixed with a residual component of the Modern Classic style.

Whereas biaxial symmetry had been a near-invariable principle of classicism—whether historical or modernistic—architecture of the late 1930's displayed a propensity for asymmetrical composition; a trend born of both Streamlining and the International style. This is best demonstrated by a series of small public institutions subsidized by the PWA. The Central Fire Station in Austin (FIG. 6.29), designed by Kreisle and Brooks in 1938, is an admirable example. The complex massing of the structure generates its own visual interest; the only ornament consists of manipulating the brick coursing, particularly the recessing of horizontal joints to suggest Streamlining. The revolutionary compositional aesthetic resolves the thorny question of the equipment bays, which had plagued

pression of construction and ornament. This same process of integral detailing was used also for the street furniture at the exposition, resulting in a dynamic equilibrium of horizontal slabs and vertical pylons in the best Streamlined manner. Such a dynamic equilibrium was more commonly found in the commercial design of the 1930's, but it was occasionally manifested in PWA-subsidized institutional architecture of the late 1930's.

Like Modern Classicism, Streamlining has a complex history, stretching back into the 1920's in Europe. The work of Eric Mendelsohn is seminal to this history, particularly the series of great German post-Expressionist department stores he designed in the period between 1926 and 1930. The Commercial Store in Oslo of 1933 (FIG. 6.28) is one of the lesser-known examples of this body of work, more widely

designers in more orthodox styles, but which now supply a change of scale that enhances the dynamic interplay of masses. The ample use of balconies and roof terraces off the second-floor crew quarters establishes the station's affinity to International Modernism, while the use of brick relates to the softening of its puritanical avant-garde aesthetic in the course of the 1930's.[24]

The Austin station is unusual in the extreme articulation of masses. Comparable public institutions are normally more simply composed, achieving formal resolution through the asymmetrical juxtaposition of component functions. One example is the Karnes City Municipal Building (FIG. 6.30), dedicated in 1941 and designed by Gordon M. Smith, DeHaven Pitts, and Charles T. Weidner. Here the functions of fire station, city offices, and municipal auditorium are accommodated by treating each as a rectangular block, with the symmetrical fronts of the fire station and the auditorium faced toward perpendicular streets, and the lower mass of the city offices placed in the reentrant corner. A common entrance to city hall and fire station is placed off-center, skewing the main facade further toward the asymmetrical and suggesting an interlocking of functional masses. Other than the stylized modernistic lettering and some vertical fluting at the auditorium entrance, the only ornament consists of the familiar banded brickwork, which establishes a horizontal strip of windows between a poured concrete grade wall and a continuous concrete header.

The City Hall and Fire Station at Mineola (FIG. 6.31) also conforms to the common asymmetry of the

FIG. 6.30
KARNES CITY MUNICIPAL
BUILDING. 1941.
Gordon M. Smith, DeHaven Pitts,
and Charles T. Weidner, architects.

FIG. 6.31
CITY HALL AND FIRE STATION,
Mineola. 1938.
Albert C. Moore and Co.,
consulting engineers.

FIG. 6.32
MUNICIPAL LIGHT AND POWER PLANT,
Baird. 1939.
Albert C. Moore and Co., consulting
engineers.

FIG. 6.33
NORTH SIDE SENIOR HIGH SCHOOL,
Fort Worth. 1937.
Wiley G. Clarkson, architect.

genre in the late 1930's, although the public safety and civic government functions are more loosely related to each other. The suggestion of Streamlining is less pronounced than at Karnes City, and the allusion to International Modernism more so, despite the massive skewing effect of the corner pavilion. The Mineola design is credited to Albert C. Moore and Co., Consulting Engineers, who designed considerable PWA-supported work in Texas, often of a more technical nature. They designed the municipal light and power plants for Baird (FIG. 6.32) and Weatherford in 1939–1940, emphasizing a crisp industrial detailing relieved by banded brick coursing and modernistic lettering. The influence of modern design as practiced by the Tennessee Valley Authority seems a likely influence on Moore and Co. and other designers of such analogous industrial installations.[25]

The Public Works Administration sponsored extensive construction of new schools. High schools in particular remained the enigma they had been to eclectic designers: buildings of unparalleled bulk difficult to resolve in any design idiom. By the 1930's there was a tendency to locate the auditorium and/or gymnasium at one or both ends of these essentially linear buildings, where they could be isolated from classroom functions for use after school hours. Two such Texas high schools illustrate alternative idioms of modernistic design in the late 1930's.

The North Side Senior High School in Fort Worth (FIG. 6.33), erected in 1937 to the design of Wiley G. Clarkson and his chief designer, Charles O. Chormaster, remains essentially classical in its ordonnance. The auditorium and gymnasium—although serving dissimilar functions—are expressed as virtually identical masses on either end of the classroom block, which is itself articulated with entrance pavilions at ends and center. Large windows set between continuous vertical piers light three floors of classroom space; a basement floor extends forward beneath a raised front terrace. North Side High School, in fact, has much in common with Trost and Trost's El Paso High School of twenty years before (FIG. 4.26). Only the details of the classical design have been modernized.[26]

By contrast, Lamar Senior High School in Houston (FIG. 6.34), designed in 1937 by John F. Staub and Kenneth Franzheim with Louis A. Glover, Lamar Q. Cato, and Harry D. Payne, bends a similar plan configuration to a more avant-garde expression. The full depth of the auditorium is projected forward of the classroom block, whereas the shop wing extends to the rear at the opposite end of the academic unit. This deliberately asymmetrical Z-plan and the horizontally banded fenestration give the composition a dynamic, decidedly unclassical aspect, which might have been derived from contemporary Streamlining or from International Modernism. The Z-plan and curtain-wall glazing of the shop wing suggest the Bauhaus at Dessau, designed by Walter Gropius (FIG. 6.35), one of the most famous exemplars of modern European architecture.[27]

The modernistic idiom and the International avant-garde can thus be seen moving toward each other in the course of the 1930's, as American architects discovered the

FIG. 6.34
LAMAR SENIOR HIGH SCHOOL,
Houston. 1937.
John F. Staub and Kenneth Franzheim,
with Louis A. Glover, Lamar Q. Cato, and
Harry D. Payne, architects.

FIG. 6.35
THE BAUHAUS,
Dessau, Germany. 1925–1926.
View of workshop wing from the
southwest.
Walter Gropius, architect.
*Photograph courtesy The Museum of Modern Art, New York.*

FIG. 6.36
ROY CULLEN BUILDING,
University of Houston. 1939.
Lamar Q. Cato, architect.

FIG. 6.37
CHEROKEE COUNTY COURTHOUSE,
Rusk. 1941.
Gill and Bennett, architects.

One manifestation of such a rapprochement is the reappearance of Spanish tile roofs on buildings of the modernistic idiom. These appear in 1939 on the first unit of the new University of Houston: the Roy Cullen Building (FIG. 6.36) by Lamar Q. Cato.[29] Despite its calculated asymmetry, this building is idiomatically related to the Modern Classic style, with very shallow moldings replacing the more robust ornamental detail experienced earlier. It seems related to the abstraction of Georgian detail in ca. 1940 residential design that is sometimes called the Moderne Regency, although in this case, the hipped tile roofs impart a vaguely Spanish character.

Another aspect of the tendency in the late 1930's to impart regional qualities to the modernistic idiom is found in the use of fieldstone, either uncoursed in more vernacular work or roughly coursed for monumental commissions. Such a finish was wedded to modernistic form conventions by Gill and Bennett at the Cherokee County Courthouse in Rusk of 1941 (FIG. 6.37). The Rusk courthouse seems relatively independent of modernistic form conventions and hence closer to avant-garde modernism. On the main facade, at least, the fieldstone reads as a sequence of panels and buttresses rather than as a field of wall into which framed window groups have been inserted.

By the time of the American entry into World War II in 1941, the modernistic idiom in its various permutations had become the dominant—although not exclusive—mode of design for Texan public institutions. Over the preceding dozen years, a consensus had developed for a modern style of architecture, if not for a

discipline of European modern architecture and as the Europeans relaxed their puritanical aesthetics to accept natural materials and regional adaptation.[28] At the same time, however, there was a search for regional adaptation and organic qualities in American architecture. Regionalists such as William W. Wurster in California, Pietro Belluschi in Oregon, and David Williams and O'Neil Ford in Texas distanced themselves alike from the modernistic idiom and from International Modernism. Also in the 1930's, Frank Lloyd Wright experienced a regeneration of creative energy and Alvar Aalto moved away from orthodox modernism toward a more organic conception of modern architecture. The full impact of these developments in Texas is discussed in Chapter 8, but in the meantime, a certain rapprochement between the modernistic tradition and regional expression should be considered.

radically new form of architecture on European models. In the process of evolution, modernistic institutional design had been cross-fertilized with commercial architecture of Zig-Zag and Streamlined detail, and with a new generation of American commercial skyscrapers.

## THE MODERNISTIC SKYSCRAPER IN TEXAS

As Henry-Russell Hitchcock observed in 1929, a fine line separated Gothic and modernistic skyscrapers, for the specific character of their ornament was less important than its architectonic function.[30] To classify the Smith-Young Tower (FIG. 4.88) as eclectic because of its Gothic ornament, and the Milam Building (FIG. 6.44) as modernistic despite its vaguely Spanish ornament, is to walk this fine line. Both respond to developments in American skyscraper design over the preceding decade.

1922 was the critical year in the evolution of the modernistic American skyscraper. In that year, Hugh Ferriss produced his *Study for the Maximum Mass Permitted by the 1916 New York Zoning Law*, which established the image of the complex, stepped-back building mass. These same considerations influenced Ralph Walker's 1922 design for the Barclay-Vesey Building in New York (FIG. 6.38; for McKenzie, Voorhees and Gmelin; also known as the New York Telephone Building). The massing and details of the Barclay-Vesey Building, completed in 1926, would influence several Texas skyscrapers later in the decade. Also in 1922, the Chicago Tribune Tower competition was held. Although won by Howells and

FIG. 6.38
BARCLAY-VESEY BUILDING,
New York. 1922.
McKenzie, Voorhees and Gmelin,
architects.
Ralph Walker, designer.
*Photograph courtesy of Richard A. Scherr.*

FIG. 6.39
CHICAGO TRIBUNE TOWER
COMPETITION.
Second place prize. 1922.
Eliel Saarinen, architect.
*Photograph reproduced by permission of the Museum of Finnish Architecture, Helsinki.*

Hood, who used a Gothic design, the second-place entry by Eliel Saarinen (FIG. 6.39) became a potent source of inspiration for subsequent skyscraper design. Saarinen's vocabulary of ornament resembled a modernistic abstraction of Gothic forms. By 1924 Raymond Hood, the winning co-designer of the Tribune Tower Competition, had abandoned explicitly Gothic detail in favor of Saarinen's abstracted ornament, which Hood applied to the American Radiator Building in New York.

FIG. 6.40
DAILY NEWS BUILDING,
New York. 1929–1931.
Raymond Hood, architect.

FIG. 6.41
R.C.A. BUILDING,
Rockefeller Center,
New York. 1933.
Raymond Hood, architect.

Hood did not long remain committed to Saarinen's synthesis, however, but in rapid succession produced a series of experiments in skyscraper form: the Daily News Building of 1929–1931 (FIG. 6.40), the McGraw-Hill Building of 1930–1931, and the R.C.A. Building at Rockefeller Center of 1933 (FIG. 6.41). All of these were attempts to style the stepped-back masses of the skyscraper form. Concurrently in Philadelphia, George Howe and William Lescaze were creating the Philadelphia Savings Fund Society Building (1929–1933; FIG. 6.42), which achieved formal resolution through the dramatic expression of function and structure. Because Lescaze was an Italian-Swiss immigrant imbued with the avant-garde tradition of European modernism, the PSFS Building was a vitally important transmission point between the modern mainstream and that quintessential American building type, the skyscraper.[31]

In Texas, as in the nation at large, a remarkable series of skyscraper office buildings and hotels rose in

FIG. 6.42
PHILADELPHIA SAVINGS FUND
SOCIETY BUILDING. 1929–1933.
Howe and Lescaze, architects.

FIG. 6.43
PETROLEUM (now SOUTHWESTERN LIFE)
BUILDING,
Houston. 1927.
Alfred C. Bossom, architect.

the later 1920's, as the commercial tower came to represent progress and modernity both in the metropolitan centers and the smaller cities. Gothic skyscrapers in Corsicana and Midland, as well as in San Antonio, Austin, Houston, and Dallas, have been examined previously in Chapter 4. This same dual aspect of urban concentration and dispersion over the prairie prevailed in the modernistic phase of skyscraper design.

Two Texas skyscrapers seem more or less indebted to the Barclay-

FIG. 6.44
MILAM BUILDING,
San Antonio. 1928.
George Willis, architect.

Vesey Building of Ralph Walker. The earlier of these is the Petroleum Building in Houston (now Southwestern Life Building; FIG. 6.43), designed by Alfred C. Bossom of New York in 1927.[32] Although the configuration of the Petroleum Building—a narrow L-shaped slab with a light court internalized within the block—owes nothing to the Barclay-Vesey Building, the roof-top termination with two stepped-back layers of double-height arcades seems based upon Walker's design. The final, hipped roof penthouse is set back once again, creating a highly successful tapering skyline that belies stylistic designation. Some of the ornament appears vestigially Meso-American.

George Willis' Milam Building in San Antonio of 1928 (FIG. 6.44), with its U-shaped plan and light court turned toward the street, is closer to the Barclay-Vesey in morphology. Although there is nothing new in this plan configuration, the ascending sequence of wings, rear slab, and arcaded penthouse suggest the New York skyscraper as a proximate model. At twenty stories high, and half a city block in breadth, the Milam became the largest reinforced concrete building in the United States.[33] Both the Petroleum Building in Houston and the Milam Building are faced in brick, however, and achieve their architectonic character primarily from the rhythm of window spacing and from the vertical expression of the piers. This brick-builder's aesthetic may be ultimately related to European Expressionism, mediated through New York models such as Barclay-Vesey.[34] Ornament per se is kept to a minimum, and confined largely to the top of each building.

A similar stylistic ambiguity may be observed in Abilene and Big Spring, where skyscraper hotels of fifteen to seventeen stories dominate the skyline and business district of both cities. Both the Wooten Hotel in Abilene (FIG. 6.45), designed by David S. Castle in 1930, and the Settles Hotel in Big Spring (FIG. 6.46), by Peters, Strange and Bradshaw in the same year, conform to the formula of a tower resting upon a broad base.[35] In each case, the detail is faintly historicist but is incorporated into a formal parti emphasizing the skyscraper proportions through continuous vertical piers and grouped fenestration. Each ascends to a stepped-back penthouse, which had become *de rigueur* by 1930.

In El Paso, Trost and Trost had two skyscrapers under construction in 1930. The Hilton Hotel, intended to provide the capstone of Conrad Hilton's Texas-based hotel chain, is a rather uninteresting structure, save for its once luxurious lobby, which was unfortunately remodeled out of existence. As a skyscraper hotel, along with the New Driskill in Austin, it culminated Henry Trost's long career as a hotel designer, extending back a decade before the Paso del Norte of 1913 to the Santa Rita in Tucson and the Gadsden in Douglas, Arizona.[36] Trost and Trost's other El Paso skyscraper, from about 1930, was the fifteen-story Bassett Tower (FIG. 6.47). In exterior massing the Bassett Tower is a virtual duplicate of the firm's contemporary Luhrs Tower in Phoenix, consisting of five parallel slabs

projecting and receding in plan, and ascending in step-backs to a central elevator penthouse. By staggering the masses in plan, Trost was able to provide a maximum of natural light and multiple exposure to twelve offices on each of the lower floors. The staggered slabs of the Bassett Tower rise from a broad, one-story plinth of commercial retail space, which isolates the tower from the encroachment of competing buildings on neighboring sites. However, the Depression prevented such neighbors from materializing, and the Bassett Tower today remains spatially isolated. In an age when many skyscrapers had only two finished facades turned to the intersecting streets, and when even the skyscraper hotels in Abilene and Big Spring occupied a higher floor area ratio, the Bassett Tower stands as testament to the symbolic qualities of the skyscraper form.

The character of ornament on the Bassett Tower differs markedly from that on the Luhrs Tower in Phoenix. At Phoenix, the ornament seems like a timid modernistic abstraction of classical or Spanish Renaissance details, similar in spirit to the San Angelo City Hall (FIG. 6.05). At the Bassett Tower, however, the vocabulary of the Zig-Zag mode developed at the 1925 Paris Exposition des Arts Decoratifs has been effectively employed. As the main entrance (FIG. 6.48) demonstrates, Trost and Trost manipulated an intricate repertoire of chevrons, bosses, and other ornamental details that bear no resemblance to Gothic or classic or Spanish sources, nor to the architectonic sculpture of Goodhue. It is a fully

FIG. 6.45
WOOTEN HOTEL,
Abilene. 1930.
David S. Castle, architect.

FIG. 6.46
SETTLES HOTEL,
Big Spring. 1930.
Peters, Strange and Bradshaw, architects.

FIG. 6.47
BASSETT TOWER,
El Paso. 1929–1930.
Trost and Trost, architects.

FIG. 6.48
MAIN ENTRANCE, Bassett Tower.

assimilated specimen of the new ornamental style.[37]

If the Bassett Tower stands aloof from its neighbors and thus creates its own context, designers in more densely congested cities like Dallas and Houston usually did not enjoy this luxury. A unique response to the problem of congestion is reflected in Lang and Witchell's planning of the 1930 office headquarters for the Dallas Power and Light Company (FIG. 6.49). The DP&L Building occupies a difficult internal site between Jackson and Commerce Streets, where it can hardly be appreciated to full advantage. This building represents yet another conception of step-back massing: a peeling away of layers of building mass from a central slab, similar to that employed at Rockefeller Center. Set-backs occur at the fourth, tenth, and twelfth floors, but not at the roofline. The structure is clad in brick, and alternating major and minor continuous piers emphasize the vertical dimension. The spandrels and the parapets of the various set-backs are monochrome terra-cotta, cast in a variety of typical art deco forms derived ultimately from Paris Exposition des Arts Decoratifs, and presumably designed for the firm by Dudley Green.

The building's tower extends half a block north from Jackson Street toward Commerce Street, the main thoroughfare of downtown Dallas. Although the office tower does not front on Commerce, a three-story public service lobby was constructed as a link between the main thoroughfare and the office tower, which turns a windowless but vertically articulated face toward Commerce. The design of this lobby link, although also part of the original

FIG. 6.49
DALLAS POWER AND
LIGHT CO. BUILDING,
Dallas. 1930.
Lang and Witchell, architects.

program by Lang and Witchell, has a somewhat different character from that of the skyscraper. Faced with white stone above a polished black granite basement, the lobby facade (FIG. 6.50) is closer to the Modern Classic style of Goodhue and Cret than to the Zig-Zag idiom of skyscraper design. The fluted pilasters read as simplified abstractions of classical orders, and the portrait busts of Edison and Watt that emerge from the piers at either party wall recall the architectonic forms of Saarinen's Helsinki station and Goodhue's Nebraska capitol, as well as those Lang and Witchell were using on Waco Hall at Baylor. The transom above the lobby entrance features an etched glass mural that

FIG. 6.50
LOBBY FACADE,
Dallas Power and Light Co. Building.

FIG. 6.51
LONE STAR GAS BUILDING,
Dallas. 1931.
Lang and Witchell, architects.

depicts an allegorical nude figure representing energy surrounded by clouds and sunlight, a typical piece of Art Deco iconography. Little of the interior detailing of the lobby survives at the DP&L Building, but such interior appointments are much better preserved at the 1931 Lone Star Gas Building, also designed by Lang and Witchell in Dallas (FIG. 6.51).

The Lone Star Gas Building enjoys a more commodious site at Harwood and Jackson Streets, and is only thirteen stories tall. It actually adjoins an earlier ten-story building for the same utility firm. Lang and Witchell exploited the amplitude to compose the building in ziggurat massing, similar to their Eastland courthouse, rather than as a tower. Six- and eleven-story masses ascend toward the thirteen-story central block. The detailing is similar in character, although somewhat more restrained, to that of the DP&L Building. At the Lone Star Gas Building, however, the interior appointments are better preserved. The elevator lobby, including the decorative ceiling in silver and gold leaf reflecting the floor pattern, and the stainless-steel and blue-enamel elevator doors in a sunburst pattern, survives virtually intact.[38]

In Fort Worth, Wyatt C. Hedrick had assumed the mantle of his former partners, Sanguinet and Staats, in 1926. As noted previously, the chief designer of Wyatt C. Hedrick and Co. was Herman Paul Koeppe. This firm's Electric Building of 1929 (FIG. 6.52) seems to make a tentative gesture toward the modernistic skyscraper while retaining a certain classical predilection. This vestigial classicism can be seen in the treatment of the ground floor and mezzanine, and in the fact that the continuous vertical piers with subordinate spandrels are employed only on the central section of each facade. The corners of the building remain monolithic pavilions with punched windows, strengthening the building mass: a classical characteristic not uncommon in institutional architecture but somewhat anomalous in the modeling of a skyscraper. Only at the attic floor does this stolidly classical articulation give way to a bit of more expressive detail, as the vertical piers become more ornamental and achieve a dynamic resolution with the horizontally banded cornice of the adjacent corner piers.[39]

Wiley G. Clarkson employed a comparable design parti of his Sinclair Building in Fort Worth of 1930 (FIG. 6.53), with the same strong corners bracketing the vertically articulated center section of each facade. Clarkson, however, employed a much more fully comprehended vocabulary of Zig-Zag ornament on the ground floor and on the stepped-back masses at the top of the building. The stepped arches of the ground floor—perhaps partly derived from Meso-American corbelled vaulting[40]—must have been among the most dramatically expressive modernistic details in 1930 Texas, although they have since been reduced to mere pattern by subsequent remodeling.

Clarkson's greater comprehension of the new style failed to drive his competitor from the scene in Fort Worth, for Hedrick and Co. soon mastered both the Modern Classic and Zig-Zag modes of the new style, as seen in their Will Rogers Memorial Coliseum and Auditorium (FIG. 6.14) and Central Fire

FIG. 6.52
ELECTRIC BUILDING,
Fort Worth. 1929.
Wyatt C. Hedrick and Co., architects.

Station (FIG. 6.16). Unfortunately, Hedrick and Co.'s great Fort Worth skyscraper masterpiece does not survive. The Aviation Building (later known as the Trans-America Life Building), along with the adjacent Palace Theater, was demolished in 1978. The main entrance and lobby, in particular, were a tour de force of modern ornamental design. Constructed largely of colorful glazed terra-cotta, the entrance combined architectonically abstracted sculpture on the jambs, a stepped arch beneath an almost Baroque cartouche supported by eagles, and chevron patterns reminiscent of American Indian art.[41]

Wyatt C. Hedrick and Co. also designed a skyscraper passenger sta-

FIG. 6.53
SINCLAIR BUILDING,
Fort Worth. 1930.
Wiley G. Clarkson, architect.

tion in Fort Worth for the Texas and Pacific Railroad. In this design, a ten-story office slab rises over the station lobby, forming a headhouse for the concourse and platforms beyond. This genre is equally represented, however, by the Santa Fe Railroad Building in Galveston (FIG. 6.54), designed by E. A. Harrison in 1931. At eight stories plus central penthouse, and broad enough to accommodate multiple tracks backed up to the concourse, the Galveston station, although not exactly a skyscraper, typifies the attempt to reconcile rational structure with modernistic expression. In any rational structural system, the column spacing will be wider than the floor-to-floor height. Hence, attempts to articulate the verticality of the skyscraper invariably imposed nonstructural piers, so that the exterior cladding became a mask of construction, rather than an expression of it. (Only around 1930, at the Mc-Graw-Hill Building, did Raymond Hood develop the alternative concept of the skyscraper as a stacking of horizontal floors, but this structure had no influence in Texas.) Because the Galveston station is not a skyscraper, Harrison therefore was free to deploy the horizontally proportioned structural bay as the primary generator of formal pattern. The station is not Streamlined, as Hood's McGraw-Hill Building is; the column lines, rather than the spandrels, are continuous, and the fenestration is subdivided by mullions into three sash per bay. The rhythm accelerates toward the center, where a three-story, stepped-back penthouse signifies the main entrance at street level below. Here the pattern of fenestration becomes more complex, and the mullions

FIG. 6.54
SANTA FE RAILROAD BUILDING,
Galveston. 1931.
E. A. Harrison, architect.

take over vertical dominance. The ornamentation is quite restrained; it is limited to a few symbolic references to the Southwest as served by the Santa Fe Railroad. This includes the main entrance "flat arch" derived from the Pueblo Revival.[42]

Alfred C. Finn of Houston seems to have drawn upon explicit models for his two Texas skyscrapers. The Gulf Building in Houston (FIG. 6.55; now the Texas Commerce Bank Building), designed with Kenneth Franzheim and J. E. R. Carpenter in 1929, was closely modeled upon Eliel Saarinen's design for the Tribune Tower Competition of 1922 (FIG. 6.39). At thirty-seven stories and 428 feet, the Gulf Building, upon completion, was the tallest building in Texas. Terra-cotta casting permitted a close replication of Saarinen's ornamental modeling, although Finn made certain changes in ap-

FIG. 6.55
GULF (now TEXAS COMMERCE BANK)
BUILDING,
Houston. 1929.
Alfred C. Finn, Kenneth Franzheim,
and J. E. R. Carpenter, architects.

plication; for example, the step-back massing begins much closer to the top than in Saarinen's design. Like the Bassett Tower in El Paso, the Gulf Building rises free on all sides above a six-story plinth, which contains major retail space and a great, three-story-high banking hall, richly decorated in Art Deco ornament and substantially intact.[43]

Finn's second Texas skyscraper represents the antithesis of Houston's urban concentration. The People's National Bank Building in Tyler of 1931 (FIG. 6.56; now the Interfirst Plaza Building) was the largest corner bank building in Texas and the epitome of the prairie skyscraper. At sixteen stories, it challenges the skyscraper hotels of Big Spring and Abilene, and dominates the courthouse square it faces and the skyline of Tyler. Finn's source for the crisply defined slabs of the bank building seems to have been Raymond Hood's Daily News Building in New York (1929–1931; FIG. 6.40), although a recent reglazing of the vertical fenestration has enhanced the similarity by suppressing the spandrels. Nevertheless, the continuous vertical piers, the layering of the slabs as they ascend to the tallest block, and the relative lack of ornamentation make the Tyler building the most modern skyscraper in Texas prior to World War II.[44] The onset of the Depression brought such ambitious commercial undertakings to a halt for fifteen years. The most progressive American skyscraper of the period from 1929 to 1933, the proto-functionalist Philadelphia Savings Fund Society Building by Howe and Lescaze (FIG. 6.42), had no imitators in Texas.

FIG. 6.56
PEOPLE'S NATIONAL BANK BUILDING,
Tyler. 1931.
Alfred C. Finn, architect.

FIG. 6.57
PETROLEUM BUILDING,
Big Spring. N.D.

## MODERNISTIC
## COMMERCIAL DESIGN

Even at an average height of fifteen stories, the skyscraper had a limited applicability to the smaller cities of Texas. Structures such as the People's National Bank Building or the Settles Hotel stand unchallenged as symbols of urban aspiration in Tyler and Big Spring. Yet, office buildings and sometimes hotels of lesser height were also built in the times of prosperity in the late 1920's. At twelve stories, Wyatt C. Hedrick and Co.'s Petroleum Building in Midland (FIG. 4.85) established that city as the capital of the Permian Basin oil field, but smaller petroleum buildings could be found throughout West Texas as commercial

Gothic forms gave way to modernistic expression on the eve of the Depression. The Petroleum Building in Big Spring (FIG. 6.57) is representative of this genre, satisfying the need for office space generated by the oil boom. At six stories, it hardly competes with the nearby Settles Hotel, but it represents a more modernistic conception of building form. The continuous brick piers establish a dominant vertical proportion, combined with terra-cotta ornament at the roofline and second floor. This creates a broken, serrated cornice characteristic of the Zig-Zag mode, although the brick piers are not modeled in any way. The ornament on the second floor and on the main office en-

FIG. 6.58
FIRST NATIONAL BANK,
Midland. 1938.
Wyatt C. Hedrick and Co., architects.

FIG. 6.59
SOUTHWESTERN BELL
TELEPHONE BUILDING,
Cisco. N.D.
Irvin Ray Timlin, architect.

trance is certainly less cosmopolitan than that of Hedrick and Co. in Fort Worth or Lang and Witchell in Dallas. Rather than being a new vocabulary derived from the Paris Exposition des Arts Decoratifs, the ornament on the Big Spring Petroleum Building seems like an abstraction of various historical sources, including Gothic aediculae, Romanesque arcading, and the Pueblo flat arch.

Banks tended to adopt the Cret-influenced, Modern Classic idiom, rather than the more flamboyant Zig-Zag forms. The First National Bank of Midland (FIG. 6.58), remodeled and expanded by Hedrick and Co. in 1938, employs fluted piers and slightly articulated end pavilions, along with a heavy but severely plain attic, all suggestive of Cret's Folger library. The bank itself is a remodeling of a Beaux-Arts Classic structure of earlier vintage, joined to a new eight-story office block.[45]

In addition to banks, utility companies usually sought an institutional presence in the Texas towns and cities they served. As described in Chapter 5, the West Texas Utility Company employed a Southwestern regional mode of expression for this purpose. Despite the Spanish Baroque detail selected for its San Antonio headquarters (FIG. 5.63), the Southwestern Bell Telephone Company generally adopted the modernistic idiom for its Texas offices and service plants, designed by its corporate architect, Irvin Ray Timlin, out of its St. Louis headquarters.[46] Their Cisco facility (FIG. 6.59) is one of the more bizarre of these buildings. Asymmetrically balanced between the blank walls of equipment spaces and fenestration for personnel areas, the Southwestern Bell building at Cisco also employs an unorthodox ordonnance of pier buttresses ambiguously decorated with terra-cotta cartouches. The ambiguity resides in their intermediate placement on the piers; they cannot be capitals because they do not cap anything. The form of these cartouches suggests the geometrical abstraction of Meso-American reliefs, although the concentration of ornament over the main entrance also evokes a suggestive Spanish character, all reinforcing the essentially eclectic character of much Art Deco ornament.

The Zig-Zag mode, as crystallized at the 1925 Exposition des Arts Decoratifs in Paris (FIG. 6.15), was very largely a commercial style. The principal demonstration pieces at the exposition were the pavilions of the major Parisian department stores. The new ornamental vocabulary of the Zig-Zag line was conceived as a modern replacement for the curvilinear forms of the Art Nouveau of a quarter century before. It was seen as the means by which French decorative artists could recapture the preeminence they had enjoyed around 1900, subsequently eclipsed by the prestige of German industrial design as promoted by the Deutscher Werkbund.[47] Although the United States did not participate in the Exposition des Arts Decoratifs, many Americans did attend, and by the later 1920's the forms of the new decorative style began to appear in American architecture. Although in America the Zig-Zag mode was frequently merged, particularly in institutional architecture, with other sources of modernistic abstraction invented by Saarinen, Goodhue, and Cret, in commercial design it often

reigned supreme. The most overtly Zig-Zag buildings are usually commercial-strip architecture, often employing glazed terra-cotta for eye-catching color. Terra-cotta was the medium par excellence of the Zig-Zag style.

Although many such structures were built in Texas in the late 1920's and early 1930's, two such projects—in Amarillo and Beaumont—stand out. The Paramount Theater Building in Amarillo (FIG. 6.60) was built in 1932 to designs of W. Scott Dunne. The building has been renovated for use by the Xerox Corporation—in the course of which the shop windows were replaced with an open loggia—and the theater has discontinued operation. The terra-cotta facing, however, has been preserved, and with it, the building's modern Zig-Zag character. The two-story strip occupies a full city block on South Polk Street, but the rhythm of major structural piers and minor vertical mullions is irregular, interrupted by the off-center theater front. The terra-cotta pier profile is cast with multiple serrated edges, and the piers rise to finials with elongated hexagonal facets. These details are repeated with less elaboration on the mullions, which also break the cornice. The tympana above the second-floor windows are cast with vertical fluting, and the coping between the piers and mullions consists of a Zig-Zag fret. These details increase in height and intensity at the theater facade. Nothing on the Paramount Theater Building suggests an abstraction of historical styles; all is originally conceived using the new ornamental vocabulary.[48]

The Kyle Block, occupying the two hundred block of Orleans Street

FIG. 6.60
PARAMOUNT THEATER BUILDING,
Amarillo. 1932.
W. Scott Dunne, architect.

in Beaumont (FIG. 6.61), is even more ambitious than the Paramount block, although its formal syntax differs somewhat. Verticality expressed by continuous pier lines and serrated edges gives way to modeling of the building mass. The long street is divided into five segments, with a two-story block on each corner, then a section of single-story shops, and finally another two-story increment in the center. Although the familiar repertoire of fluting and sunbursts does occur, the most insistent Zig-Zag features are the stepped arches over the shop windows. Windows with canted haunches also occur, recalling the Pueblo flat arch, whereas the stepped arch recalls Meso-American corbeling techniques.[49]

Glazed terra-cotta could be used to simulate more traditional materials, but it could also be used to create the brightly colored, highly artificial ambience that established corporate identity and attracted customers: the facade as billboard and the building as trademark. Such terra-cotta trademark facades did not originate with the new ornamental dispensation, however. Montgomery Ward had used such a design in a faintly abstracted classical vein in the 1920's. A number of these facades survive in Texas in Childress, Plainview, Vernon, and Hillsboro, and doubtless elsewhere. The store in Childress (FIG. 6.62) was designed in 1928 by Wyatt C. Hedrick and Co., which employed standard Montgomery Ward details

FIG. 6.61
KYLE BLOCK,
Beaumont. N.D.

as manufactured by North West Terra Cotta Co.[50]

Of the numerous American companies that sought to exploit the new style to establish recognizable identities in the 1930's, however, none used terra-cotta with fewer inhibitions than the S. H. Kress Company. Of the surviving Kress stores in Texas, that in San Antonio (FIG. 6.63) is perhaps the finest, produced by the company's designer, Edward F. Sibbert, in 1938.[51] The San Antonio Kress store combines vertical and horizontal fluting with touches of Spanish Baroque detail and prominent advertising graphics. It typifies the tendency of 1930's commercial architecture to treat the street facade, if not the entire building, as a billboard.

The Kress renovation campaign coincided with efforts to stimulate the American business environment by, among other strategies, modernizing Main Street. The 1935 Modernize Main Street Competition, a promotional ploy by the Libby-Owens-Ford Glass Company, was intended to stimulate the use not only of window glass, but also of colored structural glass, known as vitrolite, as a facing material for commercial remodeling.[52] Such structural glass tended to supplant terra-cotta as a cladding material in the 1930's, as the new aesthetic of Streamlining replaced the Zig-Zag line.

Although in the 1920's the Streamlined style had serious roots in the work of Eric Mendelsohn (FIG.

FIG. 6.62
MONTGOMERY WARD STORE,
Childress. 1928.
Wyatt C. Hedrick and Co., architects.

FIG. 6.63
KRESS STORE,
San Antonio. 1938.
Edward F. Sibbert, architect.

FIG. 6.64
TEXAS THEATER,
Seguin. 1929.
W. Scott Dunne,
architect.

6.28) and continued in the 1930's as the vehicle for significant architecture, it tended to be equated with the styling of machinery and appliances by the new breed of industrial designers. Among these designers were Norman Bel Geddes, Raymond Loewy, and Walter Dorwin Teague. Although streamlining obviously improved the efficiency and performance of transportation vehicles, its application to most forms of machinery, such as household appliances, was largely image and packaging.[53] The same might be said of much commercial architecture of the 1930's, as new materials such as structural glass, glass block, chrome, and neon tubing were used to attract customers. The neon tube, which made the Streamline visible at night as well as by day, introduced a new quality to illuminated advertising.

In the 1920's, illuminated advertising consisted of setting incandescent bulbs in regular patterns, usually to border a hanging sign. A few of these survive; the Texas Theater in Seguin (FIG. 6.64), designed by W. Scott Dunne in 1929, typifies the 1920's style of commercial advertising. No other building type would participate as completely as the motion-picture theater in the 1930's modernization of Main Street, as talking pictures drove out vaudeville and made the movies a universally available expression of American culture. Most Texas towns of any size have a theater that was constructed or remodeled in the 1930's. The Streamlined marquee and the neon-illuminated advertising beacon became the leitmotifs of this decade of modernization. The transformation in theater imagery can be examined by comparing the Texas

Theater in Seguin with the State Theater in Austin (FIG. 6.65). The tentative balance between modern Zig-Zag and classical principles of design at Seguin has given way to a balance between horizontal and vertical tendencies. A Streamlined marquee, banded in chrome and neon, floats suspended above a street level of black structural glass. The suspended electric sign has now become a vertical advertising pylon of monumental scale, dominating the street facade, defined by enameled color by day and by neon tubing at night. The theater facade itself has been modernized by the balanced application of vertical and horizontal lines, the latter as streamlined flow lines of black glass, but it is the marquee and pylon that dominate and energize the composition. The street front of the Austin theater has become a giant billboard advertising the entertainment available inside.

For commercial remodeling in the 1930's, colored structural glass and glass block became the most popular materials, after neon and chrome. They were normally used for storefronts, without necessarily affecting the rest of the building. Because structural glass could be obtained in a variety of bright, shiny colors, it could be used to extend advertising trademarks and color schemes to architectural scale. The use of blue and orange by Rexall and green by Walgreen's led William Wurster to dub the style Drugstore Modern, and despite the pejorative connotations of this term, several excellent examples of such drugstore fronts survive in Texas. Those in Eastland and Cisco (FIG. 6.66), both in black glass, also incorporate the modernistic graphic style that

FIG. 6.65
STATE THEATER,
Austin. N.D.

FIG. 6.66
DRUGSTORE,
Cisco. N.D.

FIG. 6.67
HALL FURNITURE COMPANY STORE,
Sherman. N.D.

became popular in the 1930's. The storefront remodeling of the Hall Furniture Company in Sherman (FIG. 6.67) is another excellent surviving specimen of the commercial application of structural glass, as is that of the Behearse Jewelers in Denison. In both cases, however, the accompanying hanging neon sign is a timid expression of the advertiser's art.

The concept of the building as billboard—as an immediately recognizable trademark and advertisement for the goods and services purveyed—was not limited to main street remodelings, nor was it exclusively a development of the 1930's. Both the West Texas Utility Company and Magnolia Oil have been seen using Spanish Colonial forms in pursuit of such a strategy of corporate identification in the 1920's. In 1937, the industrial designer Walter Dorwin Teague produced a modern service station design for Texaco—with consistent graphics and color scheme—many of which survive in Texas. A competing design for Conoco, although not as common as the Teague Texaco station, is more thoroughly invested with the idiom of Streamlining, with bull's-eye windows, curved corners, and horizontal flow lines rendered in recessed brick. A surviving example in Laredo (FIG. 6.68) represents the genre.

By the 1930's, widespread automobile ownership had begun to affect American commercial architecture; private-vehicle access to commercial strips and highway margins had caused many retail functions to concentrate there. The major tire companies developed "super stations," which not only sold tires but provided servicing and repairs. Characterized by multiple service bays and parking areas, such facilities were one story in height and spread out laterally, which made them ideally suited to the Streamlined aesthetic. They were also easily adapted to the corporation's color scheme and trademark. The latter was usually displayed in neon, because enterprises on the commercial strip or highway margin were often open at night for the convenience of working customers. Automobile dealerships also tended to shift from the downtown fringe to the highway strip in the 1930's, and increasingly adopted the Streamlined idiom consistent with the merchandise purveyed. The Knapp Chevrolet Dealership Building in Houston (FIG. 6.69), designed by Newell Waters in 1940, is typical of this genre.[54] In the best examples of the style, the horizontal streamlined flow is arrested by a vertical element, producing a dynamic resolution of spatial polarities. At the Knapp dealership, this vertical element is supplied by the pylon that separates the salesroom from the service department, which arrests the streamlined curves of the display windows and achieves asymmetrical balance with the subordinate service wing. The vertical slot on the pylon is filled with glass block. The sign at Knapp Chevrolet has been altered to replace the origi-

FIG. 6.68
CONOCO STATION,
Laredo. N.D.

FIG. 6.69
KNAPP CHEVROLET
DEALERSHIP BUILDING,
Houston. 1940.
Newell Waters, architect.

FIG. 6.70
RIVER OAKS COMMUNITY CENTER,
Houston. 1937ff.

nal neon advertising graphics, but the building remains an exemplary specimen of the Streamlined commercial style of the 1930's.

The supermarket was another commercial innovation to emerge during the Depression. Customers who owned automobiles could travel considerable distances to save money on food. Cheaper prices were made possible not only by self-service and the check-out system, but by economies of scale: supermarkets were much larger than conventional chain groceries. Separate departments for meat, produce, baked goods, and dairy products made one-stop shopping possible, and evening hours permitted families to shop after work. The enlarged scale of operations made a new morphology necessary, which, like the super station and auto dealership, was amenable to Streamlined design. The constantly increasing scale of supermarket operations since World War II has, however, left few such 1930's stores remaining.

The concept of the shopping center remained flexible throughout the 1930's. At the one end, strip developments like those in Amarillo (FIG. 6.60) and Beaumont (FIG. 6.61) did not incorporate private off-street parking, while at the other, Highland Park Village (FIG. 5.74) surrounded its parking lot with shopping, which served to turn the commercial functions away from the surrounding streets. Between these two extremes, most 1930's shopping centers placed their parking lots between the shopping and the public street. Such strip shopping centers were commonly designed in the streamlined idiom in the 1930's. The River Oaks Community Center on West Gray Avenue in Houston, begun in 1937 and projected eastward after World War II, is an excellent example of Streamlining applied to paired commercial shopping centers facing each other across a major street. The horizontal sweep of these matching centers is reinforced by bull-nosed corners, horizontal banding, and a continuous marquee with curving soffit. Although the original increment—designed by Stayton Nunn and Milton McGinty—has been disfigured through remodeling, the original Streamlined character is still preserved in the later additions west of McDuffee Street (FIG. 6.70).[55]

If the suburbanization of commercial functions continued to accelerate during the 1930's, it was not yet to the detriment or exclusion of downtown shopping and entertainment activities. Both the major retail chains, such as Woolworth's and Kress, and the local department stores remodeled their premises or constructed new buildings downtown during the course of the decade. The 1920's had seen the design of significant department stores in Europe by P. L. Kramer, W. M. Dudok, and above all, Eric Mendelsohn, and these were frequently studied by American designers of the genre. The streamlined corner, the continuous marquee, and the vertical arresting pylon can be found in Kramer's de Bijenkorf Store in the Hague as well as in Mendelsohn's commercial architecture (FIG. 6.28). Not all designers or their patrons accepted the dynamic imagery of Streamlining without qualification, however. Although Bartlett Cocke's new store for Joske's in San Antonio in 1937 (FIG. 6.71),[56] employed the curved corner and continuous marquee, it also introduced elements of the Modern Classic and hints of the Spanish Colonial, suggesting that to many architects, Streamlining was just another style, not a matter of fundamental conviction, and that the eclectic impulse lay not far beneath the surface.

Perhaps the modernistic idiom had a greater affinity to industry than to retailing, since the engineer's concept of functionalism interacted with the industrial designer's expression of style. The heavy industrial plants created by Albert Kahn for General Motors and Ford, which culminated in the latter's immense River Rouge plant celebrated by Charles Sheeler, established a functionalist aesthetic for factory design in which ornament of any species had no place.[57] But Kahn had also designed the Ford and General Motors pavilions at the Chicago Century of Progress, in conjunction with the exhibition design of Walter Dorwin Teague, and so functionalism and modern styling were

FIG. 6.71
JOSKE'S DEPARTMENT STORE,
San Antonio. 1937ff.
Bartlett Cocke, architect.

confounded in the public mind. Streamlining symbolized machine efficiency and looked modern. The Austin Company of Cleveland developed this pastiche of functional and Streamlined imagery in a series of highly influential plants around the country.[58] The Streamlined imagery was most readily applied to the lighter processing and service industries that were moving out of the zone of transition around the center city and seeking suburban locations with highway access.

Dairies, bottling plants, bakeries, and laundries also exploited the Streamlined look in the late 1930's. The Coca-Cola Company, Borden's Dairy, Mrs. Baird's, Buttercrust Bakeries, and various laundry companies were among the service industries in Texas that erected Streamlined processing plants.[59]

Streamlining was also widely adopted for small professional office buildings and apartment houses during the 1930's. The commercial block facing the courthouse square

FIG. 6.72
COMMERCIAL BLOCK,
San Augustine. N.D.

FIG. 6.73
APARTMENT HOUSE,
Alice. N.D.

in San Augustine (FIG. 6.72) presents a somewhat contrived asymmetrical facade to the street, with the circulation expressed as a vertical slot between horizontal bands defined by brick detail. That the left side of the street facade is slightly wider than the right—and one corner is turned in a bull-nose curve while the other is square—comes across as a slightly awkward effort to achieve asymmetrical balance.

Streamlining was also applied occasionally to collective housing types, where it is often difficult to disentangle from the influence of the International style. A small apartment house in Alice (FIG. 6.73) demonstrates this ambiguity. Streamlining is implied by the curved jambs and horizontal moldings applied to the main entrance, and by the curving line of the balcony and its pipe railing. But cantilevered balconies and pipe railings are also found in the International Modern tradition, and the strict

symmetry and closed corners of the Alice apartment house belie the asymmetrical principles of composition common to both traditions.

By the 1940's, the corner window—either squared or rounded—had come to symbolize modernity, even though in most cases a pipe column supported the corner, rather than the cantilever. Found alike in the Usonian houses of Frank Lloyd Wright and in the International Modern work of William Lescaze, such corner windows figure prominently in the residential design of the period, discussed in Chapter 7.

Abstracted classicism, Zig-Zagging, and Streamlining had become popular styles in the late 1920's and throughout the Depression decade, competing for the public's allegiance with the surviving vestiges of historical eclecticism. Purists in Europe and America might complain that these styles were just that—styles: superficial alternatives to the Spanish Colonial and the Beaux-Arts Classic rather than an authentic modern architecture, founded on the new technologies of the modern age and adapted to the social problems of the twentieth century. In the course of the 1930's, these two poles of critical appreciation—the modernistic and the modern—would move more closely together, although the dichotomy never quite disappeared. This convergence of the modernistic impulse with the demands for an authentic modernism, reinforced by a metamorphosis within the modern movement toward organic and regional concerns, comprises one of the themes of the following two chapters.

# VII

## RESIDENTIAL DESIGN: MODES AND TYPOLOGIES, 1895–1940

### THE LATE-VICTORIAN HOUSE: A RESOLUTION OF PICTURESQUE AND FORMAL VALUES

Residential architecture in Texas, as in the nation at large, alternated between the common and the monumental; developing the typologies and techniques of vernacular building on one hand, and sharing in the eclectic modes of learned architecture on the other. This ambivalence was apparent as early as the 1840's, when Greek Revival houses began to appear in East Texas, built by designing craftsmen armed with the pattern books that permitted them to reproduce the forms and details of the national style accurately. This replication of Greek temple forms for residential design was vigorously attacked in 1841 by Andrew Jackson Downing:

> In a dwelling house, the expression of purpose is conveyed by the chimney tops [and] the porch or veranda. . . . Yet how often do we meet . . . models of Greek temples . . . without the least hint . . . whether the edifice is a chapel, a bank, a hospital, or the private dwelling of a man of wealth![1]

In 1850 Downing published *The Architecture of Country Houses* which provided distinctively residential models to a new generation of designing craftsmen, and thus established domestic architecture as a separate species of design divorced somewhat from the monumental styles. Although after the Civil War a certain number of imposing houses were built in the High-Victorian modes of Second Empire, Victorian Gothic, and Italianate fashion, a larger body of work eludes such simple identification with the dominant public building styles. Vernacular and learned eclectic houses alike can be recognized as residential forms by the use of porches. The porch, as advocated by Downing in the 1840's, would survive as the most characteristic feature of American residential architecture for about seventy-five years.

Porches and eave bracketing would normally be constructed of wood, regardless of the kind of material employed in the house itself. In East Texas, for example, Victorian houses continued to be built of wood with weatherboarded exteriors. In the Hill Country, fine-dressed limestone became the characteristic medium. In West Texas, local sandstones were used, usually rough faced except for trim. Here and there brick was used as a superior material. It was either of local manufacture or transported by rail after the railroads bound Texas to the national economy in the 1870's.

FIG. 7.01
TYPICAL VICTORIAN HOUSE,
1303 West Main Street,
Waxahachie. c. 1890.

But everywhere the porches and eave brackets were of wood, and often consisted of items of stock manufacture ordered from catalogs, shipped to Texas by rail, and simply nailed up by the designing contractor. This proliferation of wooden decoration is commonly known as Victorian Gingerbread, or sometimes more descriptively as "stickwork."[2]

As the 1870's gave way to the 1880's and then to the early 1890's, the scale of this ornamental stickwork changed. Heavier, more massively proportioned elements gave way to a lighter, more delicate membering, sometimes approxi-

mating a membrane of basketry. Concurrently, the composition and proportions of the houses also evolved. Proportions in the 1880's became more steeply vertical, and the outline and configuration of the house became more irregular and picturesque. An emphasis on the corner became a pronounced value in design; large houses around 1890 often featured a corner turret or oriel (FIG. 7.01). At the same time, the stickwork porches tended to ramble across the front and side of the house, wrapping around the salient corner and drawing the passerby's attention to the diagonal aspect instead of the front elevation. The fragmentation of the classically proportioned and symmetrically disposed Greek temple facade, which Downing had attacked fifty years before, could hardly have been more thorough or more complete. Victorian taste had prevailed. But by the 1890's, a reaction in favor of formal and classical values in design was once again on the horizon.

This reaction had its roots in several sources. The United States Centennial in 1876 had focused attention on American history of the colonial period, including the Palladian classicism of the eighteenth-century American Georgian style. Many of the eastern states selected this style for their state pavilions at the next American world's fair, the Columbian Exposition at Chicago in 1893. Since the early 1880's, certain eastern architects had been cultivating an American Renaissance of formal, monumental architecture, which would prevail as the dominant style of the Chicago fair and influence American architecture for the next quarter century. Nevertheless, the state pavilions at the exposition were largely domestic in scale, and colonial rather than Renaissance in character. These pavilions perhaps did more than the Great White Way to redirect the course of American residential architecture.[3]

The first traces of a new classicism in Texas domestic architecture appeared in the stickwork details, which became more robust and correctly proportioned in the 1890's. A house in Gainesville (FIG. 7.02) demonstrates this classicizing of the stickwork detail in comparison to the earlier example. The porch supports have now become paired classical columns supporting an architrave and cornice, rather than slender posts with brackets and a skirt of fine spindles beneath the porch roof. The columns of the Gainesville house rest on a brick banister, which reduces their height and facilitates classical proportioning. This late-Victorian genre retains the wooden porch rail, but uses classical balusters to replace the slender spindles of the preceding phase.

There are subtle adjustments in composition at the Gainesville house that portend the new classicism even more strongly than the stickwork details. Although the porch rambles around both sides of the house, it is interrupted on the central axis by a pedimented entrance pavilion leading to the front door. The two sides of this central axis are dissimilarly treated, thus avoiding absolute symmetry, but there is no strong skewing to a salient corner. The opposing principles of picturesque asymmetry and formal axiality compete; the house is a monument of transition.

FIG. 7.02
LATE-VICTORIAN HOUSE,
417 South Denton Street,
Gainesville. C. 1895.

FORMALIST DESIGN: 1900–1917

By the early 1900's this transition was practically complete. Except in the Bungalow mode (see the next section in this chapter) and in some Prairie School work (see Chapter 3), formality, symmetry, and frontality had become the dominant principles of composition in domestic architecture. As in the Victorian period, however, a dichotomy existed between prestige residences in fashionable neighborhoods, often designed by architects applying the increasingly correct stylistic vocabulary of Academic Eclecticism (see Chapter 4), and housing constructed for a less elite clientele of homeowners or speculative inves-

FIG. 7.03
TYPICAL FOURSQUARE,
5702 Palo Pinto Street,
Dallas. C. 1900–1910.

FIG. 7.04
GABLE-ROOFED FOURSQUARE,
Dallas. 1910.

tors by contractor-builders following published models. The latter often evaded precise stylistic designation. The simplest form of such symmetrical, frontal houses has been called the foursquare,[4] represented by a house in Dallas (FIG. 7.03).

In its simplest form, the foursquare comprised six rooms, with a large living room across the front of the house and an entrance and stair in the front corner. Despite this asymmetrical configuration in plan, the front elevation was only slightly inflected toward the corner, if at all. The full front porch, carried over from the Victorian era, masked all such planning asymmetry. A larger,

eight-room foursquare might have a center entrance and two full rooms across the front. The basic foursquare configuration might be embellished with details drawn from one of the contemporary progressive or eclectic modes, but did not really conform to them in more fundamental respects. The front porch, part of the American suburban vernacular since the Civil War, precluded accurate rendering of most historical models.

A variant of the hipped-roof foursquare was the gable-roofed form,[5] represented by a house in Dallas (FIG. 7.04). In the gable-roofed variant of the four-square, the ornamental detail was frequently borrowed

FIG. 7.05
SCOTT MANSION
(foursquare with Mission traces
and Art Nouveau ornament),
425 South Church Street,
Paris. 1908–1910.
J. L. Wees, architect.

from the Craftsman Bungalow mode (see the next section), and low-pitched roofs, heavy rafters and eave-bracketing, and selective use of shingles or half-timbering are frequently transposed to such gabled four-squares from the bungalow mode.

Although the foursquare was intrinsically a vernacular housing form, it could be used as the basis for ornamental embellishment in any of a number of fashionable modes, from Prairie School to Mission Revival. One of the most extraordinary examples of such fashionable conflation is the Scott Mansion in Paris, erected between 1908 and 1910 to the design of J. L. Wees (FIG. 7.05). Except for a displaced side entrance, both of the elevations of the house are biaxially symmetrical and fronted by a continuous veranda. Unlike its counterparts a decade earlier, there is no inflection toward the corner, despite the intersection of streets that bound the corner lot. The construction of tan pressed brick is commonplace at this date, and the curved gable parapets and deeply overhanging red-tile roof convey suggestions of the Mission style. The ornament of the Scott Mansion is Art Nouveau, however; this is perhaps the only occurrence of this exotic European style in Texas (appropriately, in Paris).

FIG. 7.06
GEORGE PATTULO HOUSE
(Georgian Colonial),
5520 Swiss Avenue, Dallas. 1914.
Thompson and Fooshee, architects.

Despite its Mission Revival and Art Nouveau details, the Scott Mansion is fundamentally an elaborate foursquare, which as an autonomous housing form was an inappropriate vehicle for the more literal and accurate rendering of historical models that characterized Academic Eclecticism in this period. Architects who designed learned renditions of the historical modes for prosperous clients normally respected the same propensity for frontality and formal symmetry, but often found it necessary to dispense with the front porch. The George

Pattulo House in Dallas (FIG. 7.06), designed in 1914 by Thompson and Fooshee, is a Georgian Colonial design that sacrifices the front porch to greater historical accuracy.[6] The axial symmetry and Palladian classical details in red brick and white trim bring the Pattulo House very close to a literal revival. Even the central hall plan with side stair lighted by a Palladian window is adapted directly from eighteenth-century precedents. Nevertheless, the architects made some eclectic adaptations, as in the large banks of grouped windows on the first floor, which have no historical precedent. The environmentally popular porch is accommodated on the side of the house, where it occasionally was placed in the eighteenth-century Georgian style.

A more elaborate, less specifically Georgian Colonial rendition of English Palladianism is the Greer-McCutcheon House, built in 1916 (FIG. 7.07).[7] Although all of the details are derived from the English Palladian vocabulary, the house is not a revival of any eighteenth-century model, but is a twentieth-century eclectic interpretation. One-story corner porches have been placed to bracket the main housing block, thus retaining the sheltered porch without obscuring the front facade, where an open terrace connects the two projecting corner porches.

The same spirit of allusive eclecticism seen in a Georgian context could also be marshaled to evoke a Mediterranean or Spanish character. A house in Dallas (FIG. 7.08) uses the same protruding one-story porches to bracket the main facade; only now the tile roof and white

FIG. 7.07
GREER-MCCUTCHEON HOUSE
(English Palladian),
Dallas. 1916.

FIG. 7.08
HOUSE (Mediterranean),
3518 Armstrong Parkway, Dallas. N.D.

FIG. 7.09
LAURA WHITE HOUSE
(Mission Revival),
900 South Bridge Street,
Brady. 1912.

## THE BUNGALOW MODE AND ITS PERMUTATIONS

The bungalow is both a style and a type. The term originated in India, where it described a one-story building surrounded by a veranda. By the first decade of the twentieth century, the "bungalow" had become a common American domestic type, probably appearing first in California and spreading quickly throughout the West. Generically, therefore, the bungalow may be considered a one- or one-and-a-half-story house with a porch; although after 1920, as porches began to disappear from larger housing types, a one-story porchless house appeared that should also probably be classified as a bungalow. One-story "cottages" with extensive stickwork porches had been built in the Victorian period, of course, but the term "bungalow" had not been used to describe them, just as it has not been applied to the tract developers' one-story ranch houses erected since World War II. "Bungalow" thus implies not just a spatial classification, but also a set of formal characteristics occurring within a limited time period, roughly 1900–1930.[8]

Apart from its one-story plan and its porch, the attributes of a typical pre–World War I bungalow include low-pitched roofs that enclose a partial second-floor or attic space, and extensive roof overhangs with exposed eave carpentry in the form of rafters and brackets. This formal vocabulary could be applied on larger two-story houses as well. The houses of Charles and Henry Greene in California epitomize the large house in the Bungalow style. Houses of comparable scale and complexity are rare in Texas, but

plaster walls confer a Mediterranean rather than English character.

A literal quotation of Spanish Baroque detail in American architecture did not become widespread until after World War I, but the more vaguely suggestive Mission Revival style was occasionally used before then in Texas, for residential as well as public buildings. The Laura White House in Brady of 1912 (FIG. 7.09) is a good example of the Mission Revival, sometimes known in Texas as the Texian style. The flat plaster walls terminating in curved gable parapets and the tile roofs supported on heavy wooden bracketing recall the same vocabulary of forms found in public architecture of the Mission Revival. The designer has skillfully manipulated the forms to provide a full front porch while still emphasizing the picturesque aspect of the style.

the Bungalow vocabulary could be applied as alternative detailing to variations of the foursquare, as seen above (FIG. 7.04).

The California work of the Greene brothers also reflects a reciprocal relationship with the Arts and Crafts movement—a relationship they shared with their midwestern contemporary, Frank Lloyd Wright. There is no evidence that Wright and the Greenes knew each other, but both knew Gustave Stickley, who published work by both in *The Craftsman*. As editor of this journal from 1902 to 1914, Stickley became the leading American exponent of the Arts and Crafts movement. The Arts and Crafts Exhibition Society had been founded in England to carry on the work and ideals of William Morris, who died in 1896. Primary to Morris' philosophy had been the idea that the production of objects of everyday use was just as much a fine art as painting, sculpture, and architecture. There was no fundamental distinction between fine and applied arts; artifacts acquired value when labor was expended on them. This tenet, taken over from John Ruskin, placed value on craftsmanship rather than on the refinement of the finished product. For thirty-five years, Morris' firm produced furniture, metalwork, textiles, and wallpaper that disciplined late-Victorian design with a spirit of rudimentary simplicity. These values would be propagated to the European continent and to America by *The Studio*, the journal of the Arts and Crafts Exhibition Society. In the fifteen years before World War I, dozens of arts and crafts enterprises were founded in the United States. Stickley's Craftsman Enterprises were

only the best known; others included Elbert Hubbard's Roycrofters in Syracuse, Rookwood Potteries in Cincinnati, and the Auvergne Press in Chicago, founded by Frank Lloyd Wright and William Winslow in emulation of Morris' Kelmscott Press.[9]

Gustave Stickley, however, was the movement's leading American exponent. He produced a form of sturdy, rudimentary furnishings that reflected the ideals of William Morris and provided the appropriate setting for the simple but refined life-style of his adherents. The furnishings and rendered interiors published by Stickley reflect the ideal interior environment of the Bungalow style. Through his Craftsman Home Builder's Club, Stickley also purveyed construction drawings with which a client could have his or her Craftsman home built. There thus has been a tendency to equate Stickley more exclusively with the Bungalow style than facts seem to warrant. The term "Craftsman style" or "Craftsman Bungalow" are often used generically to describe a body of domestic architecture to which Gustave Stickley was only one contributor.[10]

In fact, an extensive number of organizations catered to the Bungalow movement and its middle-class clientele, purveying not only working drawings for local construction but even complete, pre-cut houses that could be shipped by rail and merely assembled on the site. Sears, Roebuck and Company was one of the largest of these merchandisers; the pre-cut kit of parts was just another commodity available through its mail-order catalogs.[11]

Perhaps the most common form the "Craftsman" Bungalow style

FIG. 7.10
BUNGALOW
(front gable with offset front-gable porch),
5401 Miller Avenue, Dallas. N.D.

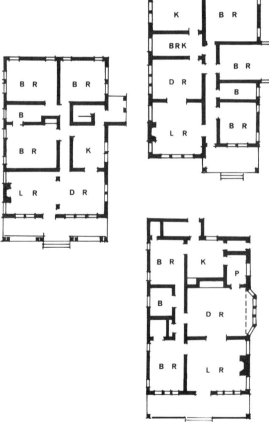

FIG. 7.11
TYPICAL BUNGALOW FLOOR PLANS.
*From Vernooy, "The Bungalow."*
*Reprinted by permission of D. Andrew Vernooy.*

took was the front-gable form with offset front-gable porch, represented by an example in Dallas (FIG. 7.10). Because bungalows were commonly built without basements, the house sits low on the ground; the siding masks the foundation. The rafters are exposed on the sides, and the roof overhang on the front gables terminates in a false rafter supported on triangular brackets. The porch supports rest on masonry pedestals.

Various plan configurations for a five- or six-room bungalow (FIG. 7.11) demonstrate its basic bipartite division: living-dining-kitchen on one side, bedrooms and bath on the other. These planning variations were predicated on standard sizes of milled lumber and standard joist spans.

Various permutations of this basic plan, roof form, and ornamental detail were possible. Bay windows, inglenooks, or alcoves could be extruded from the body of the house to provide for the refinements that made living in an Arts and Crafts house an artistic experience. The plan itself could be offset with an L to permit a separate vestibule in front or wider bedrooms behind. The plan could also be extended back to include an extra tier of rooms to the rear, which could accommodate six or seven rooms and three or more bedrooms. Roof forms could vary. The front gable porch could be juxtaposed to a side gable over the house, or jerkinhead gables or hipped-roof forms could be substituted for the triangular gable. The front porch could be centered rather than offset, or offset further to incorporate a side porch or porte cochere. Dormers and cross-gables could be used to ventilate the attic space or accommodate extruded functions. Materials could also be varied. Shingles might be substituted for weatherboarding, either on the entire house or in the gables; half-timbering was sometimes used to fill gables as well. Brick or cobblestone was often used for porches or chimneys. Thus, the possibilities for variation within the Bungalow type exceed the possibility of illustrating them all. FIGURES 7.12 through 7.14 are representative possibilities.

The bungalow in its most common form is a small, one-story, single-family house with five or six rooms. Extensive neighborhoods of such houses were developed in all Texas towns and cities from the turn of the century until the mid–1920's. It became perhaps the most pervasive and representative Texan housing type. Multiple housing forms of the bungalow type also occurred. The duplex bungalow was not uncommon, and the Craftsman Bungalow court (as opposed to the Hispanic and modernistic versions of the same type), a popular form of retirement housing in California, appeared at least once in Texas: at the Montana Courts in El Paso (FIG. 7.15).

But the bungalow was a style as well as a type, and as such might appeal also to the prosperous clientele of large houses. Various means were found to extend the bungalow form beyond the five- or six-room one-story prototype. On a national perspective, the most common way to extend the bungalow was to place a second floor of bedrooms in the attic space beneath the roof, and to light these rooms with dormers and gable windows. Squeezing the upper floor directly under the roof preserved the

FIG. 7.12
BUNGALOW (single-front gable with included full-front porch). N.D.

FIG. 7.13
BUNGALOW
(side gable with symmetrical entrance porch, jerkinhead gables), 5020 Abbott Street, Dallas. N.D.

FIG. 7.14
BUNGALOW
(front gable with offset side-gabled porch),
3511 Dartmouth Avenue, Dallas. N.D.

FIG. 7.15
MONTANA COURTS,
El Paso. N.D.

proportions of a bungalow, but deprived the bedrooms of the insulating properties of a separate attic space. Upper floors in such "semi-bungalows" were always cold in winter and hot in summer. They are rarely found in Texas, where the extreme summer heat would make these semi-attic spaces intolerable. Instead, the most common extended form in Texas is the "popped-up" bungalow, in which a partial second story with its own roof and attic space rises above the low-pitched roof forms of the ground floor. A popped-up bungalow in Dallas (since demolished) is typical of this variation of Bungalow morphology (FIG. 7.16).

As this example illustrates, the bungalow form is by no means confined to bungalow neighborhoods, where the benefits of home ownership have been made accessible to the lower middle class.[12] Bungalow forms are frequently found interspersed with other styles and types in prosperous neighborhoods as well. It is, for example, the dominant housing form in most West Texas cities, which were rapidly growing during the first quarter of the century. Extended variations of the bungalow line the main streets of these cities, just as the grand Victorian houses from the 1890's do in the towns of East Texas. An extended bungalow in Mineral Wells illustrates this phenomenon (FIG. 7.17). The house is constructed of brick, indicating its status. It has both a side-gabled porte cochere and a front-gabled porch, and the roofs are supported by tapered wooden posts resting on brick pedestals. A cross-gabled, partial second floor is "popped-up." Indeed, in its cross-axial configuration, radiating porches, and partial second floor it somewhat resembles a Prairie School house, and some such influence may have occurred.

The bungalow form, as a style and as a type, continued to be constructed well into the 1920's. Nevertheless, it did undergo some morphological changes during the course of that decade; for the most part these paralleled shifts in other residential forms. As porches became less popular in more fashionable modes, they tended to diminish or disappear on the bungalow as well. An example in Dallas (FIG. 7.18) illustrates this tendency. The porch has disappeared, to be replaced by an unroofed front terrace and a vestigial aedicula sheltering the main entrance. Details have been classicized and the character-

FIG. 7.16
EXTENDED BUNGALOW WITH "POPPED-UP" SECOND FLOOR, formerly at 3603 Harvard Avenue, Dallas. N.D.

FIG. 7.17
EXTENDED BUNGALOW WITH TRACE ELEMENTS OF PRAIRIE SCHOOL, 1001 East Hubbard Street, Mineral Wells. N.D.

FIG. 7.18
BUNGALOW
(front terrace in lieu of porch),
Dallas. N.D.

FIG. 7.19
"TUDOR" BUNGALOW WITH
FRONT CHIMNEY,
5943 Monticello Avenue, Dallas. N.D.

istic rafters and brackets have disappeared. The bungalow as a type remains, but the style has been supplanted.

A more common evolutionary form of the 1920's bungalow borrowed from the revived picturesque aesthetic of that decade (see below). The full verandas of the earlier Bungalow style have disappeared, surviving at best as small entrance or side porches, but the characteristic feature of the design has now become the front chimney. This development may be seen in a bungalow in Dallas (FIG. 7.19). The chimney had not previously figured prominently as a design element, being either centralized within the house or placed on a side wall. Now, however, as on larger housing types, the front chimney has become a powerful device for picturesque massing. It functions as a dominant vertical element, asymmetrically placed, about which the front entrance and windows are composed.[13] These houses, sometimes superficially described as Tudor,[14] are usually constructed of brick and frequently embellished with rusticated stone trim and other picturesque embellishments. In many neighborhoods, they seem to supplant the earlier bungalow forms at rather precise points. Adjacent blocks on a given street or parallel streets may suddenly change from a uniform fabric of Craftsman Bungalows to one of front-chimney brick bungalows, reflecting the chronological sequence of land development. A comparable shift in residential style is also perceivable in neighborhoods of larger homes, beginning about the time of World War I.

When America entered the Depression in 1929, the bungalow as a type had been the dominant form of residence in Texas for a quarter century. Its simplicity of construction—and aggressive marketing by bungalow brokers—had extended the benefits of home ownership to a broader clientele of the middle class. Nevertheless, a majority of American households still rented their domiciles in 1929. Even detached bungalows on separate lots, at least in less prestigious neighborhoods, were frequently rented from landlords who held landed property as investment, rather than trusting to the stock market or banks. Owners of multiple-dwelling forms, such as the duplex or bungalow court, obviously sought to lease all but one of the housing units, at the very least. By constructing multiple forms of rental housing, investors benefited from economies of land use and construction cost. Two units sharing a party wall could be constructed more cheaply than two detached units, and could be situated on less property. The tenement and the rowhouse terrace were the most efficient forms of such multiple housing, but these did not comport well with the low-density scale of neighborhoods in most Texas cities. One form of multiple dwelling did become quite popular in Texas, because it combined the economies of construction and land use with the convenience of living on one floor: the stacked duplex.

This structure seems to have flourished in Texas cities after World War I, when the expanding perimeter of urbanization led to an increased density of settlement in an intermediate ring between the center city and the most extended suburbs. The stacked duplex catered to this population influx in strategic

FIG. 7.20
STACKED DUPLEX,
6151–6153 Oram Street, Dallas. N.D.

neighborhoods, such as Oak Lawn and Highland Park in Dallas, where landlords sought to augment property rents without sacrificing genteel suburban character. The average stacked duplex, represented by one in Dallas (FIG. 7.20), looks at first glance like a large freestanding house. It may or may not disport a front chimney, but presents an asymmetrical, picturesque aspect to the street. The distinguishing feature of the stacked duplex is the separate entrances for first- and second-floor flats; the latter opens to a stair to the upper floor. Frequently, as in FIG. 7.20, corner porches are provided above each other for the superimposed flats. The lower porch may also incorporate the entrance to the ground-floor unit. Designers frequently manipulated the separate entrances and porches for picturesque effect, a strategy consistent with the evolving form conventions of the 1920's, to be discussed next.

FIG. 7.21
ENGLISH TUDOR HOUSE
WITH FRONT CHIMNEY,
Dallas. N.D.

PICTURESQUE DESIGN: 1918–1930

Sometime around the time of World War I, American residential design began to undergo a shift in values that would affect all housing types— from the bungalow with its porchless facade and front chimney to the grander homes in prestige neighborhoods designed by architects. Although domestic designers continued to employ symmetrical, formal partis throughout the 1920's, a picturesque and asymmetrical alternative became widely popular after a quarter-century of formality. In compositional terms this shift in design values entailed the suppression of the front porch and the increased prominence of stair and chimney placement on the facade. In stylistic terms, the 1920's saw new interpretations of historical models gain increased prominence, of which the English Tudor and the Spanish Colonial are perhaps the most significant. It should be noted, however, that these were eclectic

modes of design and not literal revivals, and that the popularity of these two styles seems derived in part from their susceptibility to picturesque composition.

This change from formal to picturesque expression also coincided with changes in the morphology of suburban development and housing plan types. New upper-class suburbs laid out after World War I tended to incorporate larger lot sizes with extended frontages. Residence streets were laid out from east to west, if possible, and a preference was given to lots on the south side, where sunlight could be introduced on the private, rear side of the residence. Floor plans evolved toward fewer but larger rooms, and the living room assumed functions assigned to the music room, library, and reception parlor in Victorian houses. The dining space, as well, often extended off the living room rather than taking up a separate room. Traditional center-hall plans were abandoned in favor of more informal configurations. For example, greater property frontage allowed for linear plans one room deep, which permitted through-ventilation, especially desirable in the Texas climate. As front porches were abandoned, they were supplanted by private terraces and patios to the rear of the house. Although initially relegated to the rear corner of the lot like the stables and carriage house it replaced, the garage eventually was incorporated into the body of the house, further elongating its street frontage. These generic attributes of the 1920's and 1930's suburban house are found both in eclectic and progressive modes of expression. The so-called Period House only loosely borrowed forms and details from various historical periods; in planning it had more in common with the regionalist and modernist plans than it did with the house forms of the seventeenth and eighteenth centuries, or for that matter, with the nineteenth-century Victorian house.[15]

A house in Dallas (FIG. 7.21) is typical of the fully evolved Tudor residence of the 1920's. The steeply pitched slate roofs, half-timbering, banks of leaded casement windows, and four-centered Tudor arch comprise the characteristic ingredients of this style. Although half-timbering had been an occasional element in the Bungalow mode and its larger Craftsman variants, it had been combined with gables of shallower pitch and with highly articulated rafters and brackets. These features were now suppressed in favor of a more literal evocation of a recognizable historical idiom. The new prominence of the chimney in Picturesque Eclectic practice reinforces this historical context, as the ornamental chimney had been a common feature of English fifteenth- and sixteenth-century architecture—the Tudor and Elizabethan centuries.

Not all designers applied historical details with such authenticity, however. Tudor form conventions could be more freely interpreted, as on the Eastman House in Dallas (FIG. 7.22), built in 1923.[16] Here the front chimney, which is tucked behind the entrance porch with its offset gable, is less prominent. Employed here, however, is a new picturesque compositional device: the front stair. The dominant feature of the facade is the great elevated casement window corresponding to the stair landing, placed

FIG. 7.22
EASTMAN HOUSE
(generic Tudor with front stair),
5816 Swiss Avenue, Dallas. N.D.

beneath the larger of the two steeply pitched front gables. The house is constructed of painted brick without recourse to half-timbering.

A more emphatic use of the asymmetrical forward projection is found in houses such as one in Dallas (FIG. 7.23), where the house plan has become L-shaped with a round tower in the reentrant corner. Such forms evoke French rather than English allusions, and have been associated with a Norman style.[17] The Norman style employs steep slate roofs, as does the English Tudor, but the flaring eave line and the dormers breaking into the cornice were considered French stylistic devices. When such steep and flaring slate roofs were combined with symmetrical plans and classical details, a species of French Colonial was produced, as in a house in Dallas (FIG. 7.24).[18] If a gambrel roof was used, the resulting house might be read as Dutch Colonial.

None of these styles had any particular relevance to Texas, which

FIG. 7.23
FRENCH NORMAN STYLE HOUSE
(tourelle in re-entrant corner),
3738 Armstrong Parkway, Dallas. N.D.

FIG. 7.24
FRENCH COLONIAL HOUSE,
Dallas. N.D.

had never been part of English, French, or Dutch colonial empires. It had been part of the Spanish Empire, however, and contained some of the most distinguished monuments of the provincial Spanish Baroque. The impulse for an eclectic style based on the Spanish Colonial period came from outside Texas, however. As seen in Chapter 5, it was the California missions, not the earlier ones in Texas, that prompted the Mission Revival beginning in the 1890's, and the style enjoyed a limited popularity in Texas before World War I. The impulse for a more accurate and sophisticated use of the Spanish Baroque also originated in California around 1915. Unlike the earlier Mission Revival phase, however, the Spanish Colonial Revival struck a strong and lasting chord in Texan sensibility. In addition to its extensive use in public architecture of the 1920's, the Spanish Colonial style was widely used for residential design, partly because it lent itself to picturesque composition.

Two strands of Spanish Colonial Revival may be discerned in residential architecture in Texas. One was the use of Spanish Baroque ornament, similar to its implementation on public and commercial architecture. The second strand employed vernacular forms and details derived particularly from the Andalusian region of Spain, with emphasis on plaster walls, timbered ceilings and porches, tile, and ironwork. These vernacular effects, like the half-timbering of the English Tudor and French Norman modes, condoned an informality that was foreign to the authentic Spanish Baroque. As might be expected, the prevalent eclecticism of the period encouraged a free combination of Baroque and vernacular elements. The style thus created was widely diffused throughout the Spanish borderlands, including California and Florida.

In Dallas, the premier interpreters of the new Spanish Colonial sensibility were Marion Fooshee and James Cheek, designers of the Highland Park Shopping Village in 1931 (see Chapter 5). As early as 1916, when the Spanish Colonial was just beginning to supplant the Mission Revival in California, Fooshee and Cheek designed the W. G. Sterrett House in Highland Park, an autonomous suburb of Dallas (FIG. 7.25). Here the vernacular elements—plaster walls, tile roofs, wooden balconies, ornamental ironwork—predominate, but there is no trace of Baroque detail. The facade of the house is a carefully contrived picturesque composition. The asymmetrically placed front turret accommodates both the main entrance and an ascending stair, devices later employed by other architects in the Tudor and Norman modes. The dissimilar treatment of the two ends of the facade further reinforces the picturesque variety. It is a remarkably precocious work for its early date.

The Sterrett House proved so popular with its owners that five years later Fooshee and Cheek designed another for their son, W. G. Sterrett, Jr., on an adjoining site (FIG. 7.26). Here the house form is more compact and somewhat more formal, and although the stair can be read in the asymmetrical composition of the facade, the semicircular turret is not used. The wood-framed second floor porch of the Andalusian vernacular is retained, however, along

FIG. 7.25
W. G. STERRETT HOUSE
(Spanish Colonial Revival),
Dallas. 1916.
Fooshee and Cheek, architects.

FIG. 7.26
W. G. STERRETT, JR., HOUSE
(Spanish Colonial Revival),
4208 Beverly Drive, Dallas. 1921.
Fooshee and Cheek, architects.

FIG. 7.27
THOMAS HOGG HOUSE
(Spanish Colonial Revival),
San Antonio. 1924.
Atlee B. and Robert M. Ayres, architects.

FIG. 7.28
C. D. HILL HOUSE
(Spanish Colonial Revival),
3318 Beverly Drive, Dallas. 1924.
C. D. Hill, architect.

with the customary plastered walls, tiled roof, and touches of wrought iron ornament.[19]

By the 1920's, the Spanish Colonial was becoming popular. In 1924, Atlee B. and Robert M. Ayres adopted this mode for the Thomas Hogg House in San Antonio (FIG. 7.27), the only Texas example included in Rexford Newcomb's 1928 *Mediterranean Domestic Architecture in the United States*.[20] The Ayres also used a stair turret, (as Fooshee and Cheek had done on the first Sterrett house) as well as a front chimney, but now the turret functioned as a hinge in the dogleg shift of the plan, a feature characteristic of the large suburban houses they designed. Unlike more compact and conventional configurations, this planning permitted the principal rooms of the house to have both front and rear exposures, inviting through-circulation of breezes and alternative morning and afternoon prospects. In this regard, the Ayres' regionalism seems more than a historical style, for it anticipates the planning principles of the 1930's Texas Regionalists David Williams and O'Neil Ford (see a later section in this chapter).

A more compact and conventional application of historical associations is found in the house Dallas architect C. D. Hill designed for himself in 1924 (FIG. 7.28).[21] This house is very nearly biaxially symmetrical, skewed to the picturesque by the entrance vestibule on the left. Rather than the wooden beams and porches of the Andalusian vernacular, the Hill House relies on Baroque ornament for its specific historic character. The entrance and the main parlor windows are accented by spirally fluted colonnettes, a device traceable to Bernini's Baldichino at St. Peter's and recurring frequently thereafter throughout the International Baroque.

Fooshee and Cheek, Atlee B. and Robert M. Ayres, and C. D. Hill all maintained extensive architectural practices that included the design of expensive homes in elite suburbs. But most housing in Texas—not only during the 1920's but in all previous periods—was built by designing contractors who interpreted new residential fashions for the middle class. One such contractor who eventually assumed the title of architect was Clifford Hutsell, who popularized and expanded the Spanish Colonial mode in new neighborhoods of Dallas in the 1920's and 1930's. Hutsell's interpretation of this style was personal and a bit bizarre, occasionally bordering on kitsch. Lakewood Boulevard in Dallas contains perhaps the greatest assortment of Hutsell homes, which stand out from more conventional renditions of the mode. A pair of houses, erected between 1935 and 1937, reflect Hutsell's ultimate interpretation (FIG. 7.29).[22] Hutsell normally used unplastered brick, not a historically authentic material in the Spanish Colonial world, where plaster on stone predominated. His Spanish tile roofs are frequently glazed in brilliant, even variegated, colors. L-shaped plans and double-height living rooms are characteristic, and by the 1930's Hutsell had begun to use the parabolic arch for the great front window lighting the parlor. Exposed wooden balconies and decorative ironwork continue the identification with the Spanish vernacular, however. Hutsell's interiors often include painted murals and ceilings, artificial logs

FIG. 7.29
POPULIST SPANISH COLONIAL HOUSES,
Dallas. 1935–1937.
Clifford Hutsell, architect.

hung with Spanish moss, and other bizarre furnishings eschewed by more decorous designers. By the 1930's, the garage was commonly incorporated into the house form, rather than being consigned to the rear of the lot.

The Spanish Colonial idiom could also be extended to even humbler building types. One-story houses with plaster walls and tiled roofs, bungalow in type but Spanish Colonial in character, were also built in Texas, as were bungalow courts of Spanish character. The bungalow court, like the bungalow itself, was a California innovation, intended to combine the privacy and convenience of a small, one-story bungalow with the economy of party-wall construction and common access to lawns and gardens. Many were occupied by retirees of modest incomes who came seeking a milder climate. By the teens, such bunga-

FIG. 7.30
TEXAS SHEEP AND GOAT RAISERS
ASSOCIATION BUILDING
(Spanish Colonial with traces
of Pueblo Revival),
San Angelo. N.D.

low courts in California were being rendered with plaster walls and tiled parapets. A small number of such Spanish courts are to be found in Texas. One in San Angelo was discussed in Chapter 5 (FIG. 5.75).

As seen in Chapter 5, the Pueblo Revival became widespread only in New Mexico, where it became the prevalent regional style in the 1920's. It was occasionally found in the western portion of Texas, however, and suggestive trace elements occur here and there throughout the state. The distinguishing features of the Pueblo Revival are the soft, amorphous plaster walls and the absence of Spanish tile roofs. Flat roofs, parapets, and wooden structural members such as roof beams and lintels are common. The projection of the roof beam through the wall, called a viga, is the most characteristic feature of this idiom. The

crossbreeding of the Spanish Colonial and Pueblo Revival modes may be seen in a house in San Angelo (FIG. 7.30), now occupied by the Texas Sheep and Goat Raisers Association. This house combines the tile roofs, curved gable parapet, and entrance frame of the Spanish Baroque with the parapet roofline, vigas, and wooden lintels of the New Mexico pueblos. As a one-story residence, it represents the extended bungalow type translated into a highly eclectic Spanish idiom.

In the Southwest, the Pueblo and Spanish Colonial forms of architecture had been adapted to a hot, dry environment where heavy walls, tile roofs, and limited window openings provided protection against the summer heat. But Texas also contained regions peripheral to this environment. The humid prairie and the pine woods of East Texas were closer to the ecology of French Louisiana, and the coastal plain along the Gulf of Mexico was the southwestern borderlands' only opening to the Caribbean maritime frontier. These geographical circumstances suggested other forms of eclectic residential design. Perhaps the leading architect to draw upon the historical ecology of Southeast Texas was John F. Staub of Houston. Although Staub was adept at manipulating the various period modes discussed earlier—including the English Tudor, French Norman, French Georgian, and Spanish Colonial— by the 1930's he had become something of a regionalist in more than an eclectic sense. "Ravenna," designed in 1934 for Stephen P. Farish in Houston, is a grand rendition of the Southern Plantation mode (FIGS. 7.31 and 7.32). Derived from the eighteenth-century English Palla-

FIG. 7.31
"RAVENNA," STEPHEN P.
FARISH HOUSE,
Houston. 1934.
John F. Staub, architect.
*From Barnstone,* The Architecture of
John F. Staub.
*Reprinted with permission of owner.*

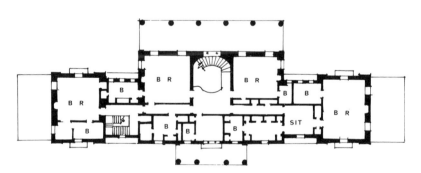

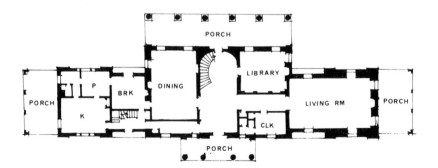

FIG. 7.32
"RAVENNA." Floor plans.
*From Barnstone,* The Architecture of
John F. Staub.
*Reprinted with permission of owner.*

FIG. 7.33
HOWARD SHANE HOUSE,
4620 Southern Avenue, Dallas. 1936.
Charles S. Dilbeck, architect.

## VERNACULAR TENDENCIES OF THE 1930'S

The stock-market crash of 1929 and subsequent Depression enforced a hiatus on most domestic construction in the United States until after passage of the FHA National Housing Act of 1934, which guaranteed mortgages for home construction and spawned a new wave of residential architecture in the latter 1930's. Although informal and linear house plans survived this hiatus, new variations of eclectic expression appeared when building resumed. One of the more popular new modes drew upon the weatherboarded houses of seventeenth-century New England for inspiration. A characteristic feature of this body of work had been the upper-story overhang, called a jetty, which resulted from the carpenter's reluctance to drill too many holes at any given point in the heavy braced frame construction commonplace in late-medieval and Tudor England and emulated by the New England colonists. Such jetties were commonly decorated at the corners by pendants of carved ornament called pendils. Both jetties and pendils began to appear in American suburbs, even in Texas, in the 1930's.

In New England, early settlers had adapted the heavy braced frame and infilled construction of English vernacular building to the more severe American climate by covering the exterior with weatherboards split from the virtually limitless virgin timber of the new continent. Such weatherboarding (or very commonly shingles, as a substitute) was also revived in the 1930's. It was often seen on upper floors above a brick or fieldstone ground floor. Such details evoked a vernacular

dian tradition as adapted to the southern colonies, Ravenna features a central block with subordinate wings and giant two-story Tuscan porticos facing both front and rear. In other respects, however, Staub departed from his historical models. Rather than consigning service functions to the dependent wings, he incorporated the wings into what becomes a long, narrow house plan, with service functions along the front (west) and principal living spaces directed to the rear (east), providing triple exposure and through-ventilation to the living room and master bedroom. Moreover, the windows are somewhat oversized in relation to Palladian proportions, with main-floor window sills carried down virtually to the floor to permit maximum circulation of air. This oversizing of windows became quite popular in the domestic architecture of the 1930's in Texas.[23]

FIG. 7.34
HOUSE,
Dallas. N.D.
Charles S. Dilbeck, architect.

tradition rather than the learned Palladianism of the eighteenth century. These devices were not utilized in a literal revival of seventeenth-century housing forms, of course, but were applied to the evolving residential house plans of the American suburbs described previously. If anything, house configuration became even more informal, with L-shaped plans and subordinate masses commonly projecting forward into the front lawn. The character of a vernacular farmstead with its artless but picturesque assemblage of sheds and outbuildings provided a rationale for informal planning that frequently incorporated the garage into the body of the house. The Howard Shane House in Dallas, designed before 1936 by Charles Dilbeck, is a representative example of this non-Regional Eclectic mode (FIG. 7.33). It is typical of the elasticity of the eclectic tradition that a house deploying obvious New England ele-ments could still be considered a ranch house in Texas, promoting confusion among those architects seeking a valid indigenous regional style for Texas (see below).[24]

This house is a relatively restrained exercise in this elastic vernacular eclecticism, at least by the normal standards of its designer. Most commentators would probably find Dilbeck's work more akin to that of Clifford Hutsell, rather than to the designs of David Williams and O'Neil Ford (see below). Like Hutsell's work in the Hispanic mode, Dilbeck brought to the Texas suburb a bizarre combination of vernacular and craftsmanlike details frequently verging on kitsch. A house in Dallas (FIG. 7.34) represents Dilbeck at his more typical exuberance.[25] It is difficult to find anything about it, however, that has been specifically adapted to the historical or environmental regionalism of Texas.

## REGIONAL AND INTERNATIONAL MODERNISM OF THE 1930'S

At Ravenna, John F. Staub had manipulated a historical model to accommodate an environmentally adapted plan. At the Ernest Bel Fay House (FIGS. 7.35 and 7.36), which Staub designed in 1937, a less rigidly historical idiom adapts more comfortably to the constraints of environmental regionalism.[26] Ostensibly designed in a Louisiana Plantation mode, the Fay House reflects a level of provincial culture comparable to that of seventeenth-century New England—certainly less sophisticated than that of eighteenth-century English America. There are no orders or proportions to trouble the designer; the house takes on a vernacular ambience. Verandas at both ground and second floor permit all main living spaces sheltered access to the outdoors, as well as ventilation, and several rooms have exposure on three sides. Although the main block of the house appears biaxially symmetrical, the plan reveals an imbalance between the left and right sides, which is carried to the three-dimensional massing by the dissimilar treatment of the dependent wings. Unlike Ravenna, where dissimilar functions were compressed into identical wings, at the Fay House the functional disparity is exploited for an informal, even picturesque, parti. The incorporation of a garage within the house form was becoming increasingly common in the 1930's, and Staub exploited this functional innovation to skew the plan and elevate the master bedroom suite to its extruded corner location on the second floor.

Elsewhere, in the quest for a French Colonial character, Staub employed decorative wrought iron for porch supports and railings in emulation of the historical architecture of New Orleans. The combination of low-silled, oversized windows, wrought-iron porches, and painted brick came to form a rather common regional idiom in East Texas.

John Staub was only one among many American architects in the 1930's who sought to renew domestic architecture by drawing upon the less academic, more vernacular strains of the historical past. But in the 1930's, certain American architects began to see regionalism as something more than historical eclecticism. They responded to the encroachment of International Modernism, itself in a process of symbiosis with more organic forms and materials, by calling for an architecture based upon the modern interpretation of the environmental imperatives and building cultures of the diverse regions of the United States. The principal interpreters of this new regionalism were Pietro Belluschi in Oregon, William Wurster in the Bay Area of California, Harwell Hamilton Harris in Southern California, and David Williams and O'Neil Ford in Texas.[27]

David Williams defined the credo of modern Southwest regionalism in 1931:

A logical regional architecture has for its origin the simple, early forms of building native to its own locale, and grows by purely functional methods into an indigenous form of art.[28]

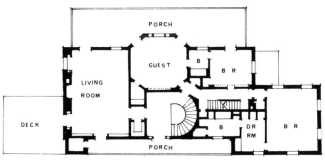

FIG. 7.35
ERNEST BEL FAY HOUSE,
105 North Post Oak Lane,
Houston. 1937.
John F. Staub, architect.
*From Barnstone,* The Architecture of
John F. Staub.
*Reprinted with permission of owner.*

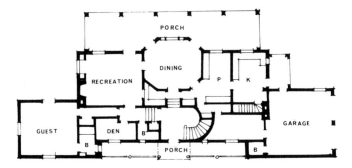

FIG. 7.36
ERNEST BEL FAY HOUSE. Floor plans.
*From Barnstone,* The Architecture of
John F. Staub.
*Reprinted with permission of owner.*

FIG. 7.37
RAY MCDOWELL HOUSE,
6292 Mercedes Avenue, Dallas. 1927.
David Williams, architect.

During the 1920's David Williams occasionally had designed in the Spanish Colonial style, but as he grew increasingly dissatisfied with the blatant eclecticism of the decade, he sought more appropriate sources for a regionalism indigenous to Texas. His "Texas Colonial" idiom, illustrated by the 1927 Ray McDowell House in Dallas (FIG. 7.37), represents one alternative. Loosely based on the antebellum architecture of East Texas and Louisiana, these houses of painted brick satisfied Williams' quest for a more indigenous form of regionalism. The interior fittings were carefully fashioned to reinforce the suggestion of frontier artisanship.[29] Williams and his young protégé, O'Neil Ford, also found indigenous roots of a Texas regionalism in the early nineteenth-century Hill Country building culture, erected by Anglo and European settlers without pretension to formal styles. As Williams described this work,

After two hundred years of trying, the Spaniards had not yet colonized the region. The land was becoming wilderness again when in 1821 Stephen Fuller Austin came with his first group of 'sober and industrious' colonists. . . . Fortunately, their own comfort demanded a little beauty and a great deal of good taste. There is not in any one of these houses built in the Southwest before 1850 an instance of imitation of foreign styles, of sham, of striving for effect, of any use of unnatural, unnecessary ornament or of material not structural and fit for its purpose. . . . Their style is modern, for it satisfies all the requirements of modern design and construction.[30]

These structures were usually one-story, gable-roofed forms, constructed of plastered stone or adobe masonry, with shed additions to the rear or wood-framed porches to the front that were included within the roof envelope. Although most had been roofed originally with wood shingles, good building timber was scarce in the sparsely wooded Hill Country, and in the 1870's most had been reroofed with tin sheets imported by rail. Somewhat incongruously, the tin roof became the icon of the Texas regional style—despite the superior insulating properties of the Spanish tile roofs, which were associated with the historical revival that Williams and Ford had come to despise.

David Williams' best-known example of the Texas regional style is the extensively published Elbert Williams House in University Park (Dallas), built in 1932 (FIG. 7.38).[31] A large, rambling house of two-and-one-half stories, the house displays the same plastered brick walls, large shuttered windows, asymmetrical facade, and frontier-artisan interior as the earlier McDowell House, but the idiom has been subtly shifted. The metal roofs, more steeply sloped than the shingled surfaces of the earlier work, have become the dominant feature, and call attention to the juxtaposition of primary gabled forms in the composition. The Williams House, however, is perhaps not as fundamentally original as is sometimes claimed, for the clapboarded upper floors and informal disposition of building masses seem similar to other forms of "vernacular" suburban architecture of the 1930's, as discussed previously.

Although David Williams left private practice in 1933 to go into public service during the Depression and subsequent world war, the lessons of the Texas vernacular were further developed by his protégé, O'Neil Ford. Several houses by Ford continue the idiom of the Elbert Williams House. Two homes in Dallas, both designed by Ford in 1932, replicate Williams' University Park house,[32] whereas Ford's 1939 house for Frank Murchison in San Antonio (FIGS. 7.39 and 7.40), designed in partnership with Arch B. Swank, Jr., illustrates both Ford's knowledge of Williams' work and his subsequent development of the idiom.[33] The massing of the Murchison House has been reduced to two stories, and the pitch of the gable reduced. The standing-seam copper roof has been retained, but stone and cedar have replaced the painted brick. Moreover, much of the house is only one-room deep, for ultimate climate control in Texas heat, and rambles over a sloping site. The predominant orientation is southeast toward the morning light and prevailing breeze, with large

FIG. 7.38
ELBERT WILLIAMS HOUSE,
Dallas. 1932.
David Williams, architect.

glazed areas and generous porches, whereas blank walls and modest windows temper the hot afternoon sun on the southwest. Although the garage is included within the roof form, a breezeway reminiscent of the dogtrots of early Texas houses separates it from the kitchen. Although evidence of explicit derivation is lacking, it seems likely that Ford was influenced by the Usonian houses of Frank Lloyd Wright, whose work experienced a remarkable regeneration during the 1930's. As the world's foremost exponent of an organic architecture, Wright could hardly fail to influence anyone seeking a new direction in American architecture.[34] Both Wright's Usonian houses and Ford's Texas vernacular seem like precursors to the ubiquitous ranch-style homes of the postwar American suburbs.

Frank Lloyd Wright built no architecture in Texas before World War II. (His considerable influence on the Prairie School in Texas has

FIG. 7.39
FRANK MURCHISON HOUSE,
9 Ironwood Road, San Antonio. 1939.
O'Neil Ford, architect.
*From Zisman,* Pencil Points *21 (April 1940).*
*Reprinted with permission of* Progressive
Architecture, *Penton Publishing.*

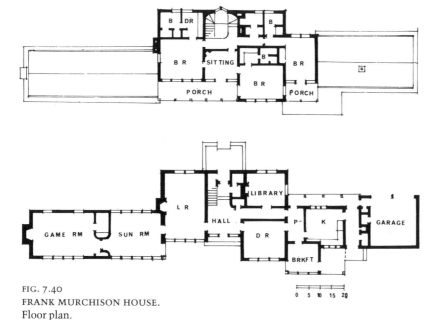

FIG. 7.40
FRANK MURCHISON HOUSE.
Floor plan.
*From Zisman,* Pencil Points *21 (April 1940).*
*Reprinted with permission of* Progressive
Architecture, *Penton Publishing.*

been discussed in Chapter 3.) His most assiduous devotee in Texas in the 1930's was Karl Kamrath of Houston, whose own house of 1938–1939 is a reasonable interpretation of Wright's own Usonian work (FIGS. 7.41 and 7.42). Faithful to Wright's precept and example, Kamrath used natural materials: horizontally split limestone and rough-sawn yellow pine. Kamrath's house plan shows some characteristic Usonian features: the slab on grade replacing the basement, the carport replacing the garage, the open plan on the first floor (not here extended to the kitchen); the fireplace near the corner of the living room establishing an implied diagonal with the corner window opposite. The screened porch is an adaptation to the climate of East Texas. The house's small lot induced Kamrath to place his bedrooms on the second floor, where a generous roof-deck is provided. The entire second floor, including the deck parapet, is clad in horizontal clapboards, recalling Wright's use of similar forms at the Herbert Johnson House in Racine and at Suntop Homes in Ardmore, Pennsylvania, among other examples.[35]

Although Karl Kamrath was the most literal interpreter of Frank Lloyd Wright in Texas, the American master also influenced other architects who sought a middle ground between abstract European Modernism and Regional Eclecticism. Howard R. Meyer was one such designer. A house by Meyer in Dallas (FIGS. 7.43 and 7.44) is an example of Meyer's domestic architecture, which combines influences from several sources.[36] The projecting ground-floor bedroom is

FIG. 7.41
KARL KAMRATH HOUSE,
Houston. 1938–1939.
Karl Kamrath, architect.

FIG. 7.42
KARL KAMRATH HOUSE. Floor plan.
*From "House for Karl Kamrath . . . ,"*
Architectural Forum *73 (December 1940).*

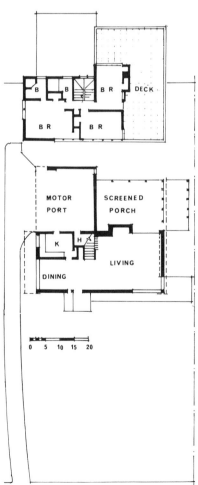

a common compositional device of the late 1930's. The shallow-pitch, standing-seam metal roofs recall those of Williams and Ford. The crisp brickwork and corner windows are commonplace modernistic mannerisms of the decade, although they are usually not combined with overhanging eaves and pitched roofs. The continuous second-floor sill line with horizontal siding above recalls Wright, whereas the second-floor roof-deck (since enclosed) might derive from either Wright or European Modernism.

Wright's regeneration in the 1930's coincided with the streamlined idiom popularized by American industrial designers, with the Modern Classic idiom for public architecture influenced by Goodhue and Cret, and with the growing American awareness of International Modern architecture of European derivation. In domestic architecture in particular, it is often difficult to separate American Streamlining from International Modern influences. Curving forms, flow lines, glass block, and bull's-eye windows seem derived from the Streamlined Commercial mode, but Le Corbusier had also introduced glass block in the 1930's, and the nautical-appearing pipe rails commonly found in this work may be traced back to the Villa Savoye. Most of the houses built in Texas in this modernistic style are of conventional masonry construction, either plastered or painted white, with flat roofs, but with quite massive-appearing wall surfaces, belying the separation of wall from structure on which the 1920's modern architecture of Europe had been predicated. The most commonly used modern feature in domestic architecture is the corner window, which became almost an icon (or cliché) of modernity in the late 1930's. The masonry wall above such windows was carried on steel shelf angles supported by a corner pipe column, conveniently concealed behind the metal sash, which

FIG. 7.43
HOUSE,
Dallas. 1940.
Howard R. Meyer, architect.

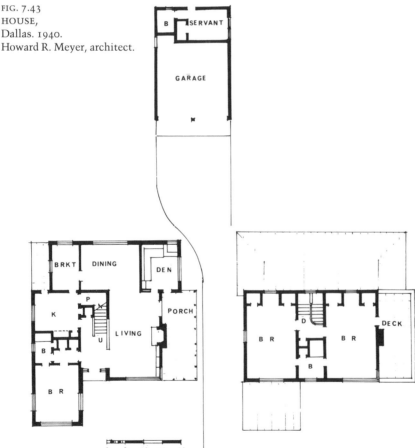

FIG. 7.44
HOUSE,
Dallas. Floor plan.
*From* Architectural Forum *72 (February 1940).*

similarly suggested modern, machine-generated technology without any fundamental commitment to an industrialized building culture. To most designers and their clients, it was simply another style.

A considerable number of such modernistic houses in Dallas were designed by Luther Sadler, who was inspired by the Texas Centennial Exposition. The International Modern image of the Magnolia Lounge by William Lescaze (see Chapter 8) seems to have had more influence on Sadler than the monumental Modern Classic forms of the main exhibition areas conceived by George Dahl and Paul Cret. A house in Dallas is typical of this series (FIG. 7.45). This residence has the painted masonry walls, flat roofs, and corner windows identified previously. The front door adjoins a reception lobby walled in glass block; the entrance itself is sheltered by a second-floor overhang supported on pipe columns. A two-car garage is incorporated into the west side of the house, beneath a second-floor porch. This facade achieves dynamic contraposto by the juxtaposition of an asymmetrically placed, semicircular stair turret with a cantilevered outside stair to the second-floor porch. These forms might have been derived from Streamlining or from the nautical imagery of Le Corbusier, an example of the stylistic ambiguity of the modern domestic idiom in 1936.[37]

From this ambiguous modernistic stance, architects might move in several directions: back to a rapprochement with traditional forms by abstracting and streamlining historical details, in what has been called the Moderne Regency, or forward to a full assimilation with

International Modernism and a possible cross-fertilization with an authentic regionalism of the Southwest.

The first of these tendencies is demonstrated by a house in Dallas (FIG. 7.46). The basic juxtaposition of two rectangular masses is similar to the parti employed by David Williams and O'Neil Ford, although now the details are compounded of modernistic and Regency sources, i.e., late Georgian of circa 1800, known in the United States as Federal. The roofs are shallowly hipped rather than flat, and the windows are double-hung wooden sash with very large panes and attenuated glazing bars—Regency characteristics. Banks of these windows are grouped at the corner of the block, however, as would be found in the modernistic work discussed previously. The bull's-eye window and horizontal flow lines are common Streamlining elements, and the double string courses between floors also reinforce the horizontality of the facade. The front chimney seems carried over from the picturesque composition of the 1920's, and the front door is detailed in manipulated brickwork, suggesting Regency attention to the entrance without replicating historical detail. Work of this kind—using brick coursing to simulate historical or Streamlined ornament and thus achieve a synthesis of the two styles—was quite common on the eve of World War II.

The alternative course of development from the ambiguous modernistic idiom of 1936 was to embrace the full rigor of International Modernism as it had been developed in Europe and now began to appear in the United States. Seminal to this

FIG. 7.45
HOUSE,
6851 Gaston Avenue, Dallas. 1936.
Luther Sadler, architect.

FIG. 7.46
MODERNE REGENCY HOUSE,
Dallas. N.D.

FIG. 7.47
CHESTER NAGEL HOUSE,
3215 Churchill Drive, Austin. 1940–1941.
Chester Nagel, architect.
*From* New Pencil Points *(January 1943).*
*Reprinted with permission of* Progressive
Architecture, *Penton Publishing.*

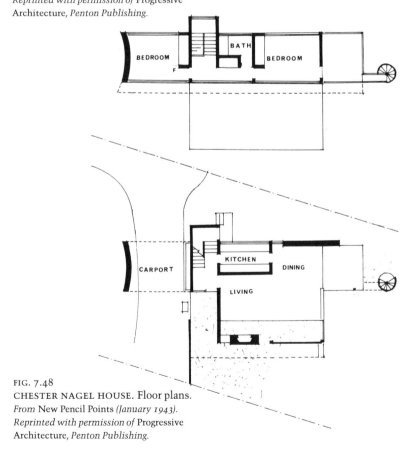

FIG. 7.48
CHESTER NAGEL HOUSE. Floor plans.
*From* New Pencil Points *(January 1943).*
*Reprinted with permission of* Progressive
Architecture, *Penton Publishing.*

process was the arrival of German émigrés fleeing National Socialism; among the most eminent were Walter Gropius and his former colleagues at the Bauhaus. Gropius, who had spent several years in England, was invited in 1937 by Dean Joseph Hudnut to assume direction of the architecture program at the Harvard Graduate School of Design. Gropius invited Marcel Breuer, a former student and teacher at the Bauhaus, to join the Harvard faculty, transforming it into the leading school of architecture in the United States. One of their first students was Chester Nagel, who had graduated with a degree in architecture from the University of Texas at Austin in 1934 and spent the intervening Depression years working for the National Park Service. In 1939 he entered Harvard, and after graduating, designed a Gropius-inspired home for himself in Austin.[38]

The Chester Nagel House (FIGS. 7.47 and 7.48), built in 1940–1941, reflects an entirely new building technology, rather than the merely novel aesthetics of the modernistic idiom. The second floor is carried on steel framing quite independently of the ground-floor living-dining areas. The openness of the main floor plan, with its flagstone paving and isolated walls of brick masonry alternating with generous expanses of glass, recalls Wright's Usonian houses. It certainly does not resemble the Bauhaus designs or the architecture that Hitchcock and Johnson had canonized as the International style in 1932.[39] In the intervening decade, International Modern architecture had undergone its own internal development, shedding much of the spartan austerity of the 1920's and rediscovering such organic qualities as the expression of natural materials. The houses that Gropius and Breuer built for themselves and a few clients in New England reflect this rapprochement between modern architecture and the tradition of artisanship; Nagel seems to have absorbed this synthesis from them at Harvard. If Nagel's house is still far removed from O'Neil Ford's Murchison House—the one having evolved from the International style and the other from the indigenous vernacular—they are both species of modern architecture. They remain closer in spirit and content than the works of each designer's mentor fifteen years before, when David Williams was still working in the Spanish Colonial Revival and Walter Gropius was designing his own Director's House at Dessau.

There was, of course, an older American fountainhead of modern architecture whom the European émigrés recognized as their spiritual mentor: Frank Lloyd Wright. When in 1924 Richard Neutra came to America to seek the roots of modern architecture, he met Wright at Louis Sullivan's funeral in Chicago. Although Neutra's professional relationship with Wright was short and stormy, he remained in Los Angeles to forge, with his Viennese compatriot Rudolf Schindler, an avantgarde modern architecture parallel to that being developed in Europe. Neutra's work was sufficiently consonant with the modernist mainstream in Europe for his Lovell House to be included in the International style exhibition at the Museum of Modern Art in 1932. Neutra's work in the 1930's represents a symbiosis between the crisp, mini-

FIG. 7.49
GEORGE KRAIGHER HOUSE,
525 Paredes Line Road, Brownsville. 1937.
Richard J. Neutra, architect.

malist forms of the International style and the lush California landscape. It was this acclimatized International Modernism that attracted George Kraigher to commission a house from Neutra in Brownsville in 1937 (FIG. 7.49).[40] The Kraigher House reveals a certain dynamic juxtaposition of horizontal and vertical planes—perhaps related in origin to De Stijl—that reflects Neutra's personal development of a rigorous modernism cut off from its European sources. In functional disposition of masses, however, the Kraigher House seems similar to the contemporaneous work of Karl Kamrath, O'Neil Ford, and Chester Nagel. All had built more or less rambling houses with partial second floors and roof decks or balconies. Each had pursued a different idiom of expression, derived from different points in the history of modern architecture, but each in his own way had expressed the site, the function, the structure, and the nature of materials. Modern architecture had arrived in Texas.

# VIII

# INTERNATIONAL AND REGIONAL MODERNISM IN THE PUBLIC SPHERE: 1936–1945

The one hundredth anniversary of Texas independence in 1936 was the occasion for monumental commemoration, not just at the Centennial Exposition at Dallas (see Chapter 6), but at various historical locations throughout the state. Memorial museums were built at the San Jacinto battleground near Houston, at Gonzales where the first battle of the War for Texas Independence had been fought, and at El Paso on the grounds of the Mining College. All of these were, of course, species of public works intended to relieve unemployment during the Depression. The San Jacinto and Gonzales memorials conform to the Modern Classic idiom commonly used for 1930's public architecture, as discussed in Chapter 6. Not all publicly sponsored architecture conformed to this modernistic style, however. The El Paso Centennial Museum was designed by Percy McGhee in the "Bhutanese Revival" that Henry Trost had introduced on the campus twenty years before, but McGhee substituted uncoursed fieldstone for plaster in the massive sloping walls.

The use of uncoursed or irregularly laid fieldstone became quite popular in the 1930's, for both domestic and public architecture. It was used extensively in those buildings of a less monumental char-

acter, subsidized by the PWA or constructed by the Civilian Conservation Corps (CCC). Such structures were built in national or state parks, both of which were significant to Texas. Big Bend National Park was created in 1935, although plans for its development were delayed by attrition in the CCC and by World War II. Even more than the national parks, state parks flourished in the Depression as a new professional arena for landscape architecture, and Texas, along with neighboring Oklahoma, developed the most elaborate state park facilities. The cabins and lodges at Bastrop State Park (FIG. 8.01) reflect the high standards of artisanship achieved within the officially sanctioned rustic style.[1]

Some of the state parks in Texas were developed in conjunction with historic monuments, whose remains and artifacts required restoration. The most significant restoration projects in Texas in the 1930's were probably the Mission Nuestra Señora del Espíritu Santo de Zuniga at Goliad (FIG. 8.02), carried out from 1935–1941 by Raiford Stripling, the San Antonio Riverwalk restoration supervised by Robert H. Hugman, and La Villita in San Antonio, a slum area restored by the National Youth Administration (NYA) under David Williams and

FIG. 8.01
LODGE,
Bastrop State Park. N.D.

FIG. 8.02
MISSION NUESTRA SEÑORA DEL
ESPÍRITU SANTO DE ZUNIGA,
Goliad. Restored 1935–1941.
Raiford Stripling, restoration architect.

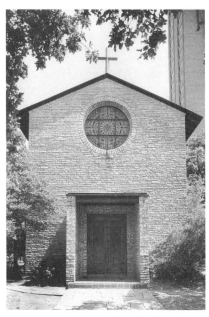

FIG. 8.03
CHAPEL IN THE WOODS,
Texas State College for Women
(now Texas Woman's University),
Denton. 1939.
O'Neil Ford and Arch Swank, architects.

O'Neil Ford.[2] All of these were public-works projects intended to put the unemployed—professional as well as unskilled—to work, but the restoration plans had the added effect of concentrating attention on indigenous techniques and craft processes. They thus reinforced the quest of the Texas Regionalists, Williams and Ford, for a valid style that would be both modern and indigenous (see Chapter 7). O'Neil Ford built his first significant nonresidential commission embodying this Regional Modernism in 1939, when he and Arch Swank designed the Chapel in the Woods for the Texas State College for Women (now Texas Woman's University) in Denton (FIG. 8.03). Like the La Villita restoration, the Denton chapel was a project of the NYA, built largely by construction trainees.

Like O'Neil Ford's early houses (see Chapter 7), the Chapel in the Woods consists of two primary blocks placed in linear sequence, one for the congregation and a smaller one for the chancel. Each is roofed in the shallow-pitched standing-seam metal that Ford thought indigenous to Texas, and projects uniformly beyond the building wall with a very shallow fascia made possible by the absence of rafters. In fact, the wooden roof-deck runs parallel to the slope, supported by longitudinal purlins that rest on four great parabolic arches in brick, except in the chancel, where a parabolic wooden ceiling is used. The dominant interior finish is a variegated red tapestry brick, but the exterior is faced in irregularly coursed fieldstone cut to the scale of brickwork and beautifully laid. The interior furnishings recall the Arts and Crafts period; its wooden furniture

and metal lighting fixtures were designed by Lynn Ford, O'Neil's brother, and executed by trainees of the NYA under his supervision. The stained-glass windows commemorating the role of women in society were rendered by art students at the university.[3]

The Texas Regionalists, Ford and Williams, despised the contemporary modernistic architecture as just another form of eclecticism: an alternative "style" to Spanish Colonial or Gothic. By the mid-1930's, however, a different strand of modernism of European derivation began to appear in America. The occasion for its advent in Texas was the Centennial Exposition in Dallas; its bearer was William Lescaze. Lescaze was one of a considerable number of European designers who emigrated to America after World War I. He was born in Geneva and studied under Karl Moser at Zurich. After working for Henri Sauvage in Paris, Lescaze came to the United States in 1920. Nine years later, he formed a partnership with George Howe of Philadelphia. Howe and Lescaze designed the Philadelphia Savings Fund Society Building (FIG. 6.42) of 1929–1932, the most progressive American skyscraper of its generation. The PSFS Building is a dynamic expression of structure and function, wholly free of the vertical or horizontal modernistic stylization typical of the American skyscraper in 1929. Included in the International style exhibition at the Museum of Modern Art (MOMA) in 1932, the PSFS Building established Lescaze's reputation as a leading American interpreter of International Modernism. With the onset of the Depression and the demise of his partnership with George Howe,

Lescaze's production was largely confined to commercial remodelings, in which the fine line separating his work from the Streamlined Commercial is sometimes obscured. In 1936 he was invited to design the Magnolia Oil Company Pavilion at the Texas Centennial Exposition (FIG. 8.04).[4]

Lescaze's original scheme was more provocative than the executed design. It would have provided a raised block supported on slender round piers, approached via a sweeping entrance ramp—an obvious reference to the work of Le Corbusier. As completed, the Magnolia Pavilion (recently restored as the Magnolia Lounge Visitor Center) bears certain traces of Streamlined Commercial, such as the porthole fenestration on the doors and the curving wall of glass block. These features are also found in European Functionalism around 1930, however, and may have been derived independently. The Magnolia Pavilion looks like no other structure at the fairgrounds. Instead of a facade, the principal elevation is dominated by an open roof terrace, supported by slender round piers (or "pilotis," as Le Corbusier called them) carried over from the original parti. This roof terrace, which is penetrated for an exposed access stair rather than the intended ramp, plainly expresses the principle of cantilevered construction. The exposed pipe railings adds to the image of spartan Functionalism, although the Magnolia Pavilion is carefully contrived for this avant-garde impression. There are no ornamental flow lines or other accessories of modernistic Streamlining, nor any suggestion of vernacular or regional building culture. The Magnolia Pa-

FIG. 8.04
MAGNOLIA OIL COMPANY PAVILION,
Texas Centennial Exposition,
Dallas. 1936.
William Lescaze, architect.

vilion was included in an exhibition of "Thirteen Years of Fair Building" organized in 1936 by Henry-Russell Hitchcock for MOMA. This show began with Le Corbusier's Pavilion de l'Esprit Nouveau at the Paris Exposition des Arts Decoratifs in 1925, and included Mies van der Rohe's Barcelona Pavilion of 1929 and Figini and Pollini's Electrical Pavilion for the Monza Trienalle of 1930—distinguished company indeed.[5]

Somewhere between the Texas Regionalists and the International Modernists stood Frank Lloyd Wright, whose rejuvenation in the 1930's provided stunning new monuments of American architecture: the Kaufmann House (Falling Water), the Johnson Wax Headquarters, Taliesin West, the Usonian house form, and Broadacre City. Wright's update of his conception of organic architecture restored his waning influence on American culture and reinforced the contemporary tendency toward the integration of

FIG. 8.05
FIRE ALARM BUILDING,
Houston (now demolished). 1938.
McKie and Kamrath, architects.

FIG. 8.06
FIRE ALARM BUILDING.

natural materials—whether described as organic, vernacular, or indigenous—in modern American architecture. Although he built nothing in Texas until after 1945, Wright's influence on younger architects is reflected in the work of Karl Kamrath of Houston, as already seen in Kamrath's own house (see FIGS. 7.41 and 7.42). Wright's long estrangement from mainstream American culture left no direct models of public architecture to emulate, however, so McKie and Kamrath's Fire Alarm Building in Houston of 1938 (demolished in 1990) represents an original improvisation, less Wrightian than their work in the domestic sphere (FIGS. 8.05 and 8.06).[6] When they designed the building, McKie and Kamrath "felt that the exterior should have a monumental character, partly because of its importance, and partly because it forms part of the new Civic Center. To this end split face Texas limestone, brick and concrete were combined."[7] Although the Civic Center referred to is not a tightly coordinated ensemble, the Fire Alarm Building did occupy a site near Cram and Ferguson's Spanish Colonial Public Library and Joseph Finger's Modern Classic City Hall, and thus some monumental character was thought appropriate. On the other hand, as a control and command center for the Houston Fire Department, it was not a building to which the public had free access. The two designers were thus called upon to resolve this dichotomy of purpose.

To instill some monumental character in the Fire Alarm Building, McKie and Kamrath treated the main facade as a symmetrical windowless frontispiece of split-face limestone (the wing to the right was a later addition), penetrated by a full-height entrance slot that led to a monumental staircase and then to the main control room on the second floor. The vestibule served as a memorial hall to fallen firemen, thus justifying the heroic gesture in ceremonial terms, and suggesting contemporary Italian Fascist architecture as a possible influence (although no single source is apparent).[8] This monumental stone frontispiece stopped short of the actual front corners of the building, however, dropping to a basement plinth to support the brickwork of the remaining wall surfaces. Yet when viewed from the left rear, the stone plinth interlocked with the brick masses in an articulated form reminiscent of both Wright and de Stijl, or their mutual interaction. Similarly, the brickwork and fenestration may have been derived from Wright or from Willem M. Dudok, whose late de Stijl Functionalism was much admired in the 1930's. Dudok's Hilversum City Hall in the Netherlands (FIG. 8.07) is another of the neglected masterpieces of modern architecture, more esteemed by contemporaries than by retrospective historians.[9]

The brickwork on the Fire Alarm Building consisted of orange Roman brick with deeply struck horizontal joints. The metal window frames and the fascia projected beyond the wall line, casting shadows on the wall in a manner suggestive of Dudok. These windows were narrow, horizontal strips that provided light and view only where required by interior functions, and that continued around the front corners in a typical expression of modernity. The result was an *almost* banal, factory-like

treatment of the functional facades, relieved by unusual details. Similarly, the monumental frontispiece has a strangely atectonic quality, as the entrance slot extends virtually to the fascia in an unorthodox and hence ultramodern denial of traditional expectations of load and support, made all the more dramatic by the texture of the stonework. Compared to the Modernized Classicism of the City Hall nearby, which is based on Paul Philippe Cret's abstraction of classical tectonics, the Fire Alarm Building became a radical statement of modern architecture outside the mainstream. It is interesting that in the initial publication of the building the front corners were not shown. Only the

FIG. 8.07
HILVERSUM CITY HALL. 1930.
William M. Dudok, architect.

FIG. 8.08
LINCOLN HIGH SCHOOL,
Dallas. 1939.
Walter C. Sharpe, architect.

dramatic frontispiece and the suggestive rear-corner view were included among the photographs. This editorial selectivity notwithstanding, McKie and Kamrath's Fire Alarm Building was a remarkable synthesis of ceremonial purpose and pragmatic function by architects who, like O'Neil Ford and William Lescaze, obviously regarded the current modernistic idiom as a style to avoid.

The influence of Dudok can also be detected in Lincoln High School in Dallas (FIG. 8.08), designed in 1939 by Walter C. Sharpe.[10] The powerfully articulated brick masses stand apart from both contemporary Streamlining and from the International style, as does the crisp fascia that defines the flat roof. Although

the use of glass block on the main stair was common to both species of modernism, the slotted entrance with cantilevered canopy recalls that on Dudok's Hilversum City Hall (FIG. 8.07), whose popularity in the 1930's lay in its traditional expectations of monumentality and symbolism on one hand, and its rigorous modernism on the other. Lincoln High School was obviously intended to be a monumentally imposing building, to a degree that the antimonumental aesthetics of orthodox modernism discouraged.

High schools were necessarily large and complex institutions, inherently imposing in size. The same was not true of elementary schools, which were increasingly viewed as neighborhood facilities—antimonumental, if not domestic, in scale. The one-story elementary school had been commonplace since the 1920's. Now, in the later 1930's, the school became a prime example of the new concepts of Regional or Organic Modernism applied to public buildings. When MOMA launched its "Built in USA, 1932–1944" exhibition, works by Harwell Hamilton Harris, Gregory Ain, Karl Koch, William Wurster, Vernon De Mars, Hugh Stubbins, Howe and Stonorov, Richard Neutra, Pietro Belluschi, and Raphael Soriano predominated. The abstract aesthetics of the International style had been replaced by more organic concerns for human use, orientation, site integration, and sympathetic natural materials. Three schools were included in the MOMA exhibition; these included Neutra's Experimental School in Los Angeles of 1935 and the Crow Island School in Winnetka, Illinois (FIG. 8.09), designed in 1940 by Eliel Saarinen in association with Perkins and Will. The latter became one of the most influential school designs of the decade, developed around the model classroom as a self-sufficient unit with direct access to outdoor playground space. Neutra, in the more benign climate of California, further simplified planning by replacing the closed corridor with a covered passage.[11]

Although no Texas buildings were included in the MOMA exhibition, the new conceptions of elementary school design nevertheless appeared in the state. In 1941 William Caudill, later senior partner of one of Texas' leading firms of school designers, published his treatise, *Space for Teaching*, as a research bulletin at Texas A&M. Caudill

FIG. 8.09
CROW ISLAND SCHOOL,
Winnetka, Ill. 1940.
Eliel Saarinen, with Perkins and Will,
architects.

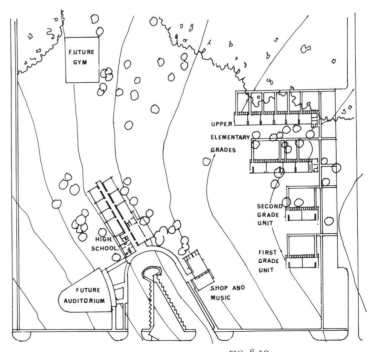

FIG. 8.10
A&M CONSOLIDATED SCHOOL,
College Station. 1940.
Finney and Langford, architects.
*From Caudill,* Space for teaching.
*Reprinted by permission of Walter Wendler.*

cited the Crow Island and Neutra schools as paradigms for his own hypothetical dispersed development plan, and used the A&M Consolidated School at College Station (FIG. 8.10), designed by Finney and Langford, as a recently completed example of a one-story school where each classroom had direct access to the outside.[12] Other schools in Houston and Austin also followed either the Neutra plan, with its covered passages, or the Crow Island model.[13]

In November 1941 all private architectural patronage in the United States came to an end as America entered World War II. Architects were drawn exclusively into defense-essential construction, including housing and related public services for defense workers and their families. Thus, the current of Organic Modernism coalesced with the relatively new and somewhat alien American development of public housing.

## PUBLIC HOUSING DURING THE DEPRESSION AND WAR

One of the effects of the Depression was that the federal government assumed responsibility for housing and human settlement. The only previous experiment in public housing in the United States had been the industrial housing constructed by the U.S. Housing Corporation during World War I, but the 60,000 units constructed were sold off to private investors in 1919. Unlike Europe, where government ownership or subsidy was responsible for a considerable segment of the housing supply, housing in the United States was regarded as a commodity in the marketplace with which the

government ought not tamper. The trend toward home ownership accelerated in the course of the 1920's, as an ever-increasing proportion of the middle class converted rent into mortgage payments. Many of these new home owners found themselves faced with foreclosure upon the onset of the Depression. One of the first measures taken by the Roosevelt administration was the Home Owners Loan Act, which refinanced mortgages and led to the National Housing Act of 1934. This legislation created the Federal Housing Administration, whose mission was to stimulate the private-housing market through mortgage insurance. This has remained the basic government housing policy in the United States ever since. Although public housing has remained a minor theme in American society, it has been a permanent fixture since the Depression.

The National Industrial Recovery Act of 1933, among other provisions, created a Subsistence Homestead Program to encourage resettlement of urban and rural workers. Part of the "Back to the Land" movement, such subsistence homesteads provided garden space where settlers could supplement their income by growing their own food and raising a few animals. Five such Subsistence Homestead communities were founded in Texas: Houston Gardens at Houston; Beauxart Gardens at Beaumont; Wichita Gardens at Wichita Falls; Three Rivers Gardens at Three Rivers; and Dalworthington Gardens at Arlington. At seventy-nine homesteads and nearly six hundred acres, the Arlington community—which was intended to settle industrial workers from Fort Worth and Dallas—was

FIG. 8.11
CEDAR SPRINGS PLACE,
Dallas. 1937.
Consortium of Texas architects.

the largest of the five. Transferred in 1937 to the National Housing Agency, Dalworthington Gardens was incorporated as a town in 1949. A few of the original houses survive.[14]

The National Industrial Recovery Act also provided for "construction under public regulation and control of low-cost housing and slum clearance projects,"[15] a mandate renewed in the United States Housing Act of 1937. A small number of public-housing projects were constructed under auspices of the PWA's Housing Division. The first PWA housing project west of the Mississippi was Cedar Springs Place in Dallas (FIG. 8.11) of 1937, designed by a consortium of Texas architects.[16] Cedar Springs Place conforms to modern planning theories of the 1930's; it was influenced by the Garden City movement and by 1920's housing in Germany, which had been warmly endorsed by Catherine Bauer in her 1934 treatise *Modern Housing.* The designs for both Garden City and German housing stressed the concept of treating the pedestrian super-block as park land, restricting vehicular access to the perimeter, and placing housing units to obtain desirable exposure to sunlight. Cedar Springs Place occupies fifteen acres lying between two streets; its cross streets are closed to form a small "superblock." It adjoins a public park on one side, which buffers the project from heavy traffic. Its short blocks of one-story row houses and two-story apartments face the southeast, alternating with communal lawn areas and shade trees. The architecture consists of white plastered walls, flat roofs, and metal casement windows, put together with a studied neutrality somewhere between Streamlined Commercial and International Modernism. Significantly, corner windows and other forms of demonstrative detailing are avoided, except for the cantilevered slabs that shelter the entrances. It is interesting that when the much larger Roseland Homes project was built in 1942, also in Dallas, face brick and pitched roofs were used, reflecting, perhaps, a resurgence of regionalism in modern architecture.

Urban public-housing projects were a form of resettlement, of course, as they complemented the slum clearance projects of the PWA, at least in theory. The resettlement programs of the New Deal went beyond such public-housing projects, however, to embrace the Subsistence Homestead Program and eventually the total planning of new towns. In 1935 the Resettlement Administration under Rexford Tugwell shifted its emphasis to suburban development near major cities. The result was the Greenbelt Towns, of which Greenbelt, Maryland, is the best known. The Greenbelt Towns reflected the evolution of principles espoused in 1898 by Ebenezer Howard, the father of the Garden City movement, which began in England. Letchworth, the first English Garden City, had been founded in 1903; Hampstead Garden Suburb followed in 1907 on the northern fringe of metropolitan London. Howard's ideals were imported

to America in the 1920's by the influential Regional Planning Association, whose members included Clarence Stein, Henry Wright, Lewis Mumford, and Catherine Bauer. The first American Garden City under private auspices had been Radburn, New Jersey, in 1928, although housing projects such as Sunnyside Gardens in New York had been established as early as 1924. During the course of its acculturation to America, Garden City planning had been crossbred with Clarence Perry's Neighborhood Concept, which had been defined in 1924 as a quarter-mile radius from an elementary school. Central to Garden City planning were two concepts: the greenbelt, which would isolate the community within the metropolitan region and limit indefinite expansion or sprawl; and the pedestrian greenway, where pedestrians could circulate separated from vehicular traffic.[17]

The pedestrian greenway had already appeared in Texas under private sponsorship when the Greenway Park Addition was created in Dallas in 1926. A pedestrian greenway replaced the conventional alley between parallel streets.[18] In the process, of course, the plan sacrificed the traditional American suburban landscape: a front sidewalk parallel to the street but separated by a curbstrip planted in trees. In Greenway Park, the sidewalk is shifted to the greenway, but many suburban communities established in the 1930's and after World War II eliminated public sidewalks entirely, partly to reduce the developers' investment in infrastructure and partly to create a more rural ambience. In fully developed communities like Radburn or Greenbelt the pedestrian greenways formed entire networks of park land, by which children could walk to school or householders to shopping or community facilities, underpassing major traffic streets. Ultimately, in the 1960's, the putative advantages of Garden City planning would be re-examined in a general attack on utopian city planning led by Jane Jacobs, who called attention to potential social dangers of unsupervised park space and reiterated the traditional role of the street as carrier of both pedestrians and vehicles.[19] In addition, by the 1960's the neighborhood school was no longer universally regarded as desirable, and so Clarence Perry's neighborhood concept was abandoned, except as a rallying cry against forced busing.

If the advantages of Garden City planning—when applied to the low-density settlement pattern of the American suburb—have come to seem dubious in historical retrospect, the same concepts appear justified when applied to the medium densities of public-housing projects, where vehicular traffic is kept to the periphery and where the density of settlement insures that community areas will always be supervised by the inhabitants. The scope of public housing, initiated with the National Housing Act of 1937, was expanded when the United States entered the war in 1941. Once again, as in 1917, housing for workers in defense industries had to be constructed. Avion Village in Grand Prairie is typical of the application of Garden City planning to such settlements (FIGS. 8.12 and 8.13). Designed by Richard Neutra, with David Williams as supervising architect for the PWA and Roscoe De Witt as resident architect, Avion Village was

FIG. 8.12
AVION VILLAGE,
Grand Prairie. 1942.
Richard Neutra, David Williams,
and Roscoe De Witt, architects.

built in 1942 to house workers at the North American Aircraft Plant. Vehicular access is restricted to a perimeter drive and service cul-de-sacs, which alternate with fingers of pedestrian greenways on which the dwelling units face. These fingers of park land lead to a central park, connecting an elementary school at the north end of the site with a community center and recreation facilities on the south. A series of two-story duplex units are located along the western edge of the site, staggered for mutual privacy and to provide a southeasterly orientation on the private side facing into the greenways. This southeasterly prospect was enhanced by porches on each floor, possibly Williams' contribution as a concession to the regional environment. These units are constructed of wood and brick veneer, and have access to grouped parking along the perimeter drive.

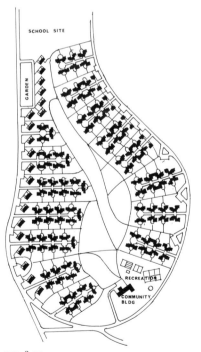

FIG. 8.13
AVION VILLAGE. Site plan.
*Adapted from Neutra,* New Pencil Points 23
*(November 1942).*

FIG. 8.14
SAN FELIPE COURTS
(greenway between parallel building rows),
Houston. 1942.
McKie and Kamrath et al., architects.

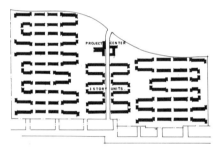

FIG. 8.15
SAN FELIPE COURTS. Site plan.
*Adapted from* Architectural Record *(May 1942).*

The majority of the units consist of one-story wood-frame duplex (occasionally quadruplex) construction, face the pedestrian greenways, and back up to the cul-de-sacs for parking and service. Although constructed to rather minimum standards—using prefabrication techniques to maximum advantage—Avion Village survives today in good condition as a mutual ownership property.[20]

Both Neutra and Williams went on to design further public housing during the course of the war. As architect for the Defense Housing Division of the PWA, Williams continued to experiment with prefabrication, including the development of the prototypical Multimax House. His largest project in Texas was for six hundred units in Beaumont.[21]

As architecture, most of this housing has a rather bland neutrality enforced by the exigencies of

prefabrication. An exception is San Felipe Courts in Houston (FIGS. 8.14 and 8.15), designed in 1942 by a consortium of local architects, including McKie and Kamrath. It seems reasonable to credit this unusually dynamic design to Karl Kamrath, the principal Texas interpreter of Frank Lloyd Wright. As in the Houston Fire Alarm Building, however, San Felipe Courts seem derived more from European Modernism than from Wright.

San Felipe Courts has a greater density than Cedar Springs Place or Avion Village, accommodating one thousand units on a superblock crossed by only one transverse street. The planning conforms to a rigorous configuration of parallel rows suggestive of German housing practice in the 1920's, where it was known as *Zeilenbau* planning.[22] The construction is reinforced concrete frame with masonry cavity wall infill, although except for projecting canopies, the concrete is not exposed. These canopies, along with projecting tile borders around openings and the use of two colors of exposed face brick, enhance the impression of dynamic forms suggestive of both Wright and Dudok. Corner conditions are exploited to dramatize spatial articulation, particularly along the central artery, where two- and three-story masses interlock. The project's community and administration center is even more dramatic (FIG. 8.16). Located on both sides of the transverse street, the center as originally conceived would have bridged the traffic artery with a floor of offices, suggesting a similar occurrence at the Dessau Bauhaus. The dynamic asymmetry of the plan and massing would have made the San Felipe

Project Center one of the most advanced modern buildings in Texas.[23]

Other Texas architects also participated in the war effort. George L. Dahl, fresh from his experience as supervising architect of the Texas Centennial Exposition, designed the enormous Red River Ordnance Depot for the U.S. Army near Texarkana at a cost of over $35 million.[24]

Most of these architects—Dahl, Ford, McKie, and Kamrath—returned to private practice after the war, more or less taking up where they had left off. Some, like Dahl, would adopt modern architecture idiomatically, as a flexible new style to replace the modernistic fashions of the 1930's, reflecting the forms of International Modernism now acculturated to America by Gropius and his fellow European émigrés. Others would continue to develop the personal manners they had initiated before the war: Ford continued to espouse a regionalism now transmuted by contact with organic tendencies outside Texas— even outside the United States. Karl Kamrath continued to interpret Frank Lloyd Wright in a state that would finally—fifty years after Wright's protégés George Willis and Charles E. Barglebaugh brought his Prairie School manner to Texas— receive three buildings by Wright himself. A few architects picked up the thread of eclecticism in the late 1940's, but a watershed had been passed. Modern architecture, no longer an alternative eclectic modernistic idiom, had now become the American mainstream, and eclecticism was banished to the status of a *retardataire* phenomenon in the arts.

Forty-five years later this triumph of modernism no longer

FIG. 8.16
SAN FELIPE COURTS.
Community and Administration Center.

seems like the unalloyed triumph of truth and beauty it once appeared to be. Modern architecture has been through its own crisis and malaise, and recently postmodernism has once again legitimized the practice of historical reference. Now that eclecticism is no longer a heresy to be repudiated, it has become possible to examine the intervening period—between the emergence of a modern architecture around 1895 and its triumph as an international fait accompli in 1945—with sympathy and understanding. No longer does the historian seek to filter out a narrow constituent mainstream while rejecting the vast bulk of built architecture. All aspects of human culture are intrinsically interesting and worthy of study. We study the past, not to predict the future, but to understand the present.

# NOTES

1. THE HISTORIOGRAPHY OF AMERICAN AND TEXAS
   ARCHITECTURE IN THE TWENTIETH CENTURY

1. Lewis Mumford, *The Brown Decades: A Study of the Arts in America*; Henry-Russell Hitchcock, *The Architecture of H. H. Richardson and His Times*; Nikolaus Pevsner, *Pioneers of Modern Design: From William Morris to the Bauhaus; An Outline of European Architecture*; Sigfried Giedion, *Space, Time and Architecture*.

2. Hitchcock, *H. H. Richardson*; Henry-Russell Hitchcock and Philip Johnson, *The International Style*. Hitchcock had previously published *Modern Architecture: Romanticism and Reintegration*, which began with 1750.

3. Previous attempts to interpret the nineteenth century included Kenneth Clark, *The Gothic Revival*, and Mumford, *Brown Decades*.

4. Andrew Jackson Downing, *A Treatise on the Theory and Practice of Landscape Gardening . . . .*

5. Scully's dissertation had been entitled "The Cottage Style." Part I, on the Stick style, was published as an article in the *Art Bulletin* in 1953; Part II as a monograph, *The Shingle Style*, in 1955. Both parts were reunited in the 1971 revised edition, *The Shingle Style and the Stick Style: Architectural Theory and Design from Richardson to the Origins of Wright*.

6. Heinrich Wölfflin, *Principles of Art History*. See also Wölfflin, *Renaissance and Baroque*.

7. Richard Longstreth, "Academic Eclecticism in American Architecture," *Winterthur Portfolio* (Spring 1982): 55–82.

8. Alan Gowans, *Images of American Living*. See Chapter 9, "Revival of the Revivals: Late Victorian Academic Realism."

9. Drury Blakeley Alexander, *Texas Homes of the Nineteenth Century*, with photographs by Todd Webb. The second volume was Willard B. Robinson and Todd Webb, *Texas Public Buildings of the Nineteenth Century*.

10. The literature on Sullivan and Wright is too vast to enumerate here. For their influence on contemporaries, see H. Alan Brooks, *The Prairie School*.

11. Among other publications, see David Gebhard, "The Moderne in the U.S. 1920–1941," *Architectural Association Quarterly* 2 (July 1970): 4–20.

12. Hitchcock and Johnson, *The International Style*.

13. David Gebhard, "The Spanish Colonial Revival in Southern California (1895–1930)," *Journal of the Society of Architectural Historians* 26 (May 1967): 131–147. For additional sources, see notes to Chapter 4.

14. The literature on the Ecole des Beaux-Arts and its influence on American design has grown in recent years until it is too great to enumerate. Its restitution to a place of importance in the history of architecture was celebrated by an exhibition at the Museum of Modern Art (MOMA) in 1975–1976, with an

accompanying book edited by Arthur Drexler, *The Architecture of the Ecole des Beaux-Arts.* Other contributors were Richard Chafee, David van Zanten, and Neil Levine.

15. For Goodhue, see Richard Oliver, *Bertram Grosvenor Goodhue.* For Cret, see Elizabeth Green Grossman, "Paul Philippe Cret: Rationalism and Imagery in American Architecture" (Ph.D. diss., Brown University, 1980). See Chapters 5 and 6 for specific sources to Cret's work in Texas. Ralph Adams Cram is regarded as the designing partner of the work of Cram, Goodhue, and Ferguson in Texas.

16. Pevsner, *An Outline of European Architecture,* 15: "A bicycle shed is a building; Lincoln Cathedral is a piece of architecture. . . . The term architecture applies only to buildings designed with a view to aesthetic appeal."

2. THE SURVIVAL OF PAST TRADITIONS

1. For Richardson, the standard texts are Mariana Griswold Van Rensselaer, *Henry Hobson Richardson and His Works* and Hitchcock, *H. H. Richardson.* For Richardson's influence in Europe, see Leonard K. Eaton, *American Architecture Comes of Age.*

2. Montgomery Schuyler, "The Romanesque Revival in America," *Architectural Record* 1 (1891): 194.

3. Henry Van Brunt, "John Wellborn Root [Obituary]," *Inland Architect* (January, 1891): 194.

4. For Gordon's courthouses, see Robinson and Webb, *Texas Public Buildings.* For the Richardsonian Romanesque in Texas, see Kenneth A. Breisch, "The Richardsonian Interlude in Texas: A Quest for Meaning and Order at the End of the Nineteenth Century," in *The Spirit of H. H. Richardson on the Midland Prairies,* pp. 86–105. I am also indebted to Glenn S. Patton and the Texas A & M University Press for the opportunity to review Patton's as yet unpublished monograph on J. Riely Gordon. The J. Riely Gordon papers and drawings have been deposited in the Architectural Drawings Collection at the University of Texas at Austin.

5. Quoted by Henry Van Brunt, Introduction to *Discourses on Architecture* by Eugene E. Viollet-le-Duc, viii.

6. For McKim, Mead and White see Leland Roth, *McKim, Mead & White, Architects.*

7. Russell Sturgis, "A Critique of the Works of Shepley, Rutan and Coolidge and Peabody and Stearns," *Architectural Record* (July 1896): 37–38.

8. Henri Focillon, *The Life of Forms in Art,* 55. For the application of Focillon's premise to Texas architecture, see Jay C. Henry, "The Richardsonian Romanesque in Texas: An Interpretation." *Texas Architect* 31 (March/April 1981): 52–57.

9. Robinson and Webb, *Texas Public Buildings,* 253.

10. Ibid., 242.

11. The great exception to this generalization is the Ashbel Smith Building ("Old Red") at the University of Texas Medical Center in Galveston, designed in 1889 by Nicholas J. Clayton. See Robinson and Webb, *Texas Public Buildings,* 188–189. See also Lawrence W. Speck and Richard Payne, *Landmarks of Texas Architecture,* 40–43.

12. Robinson and Webb, *Texas Public Buildings,* 187.

13. The Brady courthouse is illustrated in Willard B. Robinson, *The People's Architecture: Texas Courthouses, Jails and Municipal Buildings,* 156.

14. Henry, "Richardsonian Romanesque in Texas," 58.

15. Robinson and Webb, *Texas Public Buildings*, 81.

16. Henry, "Richardsonian Romanesque in Texas," 59; Texas Historical Commission, *Catalog of Texas Properties in the National Register of Historic Places*, 125; Breisch, "The Richardsonian Interlude in Texas," 104–105.

17. Karen J. Weitze, *California's Mission Revival*, 21–23.

18. Texas Historical Commission, *Catalog of Texas Properties*, 76. The catalog describes the Nolte National Bank as "Spanish Colonial Revival," overlooking its obvious Richardsonian components.

19. Curiously, University Methodist Church has been overlooked both in Roxanne Kuter Williamson, *Austin, Texas: An American Architectural History* and in Austin Chapter AIA *Austin: Its Architects and Architecture (1836–1986)*. It is mentioned by Breisch, "The Richardsonian Interlude in Texas," 103.

20. Leonard K. Eaton, *Gateway Cities and Other Essays*. Eaton's four gateway cities are St. Joseph, St. Paul, Omaha, and Winnipeg. Eaton stresses housing as the most viable adaptive function for such structures and districts. This has not occurred in Dallas, and the West End Historic District remains strictly an entertainment enclave. It was placed on the National Register in 1978. Texas Historical Commission, *Catalog of Texas Properties*, 46.

21. Stephen Fox, *Houston Architectural Guide*, 53–54. Supersedes previous edition of 1972.

22. Edward Hale, "H. H. Richardson and His Work," *New England Magazine* 2 (1894): 532.

23. For Clayton, see Howard Barnstone, *The Galveston That Was*. The Hutchings-Sealy Building is also included in Robinson and Webb, *Texas Public Buildings*, 126 and in Houston Chapter AIA, *Houston: An Architectural Guide*, 162. Stephen Fox's revised version does not include Galveston. I would not agree with Robinson's contention that the Hutchings-Sealy Building "demonstrates N. J. Clayton's adroitness in dealing with Beaux-Arts Classicism." The building seems still fundamentally Victorian, whereas the term Beaux-Arts Classicism probably should be reserved for the later phase of Academic Eclecticism.

24. Robinson and Webb, *Texas Public Buildings*, 254; Texas Historical Commission, *Catalog of Texas Properties*, 40.

25. Robinson and Webb, *Texas Public Buildings*, 252; Robinson, *The People's Architecture*, 203; Texas Historical Commission, *Catalog of Texas Properties*, 94.

26. Robinson, *The People's Architecture*, 204–205; Texas Historical Commission, *Catalog of Texas Properties*, 125. For Gordon's Arizona Capitol, see Henry-Russell Hitchcock and William Seale, *Temples of Democracy: The State Capitols of the U.S.A.*, 234–236.

27. For the Page brothers, see Austin Chapter AIA, *Austin*, 65. The Richmond courthouse is illustrated in Robinson, *The People's Architecture*, 208. The Hays County Courthouse in San Marcos of 1908 by Page and Brother is similar. Page and Brother was the firm's name of record in 1908; it later became Page Brothers.

28. The Stafford Opera House in Columbus, designed by Nicholas J. Clayton in 1886, is on the National Register. Texas Historical Commission, *Catalog of Texas Properties*, 37. That in Granbury is included in the Hood County Courthouse Historic District. Ibid., 104.

29. Scully, *Shingle Style*.

30. Andrew Saint, *Richard Norman Shaw*.

31. The only Shingle style house catalogued by Alexander and Webb is the Colonel Edward M. House Residence in Austin, since demolished. See Alexander, *Texas Homes*, 229; 263. The House Residence is also discussed in Williamson, *Austin, Texas*, 116–117.

32. Texas Historical Commission, *Catalog of Texas Properties*, 44.

33. Roth, *McKim, Mead and White*, 78–79; Scully, *Shingle Style*, 152–53.

34. For example, the H.A.C. Taylor House in Newport of 1882–1886. Scully, *Shingle Style*, 58 and Roth, *McKim, Mead and White*, 97.

35. Longstreth, *On the Edge of the World: Four Architects in San Francisco at the Turn of the Century*, 97–105. For Coxhead's churches in Southern California, see also David Gebhard and Robert Winter, *A Guide to Architecture in Los Angeles and Southern California*, 261; 320; 364; 434; 644. For those in Northern California, see David Gebhard et al., *A Guide to Architecture in San Francisco and Northern California*, 96; 169; 200; 337; 364; 446; 501–502. For Silsbee, see Joseph Siry, "Frank Lloyd Wright's Unity Temple and the Architecture for Liberal Religion in Chicago, 1885–1909," *Art Bulletin* 73 (June 1991): 257–282. Wright, of course, had worked for Silsbee before his employment by Adler and Sullivan.

36. Robinson and Webb, *Texas Public Buildings*, 164–165; Texas Historical Commission, *Catalog of Texas Properties*, 59. Upjohn was the son of Richard Upjohn, one of the pioneers of American Ecclesiology before the Civil War and designer of St. Mark's Church in San Antonio in 1859.

37. See William H. Pierson, Jr., "Richardson's Trinity Church and the New England Meetinghouse," in *American Public Architecture: European Roots and Native Expression*, 15.

38. Illustrated in Willard B. Robinson, "Houses of Worship in Nineteenth Century Texas," *Southwestern Historical Quarterly* 85 (January 1982): 235–298 and in William L. McDonald, *Dallas Rediscovered: A Photographic Chronicle of Urban Expansion 1870–1925*, 184.

39. Texas Historical Commission, *Catalog of Texas Properties*, 110. The church is now used as the Tyrrell Library.

40. Hale, "Richardson and His Work," 532.

41. For the Ecclesiology movement in America, see Phoebe B. Stanton, *The Gothic Revival and American Church Architecture*.

42. The leading liturgical interpreters of the Arts and Crafts movement in England were J. D. Sedding, W. R. Lethaby, and E. S. Prior. See Peter Davey, *Architecture of the Arts and Crafts Movement*. These men tended to revive the forms of English late or perpendicular Gothic that the Ecclesiologists and the High Victorian generation had despised as decadent, thus preparing the way for Ralph Adams Cram in America. See Chapter 4.

43. Robinson, "Houses of Worship." Watson also designed All Saints Episcopal Chapel in Austin (1899) in a similar vein. The theme is taken up again in Chapter 4.

44. Wright's great exercise in ecclesiastical design in his Prairie School period was Unity Temple in Oak Park of 1906, whose avant-garde expression was deemed suitable by the Unitarian congregation. Wright's first mentor, James Lyman Silsbee, seems to have designed a church in the Shingle style for Wright's uncle, the Reverend Richard Lloyd Jones, in the 1880's. Maybeck's preeminent church commission was the First Church of Christ Scientist in Berkeley of 1909, done in a more Ecclesiastical mode with eclectic references to Romanesque, Byzantine, Gothic, and Oriental traditions. Nothing this extraordinary was built in Texas.

45. Bobbie Joe Wise, Jr., "Trinity Methodist Church: A Historical Survey and Guidelines for Its Adaptive Use" (M. Arch. thesis, University of Texas at Arlington, 1981); Eileen Wilson Coffman, "James E. Flanders' First United Methodist Church, Pittsburg, Texas," *Perspective* 13, no. 1 (1984): 9–16.

### 3. PROGRESSIVE MODES OF DESIGN

1. The literature on Sullivan and Wright is too vast to enumerate here. The standard work on the followers of Sullivan and Wright is Brooks, *The Prairie School.* Articles in the *Prairie School Review* and monographic studies of particular regions or designers have fleshed out somewhat the picture of the diffusion of the Prairie School, but the only scholar to chart this diffusion to Texas has been Lloyd Engelbrecht in his studies on Henry Trost of El Paso. See Lloyd Engelbrecht, "Henry Trost: The Prairie School in the Southwest," *Prairie School Review* 6, 4 quarter (1969): 5–31 and Lloyd C. and June-Marie Engelbrecht, *Henry C. Trost: Architect of the Southwest.*

2. For the commercial replication of Sullivan's ornament, see Ronald E. Schmidt, "Sullivanesque Architecture and Terra Cotta," *The Midwest in American Architecture,* 163–84. Sullivan's ornament was cast by Kristian Schneider, who in 1906 left the Northwest Terra Cotta Company to work for the American Terra Cotta and Ceramic Company, which commercially marketed stock designs of Sullivanesque ornament. Sullivanesque ornament was also commercially produced by the Midland Terra Cotta Company. Schmidt also informed me of two companies in Chicago producing Sullivanesque ornament in plaster, as used extensively by J. E. Flanders. These were the Architectural Decorating Company and the Decorators Supply Company. Ronald E. Schmidt, letter to Jay C. Henry, December 10, 1990.

3. The term progressive can be applied to banks in either a social and economic sense or to describe their architecture. For the evolution of progressive banking practices, see Wim de Wit, "The Banks and the Image of Progressive Banking," in *Louis Sullivan: The Function of Ornament,* 159–198. There are no Prairie School banks in Texas. For Elmslie in relation to Sullivan, see also Craig Zabel, "George Grant Elmslie and the Glory and Burden of the Sullivan Legacy," *The Midwest in American Architecture,* 1–41.

4. For the Oak Park Studio, see Brooks, *The Prairie School.* Willis is mentioned on p. 82: "The Studio staff numbered five . . . in 1902: George Willis—a Texan who later returned home—was head draftsman (apparently leaving late in 1902 after some four years of service)." I am indebted to Stephen Fox for bringing Barglebaugh to my attention. Stephen Fox, "In Response," *Perspective* 8, no. 3–4 (1979): 17–18.

5. Wise, "Trinity Methodist Church;" Coffman, "James E. Flanders." St. James in Stamford is included in the "Historic Resources of Stamford" listing in the National Register. Texas Historical Commission, *Addendum to Catalog of Texas Properties in the National Historic Register.*

6. The Corsicana courthouse is described and illustrated in Robinson, *The People's Architecture,* 206–207.

7. The primary repository of documentation for the firm of Trost and Trost is the *Henry C. Trost/Trost and Trost Catalog* at the El Paso Public Library. This catalog was established under an NEH grant in 1988 and directed by Lloyd C. and June F. Engelbrecht in collaboration with Mary Sarber.

8. This analysis of the Henry Trost House is heavily indebted to Lloyd Engelbrecht's several publications on the building. The house is included in Texas Historical Commission, *Catalog of Texas Properties,* 54. The qualities of

prospect and retreat have recently been discussed by Grant Hildebrand, *The Wright Space: Pattern and Meaning in Frank Lloyd Wright's Houses.*

9. Engelbrecht and Engelbrecht, *Henry C. Trost,* 37–38. The Arts and Crafts movement originated in England with the theories of John Ruskin and William Morris, both of whom deplored the Industrial Revolution and sought social and aesthetic reform in a return to handicraft. Morris died in 1896, but his ideals were propagated by the Arts and Crafts Exhibition Society and its journal, *The Studio,* which was enormously influential on the European continent and in America. In the United States, the prime advocate of the Arts and Crafts movement was Gustave Stickley, through his production of Mission furniture and through publication of *The Craftsman* from 1902 until 1914. Both Sullivan and Wright knew Stickley and published in *The Craftsman,* as did the California architects Greene and Greene. For recent literature on the Arts and Crafts movement in America and the relationship of the Prairie School to this larger context, see James D. Kornwolf, "American Architecture and the Aesthetic Movement," in *In Pursuit of Beauty,* 340–383; and Wendy Kaplan, *"The Art that is Life": The Arts and Crafts Movement in America.* English contemporaries with the greatest affinity to Sullivan and Wright were A. H. MacMurdo and C. R. Ashbee; the latter wrote the Introduction to the English edition of Wright's Wasmuth monograph in 1911.

10. Engelbrecht and Engelbrecht, *Henry C. Trost,* 81–82. See also Jay C. Henry, "Trost and Trost in El Paso," *Texas Architect* 37 (March/April 1987): 34–39. The Armory in Deming, New Mexico, also by Trost and Trost in 1916, is more explicitly Prairie School in its more geometric expression of mass and absence of eclectic detail.

11. The standard work on the Chicago School is Carl Condit, *The Chicago School of Architecture.*

12. Engelbrecht and Engelbrecht, *Henry C. Trost,* 49–58. The first four concrete buildings by Trost and Trost in El Paso were the Caples Building, begun in 1909, five stories; Abdou Building, seven stories; Roberts-Banner Building, five stories; and Posener Building, five stories. All but the last survive. The Mills Building has been denatured through insensitive remodeling, however. All but the denatured Mills Building are included in "Henry Charles Trost, Commercial Structures of El Paso (Thematic Group)" in the National Register. Texas Historical Commission, *Catalog of Texas Properties,* 53–54.

13. George H. Edgell, *The American Architecture of Today.*

14. There has been little retrospective study of Lang and Witchell's Prairie School work. Contemporaneous publications include "Dallas: A City of Art and Commerce," *Western Architect* (July 1914): 65–94; and "Some Recent Architectural Work of Lang and Witchell, Dallas," *Southwestern Architectural Review* I (December 1910): 157–181. Retrospectively, their work is included in Dallas Chapter AIA, *The Prairie's Yield: Forces Shaping Dallas Architecture from 1840 to 1962,* and in William L. McDonald, *Dallas Rediscovered.*

15. "Chicago window" refers to a large fixed pane in the center flanked by two narrow, double-hung sash on either side. It filled the horizontally proportioned grid defined by column spacing and floor-to-floor height between spandrels and permitted both maximum natural light and moderate ventilation. By the 1900's, as technological evolution permitted ever wider spans, the Chicago window had lost its rationale and other combinations of structure and fenestration had to be developed.

16. Sullivan published his *System of Architectural Ornament* only in 1924, but the principles could have been derived from examination of the detail draw-

ings, if not from the finished product. Proper detailing and execution both were essential for the successful use of Sullivan's ornament. Normally he employed Kristian Schneider for casting his terra-cotta ornament, which was executed by the American Terra Cotta and Ceramic Company of Chicago. Although Frank Lloyd Wright had discontinued use of Sullivan's ornament before Barglebaugh's tenure in the Oak Park Studio, the latter would have seen Sullivan's work in Chicago. See also Jay C. Henry, "Prairie School Ornament by Lang and Witchell," *Perspective* 8, no. 2 (1979): 3–6. The Sanger building is included in Texas Historical Commission, *Catalog of Texas Properties*, 44.

17. All of these buildings were published in "Dallas, a City of Art and Commerce." The Southwestern Life Building is illustrated in McDonald, *Dallas Rediscovered*, 93.

18. Henry, "Prairie School Ornament."

19. The First National Bank Building is included in the Paris Commercial Historic District on the National Register. It is one of a colony of faintly Prairie School buildings in Paris, including the Gibraltar Hotel of 1914, the Bedford Apartments, the Cotton Exchange Building, and a store building at First North East and Bonham Streets. Texas Historical Commission, *Addendum*. A photograph of the bank building, gutted but standing amidst the rubble after the 1916 fire, is included in an album of photographs assembled by the Atlantic Terra Cotta Company donated to the Architectural Drawings Collection of the University of Texas at Austin.

20. Work of this kind is closer to the Chicago School than to the Prairie School, although such distinctions are really academic. For Nimmons and Fellows, see Condit, *The Chicago School*, 178–181. Their work was discussed in "The Modern Factory, as Illustrated in the Works of George C. Nimmons," *Western Architect* (January 1916).

21. The Sears, Roebuck Wholesale Store and Clubhouse were published in "Dallas: A City of Art and Commerce." *Western Architect* (July 1914). Other structures by Lang and Witchell in the wholesale district south of downtown Dallas included the Higgenbotham-Bailey-Logan Building, similar in expression to the Sears building, and the S. G. Davis Hat Company.

22. Dallas AIA, *The Prairie's Yield*, 29.

23. Jay C. Henry, Judy Dooley, Patricia Canavan, and Robert Canavan, "Residential Design in Typical American Architecture: The Swiss Avenue Historic District, 1905–1932," *Perspective* 10 (1981): 18. The Higgenbotham House was also published in "Dallas," *Western Architect* (July 1914).

24. Both the Gainesville and Cleburne courthouses have recently been placed on the National Register. Texas Historical Commission, *Addendum*. Of the other three Lang and Witchell courthouses, the Nacogdoches County Courthouse in Nacogdoches has been demolished, the Scurry County Courthouse in Snyder has been remodeled beyond recognition, and the Harris County Courthouse in Houston bears no evidence of Prairie School design.

25. For the ornament on the Gainesville and Cleburne courthouses, see Henry, "Prairie School Ornament." The Johnson County Courthouse is discussed and illustrated in Robinson, *The People's Architecture*, 230–233. Robinson also illustrates and discusses the Gainesville courthouse, but seems to have overlooked its Prairie School central lobby.

26. Stephen Fox, "Sanguinet and Staats in Houston, 1903–1926," *Perspective* 12, no. 1 (1983): 8. Fox illustrates one definitive Prairie School house in Houston, The Oaks, designed for Judge and Mrs. E. B. Parker in 1909–1910, which does not survive. Controversy surrounds Frank Lloyd Wright's possible

authorship of this design. See *Perspective* 12 for details. For Sanguinet and Staats in Fort Worth and Dallas, see Michael C. Hoffmeyer, "Public Buildings of Sanguinet and Staats," *Perspective* 10, no. 1 (1981): 23–27. The firm also enjoyed an extensive regional practice; however, its work outside of Dallas, Fort Worth, and Houston has yet to be systematically studied. A partial holding of Sanguinet and Staats drawings has been deposited in the Architectural Drawings Collection, University of Texas at Austin, but little of the progressive work discussed in this chapter is included.

27. For the Flatiron and Anderson buildings, see Hoffmeyer, "Public Buildings." Drawings of the Anderson building are preserved in the Architectural Drawings Collection, University of Texas at Austin. Both are included in Texas Historical Commission, *Catalog of Texas Properties*, 157–158. The firm also did a great deal of more conventional commercial work between 1900 and 1920, including the First National Bank Building (1910) and Burk Burnett Building (1914) in Fort Worth, the Carter Building in Houston (1909–1911), the Wilson Building in Dallas (1903), and the Amicable Building in Waco (1911), the tallest building of its day in Texas at twenty stories. As all of these employ historicist detail, they should be classified as Academic Eclectic, and fall within the following chapter.

28. Oscar Ruffini's Ozona High School of 1912 also responded to these new design imperatives. I have chosen to discuss it in Chapter 2 as a survival of past traditions because of Ruffini's retention of rusticated ashlar, but it is functionally and programmatically a progressive institution.

29. The school designer among the contemporaries of Sullivan and Wright in Chicago was Dwight Perkins, who occupied space in Steinway Hall along with Wright. Perkins combined influences of Sullivan and Wright in several schools in Chicago: Trumbull School of 1908, Grover Cleveland of 1909, and Carl Schurz High School of 1908. Although these were published in the *Western Architect*, they do not seem to have influenced Sanguinet and Staats' school designs.

30. Sanguinet and Staats also designed the Palestine High School in 1915–1916 and the Cleburne High School in 1918. There are possibly other school designs. The Cleburne and Palestine schools also combine a progressive program with faintly historicist details, but are less interesting than the Trimble or North Fort Worth schools. Palestine High School has been placed on the National Register. Drawings for Cleburne High School are preserved in the Architectural Drawings Collection, University of Texas at Austin.

31. A similar configuration was used for Louis Sullivan's St. Paul's Methodist Church in Cedar Rapids of 1911. For plans, see Leonard K. Eaton, *American Architecture Comes of Age*, Fig. 137.

32. For biographical data on Ayres and Willis, see San Antonio Chapter AIA, *A Guide to San Antonio Architecture*, 131–132.

33. Drawings for all seven Ayres' courthouses are preserved in the Architectural Drawings Collection, University of Texas at Austin. Of the five original commissions, only the Freestone County Courthouse in Fairfield of 1919 (significantly the youngest of the series) shows no trace of the Prairie School. The two remodelings are the Val Verde County Courthouse in Del Rio of 1915 and the Bee County Courthouse in Beeville.

34. For Maher, see Brooks, *The Prairie School*, 109 ff. Maher's institutional work for Northwestern University in Evanston, Illinois, and in Winona, Minnesota, brings a rather classical inflection to the Prairie School, which aligns it

with other contemporary tendencies toward an abstracted classicism found in the Viennese Secession and Wagnerschule.

35. Texas Historical Commission, *Catalog of Texas Properties*, 31. The drawings for the Brownsville courthouse contain no details for the skylight ornament, which was probably assembled from stock pieces available from American or Midland Terra Cotta companies. See note 2 in this chapter.

36. Drawings for the Wright House are preserved in the Architectural Drawings Collection, University of Texas at Austin. They do not bear Willis' name. The Wright and Young houses are mentioned but not illustrated in San Antonio AIA, *Guide*, 132. The Williams-Tarbutton House in San Marcos is listed on the National Register. Texas Historical Commission, *Catalog of Texas Properties*, 100.

37. Eaton, "Oscar Eckerman: Architect to Deere and Co., 1897–1942," in *Gateway Cities*, 113–128.

38. Dallas AIA, *The Prairie's Yield*, 23. As the authors observe, the John Deere (Texas Implements) Building is two years earlier than Frank Lloyd Wright's Larkin Building of 1904, with which it has a superficial resemblance. The linear edges of the Dallas building bring it closer to Sullivan's closed forms, however, and the corners lack the highly articulated massing that Wright introduced at the Larkin Building. The structure is included within the West End Historic District. Texas Historical Commission, *Catalog of Texas Properties*, 46.

39. Fox, *Houston Architectural Guide*, 52. The firm of Barglebaugh and Whitson designed the gymnasium for Texas Woman's University in Denton in 1921 in a conventional Beaux-Arts Classic mode. Their nineteen-story Medical Arts Building in Dallas, also of 1921, was one of a new generation of post-war skyscrapers emphasizing verticality in the modeling of the terra-cotta facade. It was doubtless inspired by Cass Gilbert's Woolworth Building of 1913, although the Gothic character of the Medical Arts Building was less emphatic. In many respects, it seems like a precursor of the modernistic style of the late 1920's. Unfortunately, the Medical Arts Building has been demolished.

40. Illustrated in Schmidt, "Sullivanesque Architecture and Terra Cotta," 175. The fact that the Waco building is a half-block from Lang and Witchell's Raleigh Hotel with its splendid badges of Sullivanesque ornament may account for the decision to use the same species of ornament on the garage.

41. As often happens, several other examples of Prairie School ornament occur on similar service and industrial buildings in the immediate neighborhood.

42. Once again, I am indebted to Stephen Fox for calling Curtiss to my attention. Fox, "In Response," 18. For Curtiss' work in Kansas City, see Fred T. Comee, "Louis Curtiss of Kansas City," *Progressive Architecture* 44 (August 1963): 128–134; and Kansas City Chapter AIA *Kansas City [Architectural Guide]*.

43. Texas Historical Commission, *Catalog of Texas Properties*, 76. Once again, several other specimens of Prairie School influence are found in Seguin. A commonly used Sullivanesque cartouche in terra-cotta has been retained in the remodeling of the Phillip Vivroux garage for the Episcopal Church Gift Shop, directly across from the Park Hotel. Prairie School ornament is also found at Camp Street, and in a house derived from the common paradigm of the George Barton House.

44. The modern broad-front is defined in Herbert Gottfried and Jan Jennings, *American Vernacular Design, 1870–1940*, 249.

45. Henry et al., "Residential Design," 21–22.

46. Allan Gowans, *The Comfortable House: North American Suburban Architecture 1890–1930,* 84–87. *Prairie Style,* for example, is defined as an eclectic style by Virginia and Lee McAlester, *A Field Guide to American Houses,* 438–451, which illustrates many of Frank Lloyd Wright's Prairie School houses and promiscuously confuses them with the more common foursquares. This confusion is repeated in Historic Preservation League of Dallas, *A Guide to the Older Neighborhoods of Dallas,* which does not illustrate the Higgenbotham House, but does illustrate the "Prairie Style" by a typical foursquare.

47. The distinction between "constituent facts" and "transient phenomena" was made by Giedion in *Space, Time and Architecture,* first published in 1939. Giedion had been Secretary of the International Congress of Modern Architecture (CIAM), founded in 1928 to proselytize for the new European architecture, and the book is frankly a polemical defense of the modern movement. Like all great books, it has catalyzed opposition and provoked a cycle of revisionism among modern historians, who have been burrowing into Giedion's "transient phenomena" to rewrite the history of twentieth-century architecture.

4. ACADEMIC ECLECTICISM: 1900–1940

1. Louis H. Sullivan, *The Autobiography of an Idea,* 324–325.

2. Carroll L. V. Meeks, *The Railroad Station: An Architectural History,* 3–5.

3. Longstreth, *On the Edge of the World,* 9–39.

4. Gowans, *Images of American Living,* 366–386.

5. Sullivan, *The Autobiography of an Idea,* 324–325.

6. For the operation of Hunt's atelier, see James F. O'Gorman, *The Architecture of Frank Furness,* 18–19. For Richardson's atelier, see O'Gorman, *Henry Hobson Richardson and His Office,* 2–30.

7. See June Rayfield Welch and J. Larry Nance, *The Texas Courthouse.* Unfortunately, this volume does not include the names of designing architects. Two of the courthouses have demonstrably Spanish regional characteristics: Atascosa County at Jourdanton (1912) and Hudspeth County at Sierra Blanca (1919). Several of those built late in the 1920's appear transitional to the modernistic idiom of the 1930's: Hunt County at Greenville and Rusk County at Henderson (both 1928). The list of extant courthouses includes Scurry County at Snyder (1911) and Titus County at Mount Pleasant (1900), both remodeled beyond recognition.

8. The other two early Page and Brother courthouses were those for Hays County in San Marcos (1908) and Williamson County in Georgetown (1910). Although the vestigially Victorian corner pavilions are eliminated at Georgetown, the dome is still insufficiently elevated or exposed to correct for foreshortening. An attempt to alleviate the foreshortening of the dome was apparently attempted at the Smith County Courthouse in Tyler, designed by Page and Brother in 1908–1910. The Tyler courthouse had an extremely tall, slender lantern—the opposite extreme to the previous three. It does not survive, but is illustrated in Robinson, *The People's Architecture,* Fig. 210.

9. Described but not illustrated in Robinson, *The People's Architecture,* 216.

10. Robinson mistakenly attributes the Corpus Christi courthouse to C. H. Page and Brother of Austin rather than to Harvey L. Page of Washington. *The People's Architecture,* 218; Texas Historical Commission, *Catalog of Texas Properties,* 138. It is included in Atlantic Terra Cotta Co., Photograph Album.

11. The Breckenridge courthouse is illustrated in Robinson, *The People's Architecture*, 238.

12. Described but not illustrated in Robinson, *The People's Architecture*, 268. Included in Atlantic Terra Cotta Co., Photograph Album.

13. Robinson and Webb, *Texas Public Buildings*, which illustrates only two city halls. Robinson in *The People's Architecture* illustrates city halls and markets from the 1870's in Houston, Dallas, and Austin; fire stations from Austin and Waco from the 1880's; and city halls in Galveston, Waco, San Antonio, and Fort Worth from the nineteenth century. None of these survive.

14. These ten Supervising Architects of the Treasury were: (1) A. B. Mullett, 1863–1875; (2) William A. Potter, 1875–1876; (3) James G. Hill, 1876–1883; (4) Melvin E. Bell, 1883–1887; (5) William A. Freret, 1887–1889; (6) James H. Windrim, 1889–1891; (7) W. J. Edbrooke, 1891–1893; (8) Jeremiah O'Rourke, 1893–1895; (9) William M. Aiken, 1895–1897; (10) James Knox Taylor, 1897–1914.

15. Other Texas post offices designed under Taylor's incumbency include those at Austin, Cleburne, Del Rio, Denison, Gonzales, Greenville, Hillsboro, McKinney, Sulphur Springs, and Temple, but no complete enumeration has been undertaken. Those in Greenville (1910) and Hillsboro (1910) are on the National Register; the Austin Federal Building of 1912 (now Claudia Johnson Hall of the University of Texas) is included in the Sixth Street Historic District. Texas Historical Commission, *Catalog of Texas Properties*, 102, 106, 171.

16. Texas Historical Commission, *Catalog of Texas Properties*, 92; Fox, *Houston Architectural Guide*, 48.

17. Grossman, "Paul Philippe Cret," 52, 60. For Cret, see also Theo B. White, *Paul Philippe Cret: Architect and Teacher*. Cret's work is also introduced in Carol McMichael, *Paul Cret at Texas: Architectural Drawing and the Image of the University in the 1930's*.

18. Cret had used simplified pilasters rather than complete orders on the Frankford War Memorial, Philadelphia (1922); Integrity Trust Co., Philadelphia (1923); Pennsylvania War Memorial, Varennes, France (1924); Hartford County Building, Hartford, Connecticut (1926); and the American Battle Monument, Château Thierry, France (1928). The next step in the evolution of Cret's Modern Classic style came with the Folger Shakespeare Library in Washington, D.C. (1929), an influential source for the modernistic style of the 1930's. Voelcker and Dixon's Wichita Falls Post Office falls short of the level of classical abstraction shown on the Folger library, however. Cret's work and influence on Texas architecture are discussed further in Chapters 5 and 6.

19. The Clark library is included within the Caldwell County Courthouse Historic District. Texas Historical Commission, *Catalog of Texas Properties*, p. 30.

20. Texas Historical Commission, *Catalog of Texas Properties*, 63; Houston AIA, *Houston*, 165.

21. For a comprehensive coverage of the Carnegie libraries in Texas, see John D. Sebastian, *A Survey of Texas Carnegie Libraries*. Sebastian's survey of surviving libraries catalogs Ballinger, Belton, Bryan, Cleburne, Gainesville, Houston, Jefferson, Memphis, Palestine, Stamford, Terrell, and Tyler. He has obviously missed Franklin, which does survive. In addition to the one in Belton, Smith and Moore designed the Carnegie libraries in Cleburne and Terrell. Texas cities whose Carnegie libraries have not survived, according to Sebastian, include Abilene, Brownwood, Clarksville, Corsicana, Dallas, El Paso, Fort Worth, [Franklin], Greenville, Pecos, Pittsburg, San Antonio, Sherman, Sulphur

Springs, Temple, Vernon, Waco, and Winnsboro. The Dallas library is illustrated in McDonald, *Dallas Rediscovered*, 82–83, and the Fort Worth structure in Willard B. Robinson, *Gone from Texas: Our Lost Architectural Heritage*, 257. Both appear to be larger evocations of the Belton/Beaux-Arts Classic paradigm. Those in Belton, Ballinger, Bryan, Cleburne, Palestine, and Terrell are listed on the National Register. Texas Historical Commission, *Catalog of Texas Properties* and *Addendum*.

22. Texas Historical Commission, *Catalog of Texas Properties*, 97.

23. Robinson, *The People's Architecture*, 247; included within "Historic Resources of Stamford" on the National Register. Texas Historical Commission, *Addendum*. Other examples of this formula include the Ennis City Hall, designed by Hix McCanless in 1910; the Seymour Municipal Building by Voelcker and Dixon in 1924; and the Groesbeck City Hall by A. O. Evans in 1925–1926.

24. Robinson, *The People's Architecture*, 246.

25. Ibid., Fig. 306.

26. For the architecture of the PWA, see C. W. Short and R. Stanley Brown, *Projects Constructed by Federal and Other Governmental Bodies between the Years 1933 and 1939 with the Assistance of the Public Works Administration*. Unfortunately, this compendium does not provide the names of the designing architects. Other sources of federal funding during the Depression were the Emergency Work Projects Administration (EWPA) of 1938, the Civilian Conservation Corps (CCC), and the National Youth Administration (NYA). The latter two agencies concentrated on the direct use of the unemployed in state parks and similar self-help projects. See Chapter 8.

27. Dallas AIA, *The Prairie's Yield*, 28; Robinson, *The People's Architecture*, 144.

28. The Dallas Criminal Courts and Jail Building, including plans of the jail floors, was published in "Dallas: A City of Art and Commerce," 73.

29. Atlantic Terra Cotta Co., Photograph Album.

30. Drawings for the State Office Building are in the Architectural Drawings Collection, University of Texas at Austin.

31. Fox, *Houston Architectural Guide*, 105. Watkin was the dean of architecture at Rice University. His collaboration with the prestigious New York firm dated from the plan of Rice University in 1910 (see Chapter 5). The Houston Museum of Fine Arts was published in "Museum of Fine Arts, Houston, Texas," *Architectural Forum* 47 (December 1927): 563–568.

32. For Kessler's work in Texas, see Sarah Elizabeth Campbell, "George E. Kessler, Landscape Architect to City Planner: His Work in Texas Cities" (M.S. thesis, University of Texas at Austin, 1978).

33. For El Paso High School, including the floor plan, see Engelbrecht and Engelbrecht, *Henry C. Trost*, 68–70. See also Henry, "Trost and Trost in El Paso," 34–36. The high school is on the National Register. Texas Historical Commission, *Catalog of Texas Properties*, 52.

34. See Guy Study, "The Work of William B. Ittner FAIA," *Architectural Record* 57 (February 1925): 97–124. In addition to North Dallas High School, the article illustrates Forest Avenue High School and Mt. Auburn School, both in Dallas.

35. For the history of the American campus, see Paul Venable Turner, *Campus: An American Planning Tradition*.

36. Texas Historical Commission, *Catalog of Texas Properties*, 188.

37. The master plan for Rice University by Goodhue, Cram and Ferguson of 1910 will be discussed in Chapter 5, owing to the regional idiom adopted. For

the same reason, the replanning of the campuses at the University of Texas at Austin and at El Paso (originally the El Paso College of Mines) will also be deferred to Chapter 5.

38. For Southern Methodist University, see James F. White, *Architecture at S.M.U.: 50 Years and Buildings.* Shepley, Rutan and Coolidge were the corporate successors of H. H. Richardson, and had designed the Stanford Plan in 1888. The ten Georgian Revival buildings erected at SMU between 1912 and 1928 have been entered as a thematic group in the National Register. Texas Historical Commission, *Catalog of Texas Properties,* 45.

39. For Vaughan, see William Morgan, *The Almighty Wall: The Architecture of Henry Vaughan.* For the work of Goodhue, Cram and Ferguson see Oliver, *Bertram Grosvenor Goodhue.*

40. The Oak Lawn Methodist Church is included on the National Register. Texas Historical Commission, *Addendum.* It is included in Atlanta Terra Cotta Co., Photograph Album. Similar exercises in the tan brick and terra-cotta Gothic are Sanguinet and Staats' First Methodist Church in Houston of 1910; the Laurel Heights Methodist Church in San Antonio of 1913; and Grace Methodist Church in Dallas of 1903. Many comparable examples of this popular formula could be cited. For the growing importance of educational wings in church planning, see Thomas E. Tallmadge, "The Revolution in Ecclesiastical Architecture: The Sunday School," *Architectural Record* 55 (May 1924): 416–436.

41. Fox, *Houston Architectural Guide,* 78. Cram, Wentworth and Goodhue had prepared a design for St. Matthew's Episcopal Cathedral in Dallas in 1892, which was never carried out. Oliver, *Bertram Grosvenor Goodhue,* 19. The tall lancets on the main front of Trinity Episcopal occur again on the First Methodist Church in Wichita Falls of 1928, for which William Ward Watkin, Cram Goodhue and Ferguson's Houston associate was designer. Goodhue withdrew from the firm in 1913.

42. Fox, *Houston Architectural Guide,* p. 102. Mark Lemmon designed three such ensembles for the elite Dallas suburb of Highland Park: one for the Methodists, one for the Presbyterians, and one for the Baptists. The taste for Gothic affected most denominations, regardless of sectarian liturgies.

43. For Fort Worth First Methodist, see Michael C. Hoffmeyer, "Fort Worth Architecture: A History and Guide, 1873–1933" (M. Arch. thesis, University of Texas at Arlington, 1980), 49–50.

44. For the Incarnate Word chapel, see San Antonio AIA, *Guide,* 124. Gaenslen's Catholic churches in the Romanesque mode include St. Mary's in San Antonio of 1926, and three Houston churches: Holy Name (1926), Blessed Sacrament (1924), and All Saints (1927). Fox, *Houston Architectural Guide,* 169, 173, 188.

45. Oliver, *Bertram Grosvenor Goodhue,* 145–151. As Oliver points out, Goodhue's inspiration was probably John Francis Bentley's design of 1895 for Westminster Cathedral, the seat of the Roman Catholic primate of England. Although St. Bartholomew's is Episcopalian, Bentley's Westminster design also probably influenced McGinnis and Walsh's exploration of Byzantine effects in the design for the Catholic churches in America. The most prominent example of this work is the National Shrine of the Immaculate Conception in Washington, D.C., designed in 1920.

46. First Baptist Church of Amarillo is included in the National Register in "A Thematic Group of Churches in Texas with Decorative Interior Painting." Texas Historical Commission, *Catalog of Texas Properties,* 179.

47. Included in National Register as part of "Historic Resources of Stamford." Texas Historical Commission, *Addendum*.

48. Texas Historical Commission, *Catalog of Texas Properties*, 141.

49. Included in "Thematic Grouping of Churches in Texas with Decorative Interior Painting." Texas Historical Commission, *Catalog of Texas Properties*, 178.

50. Fox, *Houston Architectural Guide*, 101–102.

51. John W. Reps, *Cities of the American West: A History of Frontier Urban Planning*, 670.

52. For Burnham, see Thomas S. Hines, *Burnham of Chicago: Architect and Planner*.

53. Texas Historical Commission, *Catalog of Texas Properties*, 54.

54. Ibid., 41. For the Kessler Plan for Dallas and the City Beautiful movement elsewhere, see William H. Wilson, *The City Beautiful Movement*.

55. Reps, *Cities of the American West*, 576–579.

56. The MKT station is included in the Denison Commercial Historic District. Texas Historical Commission, *Catalog of Texas Properties*, 73.

57. Wim de Wit, "The Banks and the Image of Progressive Banking," 159ff.

58. Included in Ellis County Courthouse Historic District. Texas Historical Commission, *Catalog of Texas Properties*, 51.

59. Texas Historical Commission, *Catalog of Texas Properties*, 163.

60. The headquarters of the Amicable Insurance Company in Waco, at twenty stories, the tallest Texas building upon its completion in 1912, was designed for a bank on the ground floor and mezzanine, and thus might be considered an extreme case of the bank-office building typology.

61. Ralph Cameron's lodge halls in Brady (1914) and Lufkin (1916) exhibit at least suggestive traces of Prairie School conventions. Drawings for the Lufkin lodge are retained in the Architectural Drawings Collection, University of Texas at Austin.

62. Texas Historical Commission, *Catalog of Texas Properties*, 159.

63. Federal Writers' Project, *The W.P.A. Guide to Texas*, 249; Atlantic Terra Cotta Co., *Photograph Album*.

64. San Antonio AIA, *Guide*, 44.

65. Included in McKinney Commercial Historic District. Texas Historical Commission, *Catalog of Texas Properties*, 36.

66. The Alhambra Theater survives; it is discussed in Chapter 5. The Hippodrome in Dallas does not. It is illustrated in McDonald, *Dallas Rediscovered*, 73.

67. Texas Historical Commission, *Catalog of Texas Properties*, 166. For Eberson's theaters, see Jane Preddy, *Palaces of Dreams: The Movie Theaters of John Eberson, Architect* [exhibition Catalog].

68. For the Majestic in Dallas, see McDonald, *Dallas Rediscovered*, 77. For the San Antonio Majestic, see San Antonio AIA, *Guide*, 36. The numerous auditorium theaters of Adler and Sullivan are compared by David Van Zanten, "Sullivan to 1890," in *Louis Sullivan: The Function of Ornament*, 36–51.

69. For the downtown as a "culture of congestion" in Texas cities, see Stephen Fox, "Lessons Learned with 20/80 Vision," *Texas Architect* 38 (March/April 1988): 17–21.

70. For the two Dallas department stores, see R. Edward Brooks, "George L. Dahl: A Critical Analysis of His Life and Architecture" (M. Arch. thesis, University of Texas at Arlington, 1978).

71. The Scott Building is included in the Paris Commercial Historic District on the National Register. Texas Historical Commission, *Addendum*.

72. The Magnolia stations in Amarillo and Fort Worth were designed by Clarkson and Gaines; that in San Antonio by Adams and Adams; and that in Houston by Alfred C. Finn. Each is adapted to its site, but all are commercial Gothic with a second floor carried over the pump islands. Atlantic Terra Cotta Co., *Photograph Album*.

73. For the corridor street, see Fox, "Lessons Learned with 20/80 Vision," 19–20.

74. The Dallas shopping center at Davis and Edgefield is included within the Winnetka Heights Historic District. Texas Historical Commission, *Catalog of Texas Properties*, 47. For the Morningside Historic District in Wichita Falls, see Texas Historical Commission, *Addendum*. For the Newport Casino, see Roth, *McKim, Mead and White*. For Roland Park, see John Dorsey and James D. Dilts, *A Guide to Baltimore Architecture*, 240–241. For Lake Forest, see Ira J. Bush, *A Guide to Chicago's Historic Suburbs*, 138.

75. For the Paso del Norte, see Engelbrecht and Engelbrecht, *Henry C. Trost*, 63. The hotel, including floor plans, was also published in *Western Architect* (July 1914). The Paso del Norte is included on the National Register within the "Henry Charles Trost Commercial Structures Thematic Group." Texas Historical Commission, *Catalog of Texas Properties*, 54. The firm of Trost and Trost had already established its reputation as hotel designers with the Santa Rita Hotel in Tucson and the Gadsden in Douglas, Arizona, and would continue to develop this building type throughout the Southwest in the 1920's. The Paso del Norte has recently been restored and expanded by the Westin chain. The old lobby is now used as a cocktail lounge, with a circular bar beneath the Tiffany skylight.

76. Dallas AIA, *The Prairie's Yield*, 26; Texas Historical Commission, *Catalog of Texas Properties*, 42. Contemporary hotels elsewhere in Texas corresponding in scale to the Paso del Norte and the Adolphus include the Gunter in San Antonio (1909) and the Rice in Houston (1912), both also designed by Mauran, Russell and Crowell, with local associates. The Raleigh Hotel in Waco (Fig. 3.14) was only slightly smaller and, except for its extraordinary Prairie School ornament, might fit generically into the same category.

77. Wyatt C. Hedrick of Fort Worth, like George Dahl in Dallas, represents the new generation of designers coming into independent practice in the 1920's. An associate of Sanguinet and Staats, he bought out the elder partners upon their retirement in 1926. Fox, "Sanguinet and Staats in Houston," 11; Texas Historical Commission, *Catalog of Texas Properties*, 41. The Galvez Hotel in Galveston is discussed in Chapter 5.

78. Texas Historical Commission, *Catalog of Texas Properties*, 163.

79. Conrad Hilton entered the hotel business in 1919, when he bought the Mobley Hotel in Cisco. The Hilton chain expanded rapidly in the 1920's, with a new hotel in Cisco and others in Dallas, San Angelo, Waco, Marlin, and El Paso. Lang and Witchell designed the Hilton hotels in Dallas and Waco. The Dallas facility is on the National Register; both are included in Atlantic Terra Cotta Co., *Photograph Album*.

80. Trost and Trost's smaller hotels built in the 1920's in the American Southwest for the motoring public include, in addition to those in West Texas, the Hassayampa in Prescott, the La Caverna in Carlsbad, the Hidalgo in Lordsburg, and the Meadows in Las Vegas, New Mexico. The Val Verde in Socorro, built in 1915 in a Mission Revival parti, was still predicated on railroad travel at a layover point between Albuquerque and El Paso.

81. Working drawings for the Gage Hotel are among the Trost and Trost Pa-

pers in the El Paso Public Library. The Gage is also included in Linda Johnson and Sally Ross, *Historic Texas Hotels and Country Inns*, 192–196.

82. For the Aurora Apartments, see San Antonio AIA, *Guide*, 103.

83. McDonald, *Dallas Rediscovered*, 84.

84. For the Amicable Life Building, see John Pastier, "The Cardboard Sky-scrapers of Texas: 1911–1932," *Texas Architect* 32 (May/June 1982): 55–57, and Jamie Lofgren, "Texas Skyscrapers in the 1920's," *Texas Architect* 38 (March/April 1988): 22–27. The lowest three floors have been obliterated by a modern renovation. Drawings are preserved in the Architectural Drawings Collection, University of Texas at Austin. The drawings give no indication whether they were prepared in the Houston or Fort Worth offices of Sanguinet and Staats. The names of both Koeppe and Finn appear on the various sheets. Koeppe would later become principal designer for Sanguinet and Staats' corporate heir in Fort Worth, Wyatt C. Hedrick and Co. Alfred C. Finn left the Houston office of Sanguinet and Staats in 1925 to establish his own practice in that city.

85. For the Busch Building, see Dallas AIA, *The Prairie's Yield*, 28. For the renovation, see "Kirby Building, Dallas." *Texas Architect* 31 (March/April 1981): 32. The client was Adolphus Busch of St. Louis, for whom Barnett, Hayes and Barnett had just designed the Adolphus Hotel. It is listed on the National Register. Texas Historical Commission, *Catalog of Texas Properties*, 42.

86. For the State National Bank Building, see Atlantic Terra Cotta Co., Photograph Album.

87. For the Houston Medical Arts Building, see Fox, "Sanguinet and Staats in Houston"; also Houston AIA, *Houston*, 25. It appears to have been demolished, for it does not appear in Fox, *Houston Architectural Guide*.

88. For the Norwood Tower, see Austin AIA, *Austin*, 18.

89. For the San Antonio Medical Arts Building, see San Antonio AIA, *Guide*, 21. It is included in the Alamo Plaza Historic District. Texas Historical Commission, *Catalog of Texas Properties*, 13. Other medical arts buildings in Texas included that in Dallas designed in 1921 by Barglebaugh and Whitson (demolished) and the Nix Building in San Antonio by Henry T. Phelps. Neither are overtly Gothic, however.

90. San Antonio AIA, *Guide*, 78. Robert M. Ayres is another representative of the new generation of designers coming to maturity in the 1920's. He joined his father as partner in 1922. Drawings for the Smith-Young Tower are preserved in the Architectural Drawings Collection, University of Texas at Austin.

91. New York Chapter AIA, *AIA Guide to New York City*, 20.

92. For the Waggoner Building, see Hoffmeyer, "Architecture in Fort Worth," 41.

93. Dallas AIA, *The Prairie's Yield*.

94. See Roth, *McKim, Mead and White*, 338.

95. Houston AIA, *Houston*, 20; Lofgren, "Texas Skyscrapers in the 1920's," 23.

96. Hitchcock, *Modern Architecture*, 103.

5. REGIONAL ECLECTICISM: 1900–1940

1. Richard Longstreth, *On the Edge of the World*, 28–31. The irony is that the Texas missions were half a century older than those in California, yet were generally unknown outside the state and ignored in Texas.

2. Karen J. Weitze, *California's Mission Revival*, 21–24.

3. Ibid., 76. Weitze illustrates the Southern Pacific depot in Burlingame and that of the Santa Fe in San Juan Capistrano, both of 1893. In the same year,

California chose A. Page Brown's Mission style design for its pavilion at the Chicago Columbian Exposition. By contrast, J. Riely Gordon's design for the Texas pavilion was in the Spanish Renaissance style, a vague pastiche somewhere between the Victorian sensibility and the Beaux-Arts Classic. See Robinson, *Gone from Texas*, 183.

4. For Burnham's work in the Philippines, see Hines, *Burnham of Chicago*, 197–216. For Cram, Goodhue and Ferguson's Washington Hotel in Colon, Panama, see "The New Washington Hotel, Colon, Panama. Cram, Goodhue, and Ferguson, Architects," *Architectural Record*, 32 (July 1912): 65–70.

5. For the origins of the Pueblo Revival in New Mexico, see Christopher Wilson, "The Spanish Pueblo Revival Defined, 1904–1921," *New Mexico Studies in the Fine Arts*, 7 (1982): 24–30. See also Carl D. Sheppard, *Creator of the Santa Fe Style: Isaac Hamilton Rapp, Architect*. Later work by John Gaw Meem, including that for the University of New Mexico at Albuquerque, is discussed in Bainbridge Bunting, *John Gaw Meem, Southwestern Architect*. The Franciscan Hotel is discussed in Engelbrecht and Engelbrecht, *Henry C. Trost*, 102–110.

6. For the Meso-American Revival, see Marjorie Ingle, *The Mayan Revival Style*. The Mayan culture in Guatemala and the Yucatan was only one phase of a long sequence of Meso-American civilizations, which were preceded by the Olmec and Teotihuacan cultures, contemporary with that of Monte Alban in the Valley of Oaxaca, and followed by the Toltec and Aztec phases. Meso-American seems more appropriate for this eclectic tendency than the narrower designation of Mayan Revival. For the Meso-American influence on skyscraper construction, see Francisco Mujica, *History of the Skyscraper*.

7. For the San Antonio Southern Pacific Station, see Weitze, *California's Mission Revival*, 87, and San Antonio AIA, *Guide*, 77. The station is on the National Register. Texas Historical Commission, *Catalog of Texas Properties*, 19.

8. Texas Historical Commission, *Catalog of Texas Properties*, 39.

9. Ibid., 78. Other Mission Revival stations in Texas that do not survive include Harvey L. Page's San Antonio station for the Great Northern of 1907 (Weitze, *California's Mission Revival*, 85); Frederick Sterner's MKT Station in San Antonio of 1917 (Robinson, *Gone from Texas*, 250); and Union Station in Wichita Falls, designed by Lang and Witchell in 1910 (Ibid., 249). Other surviving stations of comparable style and date on the National Register include the Santa Fe Depot and Eating House in Amarillo, the Texas and Brazos Valley Depot in Teague, also designed by C. H. Page in 1907, and the Texas and Pacific Depot in Marshall of 1908. The progressive work of Louis Curtiss for the Santa Fe Railroad has been discussed in Chapter 3.

10. The Galvez has been restored and put back in operation. See Michael McCullar, "The Hotel Galvez: Gulf Coast Landmark in Transition," *Texas Architect* 30 (January/February 1980): 41–43. It is also on the National Register. Texas Historical Commission, *Catalog of Texas Properties*, 65. Of other Texas hotels built before World War I, only the St. Anthony in San Antonio, designed in 1909 by J. Flood Walker, seems to have been strongly imbued with Mission Revival characteristics. These have been largely obliterated in subsequent expansions.

11. For the Fort Worth stockyards, see Hoffmeyer, "Architecture in Fort Worth," 97–100.

12. Texas Historical Commission, *Catalog of Texas Properties*, 118.

13. For Westminster Presbyterian, see Engelbrecht and Engelbrecht,

*Henry C. Trost,* 80–81. Another Mission Revival work in El Paso by Trost and Trost, the El Paso Country Club, does not survive. The Williams House is the firm's most ambitious residence in the style.

14. Engelbrecht and Engelbrecht, *Henry C. Trost,* 64–66. See also Dale L. Walker, "The Lamaseries on the Hill: The Bhutanese Architecture of U.T. El Paso," *NOVA: the University of Texas at El Paso Magazine* 6, no. 4 (August/ October 1971): 12.

15. Ralph Adams Cram, *My Life in Architecture,* 126; quoted in Turner, *Campus,* 201–203. The work at Rice is also discussed in Speck and Payne, *Landmarks of Texas Architecture,* 58–61, and Fox, *Houston Architectural Guide,* 116–121. For the definitive treatment, see Stephen Fox, *The General Plan of the William M. Rice Institute and Its Architectural Development.*

16. For the UCLA campus, see David Gebhard and Robert Winter, *Architecture in Los Angeles: A Compleat Guide,* 134–136.

17. For definitive treatment of the University of Texas at Austin campus, see Carol McMichael, *Paul Cret at Texas.* Battle Hall is also described and illustrated in Speck and Payne, *Landmarks of Texas Architecture,* 54–57.

18. Quoted in Speck and Payne, *Landmarks of Texas Architecture,* 55.

19. Quoted in McMichael, *Paul Cret at Texas,* 83. Cret was actually quoting from Werner Hegemann and Elbert Peet's *The American Vitruvius: An Architect's Handbook of Civic Art,* a great compendium of Beaux-Arts planning examples.

20. The imagery of a tower may also have been suggested by Charles Klauder's "Cathedral of Learning" for the University of Pittsburgh (1926–1929), although Klauder's Gothic style differed from Cret's subtle Regional Classicism.

21. McMichael, *Paul Cret at Texas,* 75.

22. Austin AIA, *Austin,* 42.

23. Dallas AIA, *The Prairie's Yield,* 38. The Third Church of Christ Scientist was published in "Christian Scientists Use Romanesque: Third Church of Christ Scientist, Dallas, Texas. Mark Lemmon, Architect," *Architectural Record* 83 (April 1938): 57–59.

24. Engelbrecht and Engelbrecht, *Henry C. Trost,* 81–83; Henry, "Trost and Trost in El Paso," 36.

25. For the Franciscan Hotel, see Engelbrecht and Engelbrecht, *Henry C. Trost,* 104–110. The European and American publication of the Franciscan, including the critique of George Edgell, *The American Architecture of Today,* is discussed on pp. 107–108. For Schindler's interest in Pueblo forms, see David Gebhard, *Schindler,* 27–30.

26. For both the Aztec Hotel and the UNM Chemistry Building, see Ingle, *Mayan Revival Style,* 19–27.

27. San Antonio AIA, *Guide,* 39. The authors identify the Casino Club Building as Art Deco, although they recognize the "Mayan" derivation of the relief ornament.

28. Ingle, *Mayan Revival Style,* 44.

29. In theater design, the interior was more important in conveying an exotic fairy tale environment than the exterior. The grandest Meso-American interior in Texas is the Aztec Theater in San Antonio, designed by Mey and Hollyer in 1926. See David Naylor, *Great American Movie Theaters, A National Trust Guide,* 192–193. Other Texas theaters included in this work are the Paramount in Abilene (David S. Castle, 1930); the Paramount in Austin (John Eberson, 1915); the Jefferson in Beaumont (Emile Weil, 1927); the Creighton in Conroe (Emile Weil, 1934); the Majestic in Dallas (John Eberson, 1921); the Plaza in

El Paso (W. Scott Dunne, 1930); the Alameda in San Antonio (N. Straus Nayfach, 1949); the Majestic in San Antonio (John Eberson, 1929); the Texas in Seguin (W. Scott Dunne, 1929); the Perot [Saenger/Paramount] in Texarkana (Emile Weil, 1924); and the Waco [Hippodrome] in Waco (1913). One should also note the Egyptian interiors in the Yucca Theater in Midland (Wyatt C. Hedrick, 1929) and the Metropolitan in Houston (Alfred C. Finn, 1927). For Eberson, see also Jane Preddy, *Palaces of Dreams.*

30. George Kubler and Martin Soria, *Art and Architecture in Spain and Portugal and Their American Dominions, 1500 to 1800.*

31. Oliver, *Bertram Grosvenor Goodhue,* 109–119.

32. Federal Writers Project, *The WPA Guide to Texas,* 358.

33. Austin AIA, *Austin,* 10.

34. Stephen Fox, "(Tall) Tales from the Borderland: Brownsville and the Spanish Colonial Revival," *Texas Architect* 31 (July/August 1981): 59–65.

35. San Antonio AIA, *Guide,* 43. The drawings are preserved in the Architectural Drawings Collection, University of Texas at Austin. These include alternative preliminary partis in fieldstone, cut stone, and brick by George Willis and Emmett T. Jackson, undated but presumably drawn up before Atlee and Robert Ayres had joined the consortium.

36. For the Dallas State Fair Music Hall, see Anita M. Regehr Toews, "Spanish Colonial Revival Architecture in Dallas: An Analysis of Its Historic Origins and Development" (Master's thesis, University of Texas at Arlington, 1984), 59–61. The other four entrants in the invited competition were DeWitt and Lemmon, Thomson and Swain, C. D. Hill and Co., and R. H. Hunt Co.

37. Robinson, *The People's Architecture,* 250.

38. Ibid., 251. The Wichita Falls City Hall and Auditorium is included in Atlantic Terra Cotta Co., Photograph Album.

39. Toews, "Spanish Colonial Revival Architecture in Dallas: An Analysis," 55–59. The Highland Park City Hall was published in "Dallas, Texas. Highland Park City Hall. Lang and Witchell, Architects." *Architect* 52 (December 1925): 182–183. It was also included in George F. Edgell, *The American Architecture of Today,* 237–239.

40. Fox, *Houston Architectural Guide,* 24.

41. Texas Historical Commission, *Addendum.*

42. San Antonio AIA, *Guide,* 85. See also Andrea Kirsten Mullen, "Jefferson High School up for National Register Listing," *Texas Architect* 33 (September/October 1983): 28; 74.

43. Texas Historical Commission, *Catalog of Texas Properties,* p. 63.

44. For the Brownsville station, see Texas Historical Commission, *Catalog of Texas Properties,* 32; Fox, "(Tall) Tales from the Borderland." Wyatt C. Hedrick and Co. did extensive work for the Fort Worth and Denver City Railroad, including a new station in Amarillo in 1930. Drawings for twenty-one projects are preserved in the Architectural Drawings Collection, University of Texas at Austin. The Lubbock station, which is now used as a restaurant, is not included in the collection. Hedrick and Co.'s entry to Lubbock seems to have been the Texas Tech commission of 1924, the year Hedrick bought out his retiring partners, Sanguinet and Staats. Hedrick and Co. also designed the Lubbock City Hall and Lubbock State Bank in 1924 and a hotel building for the Chamber of Commerce in 1925.

45. Texas Historical Commission, *Catalog of Texas Properties,* 145. Other small town motoring hotels in the Southwest by Trost and Trost include the La Caverna in Carlsbad, New Mexico; the Hidalgo in Lordsburg, New Mexico;

the Meadows in Las Vegas, New Mexico; and the Hassayampa in Prescott, Arizona. The Val Verde in Socorro of 1915 was still predicated on rail travel.

46. Toews, "Spanish Colonial Revival Architecture in Dallas," 87.

47. Engelbrecht and Engelbrecht, *Henry C. Trost,* 71–73; and Henry, "Trost and Trost in El Paso," 37.

48. San Antonio AIA, *Guide,* 58.

49. Fox, "Lessons Learned with 20/80 Vision," 19–20.

50. In 1932, there were 156,022 filling stations in the United States, competing with 162,221 other gasoline retail outlets for the business of 26.5 million registered motor vehicles. "Mr. Jenkins and Sir Henri," *Fortune* 6 (October 1932): 104.

51. San Antonio AIA, *Guide,* 121. Anita Toews illustrates a similar Magnolia station in Dallas, now demolished, which was designed by Fooshee and Cheek. Toews, "Spanish Colonial Revival Architecture in Dallas: An Analysis," 87. There was also originally a service station included in the design of the Highland Park Shopping Village.

52. The Bryant-Link Building is included in "Historic Resources of Stamford" on the National Register. Texas Historical Commission, *Addendum.*

53. Engelbrecht and Engelbrecht, *Henry C. Trost,* 62. As Islamic ornament is one of the frequently cited sources for Sullivan's ornament, it is not hard to appreciate how Henry Trost managed to introduce a touch of Sullivanesque detail in the Alhambra Theater decoration. Henry Phelps had previously used bits of Sullivanesque detail on the Mission Revival Atascosa County Courthouse in Jourdanton.

54. Fox, "(Tall) Tales from the Borderland," 62.

55. Ibid.

56. See Anita Toews, "Spanish Colonial Revival Architecture in Dallas: The Work of Fooshee and Cheek," *Perspective* 13 (1984): 9–15. See also Toews' thesis, "The Spanish Colonial Revival in Dallas: An Analysis," 73–86, and Speck and Payne, *Landmarks of Texas Architecture,* 62–65. For a contemporaneous publication, see "A Model Shopping Village in Texas, Fooshee and Cheek, Architects," *Architectural Record* 70 (September 1931): 197–198.

57. See Richard Longstreth, "J. C. Nichols, the Country Club Plaza, and Notions of Modernity," *Precedent and Innovation: The Harvard Architectural Review* 5 (1986): 120–135. See also William S. Worley, *J. C. Nichols and the Shaping of Kansas City.*

58. Fooshee and Cheek returned several times to design modifications to Highland Park Village. They were not responsible for the replacement in the 1950's of the original service station at the Preston Road entrance with an out-of-scale bank. After several decades of decline, Highland Park Village experienced gentrification in the 1980's. Drawings are preserved in the Architectural Drawings Collection, University of Texas at Austin.

59. Several examples of bungalow courts survive in El Paso. Montana Courts at 2400 Montana is in the Bungalow style, whereas the bungalow court at 1916–1920 North Mesa is in the Spanish Colonial mode, similar to that in San Angelo. Other examples no doubt exist, including one in Sweetwater. This court is in a modernistic design.

60. Stefanos Polyzoides, Roger Sherwood, James Tice, and Julius Schulman, *Courtyard Housing in Los Angeles.*

61. Peter C. Papademetriou, "Main Street Spanish," *Texas Architect* 17 (July/August 1974): 16–19.

62. Donald W. Curl, *Mizner's Florida: American Resort Architecture.*

63. Muriel Quest McCarthy, *David R. Williams: Pioneer Architect*, 30.

64. The Fort Bliss Quarters #1 has been placed on the National Register. Texas Historical Commission, *Addendum*.

65. Texas Historical Commission, *Addendum*. See also "The Taj Mahal: U.S. Air Force Landmark in San Antonio," *Texas Architect* 30 (July/August 1980): 95. The Randolph Field Chapel is illustrated in Lois Craig and Staff of Federal Architecture Project, *The Federal Presence: Architecture, Politics, and National Design*, 307.

6. MODERNISTIC MODES OF DESIGN: 1928–1940

1. The term "International style," although used occasionally in the 1920's for the new avant-garde modern architecture, was canonized in usage by Henry-Russell Hitchcock and Philip Johnson in their exhibition catalog of the new work for the Museum of Modern Art in 1932.

2. David Gebhard, "The Moderne in the U.S., 1920–1941": 4–20.

3. Viennese influence on the modernistic idiom in post-war America was experienced more decisively in the decorative arts than in architecture. Schindler and Neutra, both graduates of the Vienna Academy, developed avant-garde conceptions of modern architecture in California in the 1920's, abandoning the classicizing tendencies of the Wagnerschule. In the decorative arts, however, the influence of Josef Hoffmann and the Weiner Werkstatte survived the war, and is increasingly viewed as contributing to the "Art Deco" style in furnishings and interiors. Important European designers—Josef Urban, Kem Weber, Paul Frankl—emigrated to America and helped to create the modernistic decor of the 1920's.

4. For Saarinen, see Albert Christ-Janer, *Eliel Saarinen: Finnish-American Architect and Educator*. It has been suggested that Saarinen derived the central mass with graduated set-backs from the *sikharas* of Hindu temples, with which he would have been familiar through connections with the International Theosophical movement. Formal similarities to the massing of the New Mexico pueblos cannot be excluded, however. Forms may have several sources.

5. For the Nebraska capitol, see Oliver, *Bertram Grosvenor Goodhue*, 184–212. For the competition, see also Elizabeth G. Grossman, "Two Postwar Competitions: The Nebraska State Capitol and the Kansas City Liberty Memorial," *Journal of the Society of Architectural Historians*, 45 (September 1986): 244–269.

6. Grossman, "Two Postwar Competitions." Cret also competed with Goodhue in the Kansas City competition of 1921, won by H. van Buren McGonigle. Second and third prizes in the Nebraska competition went to John Russell Pope and McKim, Mead and White, respectively.

7. Elizabeth Green Grossman, "Paul Philippe Cret"; McMichael, *Paul Cret at Texas*. Richard Guy Wilson has pointed out that Bertram Goodhue's design of 1920–1924 for the National Academy of Sciences in Washington anticipates Cret's use of trabeated Modern Classic forms at the Folger Shakespeare Library by five years. Richard Guy Wilson, "Modernized Classicism and Washington, D.C.," in *American Public Architecture: European Roots and Native Expressions*, 271–303. This alternative manner to the arcuated style Goodhue had employed at the Nebraska capitol does not seem to have been widely imitated, however, until Cret popularized the usage at the Folger Library from 1929–1932.

8. Diane M. Hospodka Collier, "Art Deco Architecture: Dallas, Texas" (M. Arch. thesis, University of Texas at Arlington, 1980), 152 ff. Green had attended the Paris Exposition des Arts Decoratifs in 1925, where he presumably absorbed

the style first hand. Collier's references to Green as designer for Lang and Witchell apply specifically to the Dallas Power and Light Building and the Lone Star Gas Building, and not to institutional work such as the Eastland courthouse, where the influence of Saarinen and Goodhue seems stronger. The Eastland courthouse is included in Atlantic Terra Cotta Co., Photograph Album.

9. See Page Brothers' Hunt County Courthouse in Greenville (FIG. 4.06), also of 1928, as an uncomfortable compromise between classical aesthetics and the demand for more space.

10. Despite their considerable institutional and commercial work in the modernistic style, Lang and Witchell designed no other courthouses after Eastland. Trost and Trost never really exploited the potential of the San Angelo City Hall. Their Reeves County Courthouse in Pecos of 1936 is a timid and unsatisfactory compromise between the step-back massing of the modernistic idiom and conventional academic detail with a red-tile roof. Henry Trost's death in 1933 seems to have deprived his firm of its presiding arbiter of design.

11. The intervening Voelcker and Dixon courthouses include Midland County in Midland (1929); Gregg County in Longview (1932); Knox County in Benjamin (1935); Grayson County in Sherman (1936); Van Zandt County in Canton (1936); and Jack County in Jacksboro (1939). All are illustrated in Welch and Nance, *The Texas Courthouse*, which does not supply the names of architects. The Midland courthouse has been remodeled beyond recognition.

12. For the Potter County Courthouse, see Marcus Whiffen and Carla Breeze, *Pueblo Deco: The Art Deco Architecture of the Southwest*, 57–60, and its revised edition, Carla Breeze, *Pueblo Deco*, 58–59. For the landscape planning of Texas courthouse squares, see Sandra Kay Chipley, "Plazas and Squares of Texas: An Analysis of the Design Evolution of the Texas Courthouse Square and its Urban Context" (M.L.A. thesis, University of Texas at Arlington, 1985).

13. Intermediate between Goodhue's Nebraska capitol and such modernistic civic skyscrapers as the Beaumont courthouse lies the Los Angeles City Hall of 1926–1928, although its design, described as "Italian Classic," was less progressively modernistic than Goodhue's example. See Gebhard and Winter, *Guide to Architecture in Los Angeles*, 223.

14. San Antonio AIA, *Guide*, 53. Goodhue's Los Angeles Public Library of 1921–1926, a further development of the Nebraska capitol with regional overtones, does not seem to have influenced Herbert Green's design for the San Antonio Library. See Oliver, *Bertram Grosvenor Goodhue*, 226–233.

15. Federal Writers Project, *W.P.A. Guide to Texas*, 361. Included in Atlantic Terra Cotta Co., Photograph Album.

16. For Hedrick and Co.'s work in Fort Worth, see Judith Singer Cohen, *Cowtown Moderne: Art Deco Architecture of Fort Worth, Texas*. Cohen has identified Herman Paul Koeppe as the firm's Art Deco designer, comparable to Dudley Green's role at Lang and Witchell in Dallas. Koeppe joined the firm of Sanguinet and Staats in 1904 and became chief designer in 1925, shortly after Hedrick had bought out his partners. In view of Koeppe's role in the firm, it has been referred to in the plural.

17. Austin AIA, *Austin and Its Architecture*, p. 43.

18. Breeze, *Pueblo Deco*, 60–63.

19. Fox, *Houston Architectural Guide*, 24. The building designs were also published in "Administrative Center for Growing City: City Hall, Houston, Texas, Joseph Finger, Inc., Architects," *Architectural Record* 89 (March 1941): 104–107.

20. For the Hall of State, see Peggy Riddle, "The Texas Hall of State," *Per-*

*spective* 9, no. 2 (1980): 22–24. Collaborating architects for the Hall of State were Ralph Bryan, DeWitt and Washburn, Flint and Broad, Fooshee and Cheek, T. J. Galbraith, Anton Korn, Mark Lemmon, Walter Sharp, Arthur Thomas, H. B. Thomson, and Adams and Adams, "under the general supervision of . . . Donald Barthelme, a former student of Cret's." David Dillon and Doug Tomlinson, *Dallas Architecture 1936–1986,* 16.

21. The literature on the Texas Centennial Exposition is extensive. Among other sources, see the following: R. Edward Brooks, "George L. Dahl: A Critical Analysis of His Life and Architecture," 19–59; R. Edward Brooks and Jay C. Henry, "George L. Dahl and the Texas Centennial Exposition," *Perspective* 9, no. 2 (1980): 8–13; Dillon and Tomlinson, *Dallas Architecture,* 11–29; Speck and Payne, *Landmarks of Texas Architecture,* 70–75; and Collier, "Art Deco Architecture," 121–136.

22. "Sculptors and Muralists Finishing Gigantic Task," *Centennial News* 11 (January 1936): 4.

23. For Cincinnati Union Terminal, see Richard Guy Wilson, Diane Pilgrim, and Dikran Tashjran, *The Machine Age in America 1918–1941,* 111–122. Roland Wank, an emigrant from Hungary in 1924, was the chief designer for Fellheimer and Wagner's terminal, erected 1929–1933. He subsequently became chief architectural designer for the Tennessee Valley Authority (TVA), transferring the idiom of machine symbolism to the authority's dams and power stations. For Wank and the TVA, see Walter L. Creese, *TVA's Public Planning: The Vision, The Reality.* See also Marian Moffett, "Looking to the Future: The Architecture of Roland Wank," *Arris: The Journal of the Southeast Chapter, Society of Architectural Historians* 1 (1989): 5–17. At a less heroic scale, it is perhaps permissible to see this same aesthetic reflected in the Fair Park Outdoor Theater, particularly in its integration of construction and detailing.

24. For the Austin Central Fire Station, see Public Works Administration, *Public Buildings: Architecture under the Public Works Administration,* 85.

25. Creese, *TVA's Public Planning;* Moffett, "Looking to the Future."

26. Public Works Administration, *Public Buildings,* 230. See also Cohen, *Cowtown Moderne,* 148–151.

27. Public Works Administration, *Public Buildings,* 228; Fox, *Houston Architectural Guide,* 205.

28. For the discovery of European modern architecture by American architects, see James D. Kornwolf, ed., *Modernism in America 1937–1941: A Catalog and Exhibition of Four Architectural Competitions.* European architects who sought a rapprochement with American traditions included Richard Neutra and William Lescaze in the early 1930's, before the European refugees from Nazi Germany such as Eric Mendelsohn, Walter Gropius, Mies van der Rohe, and Marcel Breuer arrived in the late 1930's. Gropius' and Breuer's American works before World War II were much less spartan than the Bauhaus style. Other forces that created a tendency toward an authentic modernism in American architecture included the criticism of Lewis Mumford in the *New Yorker,* and the example of the TVA. Roland Wank, the TVA's chief architectural designer, had emigrated from Hungary in 1924 and thus should be regarded as part of a first wave of European émigrés, including Neutra and Lescaze and such designers as Josef Urban, Paul Frankl, and Kem Weber.

29. Fox, *Houston Architectural Guide,* 158. As a component of the university's new master plan developed by Hare and Hare, the Roy Cullen Building matches in regional modernistic idiom Cato's Science Building and Alfred C. Finn's later Ezekiel Cullen Building (1950).

30.  See page 140 above. Hitchcock, *Modern Architecture*, 103.

31.  Wilson et al., *The Machine Age in America*, 148–161. For Hood's work, see also Walter H. Kilham, Jr., *Raymond Hood, Architect*. For George Howe and the PSFS Building, see Robert A. M. Stern, *George Howe: Toward a Modern American Architecture*.

32.  Fox, *Houston Architectural Guide*, 46. Associate architects on the Petroleum Building were Briscoe and Dixon and Maurice J. Sullivan.

33.  San Antonio AIA, *Guide*, 50.

34.  The *Kontorhäuser* of Hamburg, particularly Fritz Höger's Chilehaus, although technically not skyscrapers, did suggest new forms of brick detailing appropriate to large-scale commercial architecture. The 1919 competition for a *Turmhaus* on the Friedrichstrasse in Berlin, best known for Mies van der Rohe's prescient glass prism, actually evoked a number of skyscraper designs in brick by German Expressionists, as did the Tribune Tower Competition of 1922.

35.  John Pastier, "The Cardboard Skyscrapers of Texas."

36.  The El Paso Hilton seems to be modeled on Bertram Goodhue's entry to the Tribune Tower Competition of 1922.

37.  For the Bassett Tower, see Engelbrecht and Engelbrecht, *Henry C. Trost*, 74; Henry, "Trost and Trost in El Paso." The plan of the Bassett Tower is reproduced in El Paso Chapter AIA, *Portals at the Pass: El Paso Area Architecture to 1930*, 52.

38.  See Collier, "Art Deco Architecture: Dallas, Texas," for both the DP & L (pp. 46–51) and Lone Star Gas Buildings (pp. 54–65). See also Diane Hospodka Collier, "Art Deco Architecture in Dallas," *Perspective* 11, no. 1 (1982): 8–12; and Atlantic Terra Cotta Co., Photograph Album. An earlier Lang and Witchell skyscraper in Dallas, the Collum Building at Main and Akard Streets of 1928, employs Art Deco ornament at the top floor and roofline only. A near neighbor to the DP & L and Lone Star Gas buildings is Mark Lemmon's Tower Petroleum Building, which adjoins party walls on two faces and in its set-back masses seems more closely modeled on Saarinen's Tribune Tower entry.

39.  The Electric Building was also known as the Hollywood Theater Building. Whereas Hedrick and Co. designed the tower, Alfred C. Finn of Houston designed the theater, which has been converted to use as a branch bank. Cohen, *Cowtown Moderne*, 43–46. See also Hoffmeyer, "Architecture in Fort Worth," 51–55.

40.  Cohen, *Cowtown Moderne*, 60–64. Such arcades also occur in European Expressionism, as at Fritz Höger's Anzieger Hochhaus in Hannover of 1926, and Expressionist influence has been imputed on Ralph Walker's New York skyscrapers (Barclay-Vesey et al.). Such direct influence on Clarkson of Fort Worth seems improbable. If anything, Meso-American influence on European Expressionism is more likely.

41.  Ibid., 53–59. Ironically, Hedrick and Co.'s finest surviving modernistic skyscraper is probably the Sterick Building in Memphis of 1928–1930. "The Sterick Building was financed by Hedrick's father-in-law, R. E. Sterling of Houston, as a real estate venture. The building's name is a combination of their names. At 365 feet tall, with twenty-nine floors above ground, it became the tallest building, not just in the city, but also in the South. For this design, Hedrick helped himself liberally to the massing and details of Eliel Saarinen's runner-up entry in the Chicago Tribune Building Competition." Eugene J. Johnson and Robert D. Russell, Jr., *Memphis: An Architectural Guide*, 76–77.

42.  Houston AIA, *Houston*, 162.

43.  Sally S. Victor, "The Gulf Building, Houston, Texas," *Perspective* 13,

no. 1 (1984): 2–8; Pastier, "Cardboard Skyscrapers"; Fox, *Houston Architectural Guide*, 43.

44. Pastier, "Cardboard Skyscrapers." See also "The People's National Bank, Tyler, Texas: Alfred C. Finn, Architect," *Architectural Record* 73 (April, 1933): 240–245.

45. Drawings for the First National Bank of Midland are preserved in the Architectural Drawings Collection, University of Texas at Austin.

46. Timlin designed three such buildings for Fort Worth. See Cohen, *Cowtown Moderne*, 65–69.

47. For the evolution of French decorative art from 1900 to 1925, see Nancy J. Troy, *Modernism and the Decorative Arts in France: Art Nouveau to Le Corbusier*; also Yvonne Brunhammer and Suzanne Tise, *The Decorative Arts in France: La Société des Artistes Décorateurs*.

48. Marcus Whiffen and Carla Breeze, *Pueblo Deco: The Art Deco Architecture of the Southwest*, 60, 110.

49. David Hoffman, "Art Deco Beaumont," *Perspective* 7, no. 2 (1978): 6–7.

50. Drawings of the Childress Montgomery Ward Store, along with those for Hillsboro and Shreveport, Louisiana, are preserved in the Architectural Drawings Collection, University of Texas at Austin.

51. San Antonio AIA, *Guide*, 37. Other surviving Kress stores in Texas include those in Amarillo, El Paso, Fort Worth, Laredo, and Lubbock. See Whiffen and Breeze, *Pueblo Deco*, 57, 61; Cohen, *Cowtown Moderne*, 136–138.

52. The Modernize Main Street Competition, sponsored by Libby-Owens-Ford, was conducted by *Architectural Record* in 1935. Competitors were offered a choice of four problems: The drug store, the apparel shop, the food store, and the automotive sales and service station. All of these enterprises were undergoing aggressive transformations in the 1930's. Jurors included Albert Kahn and William Lescaze. See "Modernize Main Street Competition," *Architectural Record* 78 (July 1935) and (October 1935).

53. The literature on Streamlining in industrial design in the 1930's is extensive. See, for example, Donald J. Bush, *The Streamlined Decade* and Arthur J. Pulos, *American Design Ethic: A History of Industrial Design to 1940*.

54. Fox, *Houston Architectural Guide*, 186.

55. Ibid., 203.

56. San Antonio AIA, *Guide*, 23. See also Michael McCullar, "Profile: Bartlett Cocke, FAIA," *Texas Architect* 29 (July/August 1979): 55–58.

57. For the work of Albert Kahn, see Grant Hildebrand, *Designing for Industry: The Architecture of Albert Kahn*.

58. For the Austin Company, see Martin Grief, *Depression Modern: The Thirties Style in America*, 50–54; and Wilson et al., *The Machine Age in America*, 80; 182–183.

59. "Record Poll in Dallas Produces Wide Variety of Choices," *Architectural Record* 88 (August 1940): 16+. The Borden Dairy Plant in Dallas, a premier example of Streamlining, was demolished to make way for the Arts District. See Collier's thesis, "Art Deco Architecture: Dallas, Texas," 70–73.

7. RESIDENTIAL DESIGN:
MODES AND TYPOLOGIES, 1895–1940

1. Downing, *A Treatise on the Theory and Practice*.

2. The term "Stick style" for this body of work was coined by Scully, *The Shingle Style and the Stick Style*.

3. Susan Prendergast Schoelwer, "Curious Relics and Quaint Scenes: The

Colonial Revival at Chicago's Great Fair" in *The Colonial Revival in America*.

4. Gowans, *The Comfortable House*, 84 ff. The foursquare is sometimes described as being "Prairie Style," a confused term propagated by Virginia and Lee McAlester, *A Field Guide to American Houses*, 443 ff. The term "Prairie School" should be reserved for work based upon the formal conventions of Frank Lloyd Wright, or the ornamental conventions of Louis Sullivan, or upon both. This body of work in Texas is discussed in Chapter 3. Although foursquare houses occasionally display trace elements of the Prairie School, most have no connection to this body of architecture. As Gowans demonstrates, foursquares are found throughout the United States and have no geographical relationship to the midwestern prairie.

5. Gowans, *The Comfortable House*, 94 ff. Gowans considers this a separate type, not a foursquare variant. He calls it the Homestead-Temple House.

6. Judy Elaine Schwartz Dooley, "A History and Guide to the Swiss Avenue Historic District: 1905–1914" (M. Arch. thesis, University of Texas at Arlington, 1978), 77–79.

7. Ibid., 101.

8. Gowans, *The Comfortable House*, 74–83. See also Robert Winter, *The California Bungalow* and Clay Lancaster, *The American Bungalow 1880–1930*.

9. The most comprehensive account of the Arts and Crafts movement in America is Wendy Kaplan ed., *"The Art that is Life": The Arts and Crafts Movement in America, 1875–1920*. See especially Cheryl Robertson, "House and Home in the Arts and Crafts Era: Reforms for Simpler Living," 336–357.

10. For Stickley, see Mary Ann Smith, *Gustave Stickley: The Craftsman*.

11. Katherine Cole Stevenson and H. Ward Jandl, *Houses by Mail: A Guide to Houses from Sears, Roebuck and Company*.

12. Several neighborhoods of bungalows in Dallas have been systematically investigated. For Park Row, see Cary Lawrence Young, "A History and Guide to the South Boulevard/Park Row Historic District: Park Row," (M. Arch. thesis, University of Texas at Arlington), 1980. For Bryan Parkway, see Patricia Taylor Canavan, "A History and Guide to the Swiss Avenue Historic District: 1917–1922," (M. Arch. thesis, University of Texas at Arlington), 1978. The Historic Preservation League of Dallas, *Guide*, identifies a number of neighborhoods where bungalows proliferated but does not systematically investigate the building type.

13. Jay C. Henry et al., "Residential Design in Typical American Architecture," 17–22.

14. Historic Preservation League, *Guide*, 94.

15. Jonathan Lane, "The Period House in the 1920's," *Journal of the Society of Architectural Historians* 20 (December 1961): 169–178.

16. Henry et al., "Residential Design in Typical American Architecture," 21.

17. Gowans, *The Comfortable House*, 124.

18. Ibid., 125.

19. Toews, "Spanish Colonial Revival Architecture in Dallas: The Work," 13.

20. See also John C. Ferguson, "The Country Houses of Atlee B. and Robert M. Ayres," *CITE: The Architecture and Design Review of Houston* (Spring 1986): 18–20.

21. Toews, "Spanish Colonial Revival Architecture in Dallas: An Analysis," 114–117.

22. Ibid., 134–157.

23. Howard Barnstone, *The Architecture of John F. Staub: Houston and the South*, 184–189.

24. Wayne Gard, "The Ranch House Goes to Town," *Better Homes and Gardens*, June 1937, 32–33; 67. This article also discusses work of David R. Williams and O'Neil Ford, considered later in this chapter.

25. Dallas AIA, *The Prairie's Yield*, 40.

26. Barnstone, *Architecture of John F. Staub*, 220–22.

27. William H. Jordy, "Four Approaches to Regionalism in the 1930's," in *Study of American Culture—Contemporary Conflict*. For a concise review of Texas regionalism, see Peter C. Papademetriou, "Texas Regionalism 1925–1950: An Elusive Sensibility," *Texas Architect* 31 (July/August 1987): 36–41.

28. David R. Williams, "Toward a Southwestern Architecture," *Southwest Review* 16 (April 1931): 301.

29. Muriel Quest McCarthy, *David R. Williams*, 54–67.

30. Williams, "Toward a Southwestern Architecture," 302, 306, 310–12.

31. McCarthy, *David R. Williams*, 102–117. See also Speck and Payne, *Landmarks of Texas Architecture*, 66–69, and Dillon and Tomlinson, *Dallas Architecture 1936–1986*, 60–61. For early appreciation of Williams' and Ford's houses, see Jerry Bywaters, "More about Southwestern Architecture," *Southwest Review* 18 (April 1933): 234–264.

32. See Bywaters, "More about Southwestern Architecture," 254–258.

33. S. B. Zisman, "The Architect and the House: 5—O'Neil Ford of San Antonio, Texas," *Pencil Points* 21 (April 1940): 196–210. Other Ford houses discussed in this article are the San Jose Ranch House on St. Joseph Island, the Roland Hirsh and Parill houses in Denton, and the John S. Maxon and Boazman houses in Dallas. The John Murchison House in San Antonio, designed for Frank Murchison's brother, was built in 1941. For both Murchison houses see San Antonio AIA, *Guide*, 112; 119.

34. O'Neil Ford's contribution to "Towards a New Architecture," *Southwest Review* 17 (January 1932): 209–229 was entitled "Organic Building." Although he does not mention Frank Lloyd Wright, whose Usonian work had not yet appeared in 1932, it seems curiously significant that this two-part article should allude to both Le Corbusier's *Vers Une Architecture* and to Wright's concept of organic architecture. Ford regarded the contemporary modernistic work as just another species of eclecticism.

35. "House for Karl Kamrath; House for Jesse R. Stone; Fire Alarm Building: McKie and Kamrath, Architects," *Architectural Forum* 73 (December 1940): 518–519.

36. "House for Melville S. Rose, Dallas, Texas; H. R. Meyer, Architect," *Architectural Forum* 72 (February 1940): 114–115. A nearby house for an unnamed client, also by Meyer, was published in *Pencil Points* 26 (February 1945): 85–88. The Henry Pearlstone House in Dallas has been demolished. Dallas AIA, *The Prairie's Yield*, 40. For Meyer's impact on Dallas architecture, see Dillon and Tomlinson, *Dallas Architecture, 1936–1986*, 52–58. Meyer's drawings have been deposited in the Architectural Drawings Collection, University of Texas at Austin.

37. Other Sadler houses in the same idiom may be found in Dallas. Sadler's modernistic masterpiece was the Highlander Apartments, recently remodeled beyond recognition. Research on Luther Sadler was compiled by Steve Eberly, who unfortunately never completed his thesis on this topic.

38. Austin AIA, *Austin*, 78. The Chester Nagel House was published in "House in Austin, Texas: Chester E. Nagel, Architect and Owner," *New Pencils*

*Points* (January 1943): 20–31. For Gropius' impact on American architecture see William H. Jordy, "The Aftermath of the Bauhaus in America: Gropius, Mies and Breuer," *Perspectives in American History* 2 (1968): 485–543.

39. Hitchcock and Johnson, *The International Style.*

40. Thomas S. Hines, *Richard Neutra and the Search for Modern Architecture,* 150. See also Fox, "(Tall) Tales from the Borderland," 65.

## 8. INTERNATIONAL AND REGIONAL MODERNISM IN THE PUBLIC SPHERE: 1936–1945

1. For the development of state and national parks during the Depression, see Phoebe Cutler, *The Public Landscape of the New Deal.* The Texas and Oklahoma state parks are discussed on pp. 67–69; the Big Bend National Park on pp. 99–103. An exhibition on the Civilian Conservation Corps in Texas Parks was organized in 1985 by the Texas Parks and Wildlife Department and traveled to twenty Texas CCC parks over a three-year period. The CCC also implemented development of urban parks, including Lee, Reverchon, and White Rock Lake parks in Dallas.

2. Michael McCullar, *Restoring Texas: Raiford Stripling's Life and Architecture;* Speck and Payne, *Landmarks of Texas Architecture,* 76–79. McCarthy, *David R. Williams,* 129–134. See also A. B. Swank, "The Villita Project," *Southwest Review* 25 (July 1940): 394–403. Hugman's drawings for the Riverwalk have been deposited in the Architectural Drawings Collection, University of Texas at Austin.

3. Speck and Payne, *Landmarks of Texas Architecture,* 80–83. See also "Chapel in the Woods: O'Neil Ford–A. B. Swank, Architects," *Pencil Points* 21 (February 1940): 66–72. For Lynn Ford, see Mary Lance, *Lynn Ford: Texas Artist and Craftsman.* Lyndon Baines Johnson was Texas administrator of the NYA. Eleanor Roosevelt attended the dedication of the Chapel in the Woods.

4. For Lescaze, see Lorraine Welling Lanmon, *William Lescaze, Architect.* The Magnolia Pavilion is discussed on p. 121.

5. "News of the Month: Thirteen Years of Fair Building Reviewed in Current Exhibit," *Architectural Record* 80 (July 1936): 2–3.

6. "Fire Alarm Building, Houston, Texas," *Architectural Forum* 73 (December 1940): 520–521.

7. Ibid., 522.

8. Italian Fascist modern architecture of the 1930's is again considered a legitimate field of scholarship. See Dennis Doordan, *Building Modern Italy: Italian Architecture 1914–1936* and Richard Etlin, *Modernism in Italian Architecture, 1890–1940.*

9. Dudok's best known and most influential work is the Hilversum City Hall, completed in 1930, but his later manner can also be seen in the more recent schools he designed as city architect for Hilversum and in the Dutch dormitory he designed for the Cité Universitaire in Paris in 1931. There is no monograph on Dudok in English.

10. "Record Poll in Dallas Produces Wide Variety of Choices," *Architectural Record* 88 (August 1940): 16. The poll was conducted among prominent citizens, not professional architects. The Hall of State at Fair Park was judged most popular, with eleven votes. Mark Lemmon's Spence Junior High School outpolled Lincoln, seven votes to five. It is a conventional piece of Modern Classic composition as described in Chapter 6.

11. Elizabeth Mock, ed., *Built in U.S.A.: 1932–1944,* 72–75.

12. William Wayne Caudill, "Space for Teaching," *Bulletin of the Agricultural and Mechanical College* 12, no. 9.

13. "Garden Oaks Elementary School, T. Wilson and I. Morris, Archs.," *Architectural Record* 90 (December 1942): 68–69; "South East Austin Elementary School, Jessen, Jessen and Millhouse, Archs.," *Architectural Record* 91 (March 1942): 72–73.

14. For the Subsistence Homestead Program, and Dalworthington Gardens in particular, see Herbert N. Antley, "A New Deal Experiment in Planned Utopia: A Study of Dalworthington Gardens and the Subsistence Homestead Program, 1933–1937," (M. A. thesis, University of Texas at Arlington), 1980. See also Diane Ghirardo, *Building New Communities: New Deal America and Fascist Italy.*

15. Mel Scott, *American City Planning Since 1890,* 317.

16. Dallas AIA, *The Prairie's Yield,* 57. The architects were Walter Sharp, Lester Flint, Grayson Gill, Ralph Bryan, Anton Korn, Roscoe DeWitt, Everett Welch, Herbert Tatum, and A. E. Thomas. See also "Cedar Springs Place, Dallas: Walter C. Sharp, Chief Architect," *Architectural Forum* 68 (May 1938): 397.

17. The most complete statement of the principles of Garden City planning in America is contained in Clarence Stein, *Toward New Towns for America.*

18. McCarthy, *David R. Williams,* 28–30; Dallas AIA, *The Prairie's Yield,* 36. Greenway Park is bounded by Mockingbird Lane on the south and University Boulevard on the north; the Dallas North Tollway is to the east and Inwood Road is on the west.

19. Jane Jacobs, *The Death and Life of Great American Cities.*

20. Richard Neutra, "Peace Can Gain from War's Forced Changes," *New Pencil Points* 23 (November 1942): 28–29; Hines, *Richard Neutra,* 175–80; McCarthy, *David R. Williams,* 136–139; Willis Winters, "Avion Village: Enduring Values of Community," *Texas Architect* 38 (May/June 1988): 24–29.

21. McCarthy, *David R. Williams,* 139–143; "Beaumont: 600 Demountable Units," *Architectural Forum* 76 (May 1942): 285–291.

22. For the relationship between European Zeilenbau planning and subsequent American public housing practice, see Richard Pommer, "The Architecture of Urban Housing in the United States During the Early 1930's," *Journal of the Society of Architectural Historians* 37 (December 1978): 235–264.

23. Peter C. Papademetriou, "Doldrums in the Forties: Houston Building Design in Transition," *Texas Architect* 29 (November/December 1979): 34. For the housing, see "War Needs—Housing. San Felipe Courts, Houston, Texas," *Architectural Record* 91 (April 1942): 47–50. The community center was published in "Project Center Building, San Felipe Courts, Houston, Texas," *Architectural Record* (May 1942): 52–53.

24. Brooks, "George L. Dahl: A Critical Analysis of His Life and Architecture," 60.

# BIBLIOGRAPHY

PUBLISHED WORKS

"Administrative Center for Growing City: City Hall, Houston, Texas, Joseph Finger, Inc., Architects." *Architectural Record* 89 (March 1941): 104–107.

Alexander, Drury Blakeley. *Texas Homes of the Nineteenth Century.* Photographs by Todd Webb. Austin: University of Texas Press, 1966.

"All Classrooms North-Lighted in Texas School: Southeast Austin Elementary School, Austin, Tex.; Jessen, Jessen and Millhouse, Architects." *Architectural Record* 91 (March 1942): 72–73.

Arwas, Victor. *Art Deco.* New York: Harry N. Abrams, Inc., 1980.

Austin Chapter AIA. *Austin: Its Architects and Architecture (1836–1986).* Austin, 1986.

Barnstone, Howard. *The Architecture of John F. Staub: Houston and the South.* Austin: University of Texas Press, 1979.

———. *The Galveston That Was.* New York: MacMillan, 1966.

Bauer, Catherine. *Modern Housing.* New York: Houghton-Mifflin, 1934.

"Beaumont: 600 Demountable Units." *Architectural Forum* 76 (May 1942): 285–291.

Breeze, Carla. *Pueblo Deco.* New York: Rizzoli, 1990.

Breisch, Kenneth A. "The Richardsonian Interlude in Texas: A Quest for Meaning and Order at the End of the Nineteenth Century." In *The Spirit of H. H. Richardson on the Midland Prairies,* edited by Paul Clifford Larson with Susan M. Brown, 86–105. Ames: Iowa State University Press, 1988.

Brooks, H. Allan. *The Prairie School: Frank Lloyd Wright and His Midwestern Contemporaries.* Toronto: University of Toronto Press, 1972.

Brooks, R. Edward, and Jay C. Henry. "George L. Dahl and the Texas Centennial Exposition." *Perspective* 9, no. 2 (1980): 8–13.

Brunhammer, Yvonne. *1925.* Paris: Les Presses de la Connaissance, 1976.

Brunhammer, Yvonne, and Suzanne Tise. *The Decorative Arts in France: La Société des Artistes Decorateurs.* New York: Rizzoli, 1990.

Bryan, Ralph. "Twelve Texas Buildings." *Southwest Review* 16 (April 1931): 325–328.

Bryant, Keith L., Jr. "Railway Stations of Texas: A Disappearing Architectural Heritage." *Southwestern Historical Quarterly* 79 (April 1976): 417–440.

Bunting, Bainbridge. *John Gaw Meem: Southwestern Architect.* Albuquerque: University of New Mexico Press, 1983.

Bush, Donald J. *The Streamlined Decade.* New York: Braziller, 1975.

Bush, Ira J. *A Guide to Chicago's Historic Suburbs.* Chicago: Swallow Press, 1981.

Bywaters, Jerry. "More about Southwestern Architecture." *Southwest Review* 18 (April 1933): 234–264.

"Cass Gilbert Master Plan for U.T. Austin," *American Architect* (December 2, 1914).

Caudill, William Wayne. "Space for Teaching." *Bulletin of the Agricultural and Mechanical College* 12, no. 9. College Station, Tex., 1941.

"Cedar Springs Place, Dallas: Walter C. Sharp, Chief Architect." *Architectural Forum* 68 (May 1938): 397.

Cernin, Olaf Z. "The Spanish Mexican Missions of the United States." *Architectural Record* 14 (September 1903): 181–204.

"Chapel in the Woods: O'Neil Ford–A. B. Swank, Architects." *Pencil Points* 21 (February 1940): 66–72.

"Christian Scientists Use Romanesque: Third Church of Christ Scientist, Dallas, Texas; Mark Lemmon, Architect." *Architectural Record* 83 (April 1938): 57–60.

Christ-Janer, Albert. *Eliel Saarinen: Finnish-American Architect and Educator.* Rev. ed. Chicago: University of Chicago Press, 1979 [1948].

Clark, Kenneth. *The Gothic Revival.* London: Constable, 1988.

Coffman, Eileen Wilson. "James E. Flanders' First United Methodist Church, Pittsburg, Texas." *Perspective* 13, no. 1 (1984): 9–16.

Cohen, Judith Singer. *Cowtown Moderne: Art Deco Architecture of Fort Worth, Texas.* College Station: Texas A&M University Press, 1988.

Collier, Diane Hospodka. "Art Deco Architecture in Dallas." *Perspective* 11, no. 1 (1982): 8–12.

Comee, Fred T. "Louis Curtiss of Kansas City." *Progressive Architecture* 44 (August 1963): 128–134.

Condit, Carl. *The Chicago School of Architecture.* Chicago: University of Chicago Press, 1952 [1964].

"Corpus Christi: The Alamo Remembered." *Texas Architect* 26 (March/April 1976): 12–13.

Craig, Lois A., and staff of the Federal Architecture Project. *The Federal Presence: Architecture, Politics, and National Design.* Cambridge: MIT Press, 1978.

Cram, Ralph Adams. *My Life in Architecture.* Boston, 1937.

Creese, Walter L. *TVA's Public Planning: The Vision, The Reality.* Knoxville: University of Tennessee Press, 1990.

Curl, Donald W. *Mizner's Florida: American Resort Architecture.* Cambridge: MIT Press, 1984.

Cutler, Phoebe. *The Public Landscape of the New Deal.* New Haven: Yale University Press, 1985.

"Dallas: A City of Art and Commerce." *Western Architect* 20 (1914): 65–94.

Dallas Chapter AIA. *Dallasights: An Anthology of Architecture and Open Spaces.* Dallas, 1978.

———. *The Prairie's Yield: Forces Shaping Dallas Architecture from 1840 to 1962.* Dallas, 1962.

Davey, Peter. *Architecture of the Arts and Crafts Movement.* New York: Rizzoli, 1980.

Davis, Howard. "The Regional House: Style or Substance." *Texas Architect* 36 (March/April 1986): 54–58.

DeWitt, Roscoe. "After Indigenous Architecture, What?" *Southwest Review* 16 (April 1931): 314–324.

De Wit, Wim. "The Banks and the Image of Progressive Banking," In *Louis Sullivan: The Function of Ornament,* 159–198. New York: W. W. Norton, for the Chicago Historical Society and the St. Louis Art Museum, 1986.

Dillon, David, and Doug Tomlinson. *Dallas Architecture 1936–1986.* Austin: Texas Monthly Press, 1986.

"Discovering Henry Trost." *Texas Architect* 27, no. 5 (1977): 19–23.

Doordan, Dennis. *Building Modern Italy: Italian Architecture 1914–1936.* Princeton: Princeton University Press, 1988.

Dorsey, John, and James D. Dilts. *A Guide to Baltimore Architecture.* Centreville, Md.: Tidewater Publishers, 1981.

Downing, Andrew Jackson. *The Architecture of Country Houses.* New York: n.p., 1851.

———. *A Treatise on the Theory and Practice of Landscape Gardening . . .* New York: n.p., 1841.

Drexler, Arthur, ed. *The Architecture of the Ecole des Beaux-Arts.* New York: Museum of Modern Art, 1977.

Eaton, Leonard K. *American Architecture Comes of Age.* Cambridge: MIT Press, 1972.

———. *Gateway Cities and Other Essays.* Ames: Iowa State University Press, 1989.

Edgell, George H. *The American Architecture of Today.* New York: n.p., 1928. A.M.S. reprint, 1970.

El Paso Chapter AIA. *Portals at the Pass: El Paso Area Architecture to 1930.* El Paso, 1984.

Engelbrecht, Lloyd C. "Henry Trost: The Prairie School in the Southwest." *Prairie School Review* 6 (4th quarter, 1969): 5–31.

Engelbrecht, Lloyd C., and June-Marie Engelbrecht. *Henry C. Trost: Architect of the Southwest.* El Paso: El Paso Public Library Association, 1981.

———. "Prairie School Architect: Henry C. Trost." *Texas Homes* 2 (November/December 1978): 26–30.

Etlin, Richard. *Modernism in Italian Architecture, 1890–1940.* Cambridge: MIT Press, 1988.

"Fairs." *Architectural Forum* 65 (September 1936): 171–190.

Federal Writers Project. *The W.P.A. Guide to Texas.* Austin: Texas Monthly Press, 1986 [1940].

Ferguson, John C. "The Country Houses of Atlee B. and Robert M. Ayres." *CITE: The Architecture and Design Review of Houston* (Spring 1986): 18–20.

"Fire Alarm Building, Houston, Texas." *Architectural Forum* 73 (December 1940): 520–521.

Ferriss, Hugh. *Study for the Maximum Mass Permitted by the 1916 Zoning Law.* New York: n.p., 1922.

Focillon, Henri. *The Life of Forms in Art.* 2d English ed. Translated by Charles B. Hogan and George Kubler. New York: George Wittenborn, 1948 [1942].

Forbes, J. D. "Shepley, Bulfinch, Richardson and Abbott, Architects: An Introduction." *Journal of the Society of Architectural Historians,* 17, no. 3 (1958): 19–31.

Ford, O'Neil. "Organic Building." (Part Two of "Towards a New Architecture.") *Southwest Review* 17 (January 1932): 218–229.

Fox, Stephen. "Courtlandt Place on Tour: A Look at Houston's First Elite Neighborhood." *Texas Architect* 32 (November/December 1982): 62–63.

———. *The General Plan of the William M. Rice Institute and Its Architectural Development.* Houston: Rice University, 1980.

———. *Houston Architectural Guide.* Houston Chapter AIA, 1990.

———. "In Response." *Perspective* 8, no. 3–4 (1979): 17–18.

———. "Lessons Learned with 20/80 Vision." *Texas Architect* 38 (March/April 1988): 17–21.

———. "Profile: Nicholas J. Clayton, Architect." *Texas Architect* 76 (July/August 1976): 51–52.

———. "Sanguinet and Staats in Houston, 1903–1926." *Perspective* 12, no. 1 (1983): 2–11.

———. "(Tall) Tales from the Borderland: Brownsville and the Spanish Colonial Revival." *Texas Architect* 31 (July/August 1981): 59–65.

———. "Texan 7." *Architectural Review* (November 1978): 275–279.

Frampton, Kenneth, and Yukio Futagawa. *Modern Architecture 1815–1919.* New York: Rizzoli, 1983.

———. *Modern Architecture 1920–1945.* New York: Rizzoli, 1983.

*Frank Lloyd Wright: Ausgeführte Bauten und Entwurfe.* Berlin: Wasmuth Verlag, 1910. English Edition, 1911.

Gard, Wayne. "The Ranch House Goes to Town." *Better Homes and Gardens,* June 1937, 32–33; 67.

"Garden Oaks Elementary School, T. Wilson and T. Morris, Architects." *Architectural Record* 90 (December 1942): 68–69.

Garner, John S. "Architecture at A & M: The Past One Hundred Years." *Texas Architect* 27 (March/April 1977): 33–36.

Gebhard, David. "The Moderne in the U.S., 1920–1941." *Architectural Association Quarterly* 2 (July 1970): 4–20.

———. *Schindler.* New York: Viking Press, 1972.

———. "The Spanish Colonial Revival in Southern California (1895–1930)." *Journal of the Society of Architectural Historians* 26 (May 1967): 131–147.

Gebhard, David, et al. *A Guide to Architecture in San Francisco and Northern California.* Santa Barbara and Salt Lake: Peregrine Smith, 1973.

Gebhard, David, and Robert Winter. *Architecture in Los Angeles: A Compleat Guide.* Salt Lake City: Peregrine Smith, 1985.

———. *A Guide to Architecture in Los Angeles and Southern California.* Santa Barbara and Salt Lake: Peregrine Smith, 1977.

Ghirardo, Diane. *Building New Communities: New Deal America and Fascist Italy.* Princeton: Princeton University Press, 1989.

Giedion, Sigfried. *Space, Time and Architecture.* Cambridge: Harvard University Press, 1941.

Gottfried, Herbert, and Jan Jennings. *American Vernacular Design 1870–1940.* Ames: Iowa State University Press, 1988.

Gowans, Alan. *The Comfortable House: North American Suburban Architecture, 1890–1930.* Cambridge: MIT Press, 1986.

———. *Images of American Living: Four Centuries of Architecture and Furniture as Cultural Expression.* New York: Harper & Row, 1976 [1964].

Grattan, Virginia L. *Mary Coulter: Builder upon the Red Earth.* Flagstaff: Northland Press, 1980.

Grief, Martin. *Depression Modern: The Thirties Style in America.* New York: Universe Books, 1975.

Grossman, Elizabeth G. "Two Postwar Competitions: The Nebraska State Capitol and the Kansas City Liberty Memorial." *Journal of the Society of Architectural Historians* 45 (September 1986): 244–269.

Hamlin, Talbot. *Greek Revival Architecture in America.* Oxford: Oxford University Press, 1944.

Hale, Edward. "H. H. Richardson and His Work." *New England Magazine* 2 (1894).

Harris, August Watkins. "Cass Gilbert's Old Library Building: The Eugene C. Barker Texas History Center, 1910–1960." *Southwestern Historical Quarterly* 64 (July 1960): 1–13.

Hegemann, Werner, and Elbert Peets. *The American Vitruvius: An Architect's Handbook of Civic Art:* New York: Architectural Book Publishing Co., 1922.

Henderson, Rose. "A Primitive Basis for Modern Architecture." *Architectural Record* 54 (August 1923): 188–196.

Henry, Jay C. "The Institutional Moderne in Texas: Sources and Permutations." *Texas Architect* forthcoming.

———. "The Kessler Plans for Kansas City and Dallas." *Proceedings of the Council of Educators in Landscape Architecture.* (1985): 100–103.

———. "Prairie School Ornament by Lang and Witchell." *Perspective* 8, no. 2 (1979): 3–6.

———. "The Richardsonian Romanesque in Texas: An Interpretation." *Texas Architect* 31, no. 2 (1981): 52–59.

———. "Trost and Trost in El Paso." *Texas Architect* 37 (March/April 1987): 34–39.

Henry, Jay C., Judy Dooley, Patricia Canavan, and Robert Canavan. "Residential Design in Typical American Architecture: The Swiss Avenue District, 1905–1932." *Perspective,* 10, no. 1 (1981): 17–22.

Hildebrand, Grant. *Designing for Industry: The Architecture of Albert Kahn.* Cambridge: MIT Press, 1974.

———. *The Wright Space: Pattern and Meaning in Frank Lloyd Wright's Houses.* Seattle: University of Washington Press, 1991. (Previously abstracted as "The Wright Space: The Parti of the Prairie House," in *Modern Architecture in America: Visions and Revisions,* edited by Richard Guy Wilson and Sidney K. Robinson, 112–143. Ames: Iowa State University Press, 1991.)

Hines, Thomas S. *Burnham of Chicago: Architect and Planner.* New York: Oxford University Press, 1974.

———. *Richard Neutra and the Search for Modern Architecture.* New York: Oxford University Press, 1982.

Historic Preservation Council for Tarrant County. *Tarrant County Historic Resources Survey.* Fort Worth, 1982.

Historic Preservation League of Dallas. *A Guide to the Older Neighborhoods of Dallas.* Dallas, 1986.

Hitchcock, Henry-Russell. *Architecture: Nineteenth and Twentieth Centuries* [The Pelican History of Art]. Baltimore: Viking Penguin, 1958.

———. *The Architecture of H. H. Richardson and His Times.* New York: Museum of Modern Art, 1936.

———. *Modern Architecture: Romanticism and Reintegration.* London: Payson and Clarke, 1929.

Hitchcock, Henry-Russell, and Phillip Johnson. *The International Style.* New York: Museum of Modern Art, 1932.

Hitchcock, Henry-Russell, and William Seale. *Temples of Democracy: The State Capitols of the U.S.A.* New York and London: Harcourt Brace Jovanovich, 1976.

Hoffman, David. "Art Deco Beaumont." *Perspective* 7, no. 2 (1978): 6–7.

Hoffmeyer, Michael C. "Public Buildings of Sanguinet and Staats." *Perspective* 10, no. 1 (1981): 23–27.

"House for Karl Kamrath; House for Jesse R. Stone; Fire Alarm Building: MacKie and Kamrath, Architects." *Architectural Forum* 73 (December 1940): 518+.

"House for Melville S. Rose, Dallas, Texas; H. R. Meyer, Architect." *Architectural Forum* 72 (February 1940): 114–115.

House in Austin, Texas: Chester E. Nagel, Architect and Owner." *New Pencil Points* (January 1943): 20–31.

Houston Chapter AIA. *Houston: An Architectural Guide.* Houston, 1972. For new edition, see Fox, Stephen. *Houston Architectural Guide,* 1990.

Ingle, Marjorie. *The Mayan Revival Style.* Salt Lake City: Peregrine Smith, 1984.

Jacobs, Jane. *The Death and Life of Great American Cities.* New York: Random House, 1961.

Johnson, Eugene J., and Robert D. Russell, Jr. *Memphis: An Architectural Guide.* Knoxville: University of Tennessee Press, 1990.

Johnson, Linda, and Sally Ross. *Historic Texas Hotels and Country Inns.* Austin: Eakins Press, 1982.

Jordy, William H. "The Aftermath of the Bauhaus in America: Gropius, Mies and Breuer." *Perspectives in American History* 2 (1968): 485–543.

———. "Four Approaches to Regionalism in the 1930's," In *The Study of American Culture: Contemporary Conflicts,* edited by Luther S. Luedtke. Delano, Fla.: Everett Edwards, 1977.

"Julia Ideson Building, Houston." *Texas Architect* 30 (July/August 1980): 48–49.

Jutson, Mary Carolyn Hollyers. *Alfred Giles: An English Architect in Texas and Mexico.* San Antonio: Trinity University Press, 1972.

Kansas City Chapter AIA. *Kansas City [Architectural Guide].* Kansas City, 1979.

Kaplan, Wendy, ed. *"The Art that is Life": The Arts and Crafts Movement in America, 1875–1920.* Boston: Museum of Fine Arts, 1987.

Kidney, Walter C. *The Architecture of Choice: Eclecticism in America, 1880–1930.* New York: George Braziller, 1974.

Kilham, Walter H., Jr. *Raymond Hood, Architect.* New York: Architectural Book Publishing Co., 1973.

Kimball, Fiske. "Recent Architecture in the South." *Architectural Record* 55 (March 1924): 209–271.

"Kirby Building, Dallas." *Texas Architect* 31 (March/April 1981): 32.

Klauder, Charles Z., and Herbert C. Wise. *College Architecture in America and Its Part in the Development of the Campus.* New York: Charles Scribners Sons, 1929.

Kornwolf, James D. "American Architecture and the Aesthetic Movement." In *In Pursuit of Beauty: Americans and the Aesthetic Movement,* 340–383. New York: Metropolitan Museum of Art/Rizzoli, 1986.

Kornwolf, James D., ed. *Modernism in America 1937–1941: A Catalog and Exhibition of Four Architectural Competitions.* Williamsburg, Va.: Muscarelle Museum of Art, College of William and Mary, 1985.

Kubler, George, and Martin Soria. *Art and Architecture in Spain and Portugal and Their American Dominions, 1500 to 1800.* Pelican History of Art Series. New York: Viking Penguin, 1959.

Lancaster, Clay. "The American Bungalow." *Art Bulletin* 40 (September 1958): 239–253.

———. *The American Bungalow, 1880–1930.* New York: Abbeville Press, 1985.

Lance, Mary. *Lynn Ford: Texas Artist and Craftsman.* San Antonio: Trinity University Press, 1978.

Lane, Jonathan. "The Period House in the 1920's." *Journal of the Society of Architectural Historians* 20 (December 1961): 169–178.

Lanmon, Lorraine Welling. *William Lescaze, Architect.* Philadelphia: Art Alliance Press 1987; distributed by Associated University Presses.

Leavenworth, Geoffrey, and Richard Payne. *Historic Galveston.* Houston: Herring Press, 1985.

Le Corbusier. *Towards a New Architecture.* Translated by Frederick Etehells. London: John Rodker, 1931. Originally published as *Vers une architecture* (1922).

Lofgren, Jamie. "Texas Skyscrapers in the 1920's." *Texas Architect* 38 (March/April 1988): 22–27.

Longstreth, Richard. "Academic Eclecticism in American Architecture." *Winterthur Portfolio,* Spring 1982, 55–82.

———. "J. C. Nichols, the Country Club Plaza, and Notions of Modernity." *Precedent and Innovation: The Harvard Architectural Review* 5 (1986): 120–135.

———. *On the Edge of the World: Four Architects in San Francisco at the Turn of the Century.* Cambridge: MIT Press, for the Architectural History Foundation, 1983.

McAlester, Virginia, and Lee McAlester. *A Field Guide to American Houses.* New York: Alfred A. Knopf, 1986.

McCarthy, Muriel Quest. *David R. Williams: Pioneer Architect.* Dallas: Southern Methodist University Press, 1984.

McCullar, Michael. "The Hotel Galvez: Gulf Coast Landmark in Transition." *Texas Architect* 30 (January/February 1980): 41–43.

———. "Profile: Bartlett Cocke, FAIA." *Texas Architect* 29 (July/August, 1979): 55–58.

———. "Profile: George L. Dahl, FAIA." *Texas Architect* 30 (November/December 1980): 72–74.

———. *Restoring Texas: Raiford Stripling's Life and Architecture.* College Station: Texas A&M University Press, 1985.

McDonald, William L. *Dallas Rediscovered: A Photographic Chronicle of Urban Expansion, 1870–1925.* Dallas: Dallas Historical Society, 1978.

McMichael, Carol. *Paul Cret at Texas: Architectural Drawing and the Image of the University in the 1930's.* Exhibition Catalog. Archer M. Huntington Art Gallery, University of Texas at Austin, 1983.

"Majestic Theater Renovation." *Texas Architect* 34 (November/December 1984): 78.

Meeks, Carroll L. V. *The Railroad Station: An Architectural History.* New Haven: Yale University Press, 1956.

Mock, Elizabeth, ed. *Built in U.S.A.: 1932–1944.* New York: Museum of Modern Art, 1945.

"A Model Shopping Village in Texas, Fooshee and Cheek, Architects." *Architectural Record* 70 (September 1931): 197–198.

"The Modern Factory, as Illustrated in the Works of George C. Nimmons." *Western Architect* (July 1914).

"Modernize Main Street Competition." *Architectural Record* 78 (July 1935).

Moffett, Marian. "Looking to the Future: The Architecture of Roland Wank." *Arris: The Journal of the Southeast Chapter, Society Architectural Historians* 1 (1989): 5–17.

Morgan, William. *The Almighty Wall: The Architecture of Henry Vaughan.* Cambridge: MIT Press, 1983.

"Mr. Jenkins and Sir Henry." *Fortune* 6 (October 1932): 104.

Mujica, Francisco. *History of the Skyscraper*. New York: De Capo Press, 1977 [1929].

Mullen, Andrea Kirsten. "Jefferson High School up for National Register Listing." *Texas Architect* 33 (September/October 1983): 28; 74.

Mumford, Lewis. *The Brown Decades: A Study of the Arts in America*. New York: n.p., 1931.

"Museum of Fine Arts, Houston, Texas." *Architectural Forum* 47 (December 1927): 563–564.

Naylor, David. *Great American Movie Theaters: A National Trust Guide*. Washington, D.C.: Preservation Press, 1987.

Neutra, Richard J. "Peace Can Gain from War's Forced Changes." *New Pencil Points* 23 (November 1942): 28–41.

Newcomb, Rexford. *Mediterranean Domestic Architecture in the United States*. Cleveland: J. H. Jansen, 1928.

———. *Spanish Colonial Architecture in the United States*. New York: J. J. Augustin, 1937.

"News of the Month: Thirteen Years of Fair Building Reviewed in Current Exhibit." *Architectural Record* 80 (July 1936): 2–3.

New York Chapter AIA. *AIA Guide to New York City*. Rev. ed. New York, 1978 [1967].

"The New Washington Hotel, Colon, Panama. Cram, Goodhue, and Ferguson, Architects." *Architectural Record* 32 (July 1912): 65–70.

Ochsner, Jeffrey Karl. "Tall Buildings: Houston as a Case in Point." *Texas Architect* 32 (May/June 1982): 38–45.

———. "The Renewal of Sutton Hall." *Texas Architect* 33 (March/April 1983): 60–63.

O'Gorman, James F. *The Architecture of Frank Furness*. Philadelphia: Museum of Art, 1973.

———. *Henry Hobson Richardson and His Office*. Boston: David R. Godine, 1974.

Oliver, Richard. *Bertram Grosvenor Goodhue*. American Monograph Series and Architectural History Foundation and Cambridge: MIT Press, 1983.

Papademetriou, Peter. "Doldrums in the Forties: Houston Building Design in Transition." *Texas Architect* 29 (November/December 1979): 28–35.

———. "Main Street Spanish." *Texas Architect* 17 (July/August 1974): 16–19.

———. "Nationalism-Regionalism-Modernism: In Search of a Texas Architecture." *Texas Architect* 28 (May/June 1978): 17–21.

———. "Texas Regionalism 1925–1950: An Elusive Sensibility." *Texas Architect* 31 (July/August 1981): 36–41.

———. "Varied Reflections in Houston." *Progressive Architecture* 56 (March 1975): 52–57.

Papademetriou, Peter, and Paul Hester. *La Arquitectura: Spanish Influences on Houston's Architecture*. Houston: Houston Public Library, 1979.

"Paso del Norte Hotel, El Paso. Trost and Trost, Architects." *Western Architect* 19 (November 1913).

Pastier, John. "The Cardboard Skyscrapers of Texas: 1911–1932." *Texas Architect* 32 (May/June 1982): 55–57.

———. "The Regionalism of Henry Trost: A Legacy for Arid America." *Texas Architect* 31 (July/August 1981): 71–73.

"The People's National Bank, Tyler, Texas: Alfred C. Finn, Architect." *Architectural Record* 73 (April 1933): 240–245.

Pevsner, Nikolaus. *An Outline of European Architecture* 1st ed. London: Harmondsworth, 1943.

———. *Pioneers of Modern Design: From William Morris to the Bauhaus*. Rev. ed. New York: Penguin Books, 1960 [1949].

Pierson, William H., Jr. "Richardson's Trinity Church and the New England Meetinghouse." In *American Public Architecture: European Roots and Native Expression*, 12–15. Papers in Art History, vol. 5. University Park: Pennsylvania State University, 1989.

Polyzoides, Stefanos, Roger Sherwood, James Tice, and Julius Schulman. *Courtyard Housing in Los Angeles*. Berkeley and Los Angeles: University of California Press, 1982.

Pommer, Richard. "The Architecture of Urban Housing in the United States During the Early 1930's." *Journal of the Society of Architectural Historians* 37 (December 1978): 235–264.

Preddy, Jane. *Palaces of Dreams: The Movie Theaters of John Eberson, Architect*. Exhibition Catalog. San Antonio: McNay Art Museum, 1989.

Price, C. Matlock. "The Panama-California Exposition, San Diego, California. Bertram G. Goodhue and the Renaissance of Spanish Colonial Architecture." *Architectural Record* 37 (1915): 229–251.

"Project Center Building, San Felipe Courts, Houston, Texas." *Architectural Record* 91 (May 1942): 52–53.

Public Works Administration. *Public Buildings: Architecture under the Public Works Administration, 1933–1939*. Reprint of vol. 1, *Projects Constructed by Federal and Other Governmental Bodies between the Years 1933 and 1939 with the Assistance of the Public Works Administration*, with new introduction by Richard Guy Wilson. New York: Da Capo Press, 1986.

Pulos, Arthur J. *American Design Ethic: A History of Industrial Design to 1940*. Cambridge: MIT Press, 1983.

"Record Poll in Dallas Produces Wide Variety of Choices." *Architectural Record* 88 (August 1940): 16; 18.

Reps, John W. *Cities of the American West: A History of Frontier Urban Planning*. Princeton: Princeton University Press, 1979.

Riddle, Peggy. "The Texas Hall of State." *Perspective* 9, no. 2 (1980): 22–24.

Robertson, Cheryl. "House and Home in the Arts and Crafts Era: Reforms for Simpler Living." In *The Art That Is Life: The Arts and Crafts Movement in America 1815–1820*, 336–357. Boston: Museum of Fine Arts, 1957.

Robinson, Cervin, and Rosemarie Haag Bletter. *Skyscraper Style: Art Deco New York*. New York: Oxford University Press, 1975.

Robinson, Willard B. *Gone from Texas: Our Lost Architectural Heritage*. College Station: Texas A&M University Press, 1981.

———. "Houses of Worship in Nineteenth Century Texas." *Southwestern Historical Quarterly* 85 (January 1982): 235–298.

———. *The People's Architecture: Texas Courthouses, Jails and Municipal Buildings*. Austin: Texas State Historical Association, 1983.

———. "Temples of Knowledge: Historic Mains of Texas Colleges and Universities." *Southwestern Historical Quarterly* 77 (July/August 1974): 445+.

Robinson, Willard B., and Todd Webb. *Texas Public Buildings of the Nineteenth Century*. Austin: University of Texas Press, 1974.

Roth, Leland. *McKim, Mead & White, Architects*. New York: Harper & Row, 1983.

Saint, Andrew. *Richard Norman Shaw*. New Haven: Yale University Press, 1976.

San Antonio Chapter AIA. *A Guide to San Antonio Architecture.* San Antonio, 1986.

Schaar, Kenneth W. "The Texas and Pacific Terminal in Fort Worth." *Perspective* 9, no. 2 (1980): 25–27.

Schmidt, Roland E. "Sullivanesque Architecture and Terra Cotta." In *The Midwest in American Architecture,* edited by John S. Garner, 163–184. Urbana and Chicago: University of Illinois Press, 1991.

Schmidt, Yolita. *The Moderne Style in Architecture: A Houston Guide.* Houston: Houston Public Library, 1978.

Schoelwer, Susan Prendergast. "Curious Relics and Quaint Scenes: The Colonial Revival at Chicago's Great Fair." In *The Colonial Revival in America,* edited by Alan Axelrod, 184–216. New York: W. W. Norton, for the Winterthur Museum, 1985.

Schuyler, Montgomery. "The Romanesque Revival in America." *Architectural Record* 1 (1891): 194+.

———. "The Works of Cram, Goodhue and Ferguson." *Architectural Record* 29 (January 1911): 1–112.

Scott, Mel. *American City Planning since 1890.* Berkeley and Los Angeles: University of California Press, 1969.

Scully, Vincent J., Jr. "Doldrums in the Suburbs." *Journal of the Society of Architectural Historians* 24 (March 1965): 36–47.

———. *Modern Architecture.* New York: George Braziller, Inc., 1966.

———. *The Shingle Style and the Stick Style: Architectural Theory and Design from Richardson to the Origins of Wright.* Rev. ed. New Haven: Yale University Press, 1971 [1955].

"Sculptors and Muralists Finishing Gigantic Task." *Centennial News* 11 (January 1936): 4.

Sebastian, John D. *A Survey of Texas Carnegie Libraries.* Austin: Texas Architectural Foundation, 1981. [Texas Historical Resources Fellowship, Texas Tech University].

Sheppard, Carl D. *Creator of the Santa Fe Style: Isaac Hamilton Rapp, Architect.* Albuquerque: University of New Mexico Press, 1988.

Short, C. W., and R. Stanley-Brown, eds. *Projects Constructed by Federal and Other Governmental Bodies between the Years 1933 and 1939 with the Assistance of the Public Works Administration.* Washington, D.C.: U.S. Government Printing Office, 1939.

Siry, Joseph. "Frank Lloyd Wright's Unity Temple and the Architecture for Liberal Religion in Chicago, 1885–1909." *Art Bulletin* 73 (June 1991): 256–282.

Smith, Mary Ann. *Gustave Stickley: The Craftsman.* Syracuse, N.Y.: Syracuse University Press, 1983.

"Some Recent Architectural Work of Lang and Witchell, Dallas." *Southern Architectural Review* 1 (December 1970): 157–181.

"South East Austin Elementary School, Jessen, Jessen and Millhouse, Architects." *Architectural Record* 91 (March 1942): 72–73.

Speck, Lawrence W., and Richard Payne. *Landmarks of Texas Architecture.* Austin: University of Texas Press, 1986.

Stanton, Phoebe B. *The Gothic Revival and American Church Architecture.* Baltimore: Johns Hopkins University Press, 1968.

Staub, John F. "Latin Colonial Architecture in the Southwest." *Civics for Houston* 1 (February 1928): 6.

Steely, Jim. "Rediscovering the Railroad Station." *Texas Architect* 34 (May/June 1984): 52–55.

Stein, Clarence. *Toward New Towns for America.* Rev. ed. Cambridge: MIT Press, 1971.

Stern, Robert A. M. *George Howe: Toward a Modern American Architecture.* New Haven: Yale University Press, 1975.

Stevenson, Katherine Cole, and H. Ward Jandl. *Houses by Mail: A Guide to Houses by Sears, Roebuck and Company.* Washington, D.C.: Preservation Press, 1986.

Study, Guy. "The Work of William B. Ittner, FAIA." *Architectural Record* 57 (February 1925): 97–124.

Sturgis, Russell. "A Critique of the Works of Shepley, Rutan and Coolidge and Peabody and Stearns." *Architectural Record* (July 1896): 1–52.

Sullivan, Louis H. *The Autobiography of an Idea.* New York: Dover, 1956 [1924].

———. *A System of Architectural Ornament According with a Philosophy of Man's Powers.* AIA Press, 1924.

Swank, A. B. "The Villita Project." *Southwest Review* 25 (July 1940): 394–403.

"The Taj Mahal: U.S. Air Force Landmark in San Antonio." *Texas Architect* 30 (July/August 1980): 95.

Tallmadge, Thomas E. "The Revolution in Ecclesiastical Architecture: The Sunday School." *Architectural Record* 55 (May 1924): 416–436.

Texas Historical Commission. *Addendum to A Catalog of Texas Properties in the National Register of Historic Places,* 1991.

———. *A Catalog of Texas Properties in the National Register of Historic Places,* 1984.

Tiller, de Teel Patterson. "Henry Trost and the Question of Historic Styles." *Perspective* 6, no. 1 (1978): 9–11.

Toews, Anita M. Regehr. "Spanish Colonial Revival Architecture in Dallas: The Work of Fooshee and Cheek." *Perspective* 13, no. 2 (1984): 9–15.

Troy, Nancy J. *Modernism and the Decorative Arts in France: Art Nouveau to Le Corbusier.* New Haven: Yale University Press, 1991.

Turner, Drexel. *Houston Architectural Survey.* 6 vols. Houston: Southwest Center for Urban Research, 1981.

Turner, Paul Venable. *Campus: An American Planning Tradition.* Cambridge: MIT Press, 1984.

Van Brunt, Henry. "John Wellborn Root [Obituary]." *Inland Architect* 16 (January 1891): 85–88.

Van Rennselaer, Mariana Griswold. *Henry Hobson Richardson and His Works.* New York: 1888.

Van Zanten, David. "Sullivan to 1890." In *Louis Sullivan: The Function of Ornament,* edited by Wim de Wit. New York: W. W. Norton, for the Chicago Historical Society and St. Louis Art Museum, 1986.

Victor, Sally S. "The Gulf Building, Houston, Texas." *Perspective* 13, no. 1 (1984): 2–8.

Vieyra, Daniel. *Fill 'Er Up: An Architectural History of America's Gas Stations.* New York: MacMillan, 1979.

———. "Places for Pumping Gas." *Texas Architect* 29 (September/October 1979): 34–39.

Viollet-le-Duc, Eugene E. *Discourses on Architecture.* Translated by Henry van Brunt. Boston: n.p., 1875.

Von Eckardt, Wolf. *Eric Mendelsohn.* New York: George Braziller, Inc., 1960.

Walker, Dale L. "The Lamaseries on the Hill: The Bhutanese Architecture of

U.T. El Paso." *NOVA: The University of Texas at El Paso Magazine* 6, no. 4 (August/October 1971): 12.

"War Needs—Housing: San Felipe Courts, Houston, Texas." *Architectural Record* 91 (April 1942): 47–50.

Weitze, Karen J. *California's Mission Revival.* Los Angeles: Hennessey and Ingalls, 1984.

Welch, June Rayfield, and J. Larry Nance. *The Texas Courthouse.* Dallas: G.L.A. Press, 1971.

Whiffen, Marcus, and Carla Breeze. *Pueblo Deco: The Art Deco Architecture of the Southwest.* Albuquerque: University of New Mexico Press, 1984.

White, James F. *Architecture at S.M.U.: 50 Years and Buildings.* Dallas: Southern Methodist University Press, 1966.

White, Theo B. *Paul Philippe Cret: Architect and Teacher.* Philadelphia: Art Alliance Press, 1973.

Williams, David R. "An Indigenous Architecture: Some Texas Colonial Homes." *Southwest Review* 14 (October 1928): 60.

———. "Toward a Southwestern Architecture." *Southwest Review* 16 (April 1931): 301–313.

Williams, David R., and O'Neil Ford. "Architecture of Early Texas." *Southwest Architect* 1 (October 1927): 5.

Williamson, Roxanne Kuter. *Austin, Texas: An American Architectural History.* San Antonio: Trinity University Press, 1973.

Wilson, Christopher. "The Spanish Pueblo Revival Defined, 1904–1921." *New Mexico Studies in the Fine Arts* 7 (1982): 24–30.

Wilson, Richard Guy. "Modernized Classicism and Washington, D.C." In *American Public Architecture: European Roots and Native Expression,* 271–303. Papers in Art History, vol. 5. University Park: Pennsylvania State University, 1989.

Wilson, Richard Guy, Diane Pilgrim, and Dikian Tashjian. *The Machine Age in America: 1918–1941.* New York: Abrams, 1986.

Wilson, William H. *The City Beautiful Movement.* Baltimore and London: The Johns Hopkins University Press, 1989.

Winter, Robert. *The California Bungalow.* Los Angeles: Hennessy and Ingalls, 1980.

Winters, Willis. "Avion Village: Enduring Values of Community." *Texas Architect* 38 (May/June 1988): 24–29.

Wölfflin, Heinrich. *Principles of Art History.* Translated by M. D. Hoffinger. 1st German ed., 1915. New York: Dover, 1932.

———. *Renaissance and Baroque.* Translated by Katherin Simon. Ithaca, N.Y.: Cornell University Press, 1966.

Worley, William S. *J. C. Nichols and the Shaping of Kansas City.* Columbia: University of Missouri Press, 1990.

Young, Melanie. "Viva San Antonio." *CITE: The Architecture and Design Review of Houston* (Spring 1986): 13–17; 23.

Zabel, Craig. "George Grant Elmslie and the Glory and the Burden of the Sullivan Legacy." In *The Midwest in American Architecture,* edited by John S. Garner, 1–41. Urbana and Chicago: University of Illinois Press, 1991.

Zisman, S. B. "The Architect and the House: 5—O'Neil Ford of Dallas, Texas." *Pencil Points* 21 (April 1940): 196–210.

Zukowski, John. *Chicago Architecture: 1892–1922.* Exhibition Catalog, The Art Institute of Chicago. Munich: Prestel Verlag, 1987.

UNPUBLISHED WORKS

Antley, Herbert N. "A New Deal Experiment in Planned Utopia: A Study of Dalworthington Gardens and the Subsistence Homestead Program, 1933–1937." Master's thesis, University of Texas at Arlington, 1980.

Atlantic Terra Cotta Company. Photograph Album. Architectural Drawings Collection, University of Texas at Austin.

Brooks, R. Edward. "George L. Dahl: A Critical Analysis of His Life and Architecture." Master's thesis, University of Texas at Arlington, 1978.

Campbell, Sarah Elizabeth. "George E. Kessler, Landscape Architect to City Planner: His Work in Texas Cities." Master's thesis, University of Texas at Austin, 1978.

Canavan, Patricia Taylor. "A History and Guide to the Swiss Avenue Historic District: 1917–1922." Master's thesis, University of Texas at Arlington, 1978.

Canavan, Robert Linus. "A History and Guide to the Swiss Avenue Historic District: 1923–1932." Master's thesis, University of Texas at Arlington, 1978.

Chipley, Sandra Kay. "Plazas and Squares of Texas: An Analysis of the Design Evolution of the Texas Courthouse Square and Its Urban Context." Master's thesis, University of Texas at Arlington, 1985.

Collier, Diane M. Hospodka. "Art Deco Architecture: Dallas, Texas." Master's thesis, University of Texas at Arlington, 1980.

Dooley, Judy Schwartz. "A History and Guide to the Swiss Avenue Historic District: 1905–1916." Master's thesis, University of Texas at Arlington, 1978.

Grossman, Elizabeth Green. "Paul Philippe Cret: Rationalism and Imagery in American Architecture." Ph.D. diss., Brown University, 1980.

Henry, Jay C. "Accommodations for Travelers in the Southwest: the Hotels of Trost and Trost." Paper presented at the annual meeting of the Society of Architectural Historians, 1980.

———. "George L. Dahl and the Advent of the Modern Idiom in Texas Architecture: 1925–1955." Paper presented at the annual meeting of the Society of Architectural Historians, 1983.

———. "The Moderne in Texas: An Overview." Paper presented at the annual meeting of the Texas chapter of the Society of Architectural Historians, 1981.

———. "The Prairie School in the Southwest." Paper presented at the annual meeting of the Society of Architectural Historians, 1978.

Hoffmeyer, Michael. "Architecture in Fort Worth: A History and Guide, 1873–1933." Master's thesis, University of Texas at Arlington, 1978.

Little, Emily Browning. "Art Deco Architecture in Texas." Master's thesis, University of Texas at Austin, 1979.

Prestiano, Robert, and Jay C. Henry. "Self-Guided Walking Tour of Downtown San Angelo." Paper prepared for the Texas chapter of the Society of Architectural Historians, 1983.

Schmidt, Roland E. Letter to Jay C. Henry. 10 December 1990.

Smith, David Franklin. "Indigenous Architecture of the Southwest: The Basis for a Regional Expression." Master's thesis, University of Texas at Austin, 1984.

Texas Parks and Wildlife Department. "The Civilian Conservation Corps in Texas Parks." Exhibition, 1985.

Toews, Anita M. Regehr. "Spanish Colonial Revival Architecture in Dallas: An Analysis of Its Historic Origins and Development." Master's thesis, University of Texas at Arlington, 1984.

Vernooy, David Andrew. "The Bungalow: A Southwestern Vernacular Perspective." Master's thesis, University of Texas at Austin, 1978.

Watson, Charles. "A History and Guide to the South Boulevard Historic District in Dallas: South Boulevard." Master's thesis, University of Texas at Arlington, 1980.

Weitze, Karen Jeanine. "Origins and Early Development of the Mission Revival in California." Ph.D. diss., Stanford University, 1977.

White, Robert Leon. "Mission Architecture of Texas, Exemplified in San Jose y San Miguel de Aguayo." Master's thesis, University of Texas at Austin, 1930.

Wise, Bobbie Joe, Jr. "Trinity Methodist Church: A Historical Survey and Guidelines for Its Adaptive Use." Master's thesis, University of Texas at Arlington, 1981.

Wise, Bob, ed. "Oak Lawn, 1880–1976: A Historical Study." Student report prepared for the School of Architecture, University of Texas at Arlington, 1976.

Young, Cary Lawrence. "A History and Guide to the South Boulevard Historic District in Dallas: Park Row." Master's thesis, University of Texas at Arlington, 1980.

# INDEX

**Boldface page numbers indicate illustrations.**

Highland Park City Hall, **175**
Highland Park Methodist Church, 303n.42
Highland Park Pharmacy, 188
Highland Park Presbyterian Church, 303n.42
Highland Park Shopping Village, 188–190, **189**, 259; service station, 310n.51
High schools, 10; as an Academic Eclectic type, 94–96; as a Progressive institution, 59–60
Alice High School, 149
Cleburne High School, 298n.30
Denison High School, 149
El Paso High School, 94–96, **95**, 215
Forest Avenue High School, Dallas, 302n.34
Jefferson High School, San Antonio, 177–**178**
King High School, Kingsville, 148–**149**
Lamar Senior High School, Houston, **215**
Lincoln High School, Dallas, **282**
Lubbock High School, 177–**178**
North Dallas High School, **96**
North Fort Worth High School, **60**–61
North Side High School, Fort Worth, **214**–215
Ozona High School, 22–**23**, 298n.28
Ozona High School Auditorium, **162**
Palestine High School, 298n.30
Schurz High School, Chicago, 298n.29
Trimble High School, Fort Worth, 59–**60**
Highway strip, 237
Hill, C. D. [and Co.], 7; invited competitor for State Fair Music Hall, 173n.36
Dallas City Hall, **89**–90
Galveston City Hall, 90
Hill Residence, Dallas, **260**–261
Oak Lawn Methodist Church, **103**–104
State National Bank Building, Corsicana, **136**–137

Hill Country building culture, 241, 268
Hill Residence, Dallas, **260**–261
Hillsboro: Hill County Courthouse, 16
Hilton, Conrad, 128–129
Falls Hotel, Marlin, 128, 305n.79
First Hilton Hotel, Cisco, 305n.79
Hilton Hotel, Dallas, 305n.79
Hilton Hotel, El Paso, 221, 305n.79
Hilton Hotel, San Angelo, 128–**129**
Hilton Hotel, Waco, 305n.79
Hilversum City Hall, **281**–282
Hindu temple architecture, 311n.4
Hippodrome Theater, Dallas, 119, 168
Hirsch House, Denton, 317n.33
Hitchcock, Henry-Russell, 1–2, 217; organized Thirteen Years of Fair Building for MOMA in 1936, 279; quoted, 140
Hitchcock and Johnson, 2, 7, 311n.1; International Style Exhibition, MOMA, 274
Hodges, T. S., designing contractor: Clark Library, Lockhart, **85**
Hoffmann, Josef, 311n.3
Höger, Fritz, 314nn.34,40
Hogg, James Oliver: First Presbyterian Church, Orange, **107**–108
Hogg Building, Houston. *See* Armor Building
Hogg Hall, University of Texas at Austin, 158, 160
Hogg House, San Antonio, **260**
Hollywood Theater, Fort Worth, 314n.39
Hollywood Theater Building, Fort Worth. *See* Electric Building
Home Economics Building, University of Texas at Austin, 160–162, **161**
Home Owners Loan Act, 284
Homestead-Temple House, 316n.5
Hood, Raymond
American Radiator Building, New York, 217
Daily News Building, New York, **218**, 228
McGraw Hill Building, New York, 218, 226
RCA Building, Rockefeller Center, New York, **218**

Hoover, Herbert, 73
Hopkins County Courthouse, Sulphur Springs, 14, 17
Horatio West Courts, Santa Monica, 190
Horta, Victor, 1
Hotels, 10, 68–69, 125–131; modern technology, 125
Adolphus Hotel, Dallas, **127**
Alhambra Hotel, St. Augustine, Fla., 147
Aztec Hotel, Monrovia, Calif., **166**
Baker Hotel, Mineral Wells, **128**
Castenada Hotel, Las Vegas, N.Mex., 141–**142**, 147
Chamber of Commerce Hotel, Lubbock, 309n.44
Cortez Hotel, El Paso, **182**
Driskill Hotel, Austin, 125, 221
El Capitan Hotel, Van Horn, 130, **164**, 179
El Paisano Hotel, Marfa, 130, 179–181, **180**
Falls Hotel, Marlin, 128
Franciscan Hotel, Albuquerque, **143**, 164
Gadsden Hotel, Douglas, Ariz., 305n.75
Gage Hotel, Marathon, **130**, 179
Galvez Hotel, Galveston, 146–147
Gunter Hotel, San Antonio, 305n.76
Hilton Hotel, Cisco, 305n.76
Hilton Hotel, Dallas, 305n.76
Hilton Hotel, El Paso, 305n.76
Hilton Hotel, San Angelo, 128–**129**
Hilton Hotel, Waco, 305n.76
La Posada Hotel, McAllen, 181
Las Lomas Hotel, Junction, **181**
Mission Inn, Riverside, Calif., 143, 147
Mobley Hotel, Cisco, 305n.79
Paso del Norte, El Paso, **126**–127
Plaza Hotel, Seguin, **69**, 125
Ponce de Leon Hotel, St. Augustine, Fla., 141, 147
Raleigh Hotel, Waco, **51**–52
Redlands Hotel, Palestine, 69
Rice Hotel, Houston, 305n.76
Rogers Hotel, Waxahachie, 69
St. Anthony Hotel, San Antonio, 307n.10

North Fort Worth Coliseum, 148

North Fort Worth High School, 60–61

North Side Senior High School, Fort Worth, **214**–215

Northwestern University, Evanston, Ill., 298n.34

North West Terra Cotta Company, 233

Norton, Charles Elliot, 1

Norwood Tower, Austin, **137**, 204

Nueces County Courthouse [Old], Corpus Christi, **79**

Nunn, Slayton: River Oaks Shopping Center, Houston, **238**

Oak Lawn district, Dallas, 255

Oak Lawn hospital district, Dallas, 92

Oak Lawn Methodist Church, **103**–104

Oak Park Studio, 7, 42, 61

"Oaks," Parker House, Houston, 297n.26

Office buildings, 131–140; Texas skyscrapers in 1917 (tabulated), 133

Amicable Building, Waco, **133**

Auditorium, Chicago, 120, 133

Bassett Tower, El Paso, 221–223, **222**, 228

Burk Burnett Building, Fort Worth, 58, 133

Busch Building, Dallas, 133–**134**

Casino Club Building, San Antonio, **167**–168

Equitable Building, New York, 139

Esperson Building, Houston, **140**

Guaranty Building, Buffalo, **48**, 133

Magnolia Oil Building, Dallas, 139–**140**

Medical Arts Building, Dallas, 299n.39

Medical Arts Building, Houston, 137

Medical Arts Building, San Antonio, **137**

Mills Building, El Paso, 47–**49**, 58, 143

Monadnock Building, Chicago, 133

Municipal Building, New York, 140

Nix Building, San Antonio, 306n.89

Norwood Tower, Austin, **137**

Petroleum Building, Midland, **137**, 229

Praetorian Building, Dallas, 133

Rookery, Chicago, 133

Santa Fe Building, Amarillo, 137

Smith-Young Tower, San Antonio, 138–140, **139**

Southwestern Bell Telephone Building, San Antonio, **183**

Southwestern Life Building, Dallas, 51, 133

State National Bank Building, Corsicana, **136**–137

Tribune Tower, Chicago, 136–137, **217**

Waggoner Building, Fort Worth, 139

Wilson Building, Dallas, **132**

Woolworth Building, New York, **135**, 137, 299n.39

Office of Supervising Architect of U.S. Treasury, 13, 82–83, 301n.14

Old Mains, 97

Baylor University, Waco, 97

Southwestern University, Georgetown, 17–**18**

Texas Woman's University, Denton, 97–**98**

University of Texas at Austin, 97

University of Texas at El Paso, **152**

University of Texas Medical School at Galveston, 97

Opera Houses, 10

Anson, **29**

Columbus, 293n.28

Granbury, 29

Orange: First Presbyterian Church, **107**–108

Organic architecture, 317n.34

Orndorf Hotel, El Paso. *See* Cortez Hotel

Outdoor Theater, Texas Centennial Exposition, Dallas, **211**–212

Overbeck, H. A.

Dallas Criminal Courts and Jail Building, **91**–92

MKT Building, Dallas, 23, **25**

Southern Supply Company, Dallas, 23, **25**

Overbeck, J. Edward: employer of George Willis, 42; Sacred Heart Cathedral, Dallas, 35–**36**

Owatonna, Minn., Bank, 42

Owls Clubs, Tucson, 44

Ozona

Crockett County Courthouse, **16**

High School, 21–**23**, 298n.28

High School Auditorium, **162**

West Texas Utility Building, **165**

Paducah: Cottle County Courthouse, 198–**199**

Page, C. H., and Brother [later Page Brothers], 6, 14

Anderson County Courthouse, Palestine, **78**–80

Aziz Brothers Building, Brownsville, **187**–188

Fort Bend County Courthouse, Richmond, **28**, 78

Hays County Courthouse, San Marcos, 297n.27, 300n.8

High and Ward School, Refugio, 176–**177**

Hunt County Courthouse, Greenville, **81**, 312n.9

Mexia City Hall and Municipal Auditorium, **174**

Mood Hall, Southwestern University, Georgetown, 97–**98**

Quanah, Acme and Pacific Railroad Station, Quanah, 145–**146**

Smith County Courthouse, Tyler, 300n.8

Sweetwater City Hall and Municipal Auditorium, 173–**174**

Texas and Brazos Valley Depot, Teague, 307n.9

Williamson County Courthouse, Georgetown, 300n.8

Page, Harvey L.

Great Northern Railroad Station, San Antonio, 307n.9

Nueces County Courthouse [Old], Corpus Christi, **79**

Paint Rock: Concho County Courthouse, 16

Palestine

Anderson County Courthouse, **78**–80

High School, 298n.30

Redlands Hotel, 69

U.S. Post Office, **82**